T0329790

Yale Agrarian Studies Series

JAMES C. SCOTT, SERIES EDITOR

The Agrarian Studies Series at Yale University Press seeks to publish outstanding and original interdisciplinary work on agriculture and rural society—for any period, in any location. Works of daring that question existing paradigms and fill abstract categories with the lived experience of rural people are especially encouraged.
—James C. Scott, *Series Editor*

For a complete list of titles in the Yale Agrarian Studies Series, visit yalebooks.com/agrarian.

Legions of Pigs
in the
Early Medieval
West

~

Jamie Kreiner

Yale UNIVERSITY PRESS   NEW HAVEN AND LONDON

Publication is made possible in part by a grant from the Barr
Ferree Foundation Publication Fund, Department of Art and
Archaeology, Princeton University.

Published with assistance from the foundation established
in memory of Calvin Chapin of the Class of 1788,
Yale College.

Yale University Press books may be purchased in quantity
for educational, business, or promotional use. For information, please e-mail sales.press@yale.edu (U.S. office) or
sales@yaleup.co.uk (U.K. office).

Set in Scala type by Newgen North America, Austin, Texas.
Printed in the United States of America.

Library of Congress Control Number: 2019956861
ISBN 978-0-300-24629-2 (hardcover : alk. paper)

A catalogue record for this book is available
from the British Library.
This paper meets the requirements of
ANSI/NISO Z39.48-1992 (Permanence of Paper).

10 9 8 7 6 5 4 3 2 1

For the birds

CONTENTS

PREFACE

It was the pigs who pushed me into this. Not living ones but the dead. When I was researching other stuff, they'd wander into the texts I was reading, true to the troublemakers they were when they were alive a millennium and a half ago. Eventually they got me here, to this book, which is about the ecologies of the early medieval West and what they meant to the people who were part of them. Pigs are at its center because they were critical members of those ecologies and also because they deeply affected the ways that humans experienced and thought about the physical world. Even today we are living with some of the legacies of those human-pig relationships. It's not just me.

Pigs are fascinating subjects, and they, like humans, have histories. But they can also help us make up a deficit in the way we've thought about the human past. We don't often ask what the early Middle Ages had to say about nature (let alone about pigs). Maybe that's because we think we know the answer—that humans in these centuries, especially Christians, saw themselves as superior to everything else that God had created; that they were incurious about the world; that in the wake of the Roman Empire their only concern was survival. But in this book I suggest a different situation. Early medieval communities were thinking seriously about their environments. They saw themselves as part of a complex and dynamic universe that was propelled by interconnected organisms and forces. In that system, even the smallest creatures or events could have far-reaching consequences. The big picture was tied to hyperlocal circumstances.

The people who lived in the early medieval West—in what is now northwest Africa and Europe—brought these perspectives to bear on their farming, policy making, and philosophizing. And pigs were both a means and a motivation for doing this. They were a flexible species that could handle a diversity of ecologies. They illustrated the benefits of being adaptable. But they were also a constant reminder that humans *had* to adapt to their animals and landscapes: total control or assimilation was unthinkable.

In this book I track the interlocking relationships between pigs and humans and the ecologies that interwove them by drawing on texts and images, bioarchaeology, settlement archaeology, and mammal biology. I wrote it with different groups of readers in mind: historians of the early Middle Ages, obviously, but also scholars and general readers who are interested in animals, agriculture, environmental history, religion, and the history of science. These might be separate categories of thinking today, but they were intuitively linked in the early Middle Ages. And I have tried to make these centuries accessible to readers who do not have a background in early medieval history.

As I worked on this project, my book was parasitic on three people especially: Chris Shannon, because we talk about trees a lot, and because we tried to be good to two raucous monk parrots as long as they lived. Henry Cowles, because he's the best writing and reading partner a person could have. Bill Jordan, because he made the medieval history of rural Europe something to love.

I am grateful to Umberto Albarella, Kim Bowes, Pam Crabtree, Caroline Goodson, and Jean-Hervé Yvinec, as well as to the many other archaeologists whose work and images appear here. Helmut Reimitz and Marios Costambeys were always happy to talk pig. Jean Thomson Black "got" this book right away and has been a truly invested editor. Susan Laity edited this manuscript masterfully. Lindsay Holman of the Ancient World Mapping Center made the maps. Many friends and colleagues passed along references and tips over the past decade, but I'd like to single out Brent Shaw for his enthusiasm. I'm also grateful to audiences at the University of Georgia, Princeton University, Ben-Gurion University of the Negev, Northern Illinois University, the University of Liverpool, New York University, Yale University, the University of Michigan, and the medievalist group at the Institute for Advanced Study (especially Cecily Hillsdale, who read more of this book than she had to, and Adam Izdebski, who shared research in advance of its publication). And Leah Wolfe, butcher at the Meat Hook, in Brooklyn, showed me how a pig's meat and bones fit together. I want to thank that pig, too, even though she is dead.

This project was supported by funding from the Department of History and the Willson Center for the Humanities and Arts at the University of Georgia, the Special Collections Research Center at the University of Chicago Libraries, the Huntington Library, the Center for Medieval and Renaissance Studies at the University of California, Los Angeles, the Barr Ferree Publication Fund at Princeton University, and a Mellon Fellowship for Assistant Professors in the School of Historical Studies at the Institute for Advanced Study. Portions of an article I published, "Pigs in the Flesh and Fisc: An Early Medieval Ecology," *Past & Present* 236 (2017): 3–42, have been reproduced across various chapters with permission from Oxford University Press.

Finally, thanks to Claudio Saunt for getting me to get this book done. Thanks to Anne O'Donnell and Ben Schmidt and little Henry for my home away from home. And thanks to Peter Brown for continuing to read and listen to my work in the generous and rigorous way he always has, for sharing his own work back, and for being a preternaturally savvy herder—of ideas, books, and students like me.

Maps

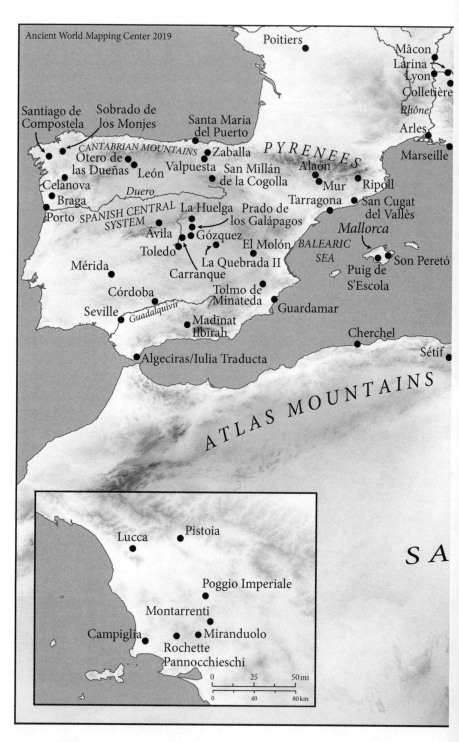

Map 1. Southern sites mentioned in the book

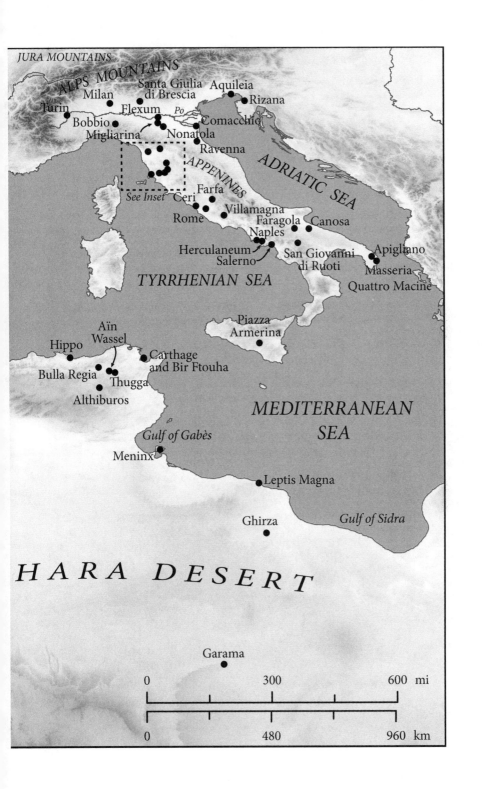

JURA MOUNTAINS

ALPS MOUNTAINS

Turin
Milan
Santa Giulia
di Brescia
Aquileia
Rizana
Flexum
Po
Bobbio
Migliarina
Nonatola
Comacchio
Ravenna
APPENINES
ADRIATIC SEA
See Inset
Ceri
Farfa
Rome
Villamagna
Faragola
Naples
Canosa
Herculaneum
Salerno
San Giovanni
di Ruoti
Apigliano
Masseria
Quattro Macine

TYRRHENIAN SEA

Piazza
Armerina

Aïn
Wassel
Hippo
Carthage
and Bir Ftouha
Bulla Regia
Thugga
Althiburos

MEDITERRANEAN
SEA

Gulf of Gabès
Meninx

Leptis Magna

Ghirza
Gulf of Sidra

H A R A   D E S E R T

Garama

| 0 | | 300 | | 600 | mi |

| 0 | | 480 | | 960 | km |

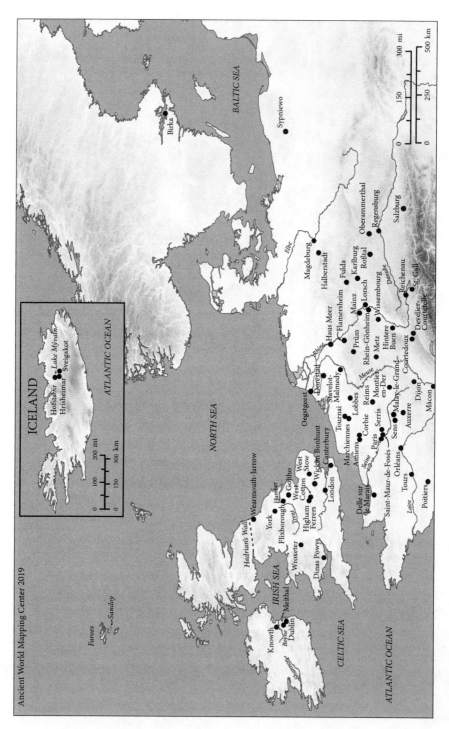

Map 2. Northern sites mentioned in the book

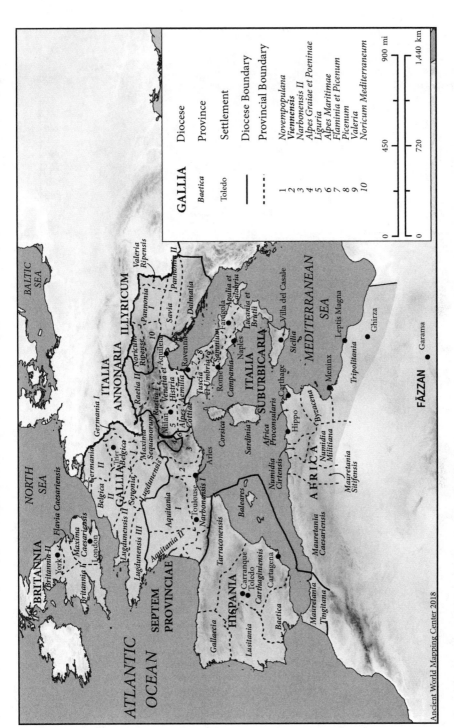

Map 3. The provinces of the western Roman Empire, ca. 400

GALLIA   Diocese

Baetica   Province

Toledo   Settlement

———   Diocese Boundary

--------   Provincial Boundary

1   *Novempopulana*
2   *Viennensis*
3   *Narbonensis II*
4   *Alpes Graiae et Poeninae*
5   *Liguria*
6   *Alpes Maritimae*
7   *Flaminia et Picenum*
8   *Picenum*
9   *Valeria*
10   *Noricum Mediterraneum*

0   450   900 mi

0   720   1,440 km

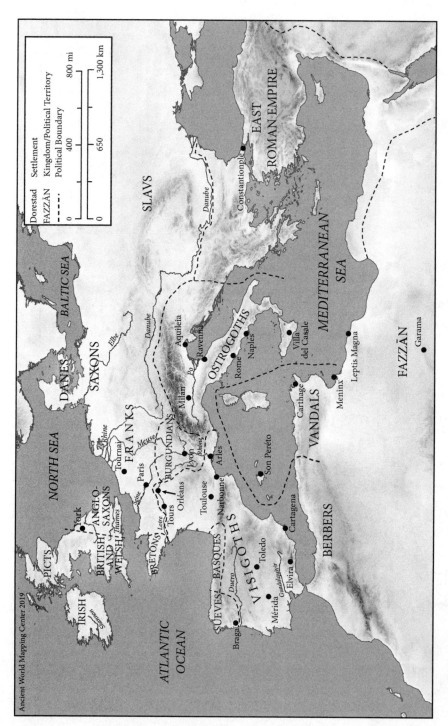

Map 4. The early medieval West, ca. 500

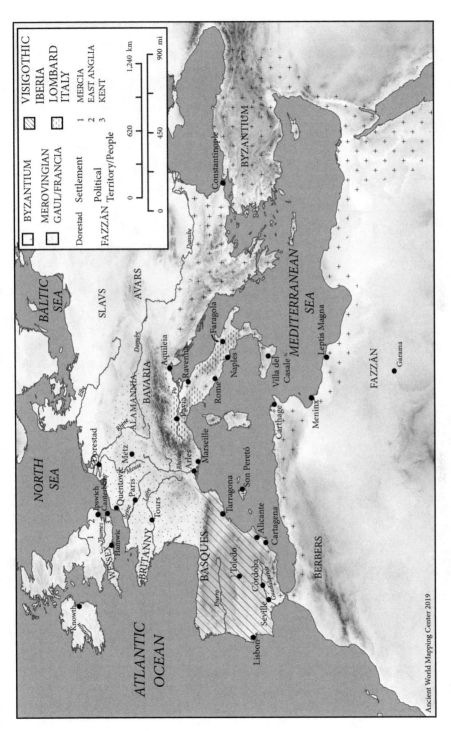

Map 5. The early medieval West, ca. 600

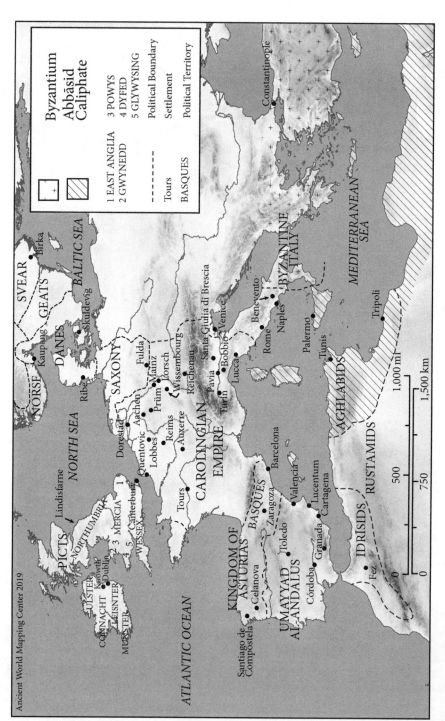

Map 6. The early medieval West, ca. 800

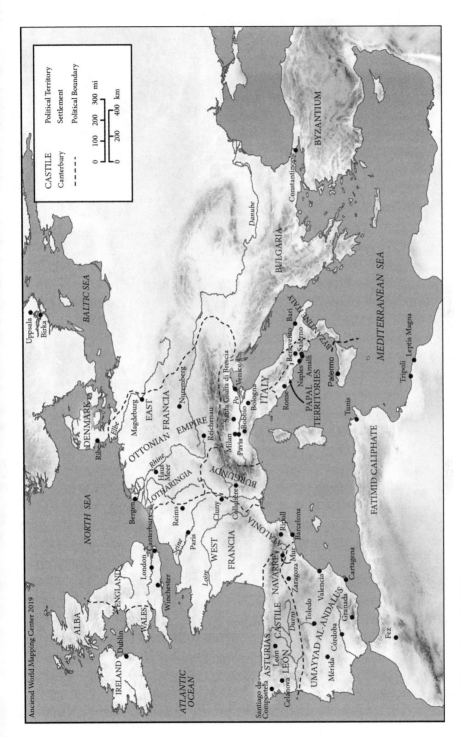

Map 7. The early medieval West, ca. 1000

Legions of Pigs in the Early Medieval West

Introduction

In the early Middle Ages almost everyone would have had a story about a pig. About the trouble a certain pig caused, or the smart thing it did, or the personality it had, or the weird stuff it ate, or the large litter it reared, or the delicious meat it eventually became. But this book does not start with anything like that. This is partly because the stories that people must have told each other about their pigs in the early Middle Ages, let alone the everyday shoptalk about them, were hardly ever written down. It is also because pigs were a sort of anti-synecdoche when it came to the way people thought about the world. No single pig could stand for the whole. Instead, pigs called attention to the particularity of things. Every pig was different, every farm and landscape and community through which pigs moved was different, and what pigs often forced humans to see was that a world in flux required flexibility rather than formulas. The rhetoric of ecology is very unlike the rhetoric of the archetype and the anecdote. The details make all the difference. In the early Middle Ages, thinking big meant thinking small.

Take the city of Meninx. It lay on the southern coast of the island of Jerba, which itself sat about 2.5 miles (4 km) off the coast of mainland Tunisia. There were not many pigs in Meninx. Their bones amount to about 5.5 percent of all the animal remains found in a sixth-century sample there, and this figure is similar to what we find in cities that more properly belonged to the pre-desert and desert of Libya, such as the Roman city of Leptis Magna and the Garamantian city of Garama (today Jarma), the capital of Fazzān. But pig statistics aside, there was no place quite like Meninx. Trade from both the Mediterranean and the Sahara converged there, and its prosperity made it one of the standout towns of late antique North Africa. The heartbeat of its economy was the production of purple dye and cloth, which relied on mollusks of the genus

Murex. If visitors had somehow overlooked the huge industrial zones dedicated to murex processing that ringed the city with their dunes of discarded shells, they would probably still have gotten the idea from the purple and red limestone that adorned the public spaces at the urban core: a wink to its leading export. The dye industry was knitted together with the fishing industry for obvious reasons, and also with salt production (because murex had to be macerated with salt for three days) and sheep husbandry, because the salt flats along the island's coasts became grasslands for grazing in the rainy season, and because sheep provided wool for what would eventually become purple fabric. Not surprisingly, sheep outnumbered pigs in Meninx.[1]

What do the pigs of this panorama tell us? Only that the panorama is incomplete, not simply because other communities raised proportionally more pigs than Meninx did, but also because the environmental and economic matrices of other settlements—even the ones nearby, even the ones with comparable pig populations—would have been qualitatively different. A snapshot like Meninx is precious because it is irreducible, a case that does not quite encapsulate. There can be exemplarity here, but it is not all-encompassing. Specific pigs and places are not stand-ins for the whole of the early Middle Ages. Instead, they move us from one scale to another, from the pigs that fed a murex workshop to the salt flats of Jerba to the Gulf of Gabès to the cross-imperial trading networks running from Sicily to the Saharan wadis of Fazzān. They are our guides to an extensive ecological gearwork. And that is how they struck their caretakers in the early Middle Ages.

So let's start small, even though it might seem that the subject of premodern pigs is a *very* small matter. Technically, this is true: in early medieval legalese, pigs fell into the category of "minor" or "lesser" livestock. If a person was giving away a piece of land, the animals usually went with it, and they were mentioned in passing, in the appurtenance clauses of the contracts that recorded the transaction. Individual species, let alone individual animals, were not often singled out in these documents. Instead animals usually appear in aggregate, flocked together, as "beasts of burden and livestock of both sexes, great and small."[2] Beneath this sort of legal boilerplate, which purported to describe a property in full, was a teeming world of animal life that humans thought about deeply, much more deeply than even their charters made of skin would suggest. And although pigs counted as lesser livestock—which put them in the company of goats, sheep, chickens, and geese, and set them against larger and pricier animals such as oxen, bulls, cows, horses, and donkeys—they occupied an outsized presence in the lives and minds of early medieval communities.

Pigs had carved out some of that space for themselves, but their influence also resonated because the littlest things mattered in Christian theology at this time. All creation was part of the divine jigsaw that God encouraged humans to piece together intellectually for the benefit of their own spiritual growth. This was one of the reasons people paid attention to their animals: they had implications for the cosmic order. Augustine of Hippo had insisted in the early fifth century that just because something was inferior to something else did not mean that it was worthless or even replaceable. To think differently would be akin to saying that because sight surpasses hearing, there should be four eyes and no ears for every human body. One of the special things about the universe was that good things were not equivalent. The presence of differently good things, the fact that the cosmos was so varied, meant that there were more kinds of good in total. If good things were truly equal and substitutable, the world—and, by extension, human understanding—would be impossibly narrowed.[3]

Pigs (sometimes "good," sometimes not) were small in one sense and large in many others; they were a species that challenges our sense of scale. This book is about the relationship between humans and pigs in agrarian life in the early medieval West, but it is also about the practices and ideas that humans developed about their lived environments as a result of their interactions with these animals. The idea that emerged most conspicuously was an "ecological" ethic that restructured policies from local to imperial levels. Centuries before the rise of environmentalism, animal-rights activism, and local-farm advocacy, early medieval societies were embracing their own distinctive interest in anchoring human perspectives to things that were smaller and greater than them.

This is not to say that the "ecological ethic" of the early Middle Ages resembles modern Western ideas of environmental protectionism or animal rights. It doesn't. But the early medieval consideration of humans' position in the world *was* informed by how other beings worked.[4] Even in a culture in which humans alone were said to be created in the image of God, ethics was fundamentally a form of ecological thinking. The things that humans paid attention to, evaluated, and worried about were *supposed to* reckon with the whole connective tissue of creation, and pigs are both a general and a particular case for understanding this. General, because pigs give us one of many possible opportunities for understanding the ways early medieval societies approached their lived environments. Particular, because they made a unique impression on early medieval culture.

After all, humans are not the only species to have histories. Other animals can also develop new forms of knowledge, new habits, and new patterns of sociability which make their lives different from the lives of their ancestors. In a suburb of Seattle, for example, more than thirty Brewer's blackbirds show up at a local Costco just before it opens, waiting along with human customers to enter the store, where they can pick up crumbs off the floor of the café or simply get out of the rain! They know the store's hours and have figured out how to exploit it. John Marzluff, the urban ecologist who observed them, sees this case as one of countless changes that resilient avian species are making all the time in response to the shifting environments they share with humans. Across the Pacific, a community of *Octopus tetricus* has settled off the east coast of Australia, fifty feet down, in a place that researchers call Octopolis. Although octopuses are typically solitary animals, this "village" coalesced around the remains of what probably used to be a boat, and now it is buried in scallop shells that the octopuses have discarded after eating their soft insides. Through a mix of improvisation and learning—and probably also a biological disposition to communication that researchers had overlooked until recently—the residents of Octopolis have figured out how to live in a group.[5]

The pigs that lived and died one thousand to fifteen hundred years ago are even more elusive than a community of octopuses in the deep, but it is possible to track elements of their histories, too. Pigs were found nearly everywhere in the early medieval West. They were the only livestock that did not produce "secondary" products in addition to meat, but they were highly adaptive to different circumstances, willing to eat almost anything, and fertile, all of which made them inexpensive to raise. In that sense they were ideal commodities. But they were also smart and delinquent animals that scrambled the plans humans set for them. They escaped from their pens and herders, destroyed crops, raided stores of food, injured people, and defiled corpses. And yet, despite their costs, most people were still willing to keep pigs, and they made continuous adjustments to accommodate them. Medieval communities' interactions with their animals also inspired new ways of managing the economies and cultures of the farm, forest, city, and court. The history of pigs in this period is also a history of the counterintuitive connections that developed between the micro-universes of pig husbandry and early medieval institutions and ideas on a wider scale.

The period I focus on used to be called the "Dark Ages" or the age of the "barbarian" kingdoms. But the early medieval West is a classic case of mistaken identity. The fracturing of the western Roman Empire did not leave an impoverished and simple society in its wake. Instead, what scholars of the early Middle Ages have found, from North Africa to the British Isles, are thousands of communities that developed ways of working and living that were specific to their local environments. Both the politics and the ecologies of this period were fragmented—though not entirely detached from one another—and the humans who moved within them were experimental, inventive, and more sensitive to the scales of the possible.[6] So this history begins with the fissure of the Roman West in the course of the fifth century, and it ends around the year 1000. My focus is on the communities and small kingdoms that succeeded the empire in Europe and North Africa (the Maghreb), with comparative attention to adjacent areas the Roman emperors never controlled, including the Libyan Sahara, Europe east of the Rhine, Ireland, and Scandinavia.

This half-millennium saw the survival of the eastern wing of the Roman Empire, which today we call Byzantium. It saw the flourishing of rabbinic culture and the compilation of the Babylonian Talmud at the western edge of Sasanian Persia. It saw the birth and maturation of Islam. It saw the creation of punctuation, the invention of musical notation, and the codification of Roman law. In these centuries, the conquests of the Arab, Syrian, and Berber armies produced a caliphate stretching from Transoxania at the edge of the Eurasian steppe to the Iberian Atlantic in the west. At the same time, hundreds of monasteries were founded where no monasteries had existed before. The inhabitants of Britain began to speak Old English, and Latin slowly evolved into the proto-Romance languages. Trading networks began cropping up in the North Sea and Baltic, and through them Scandinavian entrepreneurs got wind of wealth farther south: they raided and sometimes settled in western Europe, set up settlements and trading depots in eastern Europe and Rus', and colonized Iceland and Greenland. They even ventured out to North America. Paris first became a capital in the sixth century. Baghdad was built from nothing in the eighth, and Cairo was created in the tenth. These were the centuries of the golden basilicas of Ravenna, the magnificent mosques at Damascus and Córdoba, the Lindisfarne Gospels, the *Shahnameh,* and the translations and commentaries of Greek philosophy into Syriac and Arabic. They were the prime years and the final years for the kingdoms of the Ostrogoths, the Sueves, the Burgundians, the Sasanians, the Visigoths, the Merovingians, the Lombards, the Saxons, the Avars, the Carolingians, Essex, Kent, Sussex, East Anglia, Mercia, Northumbria, Wessex, the Ottonians, the Umayyads, and (by some measures) the 'Abbāsids—to give only a very partial list.[7]

But this book is not a political history in the traditional sense. Instead I offer a different kind of narrative about influence that works from the ground up. Across the early medieval West, pig husbandry thrived in a wide range of environmental and social conditions. And the core argument of the book is that pigs' great flexibility and intelligence, and medieval communities' engagement with those capabilities, resulted in new approaches to environments, economies, and culture that can be fairly characterized as ecological. Farmers, consumers, policy makers, and philosophers noticed that they were part of a world whose countless biotic inhabitants, inorganic features, and human institutions were fluctuating and interdependent. And what pigs in particular taught humans was that it was worth accommodating this multivariable, dynamic system—to try to be as versatile as pigs were in order to thrive. So although the pig may seem marginal or even cartoonish to us today, it was a significant player in the early Middle Ages, and the working relationships between humans and pigs came to shape not only patterns of farming and eating but also regional economies, legal culture, fiscal policies, identities, and philosophies of the cosmos.

The term *ecology* entered the English language in the last quarter of the nineteenth century as a loanword from German, and German biologists and advocates of science for the general public had coined and popularized it only a short while previously, starting in the middle of the nineteenth century. As the historian of science Lynn Nyhart has shown, fin-de-siècle Germans looked to the biological society (which they called a *Gesellschaft*) as a remedy for the social one (also a Gesellschaft). They figured that acting with an ecological sensibility would counteract the ruptures that industrialization had created within human communities. They insisted that human society was supposed to be true to its own nature by acknowledging its embeddedness in the world and by working "to interact successfully with both its physical environment and the other organisms around it."[8]

So on one hand, the concept of ecology is specific to a particular historical context, and it postdates the early Middle Ages by eight hundred–plus years. But on the other, it is not totally alien to early medieval sensibilities. Most basically, an ecology is a system of constant energy transfer, of contingent and changing relationships between different organisms and between organisms and nonliving things, and this sort of dynamic was certainly characteristic of rural and urban communities in the early Middle Ages. Human communities were embedded in environments that created opportunities and constraints on their lives and their work. And the exploitation of certain resources—say, the choice to fell oaks for fuel and timber, or to harvest murex for its color—had consequences for other entities and organisms. Just as significant, early medieval farmers and lawmakers knew this. They approached their lived environments as overlapping and interrelated systems. They developed practices and policies to accommodate regional variations, fluctuations in resources, and multifocal interests. They were not simply involved in shifts in scale. They were also thinking about scale and why it mattered.

In other words, when *we* think ecologically it becomes easier to notice that communities in the early medieval West were also thinking ecologically, even though they would not have used this term and even though their views were not identical to ours. As an analytic, ecology helps make sense of a world that was both variable and contingent, and it helps make sense of societies that saw *themselves* as variable and contingent. So although the field of ecocriticism—the study of critical perspectives toward nature and culture—is fairly new, the ideas ecocritics examine are not. Ancient and medieval thinkers were fascinated by the interdependency of physical and cosmic systems, and sometimes their sense of humanity itself became more porous as they thought about the nature of nature.[9]

Such a view was even characteristic of the intellectual circles of the early Middle Ages that were deeply committed to Christianity. And yet the early Middle Ages is often skipped over in more sweeping intellectual histories, environmental histories, and histories of science.[10] That neglect has a lot to do with the fact that early medieval writers were not interested in writing what modern writers consider science and philosophy. Instead they enthusiastically produced biblical commentaries, histories, hagiographies, liturgical poetry, monastic Rules, sermons, and curated anthologies of older works. Modern readers have mostly neglected those materials on the mistaken assumption that they would not contain much worth reading, because (so the supposition goes) Christianity automatically instilled in its believers a sense of contempt for nature—or at least made them uninterested in it. But early medieval Christians would have been shocked to hear this. They saw the study of nature as something that enriched their faith. And because they were attentive to the complexity of the universe, the Christian ethics they formulated (about their sense of cosmic hierarchies, or about the soul's salvation) were deeply relational. They took for granted that humans were part of an interactive universe of endlessly divergent perspectives. Curiosity and constant reference to other points of view were essential.

To unearth this history, then, some of the richest sources include exegeses of the creation stories in Genesis and other texts that were invested in natural history and philosophy; early medieval legal and administrative documents (law codes, decrees, charters, and property inventories); and bioarchaeology—in particular the analysis of bones, pollen, seeds, and charcoal. Because paleo-botany and osteoarchaeology have made tremendous advances in recent de-cades, this book could not have been written twenty years ago. Now large-scale field surveys and rescue archaeology are giving us glimpses of the plant and animal life on early medieval sites, and they are illuminating the early medi-eval landscape. They also make clear that it was *not* a world of interchangeable farms and farmers, and that the concept of the "average person" of the early Middle Ages (which one finds in many academic and popular histories) does not actually make much sense. Not only are early medieval farmers mistak-enly presumed to have led miserable lives, they are also treated as a uniform bloc. But the different opportunities and challenges that early medieval com-munities faced, and the ways they responded to them, suggest that rural com-munities were diverse, adaptive, and thoughtful.

Pigs are not the only possible entry point into these agrarian cultures, but they are an especially good focal point for investigating how early medieval communities thought about their lived environments. There are several rea-sons for this. First, pigs loomed disproportionately large in ancient and medi-eval imaginations. People wrote and presumably talked about them more than other livestock and even more than most other animals, although they were rarely the commonest on a farm. In addition, pigs routinely forced humans to appreciate that they were dealing with interlocking, fluctuating, and variable resources that required a correspondingly flexible approach to handling them. And they were adaptive, most noticeably in their diet but also in their behav-iors, which enabled their owners to take advantage of different ecologies. Fi-nally, unlike other livestock, pigs were consistently difficult to manage, so their caretakers could not help but notice that domestication did not fully transform animals into commodities. Humans made tradeoffs and sacrifices in order to keep raising and eating pigs, and that, more than any other animal-human relationship in this period, attests to a long-term process of coevolution.

The main pig "breed" in the early Middle Ages was a long-legged, hairy animal whose back usually rose to about 30 inches (or about mid-thigh on a 5′6″ human). Because pigs were partly free-ranging animals, they sometimes interbred with wild boars, which in this period still roamed the woodlands of North Africa and Europe. They favored acorns, beech mast, grubs, worms, and summer-autumn crops like legumes and grains, but (like pigs now) they would eat nearly anything else besides. Their diets were not the only adaptable thing about them. As modern biobehavioral research on industrial, free-range, and wild pig populations attests, pigs are social and responsive animals. They have good memories, can learn quickly, and practice what could fairly be called analytical decision making: they make effective choices by selectively applying what they have learned about past situations to new scenarios. These qualities mean that not only single pigs but whole herds of pigs can have individual characteristics and abilities, can learn new things, and can change.

The inhabitants of the early medieval West had their own insights about pigs' abilities. They knew that a simple designation like *species* did not do justice to the range of abilities that animals of the same kind could exhibit depending on their individual aptitudes and circumstances. And they were acutely aware that pigs were ingenious escape artists and food finders, so much so that early medieval societies developed extensive legislation to manage the damage pigs caused in the course of escaping from their pens, uprooting neighbors' crops, and attacking human beings.

There is no better sign of how greatly communities valued their pigs than the enormous effort that they put into accommodating these tricky animals, rather than ditch pig husbandry entirely. Early medieval kingdoms throughout the West developed new protocols of legal behavior on the logic that, because pigs would inevitably get loose and do damage, the best thing for humans to do would be to take more responsibility in the aftermath. They issued laws about the measures farmers should take when they found animals in their fields, how to deal efficiently with the animals and their owner in order to reach a nonviolent solution, and how to handle the situation if it happened a second or third time. There were times when both pigs and humans misbehaved, and these incidents sometimes show up in court records. But whether or not laws were broken, pigs were clearly shaping human institutions, even though they were ostensibly the ones under domestication.

Farmers and lawmakers were not the only people paying attention to the grit of rural life. Natural philosophers and theologians were interested in the details, too, but for different reasons. The book of Genesis narrated the origin of the universe as a six-day event in which God created everything out of shapelessness and darkness. This account fascinated and perplexed the people who read it in Late Antiquity and the early Middle Ages. It had the effect of infusing the physical world with divine significance, but it also raised countless questions that intellectuals energetically tried to answer. What did it mean that birds were created from water, for instance? When were the grubs that fed on corpses brought into being? Were the stars hot or cold?

To investigate questions like these, Christian naturalists looked beyond the Bible. They consulted scientific, poetic, and philosophical sources. They made their own observations and studies of physical phenomena. And they spoke to specialized experts, not only elites such as physicians but also farmers, fishermen, arborists, distillers, ditchdiggers, and even old men who could remember when their environments looked a little bit different.

One of their main conclusions was that the world was a highly complex system of interrelated but constantly changing parts. This meant that although certain features of the universe seemed cyclical—the seasonal winds, the celestial orbits, the growth of plants in the spring—it also contained enormous geographical diversity, and the state of any particular organism, geomorphic feature, or atmospheric phenomenon would change over time because it was connected to so many other forces. This ecological perspective also led its analysts to conclude that although humans were near the top of the hierarchy of creation, any given perspective or conclusion they formed about the world was inescapably partial. Even animals saw the world in different ways, and thinking about what their views might be could help humans piece together a more comprehensive picture of the cosmos and in the process get another step closer to the divine power that had created it. So although we might assume that pigs matter only to agrarian history, early medieval philosophers would have set us straight: they were one of many keys to a complex and spiritually charged universe.

It is not so hard to see why intellectuals in this period emphasized the intricacy of the physical world. The landscapes they lived in were a kaleidoscope of micro-ecologies, settlement types, and farming systems. Rural life was strikingly diverse. Some contrasts are obvious to us today. The vibrant oasis villages of the Libyan desert that cultivated dates and trafficked in Saharan gold and Mediterranean glass were a far cry from the settlements in Greenland that depended almost entirely on walrus hunting. But even within a single region—such as the plains and coasts of Apulia or the massif of central Spain—forms of life were so variable that it is neither helpful nor interesting to generalize about them.

Communities also adopted forms of resource management that treated their ecologies systemically. Generically speaking, this was an age of agropastoralism: early medieval settlements mixed the cultivation of grains and other plants with animal husbandry, foraging, and hunting. They also worked with pottery, metals, textiles, and glass. But each farm or village calibrated its forms of farming and craftworking to its surroundings. Whereas Meninx took advantage of its coasts and salt flats to pasture sheep in order to complement its economy of purple dye, the Libyan city of Leptis Magna was catching barbary sheep, gazelles, and Saharan striped polecats, and a royal ringfort in Ireland was taking advantage of the plovers, water rails, corncrakes, herons, snipes, ducks, and geese that frequented the nearby Boyne River.[11]

Pigs were part of nearly all of those micro-ecologies because they were versatile animals. But pig husbandry can tell modern researchers more than the ways communities fit a particular commodity into larger systems of survival. The work that humans did with pigs also transformed their sense of the ecologies they inhabited. Pigs helped settlements in a wide swathe of ecological niches "salvage" their environments, to borrow a term from the anthropologist Anna Lowenhaupt Tsing.[12] They enabled humans to profit from resources they did not produce (acorns, grubs, fish bones . . . the list is nearly endless), while also teaching them that these resources depended on far-reaching ecological forces. Some early medieval communities, in particular the ones that relied heavily on acorn-rich woodlands, developed economic strategies and fiscal policies that took these ecologies into consideration. Even in the upper echelons of early medieval society, kings and their advisers were trying to orient themselves to local perspectives, and the pig was one of their guides.

Thinking about geographies and economies offers a large-scale view of how important pigs were in the early medieval West, but on a more local level, humans' interactions with pigs also transformed their personal lives and even their identities. Anthropologists and biologists now describe domestication and evolution as multi-vectored processes. Humans may bring about changes in other animals, but in the course of things they are transformed as well. We can also see this happening on a conceptual level, not just a physical one. Humans' perceptions of the world and their ideas about themselves were in part shaped by their engagement with animals.

Swineherds are especially conspicuous for the partnerships they formed with pigs. Most of the people who herded pigs professionally in the early Middle Ages were unfree or enslaved workers. They were responsible for supervising the animals, especially in the interest of preventing escapees from damaging crops. But they also needed to manage pigs' breeding cycles, become intimately familiar with open-field and woodland topography, herd animals that were not easy to herd, and even perform basic veterinary care. As a result, like the animals they cared for, swineherds acquired a kind of double status.

They were low ranking by virtue of their legal status and by association with a dirty profession, but they were treated with respect in recognition of their skilled approach to work that was notoriously difficult.

Soldiers and states also became intertwined with pigs. In Late Antiquity, Roman soldiers had tended to eat more pork than local inhabitants wherever they were stationed, and the government even incorporated pigs into its tax system. Along with grain and wine, pigs were paid to the city of Rome and to military camps at the empire's borders. When the western half of the empire began to fracture in the fifth century, the role of pigs changed in tandem with politics. Most striking, one of the earliest law codes issued in the post-imperial West, the *Lex Salica*, which was issued in what is now northeast France, made pigs into a manifesto for its vision of a post-imperial kingdom. Its authors opened the code with an elaborate set of terms about pig theft, not so much to make clear that these acts were illegal—everyone would have already known that—but more to suggest that even pigs had consequences for the public order.

Another group of people who participated in mutual interactions with pigs were a looser category of pork eaters. A majority of people in the early medieval West ate at least a little pork, with the exception of Jews, Muslims, and Greenlanders. But a few groups focused on pork as a key part of their identity: landed elites above all, and to a lesser extent all Christians. Pigs were a transformative force even in the form of food. Pork was not an inactive substance as medieval eaters saw it. Meat was capable of interacting with live bodies in ways that influenced and changed them. Taste was the only sensory process that dissolved the boundary between subject and object. It was an intermixing of living and posthumous organisms, and in late antique and early medieval epistemologies, the things people tasted and digested also acted upon *them*.

Because Jews and Muslims do not eat pork, it might seem as if the pig has always been a touchstone for the differences between the monotheistic religions. But historically, in Late Antiquity and for most of the early Middle Ages, this was not the case. Rabbinic commentators saw the pig as a distinctly *Roman* animal, and even into the early Middle Ages, when the western empire had faded, the Romanness of the pig was its prevailing cultural identity.

It was probably first in the Visigothic kingdom of Iberia that the idea was floated that pigs were essential to Christian identity. Not all Christians ate pork, and not all pork-eating Christians thought that eating pork was necessary for being a Christian, but there were debates about the relationship all the same. (This is even more striking because Iberians were eating significantly

less pork than people in any other part of western Christendom.) But generally speaking, Christians in the early medieval West were more likely to be
arguing with each other about the risks or reasons for eating pork and other
meats than thinking about pigs as a measure of difference between Christianity, Judaism, and Islam.

Closer to the turn of the millennium, Christians increasingly used the
metaphor of meat to think about a range of complicated and sometimes contradictory issues, and because pork was seen as the quintessential meat, pigs
became entangled in Christian culture through this imagery. One way of
thinking about meat was to see it as a deadly distraction. Flesh, *carnis*, evoked
carnality: meat stood for a world of physical weakness and decay in contrast to
the eternal life of the soul. But meat could also help Christians think about the
dizzying notion of sacrifice. Meditating about more familiar forms of energy
transfer, like slaughtering and eating pigs, was a way to appreciate how Jesus
had sacrificed himself and in the process saved humankind. And by way of the
analogies of meat and slaughter to salvation, Christians thought more about
how animal bodies, especially pigs' bodies, constituted a kind of sacrifice for
humanity, too. In Christian theology, pigs were helping people transfer between spatial and temporal scales once again, from single acts of eating to a
vision of paradise and eternity.

The paradox of meat as simultaneously salvific and deficient swung into vicious forms of anti-Semitism in the late Middle Ages and early modern period.
At the same time pigs became Christianized, they also became Judaized. They
came to represent the Christian caricature of Judaism as a literal reading of
scripture, in contrast to Christianity's spiritual understanding of its true messages. But if pigs came to be seen as analogous to Jews, they were also viewed
as representatives and conduits of the very flesh that made Christian salvation
possible. In the process, the species became central to the ways that monotheists identified themselves against one another, though this understanding
came to the fore only in the eleventh or twelfth century. But the mixed and
intense meanings of pigs in Christian culture that emerged after the year 1000
or so were rooted in the early medieval world's long-standing knowledge of the
animals' complexity and versatility and ability to recast specific environments
into something new.

In short, pigs enrich our sense of early medieval human history because
they are historical subjects themselves. It might seem strange to suggest
such a thing: pigs have been tagged to certain symbols for such a long stretch
of time that they seem timeless. Even their ancient persona still makes an

immediate, rough sense to us: in three of the four Gospels, a demon that Jesus exorcized was driven straight into a herd of pigs, and the story would seem stranger today if those pigs had been horses, say, or bees or peacocks.[13] But there was another side to these animals. In the early Middle Ages they were seen as more than ciphers for greed and contamination. Before Jesus drove out that demon, he asked it who it was. "My name is Legion, for we are many": the pigs might as well have said the same thing. The herds and hordes of pigs that actually existed, and the communities they possessed, were many. And their stories were never exactly the same.

1 • A Singular and Plural Beast

"Three deaths are better than life," an Old Irish riddle runs: "the death of a salmon, the death of a fat pig, the death of a robber."[1] Of these three deaths, the fat pigs fell the most frequently: across the early medieval West, they were ubiquitous. Pigs were the consummate meat of the early Middle Ages. Horses and oxen have pulling power, cows and goats and sheep make milk and manure (and skin for parchment and packaging), sheep grow wool, and poultry lay eggs.[2] But domesticated pigs were only destined to be butchered. It took them less than two years to reach their maximum weight, so efficient were they in converting whatever they found or were fed into meat. The osteoarchaeological record shows that farmers slaughtered almost all their pigs before they reached their third birthday, and many of them much earlier, with the exception of breeding sows and stud boars.[3]

But pork was not the meat that everyone ate most. That distinction, as we will see in Chapter 3, generally went either to beef or to mutton. Some people did not keep pigs at all: Greenlanders, for instance, and Jews and Muslims, as far as we can tell. There were also some Christians who did not own pigs—or at least, there were Christians who drew up wills that listed their livestock but did not mention any pigs.[4] But because pigs were only ever raised for their flesh, they were a kind of metonym for meat more generally. Pork inspired rhapsodies, and even miracles; in Saint Brigit's Ireland, tree bark was turned not into fishes and loaves but bacon in order to feed a crowd. And when the scholar al-Jāḥiẓ wrote a massive collection about animals at the 'Abbāsid court in Baghdad, he had plenty of faults to find with pigs, both as a Muslim and as a naturalist. But he had also heard so many paeans to pork that he was fascinated by what it might taste like.[5]

Even the Christians who loved to eat pigs vilified them as greedy, dirty, destructive animals. This reputation was woven into the scriptures that early medieval readers studied and quoted and incorporated into their own stories and texts. We have already seen that in the Synoptic Gospels' account of the exorcism of Legion the demons were driven into pigs—not chickens or sheep or fish. Elsewhere in the Bible, the Prodigal Son hits rock bottom when, after spending his way through his inheritance, he is forced to take employment as a swineherd and eat what his pigs eat (Luke 15:11–32). In 2 Peter 2:22, building on one of the Proverbs (26:11), heretics are described as dogs who return to their vomit, and as clean pigs who turn right back to the mud. And the Gospel of Matthew (7:6) captures the concept of squandered resources with the image of casting pearls before swine. Augustine winked at this passage in his infamous story in the *Confessions* about stealing pears as a boy in North Africa—his second delinquent act was to waste what he had stolen by tossing most of his haul to a herd of pigs.[6]

The pig makes what is probably its most prominent appearance in the Judeo-Christian tradition in Psalm 80 in the Hebrew Bible (Psalm 79 in the Septuagint and Vulgate). In this psalm, the people of Israel ask God to show them favor again because they believe he has turned away from them. They compare themselves to a great vine that he has transplanted from Egypt. He has cleared the soil for them by removing other peoples from it, and the vine has grown so large and strong that it has come to cast shadows on the mountains and the great cedars, and it stretches from the river to the sea. But now, the Israelites lament, the vast vineyard is under siege. God has knocked down the wall that protected it, and its grapes are being harvested by passersby. Insects are swarming it. And the boar of the forest is destroying and devouring it (fig. 1.1).[7] In Hebrew, only the animal itself is mentioned—*ḥazir mi-ya'ar*—but in Greek and Latin, the boar gets an additional epithet: it is not only the *aper de silva* but also the *singularis ferus*, the singular beast.

These are ancient texts, but the pig's characterization as a ravenous and dirty animal has transcended particular historical moments. Christians in early medieval Europe made the same associations, and so do we. More than one historian has pointed this out over the years, partly with the goal of rehabilitating the animals' reputation.[8] But this flat stereotype, this singular beast, was not the only profile a pig could have, even in the past: "premodern" views were subtler than the shorthand symbolism suggests. In Late Antiquity and the early Middle Ages, farmers, policy makers, and philosophers

xtterminauit eam aper defilua .

&singularif ferut depaftuf eft eam

Fig. 1.1. Psalm 79[80]:13: "The boar from the woods has destroyed [the vine] and the singular beast has devoured it." This illustrated psalter, known as the Stuttgart Psalter after its current home, was made at the monastery of Saint-Germain-des-Prés in Paris in 820–830. The monk who illuminated this passage would have known both boars and vines well: in the same decade that the monastery produced this book, it also drew up a polyptych that attests to widespread viticulture on its tenancies and to extensive woodlands that were capable of feeding more than eight thousand pigs. (Stuttgart, Württembergische Landesbibliothek, Cod. bibl. 23, fol. 96v.)

were perfectly capable of holding multiple views of pigs simultaneously, of playing into a familiar caricature but also of homing in on the complexities of the species. They saw that pigs were not merely commodities that provided humans with meat, or symbols that worked as handy metaphors. They were also creatures that were capable of adapting to and altering their environments, including the human environments that only partially constrained them. Pigs were difficult to fully domesticate, both physically and conceptually. They called attention to themselves and required some engagement with their complex lives.

As a result, in these centuries pigs had both singular and plural meanings. "The" pig was a category of human understanding. It was a shorthand for thinking about a species that humans manipulated and evaluated. But early medieval societies also engaged with pluralized pigs, with specific and various individual pigs that had some control over the worlds they inhabited. In short, the history of the pig or pigs is a contrapuntal one.

Identifying the Animals

Genesis credits Adam with naming the animals, and in the seventh century Isidore of Seville would say that the names Adam had bestowed reflected something about each species' nature. And although Adam spoke Hebrew, Isidore was certain that his own native Latin still captured an essence of the things it named, too.[9] But pigs went by many names in the Latin-speaking West, and in a way this capacious lexicon is symptomatic of something we will see again and again: where there were pigs in the early Middle Ages, there was diversity. *Porcus* and *sus* were the most common terms; *sus* shares an Indo-European root with English "swine" (Old English: *swyn*). *Porcellus* was a piglet, *verres* a boar.[10] An adult pig—or more properly, a hog—could also be called *maialis* and *sualis* (or *soalis* or *sogalis*). A very little piglet could be a *nefrens* or *lactans* (literally "toothless" or "milking," a suckling piglet), and a piglet up to a year old or so could be a *bevralis, genalis,* or *friskinga.* (In modern terminology these might be "gilts" or "barrows," except that a *bevralis* in particular does not seem to have been castrated.)[11] A sow could simply be a *sus,* but sometimes she was a *troia, scrofa,* or *ductrix,* literally a "leader" or "deliverer." And then there was the burly beast known as the *sonorpair:* according to a massive law code issued by the Lombard king Rothari in 643, this was a boar (*verres*) that had fought and defeated all the other boars in a herd. No matter how large the herd, Rothari noted, there would only ever be one sonorpair—unless the herd had fewer than thirty pigs, in which case there would be no sonorpair at all. This word and this concept are not attested anywhere else, so it is hard to be sure what exactly Rothari meant. He may have been stressing the breeding value of an animal that had proven itself to be this tough: hence the penalty of twelve gold solidi, plus damages and replacement costs, owed by anyone who killed it.[12]

Nobody would have used all these words personally. The varieties reflect the fact that farming vocabularies were localized. *Maialis* tended to occur most on the Italian peninsula, for example, which is why *maiale* made it into modern Italian but not into Spanish, Catalan, French, German, or English. *Sualis* and its variants, and *bevralis, genalis,* and *friskinga,* were concentrated in the heartlands of Carolingian Francia (what is now northern France, northern Switzerland, and western Germany). In northern Iberia in the ninth and tenth centuries, *porca* was almost as likely to appear in a document as *porcus*—even though in classical Latin, *porca* usually designated the ridge that was formed between plowed furrows and only rarely pointed to a pig. And Ireland, which

had never been part of the Roman Empire and so never took up Latin as a native language, had its own set of terms, including *mucc* (pig), *cráin* (sow), *céis*
(gilt) *torc* (boar), *orc* (piglet), and *comlachtaid* (suckling piglet). More obscure
terms for pigs could be found in books. In the eighth century, a well-connected
monk and scholar named Paul the Deacon produced an abridged version of
a second-century dictionary that included words such as *cicur* (the hybrid offspring of a wild boar and domesticated sow), *colluviaris* (a pig that ate both
regular food and swill), and *dissulcus* (a pig whose bristles parted at its neck).[13]

And then there was *aper*: wild boar. In the early fifth century Augustine of
Hippo noted that wild boars were an in-between kind of animal: they were
obviously not livestock (*pecora*) like oxen, horses, sheep, and pigs, but they
also did not seem to count as wild animals (*bestiae*) in the same way that lions
and tigers and snakes did. This was an unusually moderate position. For most
ancient and medieval writers, the wild boar was unambiguously, thrillingly
wild, something whose "whole body had the force of a lightning bolt," as Apuleius had put it in the second century.[14] It was typically seen to be an entirely
separate animal from the pig—and very much a wild beast.

This distinction may not come as a surprise. Our own taxonomies allow us
to differentiate today between *Sus scrofa* and *Sus domesticus*. But before stall
raising and industrialized farming became the norm, wild and domesticated
pigs had been crossing their genes for about ten thousand years, and they can
still interbreed today. Even though medieval farmers would not have known
that deeper history, they must have been aware that wild boars sometimes
mated with domesticated pigs, because most of them lived in partial or fully
free-range conditions, which meant foraging in open spaces and woods. Occasionally zooarchaeologists will find the bones of animals that are manifestly
larger than those of the other domesticated pigs in a group, but smaller than
those of a typical wild boar: these were plausibly hybrid offspring.[15]

Pigs were not the only domesticated mammal to have wild counterparts
roaming the early medieval landscape. The aurochs, a species of wild cattle,
could be found in Europe until the seventeenth century (although it has only
left trace signs on early medieval sites). In North Africa, both aurochs and Barbary sheep were eaten alongside their domesticated relatives.[16] But for many
people, the wild boar was far more captivating. This was because across Eurasia throughout antiquity and for most of the Middle Ages poets and hunters
celebrated the wild boar as a premier big-game animal. They admired and
feared it for its strength and fury. Boars could easily kill men; more than one
medieval king died trying to hunt them. And even the men who killed their

boars usually sustained some kind of injury in the close combat that the final kill required. Only in the fourteenth century would the deer surpass the boar as the favorite aristocratic game in Europe.[17]

As a result, wild boars were asymmetrically gendered in medieval culture. People obviously knew that there were wild pigs of both sexes, but the subspecies as a whole was always thought of as masculine: the animals were boars, never sows. The Latin terms that writers used also tended to conflate species and gender in this way. Their terms for wild boar (*aper*) and the domesticated male pig (*verres*) were sometimes used interchangeably. So were the terms for domesticated pig (*porcus*) and sow (*sus*). But nobody ever called a wild pig a sow. Because of its masculine overtones, the Germanic name element **ebur-*, "Boar," was seen to be a respectable one to bestow on a boy, from tenant farmers to royal officials. Occasionally we meet an Ebretrudis, Ebrehildis, or Ebreverta—these were women's names—but on the whole, **ebur-* was much likelier to be attached to a man.[18]

Class distinction was another force splitting wild and domesticated pigs from each other. Among medievalists it is fairly well known that wild boars were a favored insignia for military gear among so-called Germanic peoples in antiquity and the early Middle Ages (so-called because "Germanic" is an agglomeration of the non- or pre-Roman societies of northern and eastern Europe that flattens their engagement with Roman culture and also their differences from one another).[19] But Romans celebrated the wild boar in the same spirit of martial elitism. The animal was the emblem of three legions (I Italica in Italy, X Fretensis in Jerusalem, XX Valeria Victrix in Pannonia and Illyricum, Germania, and finally Britain), and so it appeared on *their* equipment, too, not to mention their coinage and even their building materials.[20] And when imperial aristocrats decorated their rural villas and urban homes in Late Antiquity, they so frequently commissioned mosaics depicting wild boar hunts that art historians have warned us not to take these as straightforward signs of actual hunting on the premises. Instead such scenes were strategically placed in receiving rooms as images of pure masculine power, or *virtus*. The hunters may even have been Christian figures: although the mosaics often incorporate themes from ancient mythology—which was part of the shared culture of the Mediterranean world—they were also compatible with a sense of Christian triumphalism over death. A similar idea was at play on Roman sarcophagi that featured boar hunts. The hunters' courage spoke to the resolve of the occupants of the tombs, who were invariably men and boys.[21] The more formidable the boar, the more admirable the hunter and patron, and so the boars on these pieces are colossal and savage (figs. 1.2–1.5): barreled bodies,

Fig. 1.2. Mosaic of boar hunt from the Villa del Casale at Piazza Armerina in Sicily, fourth century. This massive villa complex may have been built by a military officer and former prefect of the city of Rome. This scene is part of a mosaic called "Small Hunt" (*Piccola Caccia*), which fills the floor of a large receiving room that measures about 26 × 33 ft. (8 × 10 m). The Small Hunt depicts a lively, loose narrative of hunts and of sacrifices to Diana, the goddess of hunting. This particular episode spans about 8 × 5 ft. (2.6 × 1.6 m). Across the mosaic, in the top-left corner, two hunters haul a captured boar to the altar: there the animal is markedly smaller (fig. 1.3). (Photo: LaurPhil on flickr, CC BY 2.0, https://www.flickr.com/photos/51417107@N03/11748447616/.)

Fig. 1.3. The vanquished (and diminished) boar en route to sacrifice, in a detail from the mosaic of the Small Hunt at the Villa del Casale. This scene is about 5.5 × 5 ft. (1.7 × 1.5 m). (Photo: Herbert Frank on flickr, CC BY 2.0, https://www.flickr.com/photos/liakadaweb/24465893287/.)

Fig. 1.4. This mosaic was installed in the late fourth century in the central reception space (*oecus*) of the villa of Carranque, near Toledo. Its owner was Maternus, probably the same Maternus who served as pretorian prefect of the East during the reign of Theodosius. The scene alludes to the myth of Adonis, a human lover of Venus who was gored to death by a wild boar. Mars and Venus stand in the left corner, and the protagonist appears in the guise of heroic nude hunter. But the battle is not going well: one spear has already snapped, and (following the myth) an anemone by Adonis's left foot sprouts up where his blood has spilled. There are also two injured hunting dogs, which the mosaic was careful to identify as Leander and Titurus. These names are drawn from ancient myth and literature, but they may have been Maternus's actual dogs. Other hunting mosaics around the empire also labeled their dogs, and the names are always different. Note the boar in the lower-right corner who is getting away: another win for the pigs. (Photo: Samuel López Iglesias.)

enormous heads, glinting tusks. And unlike domesticated pigs, which are usually depicted with curly tails, these boars are usually shown with straight tails. So when the North African poet Luxorius spoke of a "wild boar of Mars" eating fodder from the hand of its master in the marbled rooms of a villa, both his Vandal and his Roman (and Roman-Vandal) audiences would have easily understood the message. This pig might act like an aristocrat, but it had gone soft.[22]

Anyone was allowed to hunt wild boar in the early Middle Ages, and it is not unusual to find a few wild mammals, sometimes even wild boar, in settlements that were not populated by conspicuous consumers. But elites so greatly prized big game animals that in the course of the Middle Ages, European governments, starting with the Merovingians in the seventh century, increasingly cordoned off specific tracts of woodland as "forests." Doing so made them special legal spaces in which only kings and their friends could hunt—although this right was transferable to private landowners when rulers gave forests away as gifts, and sometimes elites tried to create their own private hunting parks by monopolizing woodlands for themselves.[23] In the ninth century, the Carolingian court in Francia became fixated on hunting as both a metaphor and a proof-test for military and imperial exercise. In the process, forest rights became such a vital form of political legitimacy that Charles the Bald would restrict his own son's access to key hunting grounds while Charles was away in Italy, to forestall the possibility of a usurpation. (In the same pronouncement Charles also restricted his son's ability to "receive pigs," *porcos accipere*. That might have meant picking off domesticated pigs

Fig. 1.5. This colossal wild boar appears as part of a panorama of animal hunts on a Roman sarcophagus dating to ca. 370–380. This portion of the scene runs about a third the length of the sarcophagus (which measures 6.8 ft. [2.08 m] in all). (Rome, Musei Capitolini, Centrale Montemartini, inv. MC 837/S. Image provided by the Archivio Fotografico dei Musei Capitolini; photo by Araldo De Luca. © Roma, Sovrintendenza Capitolina ai Beni Culturali.)

that fed in the same forests as their wild cousins, but it is likelier that it points to collecting the tax-in-kind that people paid for grazing their pigs in private and state-owned woodlands. If so, Charles was also restricting his son's ability to collect the fiscal revenue the king was expecting in late fall, about five months after this capitulary was issued.)[24] In the high Middle Ages the kings of England would eventually designate wild boars, regardless of their haunts, as off-limits to all but the court. There were probably not very many wild pigs around in England by the thirteenth century, when those laws were first issued. This is what the bone records suggest, at least: wild boars disappear from the animal remains on medieval settlements. Perhaps as far as the kings saw it, it would be unconscionable for the few that were left to end up in the hands of peasants.[25]

But even before wild boars became a legal entitlement, elites hunted them almost monomaniacally—or at least this is how such hunts were characterized by the people who watched from the sidelines. A hagiographical text written in the mid-sixth century about the bishop Caesarius of Arles complained that when wild boars filled the cultivated fields of a monastery, on an island just outside the city, the farmers working the fields tried to drive them away. But more powerful men (the counts of Arles, some Visigothic administrators, and their hunting buddies) had forced the farmers, sometimes brutally, to leave the animals alone, so they could hunt them for sport. This sort of physical abuse was probably rare, or so the hagiographers' outrage implies, but hunters were known to let their enthusiasm run wild. They made target practice of eagles and other scavengers, even when the birds were perched on human corpses. And well into the high Middle Ages, it was not unusual for hunting parties to trample through crops in the heat of a chase. Although hunters were obligated to compensate farmers for their losses, their privilege of right-of-way was nevertheless plain and sometimes legally mandated.[26]

So there was an imaginative chasm between wild boars and pigs, even though wild and domesticated pigs shared land and sometimes even bloodlines in common. And to an extent, the iconography hints at this relationship. From the fifth to the fifteenth century, the image of "the" pig was fairly consistent, from the few representations of pigs that survive in late antique and early medieval mosaics and manuscripts (figs. 1.6, 1.7, 1.8; see also fig. 4.3) to the windfall of images in the high Middle Ages in sculptures and manuscript paintings of the agricultural calendar. These are not pigs as they are commonly sketched today. These pigs are leggy, long-snouted, thickly bristled, curly tailed, and slender but brawny. Sometimes they have tusks. Often they have short manes limning the length of their spines.[27]

Fig. 1.6. Two pigs in the margins of a mass book called the Sacramentary of Gellone, which was produced in Gaul between 780 and 800. The pig on the left accompanies a feast for Saint Peter, the pig on the right, for the birthday of Saints John and Paul. (Paris, Bibliothèque nationale de France, Ms. Lat. 12048, fols. 38v and 91r.)

Fig. 1.7. November and December in the "Calendar of Salzburg," 818 CE. The slaughter of pigs typically took place at the start of winter, after the animals had fattened on the autumn windfall of tree nuts, and at the start of the cold weather that could facilitate the preservation process. Most adult humans would have barely needed to bend over to touch an adult pig's head, so the artist has depicted a fairly large but realistically sized specimen here. (Copyright © Österreichische Nationalbibliothek Vienna, Cod. 387, fol. 90v.)

Fig. 1.8. A pair of pigs appears among the "wild beasts and cattle, creeping things and winged" of Psalm 148. The drawing appears in the Utrecht Psalter, which was made at Reims between 816 and 823. (Utrecht University Library, Ms. 32, fol. 82v.)

There are some variations within this iconography that might point to actual differences in pig populations—though formal and rhetorical choices were also behind every artist's work, which is crucial to keep in mind.[28] Most of the time artists painted brown or red-brown pigs, but the leaf of an English gospel lectionary painted around the turn of the millennium shows pigs in an array of colors (fig. 5.8), which are quite similar to the coat colors of pigs mentioned in the Middle Irish *Bríatharogam* (white, gray, black, reddish brown, and blue-black). The pigs in the British Isles were not the only multicolored herds around the turn of the millennium: a charter drawn up in the kingdom of León in 1001 mentions the countergift of one white sow (*pork[a], per color[e] alba*) as part of a land transaction—the implication being that there were other colors of pigs to choose from.[29] And by the fourteenth century we find images of black-and-white-spotted pigs, which is a sign of particular patterns of cross-breeding between domesticated and wild lineages, and pigs with single white stripes circling their bellies, which seems to have been characteristic of pigs that were bred especially for truffle hunting.[30]

But it is hard to tell what pig breeds were around in the early Middle Ages—what colors they came in, their postures, their dispositions, and the qualities of their meat and fat. None of these details is recoverable from their bones.[31] It is hard enough to know how tall they were. By the time a cache of early medieval animal bones is excavated, a millennium or more after they were butchered, cooked, chewed, and thrown away, they are in a highly fragmentary state. It is not uncommon for pig bones to be so broken up that archaeologists have to estimate the animals' heights—when it is possible at all—on the basis of the bones in their feet. The figures we do have suggest that a pig's withers or shoulder height could range from about 21 to 32 inches (53–82 cm), with a rough mode of 29 inches (74 cm). A withers height of 32 inches or more was the sign of a very large pig, a wild boar, or the hybrid offspring of both. In central Europe, where the woodlands were deep and full of wild boars, the pigs seem to have run larger. Thirty-two and a half inches was actually the *average* height at the Carolingian fortress of Roßtal in northern Bavaria, and pigs on some settlements in Poland were so massive, topping out at 40 inches or so (99–104 cm), that they may have been regularly rather than intermittently breeding with their wild neighbors. This was the case with several individuals at the hillfort and hinterland of Sypniewo, for instance, in Mazovia in the tenth and eleventh centuries.[32] So in a rare Carolingian illustration of the agricultural cycle, the size of a pig held fast between a swineherd and butcher is on the larger side, but it's still entirely realistic (see fig. 1.7).

The situation had been different in antiquity. The archaeologist Michael MacKinnon discovered that Italians in the Roman Empire had bred two distinct types of pigs: a free-ranging breed that looked a lot like its early medieval successors, and a fat, smooth-skinned, short-nosed, floppy-eared pig that was fattened on the farm. Each breed had a different purpose. The hairier, slenderer ones were for everyday eating, and the big pinkish ones were slated for sacrifices. Italians may not have been the only farmers doing this. In addition to the textual and visual evidence that pointed to the existence of two pig breeds, MacKinnon took the wide range of withers heights as another indication of the split. In Italy pigs' heights ran from roughly 22 to 34 inches (57–86 cm)—which might not seem much different from the early medieval figures were it not that the maximum sizes in the early Middle Ages are outliers rather than clusters (this is why they are likelier to represent wild animals than a different breed, unlike the Roman pigs). We find similar ranges in the western provinces, coinciding with the empire's colonization of these territories. In Iberia, pig sizes ranged from roughly 23 to 32 inches (59–81 cm) in the Middle Iron Age and expanded to 25.5 to 36.5 inches (65–93 cm) after the conquest. In Gaul in the first century CE, the size of pigs "rapidly" increased while also growing increasingly diverse up to the third century. The Romans also seem to have introduced a larger pig breed to Britain.[33]

After the Roman emperors lost control over the western provinces, livestock throughout these regions tended to get smaller—cattle, most noticeably, but also sheep, goats, and pigs. This was not necessarily a sign of a civilization in decline. Larger cattle are good for plowing, but they tend to produce less milk, fat, and protein. Bigger livestock also require more fodder and water. So there are advantages to smaller animals.[34] And in the case of pigs, the disappearance of the fat stall-fed variety could reflect a change in religious practice more than anything else. Historians are starting to find that in the third century animal sacrifice began to wane across the empire. (Or as the art historian Jás Elsner put it, ritual sacrifice "became significantly more vegetarian.") By the time a stream of Christian emperors began legislating against animal sacrifice in the fourth and fifth centuries, they were condemning rituals that had mostly fallen out of style in the civic and religious life of the empire, even among polytheists. ("Mostly," because this trend was not uniform across the provinces. An inscription from one of the cemeteries of the large Roman-Libyan settlement of Ghirza, for example, attests to a sacrifice of fifty-one bulls and thirty-eight pigs in a single day, probably in the fourth century, as part of the ancestral celebration of Parentalia. Then again, such a spectacular slaughter would not have been commemorated in stone if it were routine.)[35] So although the research on pig biometrics in Late Antiquity and the early Middle Ages is still very much in progress, for now it seems plausible that farmers across the Roman West (not just Italians) were originally breeding fat, pink pigs, and then stopped—in large part because there were no longer political and religious reasons to do so.

The Spaciousness of Species

Generalizing about pig breeds will get us only so far, though, because even pigs of a similar phenotype lived in vastly different circumstances across the post-imperial West. They were able to do this because they were, and are, a flexible species. Pigs were individual, social, and adaptable creatures that changed according to their contexts.

Every pig needs to eat, for example, but what it eats and how it eats depends on the situation. Pigs' diets are notoriously ecumenical. They seem to prefer acorns, beech mast, grubs, worms, summer-autumn crops like legumes and grains, and chocolate-covered raisins. (The last is specific to modern pigs: researchers use this treat as a reward.) But depending on the season and where they are raised, they will also eat other nuts, roots, rhizomes, fruits, mushrooms, sedges, grasses, arthropods, amphibians, reptiles, eggs, rodents, mollusks, fish, whey, kitchen slops of all kinds, and, if necessary, carrion and feces, including human carrion and human feces. They will chew on the bones of other livestock, including pig bones, if they come across them in the trash. According to ancient and late antique authors of agrarian manuals, sows would even eat their own piglets if no other food could be found.[36] Tenants of the Rhineland monasteries of Wissembourg and Prüm were obligated to feed oats to the monks' pigs in the winter. Millers seem to have routinely raised pigs—they often owed fattened pigs as part of their annual rent pay-

ments—and probably fed them grain waste at least part of the year, in addition
to sending them out to the woods to feed near their riverine properties. Pigs in
Ireland gorged on dandelion roots. On the Faroes it was the roots of buttercup
and tormentil. In Iceland and the Scottish Isles, the Norse (that is, Viking)
colonists fed their pigs mostly fish or mostly plants, depending on the farm.[37]

The thing was, a pig could be happy almost anywhere, even in environments that were relatively new to it. In 2005 the *New Yorker*'s Ian Frazier took
a long look at feral hogs in the U.S. South and reported that they

> root up rare and diverse species of plants all over, and contribute to the
> replacement of those plants by weedy, invasive species, and promote ero-
> sion, and undermine roadbeds and bridges with their rooting, . . . and
> root up the hurricane levee in Bayou Sauvage, Louisiana, that kept Lake
> Pontchartrain from flooding the eastern part of New Orleans, and . . .
> root up American Indian historic sites and burial grounds, and root up a
> replanting of native vegetation along the banks of the Sacramento River,
> and root up peanut fields in Georgia, and root up sweet-potato fields in
> Texas, and dig big holes by rooting in wheat fields irrigated by motor-
> ized central-pivot irrigation pipes, and, as the nine-hundred-foot-long
> pipe advances automatically on its wheeled supports, one set of wheels
> hangs up in a hog-rooted hole, and meanwhile the rest of the pipe keeps
> on going and begins to pivot around the stuck wheels, and it continues
> and continues on its hog-altered course until the whole seventy-five-
> thousand-dollar system is hopelessly pretzeled and ruined.[38]

The despoliation that wild pigs have wrought on the U.S. South and Texas
is the sign of a relative newcomer. These pigs are mostly the descendants
of Eurasian wild boars that hunters imported in the late nineteenth century,
prowling areas where human and nonhuman environments have not adapted
to or learned to control them, at overpopulated levels. But although the scale of
this problem is a consequence of colonialism and global trade, and therefore
not representative of the early medieval situation, it speaks to the talent that all
pigs have for trying, and eating, new things.[39]

What a pig decides to do depends on the landscape, then, but also on
the pig. Pigs have demonstrably personal preferences when it comes to the
ways they explore, socialize, and respond to change.[40] And their habits can
change, too, because pigs are strategic improvisers. They make on-the-spot
choices based not only on what they already like but also on calculations that
account for predators, seasons, landscapes, and the food supply relative to

their population. All mother sows, for instance, will try to conserve resources by reducing the frequency of their nursing sessions after their piglets are two days old. Sows in industrial crates, who cannot actually move away from their litters, will instead try to sit or stand or rest on their sternums to cover their teats. (This helps, but the piglets still manage to suckle more than in the wild and in the process reduce their mother's weight more than she would like.)[41] A study that compared wild pigs living in the primeval forest of Białowieża, in Poland, to a population of wild pigs living on the edges of Kraków, found pigs' capacities to be similarly plastic. The forest-dwelling pigs ranged farther in old-growth forests largely undisturbed by human activity, switching between eating and napping day and night. The pigs who lived in the green spaces of Kraków established a smaller home range, but they walked twice as many miles per day and restricted their movements to nighttime.[42]

Pigs also respond to one another, especially the pigs they know personally, by smell, sound, and sight. They have a vocal repertoire of different grunts, squeals, "grunt-squeals," and trumpeting calls that humans are only just beginning to decode. Pigs are highly social animals in captivity (when they are permitted to socialize), as are females and their young, and groups of males, in the wild. They tend to adopt the behavior of other pigs in their group when they forage, with some variation according to their social rank, individuality, and environment.[43] A miracle story recorded in the ninth century by Walahfrid Strabo, a monk and Carolingian courtier, mentions the unmiraculous fact that the herd of pigs belonging to the monks of the monastery of Saint Gall always followed one particular sow around, "as if she were their leader." Some groups might opt for a division of labor: in late summer and early fall, in the large herds that congregate today in forested areas of Italy and Bulgaria, males and young pigs will be the first to explore an area for food, and once they find a safe and nutritious place the females and subadults will join them. (Wild pig societies also tend to be matriarchal.)[44] So it should not be surprising that in the lab, pigs are less anxious in new places if they have another pig alongside them, and they are motivated to solve puzzles more quickly when they are rewarded with a shortcut back to their friends.[45]

Every pig's capacities and choices are substantially affected by its history, too, which is another reason why pigs are both highly capable and highly variable. A pig's experiences shape its nonconscious or implicit memories, which enable the pig to acquire skills and improve its performance in familiar activities. But it also deliberately retrieves memories of its experiences to solve new problems, and it can "reverse-learn" those patterns—meaning that a pig will undo prior associations it has made when it realizes that a cause-and-effect relationship no longer holds.[46] Pigs' spatial memories are complex and constructive. As wild animals they can find food in new locations by drawing on their memories of food finding in the past to make new inferences and conclusions—although we still have a lot to learn about what kinds of comparisons and connections pigs make when they navigate.[47] And as lab animals, they have proved that they like to explore and learn, not only in pursuit of a goal but also for curiosity's sake. They prefer new objects to old ones. They prefer mazes to "environmentally impoverished" places in which there is nothing for them to do.[48]

This single species was therefore capable of generating many conceivable scenarios that could count as "typical" or "natural," not only because the world itself was a vast and variable place but also because pigs responded to that dynamism with intelligence and versatility. This observation is the fruit of years of biobehavioral research, but its insights are not exclusively modern. Late antique and early medieval observers employed the idea of "species," too—or what they usually called *genus* in Latin—and they also saw that these generalizations fell short.

In the fifth century Augustine of Hippo proposed one working definition of species that was based on sociability. He argued that all animals, including humans, naturally seek peace among their own kind (*genus*). That is obvious in the case of gregarious animals like sheep, starlings, or bees. But it is also true of inveterate loners. Even tigers will come together to mate, and the female will pacify her own fierceness to nurture her cubs when it is time.[49]

But Augustine also ventured this theory of species in order to point out, as part of a larger argument he was making in *City of God,* that humans were not particularly adroit in thinking about larger scales and structures. Any given person's plans for a social order might suit that person and a handful of other people, but that ostensible peace would never work for everyone. Part of the problem was that an individual's perspective was inescapably limited. Another handicap was the fact that humans are inherently self-serving. So although we *should* reach conclusions and make policies only after considering multiple perspectives and acknowledging that our sense of justice is necessarily provisional and imperfect, we instead favor snap judgments that dismiss tigers as ferocious or other human beings as monstrous. Species-ness is hard to recognize and even harder to respect.

Another taxonomic approach to the concept of species is perhaps more familiar to us. Species could also be defined by the unique forms and behaviors that a set of organisms shared and reproduced in their offspring.[50] One well-known adoption of such a classification system was Isidore's encyclopedic *Etymologies,* which the bishop compiled in the seventh century and Europeans enthusiastically read, copied, excerpted, and rewrote throughout the Middle Ages:

> The pig/sow (*sus*) is so called because she roots up (*subigat*) pasture, that is, she searches for food by rooting the earth up. The boar (*verres*) [is called that] because he has great strength (*vires*). The pig (*porcus*) [is named] as if he were dirty (*spurcus*), for he gorges himself on filth, immerses himself in mud, and smears himself with slime. Horace says: "And the sow is a friend to mud." This is also the source of the terms for "uncleanness" (*spurcitia*) and "illegitimate children" (*spurii*).[51]

Isidore's characterizations here were obviously guided by lexicon as much as by nature, because his *Etymologies* was predicated on the idea that sign and signified had a meaningful rather than arbitrary relationship. But although we should not treat this as a straightforwardly naturalistic text, it was nevertheless the case that pigs' familiar behaviors helped Isidore and his readers triangulate the everyday world and the Latin language to get closer to the ideas that Adam had intended to inscribe. Animals and words together were a key to divine taxonomies.

Identifying species as a set of organisms with reproducible traits was analytically useful, but in Late Antiquity critics had already begun to be troubled by the limitations of this approach. According to the first creation story in Genesis, God had made all things that would ever exist "according to its kind (or species)"—or in the language of the Vulgate, *secundum genus* (Gen. 1:21). But it was not clear how the intangible properties of an animal species were reproduced generation after generation. Basil of Caesarea's explanation to his own congregation in Cappadocia in the late fourth century was that God had assigned a single soul to every species of land animal. It was because of a shared soul, for example, that all lions were courageous, solitary, proud, terrifying, and picky about their meat. All bears were lazy and secretive for the same reason. Each species' soul determined its unique mix of sense perceptions, memories, and emotions. So although animals were not capable of reason (or education, as Basil's Latin translator would add), they were sensitive to their environments and knew what was good for themselves, thanks to the soul that God had given them.[52]

Basil's language of animal souls drew on the Aristotelian tradition of thinking about the "soul" as a life-giving force that enabled a living thing to fulfill its purpose, but it was not explored extensively in the Latin West. His own translator tended to blunt the force of the Greek *psyche* by waffling between *anima* and *animus*, the second of which reduced the "soul" to something more mental and metaphorical. Other Christians did not hesitate to say that animals had souls, but their interests usually lay elsewhere, and, again, their language was somewhat slippery. When Gregory the Great explained in the late sixth century that animals had souls, his preferred word was "vital-" or "life-spirit," *vitalis spiritus,* a lexical choice that one of his later readers noticed was an equally polysemic term. (This reader was Dhuoda, an elite woman living in Francia in the ninth century, who discussed the passage in a book of advice for her son.) But Gregory was very much talking about souls here: he was arguing that the difference between human and animal souls was that animal souls died when their bodies did—a point that Basil had also made—whereas human souls were immortal. It was actually this latter claim that was more hotly contested in Gregory's day. The bishop of Rome was writing to rebut Aristotelian circles across the Mediterranean who were skeptical about the afterlife of human souls. But later readers would take issue with the first assumption as well. John Scottus Eriugena, who had read the work of both Basil and Gregory and wrote his own natural-philosophical texts in Francia in the ninth century, was not so sure that *animal* souls were mortal, either.[53]

The language of the soul aside, other accounts of species generation still shared Basil's conviction that God had set something in motion that could continue to reproduce itself down to the very mental activities of individual animals. But this proposition provoked an additional criticism, which was that individual creatures varied considerably even within a single species. For Boethius, an aristocrat and a politician writing in the Ostrogothic kingdom of Italy in the early sixth century, this taxonomical problem was unavoidable because this was how categorical thinking worked. In his commentary on Porphyry's *Isagoge,* which was itself a third-century commentary on Aristotle's *Categories,* the concepts of *genus* and *species* were not absolute or fine-grained. They were only meant to describe relationships between things. If you asked a man what he was, he would never say he was an animal—that's not how conversations usually go!—but if you asked him what he and a horse and an ox were, you would get the category you were looking for. The same is true for things grouped together as a species (*species:* Boethius is not leaning on the *genus*-language of the Bible here). Members of a species have a form in common, but even then their shared taxon is a conceptual distinction that is not attached to any individual's actual existence (*natura*). Humans were capable of laughter, for instance, but some people never thought anything was funny.

The only time it was possible to generalize while *also* being fully specific was when you were talking about a "grouping" or category that consisted of lone representatives—such as the phoenix or the moon. Otherwise, when you described a species you would only ever be approximating.[54]

Variation was not simply a problem with humans and their uniquely willful behavior. It was also observable in nonhuman animals. An animal might be said to act "unnaturally" and therefore hint at the presence of the *super*natural, but even the "natural" order itself encompassed a great variety of possibilities.[55] Augustine's response to this in his own commentary on Genesis was that although God had established a set of finite possibilities or *termini* for every species, those parameters did not confine any individual creature to a single trajectory. Members of a species could differ noticeably from one another. They might even resemble members of another species in some ways. But crucially from Augustine's point of view, they never became so different as to transgress the species boundary. And it is striking that one of the species Augustine singles out in this discussion was the pig: a pig, he insisted, would never be more like a human than a pig.[56] He was making his argument to a culture that was all too familiar with pigs' many possible behaviors.

These were all ways of thinking about pigs categorically, as "the" pig in the singular, whether pigs were joined by their sociability or reproducible likeness or even their iconography. But these writers and their contemporaries were also aware that such taxonomies had certain explanatory and predictive limitations—that they were inexact sciences, in other words. Such shortcomings would have been especially obvious to them in the case of animals they knew well, including pigs, and it was even more common to find medieval societies seeing pigs in the plural, rather than generalizing about them. The animals' changeability, and their sheer numbers, mattered. Although pigs were very nearly everywhere in the early medieval West, if you'd seen one, you hadn't seen them all.

Unruly Commodities

Because pigs were able to change in response to other pigs and to their surroundings, we cannot capture precisely what any given group of pigs was like or what it was like to work with them. But the early medieval evidence we have confirms that the cognitive and behavioral capacities of modern populations of domesticated and wild pigs do have striking parallels to those of pigs in the past, even though their contexts and histories are not identical. Early medieval pigs also had a knack for learning, exploring, and taking advantage of new situations—and early medieval humans knew this, because those behaviors were taxing. But people were willing to work with pigs anyway, and their own ideas and behaviors changed in the process.

Incidentally, pigs' health was almost never a concern for the humans who raised and ate them.[57] Not only were pigs generally slaughtered before the aging process set in, with all its attendant injuries and ailments. Pigs were also raised in low-density and outdoor environments that did not make them highly vulnerable to illness, in contrast to the industrial conditions they endure today.[58] Sometimes pigs did get sick. Columella and Palladius, Italians who wrote farming handbooks in the first and later fourth or fifth centuries, respectively, mentioned that pigs could experience fevers, dizziness, vomiting, engorged spleens, tumors, and lung problems. Pliny the Elder, who wrote his massive Natural History in the first century, added that they were also susceptible to madness and sore throats. Early medieval encyclopedic and legal texts identified rabies, contraction of the leg tendons, and blisters (caused by the bites of a parasite called the usia) as additional risks.[59] And osteoarchaeologists occasionally find evidence of pig pathologies in the animals' bones: an intestinal parasite (Trichuris suis), a broken bone here and there, a diseased bone with abnormal growth, sets of crowded teeth, and cases of linear enamel hypoplasia—a deficiency in the calcium development of teeth that indicates stress on a pig's diet and health. There is also a passing reference in a late antique medical text that treats a remedy of radishes for sick pigs as common knowledge.[60] But when it came to internal medicine especially, medical theorists were certain that pigs could generally take care of themselves—in particular, by feeding on river crabs, which was reported to be a panacea for whatever problems they might have.[61]

Such theories may not have been accurate, but farmers had other things to worry about, mostly involving the animals when they were rambunctiously healthy. Pliny had snickered that no animal was more brutus (that is, fatter and dumber) than a pig, but in the early Middle Ages such a comment did not have much traction.[62] For just about every kind of boundary that humans devised to pen or restrain their livestock—wood fences, "islands" of pasture surrounded by trenches or ditches, pens with stone walls—pigs figured out ways to escape. Not only are pigs good at solving their way out of spatial puzzles. They can jump up to four feet high. They can swim a few miles at a time. And if one pig was able to figure its way out of a pen, the animals' ability to learn from one another meant that others would bring up the rear. An eighth-century Irish

Fig. 1.9. In the late Middle Ages the city of Pistoia outlawed the tying of pigs to a weight in the open-air market of the Piazza del Sala, a practice that the scribe helpfully sketched in the margin here. In the early Middle Ages, this sort of tethering could result in a broken leg, and it was apparently not practiced often. (Archivio di Stato di Pistoia, Comune di Pistoia, Raccolte 5, fol. 225r [late fourteenth century]. Photo and find: Guy Geltner. Reproduced with permission from the Ministero dei beni e delle attività culturali e del turismo, Archivio di Stato di Pistoia, authorization no. 1999.)

law text known as *Bretha Comaithchesa* anticipated this problem and outlined what the fines would be when a piglet jumped the fence into a tasty field of grain four times in a single day, "lead[ing] the herd each time." A few frustrated farmers even tried to tether their pigs by the hind leg in an attempt to anchor them to a spot in the farmyard (fig. 1.9), but pigs would work so energetically to free themselves that they could break their legs in the process, and their struggle shows up in their bones.[63]

Stray and lost animals were only a fraction of the problem. The mastermind piglet of the *Bretha Comaithchesa* points to a more serious concern, which centered on the "moveable disc at the top of the muzzle": pigs were rooters.[64] All livestock were capable of escaping and doing damage, but pigs were considered especially pernicious culprits. We have already seen that Isidore of Seville classified a pig's manner of rooting as one of its defining characteristics as a species. That rooting made them valuable, because the dexterity of their snouts extended their dietary range to the realm of the subterranean. But it was also a real liability, as Ian Frazier's informants knew all too well. Once pigs escaped their pens, they were capable of what the Old Irish laws called "root trespass" (*fochlaid*), which was worse than the kinds of damage that other livestock were capable of. Pigs could eviscerate a field of crops rather than merely trim it down. They could reengineer a landscape by digging ditches, turning a carefully plowed field or flat meadow into a completely different terrain. This would have been a risk in cities, too, because many towns in the early Middle Ages were filled with food gardens—in residential yards, between homes, in abandoned lots, even in repurposed theaters and fora.[65]

There were other disturbing possibilities for a pig on the lam. They could bite people. They could kill adult men and women, not to mention children. They were known to defile the dead by munching on their corpses before anybody had had a chance to bury them. They killed one another on occasion. It also went on the record that one particular pig had been locked up in a pen after causing damage—only to attack and kill a calf that happened to be inside the pen, too.[66]

These were worst-case scenarios, but not all pigs caused so much trouble, at least not all the time. In Ireland, some women hand-fed runt piglets and treated them as pets, for example, although once the pigs got older, their habit of "follow[ing] everybody" around could also make them a nuisance.[67] This practice is not attested anywhere else in the early medieval West, but as we will see, the pigs of these centuries were generally capable of being managed and herded in ways that made them collaborative and productive members of agrarian society. So the risks of pig husbandry rarely seemed to outweigh the benefits.

But the risks were there all the same, and farming communities looked for ways to reduce them and to limit the damage their animals were capable of doing. The Visigothic village of Gózquez, for example, which was home to ten to twelve households in central Spain, channeled the movement of its livestock—mostly sheep, goats, and cattle, in this case—along a fenced trail that ran through the center of the village in order to reduce the opportunities for stray animals to interfere with the farming plots scattered throughout the area (fig 1.10).[68] In a more famous and fictional map, the containment of livestock was handled in a different way. The Plan of Saint Gall (a monastery in what is now Switzerland) represents the idealized architecture of livestock and unfree workers in an orderly grid (fig. 1.11). The plan was drawn up at the imperial monastery of Reichenau in the ninth century to encourage the monks of Saint Gall to meditate on the meanings and functions of their monastic space. In the quadrant at the bottom of the parchment, the pig house (*domus*) shares the same elegant geometry as the buildings for the other livestock. It features a central courtyard surrounded by stables on three sides and fronted with living spaces for the swineherds. The text above the pig house reads, "This place nourishes the [young] pigs and watches over the adults." Even in the plan's serene vision, swineherds had to monitor their charges closely.[69]

Fig. 1.10. The eastern half of the village of Gózquez (525/40 to 750), with its parallel lines of fences proactively limiting the ability of animals to stray into crops as they were herded to other places. (Reproduced by permission of Alfonso Vigil-Escalera Guirado.)

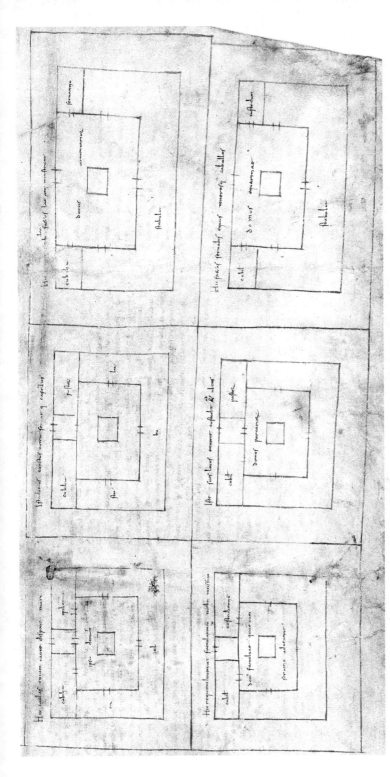

Fig. 1.11. Livestock and the unfree in harmony in the Plan of Saint Gall, made at Reichenau in the 820s. The buildings include, moving clockwise from top left: the houses of sheep and shepherds; goats and goatherds; dairy cows and cowherds; horses and grooms; pigs and swineherds; and the servants who arrive with guests of the monastery. (St. Gallen, Stiftsbibliothek, Cod. Sang. 1092 fol. 1r.—Plan of Saint Gall.)

When lawmakers began writing a flurry of codes in the early Middle Ages, sometimes in the spirit of Roman law but always in the interests of communities who recognized themselves as post-imperial, they were keenly sensitive to the havoc that livestock were capable of causing. They made a few recommendations for how to avoid animal destruction. Gates should not be left open. Fences should be fixed. (They should also be built competently to begin with.) And people who damaged or destroyed other landowners' fences would pay high penalties.[70] These were obvious solutions, but sometimes it was necessary to remind communities of their own obligations to be proactive: in the 930s or 940s, the Anglo-Saxon king Æthelstan complained to the city of London that many people were unconcerned about what their livestock were up to, because they were overly confident in the ability of the city's "police" force or security guild to work without any effort on their part.[71] But lawmakers were even *more* interested in developing protocols for the aftermath—for dealing with the damages that animals were inevitably going to cause rather than reminding people how to prevent them in the first place—because no matter how many precautions a farmer might take, they almost certainly were not going to be enough.

When a farmer did find an animal in his or her crops, the procedures for handling the situation were fairly consistent across legal cultures. Above all, whoever owned the animals was held liable for their actions. But the victim was also expected to handle the situation with a cool head: he or she should carefully drive the animals out of the field, perhaps into an enclosure, and immediately notify their owner, who usually owed fines in addition to the damages. The animals were returned only after restitution was made. (In Visigothic Iberia, the fines escalated if the owner did not respond promptly.) Sometimes arbitrators were employed to set a price on the losses, and the fines were higher if the animals' owner had intentionally loosed them into the field. It was also considered a good idea to summon neighbors to the scene straightaway, so that they could serve as witnesses.[72]

In some communities, a farmer was allowed to kill an intrusive animal under certain circumstances. In the Rhône valley in the early sixth century, Burgundian lawmakers set a three-strikes rule for pigs: if an owner's pigs traipsed through another farmer's vineyards, meadows, grain, or oak woods, the owner would receive up to two warnings to watch them properly. But if it happened a third time, the farmer who suffered the losses was entitled to kill the best pig of the entire herd and keep the meat for himself. Evidently this policy struck some farmers or lawmakers as too lenient: a later modification of this code added that the owner of a vineyard could kill one pig immediately if a herd was found in that painstakingly cultivated space. In Lombard Italy, it was permissible to kill a trespassing pig if it was part of a herd of more than ten animals; and if the pigs were earnestly digging ditches it was lawful to kill one no matter how small the herd. King Ine of Wessex (688–694) showed even more sympathy to the victims of loose livestock: if a cow broke through a well-maintained fence to graze on someone's crops, the landowner could kill it because its owner was, to the king's mind, unable or unwilling to watch it properly. (Ine did not make special provisions for killing pigs.)[73]

The damages a domesticated animal caused were almost never treated as an accident—that is, as unactionable. There were only a few cases, depending on the legal culture, in which lawmakers were willing to lay all the blame on animals themselves. Irish jurists were the most permissive, although disagreements arose among them about what counted as an extenuating circumstance. They suggested that if an animal were being chased, or in heat, or frightened by thunder and lightning the trespasses it made was not a punishable offense. Likewise injuries that pigs inflicted were not actionable if the animals had been disturbed from their (routine) digging or eating, if they were already injured, or if they were defending their piglets. And in Lombard Italy, nobody was liable for an animal if it was rabid or possessed by a demon—in other words, if it was out of its mind.[74]

Lawmakers were arguing here that animals usually thought and behaved in predictable or at least legible ways, which humans needed to anticipate. In most cases, they took the position that owners were obligated to constrain that behavior for the benefit of their neighbors—but they were still responsible when their animals outmaneuvered them. Such strictures were not imposed because humans were thought to be capable of complete control over their animals. As the rabbinic compilers of the Babylonian Talmud, working in western Persia around the same time as the production of these law codes, which were mostly developed in the fifth to eighth centuries, had observed, one problem with agricultural tort law was that it presumed that animals were transparent, but in reality they were sometimes inscrutable.[75] In the legal cultures of the early medieval West, the assignment of guilt was only a legal exigency. *Somebody* needed to be at fault, because conflicts were resolved almost exclusively through the payment of fines. It might make a difference in the fine if the animal owner had been negligent, but the truth was that even cautious owners could not outsmart their animals every time. Either way, they had to pay.

Whatever the animals' owners might have felt about the laws' definition of justice, it is clear that the farmers who found their investments destroyed by another's livestock thought the laws did not go far enough. The law codes are full of instructions about what *not* to do if you find animals in your fields. *Don't* chase the animals off in a state of "excessive rage" and thereby cause even more damage. *Non moleste sed modeste,* went the rule in one farming community: a farmer should kick the animals out "not madly but measuredly." Don't send your dogs after them. Don't cut the lips off the livestock munching your crops, or an eye or an ear or a horn or a tail. Don't kill them outright—or as a Bavarian law code from the eighth century put it sympathetically, "Nobody should dare kill someone else's animal, not even a pig, despite the damages it is found to have done." And it did not go without saying that an aggrieved farmer should not beat up or kill the animals' herder.[76]

All told, these laws show that different legal communities, and even different members of the same community, had some conflicting views about what was possible or reasonable to do when pigs and other livestock escaped. But no matter what position a person took, those legal discourses were shaped by animals that were happily, irredeemably transgressive. The result was an ongoing process of co-domestication: in the effort to raise pigs for their meat, humans bent their practices and policies to accommodate them.

And it is no surprise that the conflicts that pigs triggered were not always resolved in line with the transactional formalities the lawmakers prescribed. Some cases ended up in court, and records of a few of those cases survive, though the details are frustratingly vague. There is a patchy document, for example, scratched on slate in the 640s that was found in Ávila, in central Spain. The slate identifies itself as a *securitas,* which (as we can tell from other formulaic arrangements of this kind drawn up in Gaul) was a contract that confirmed a party's ownership of some disputed property and recorded the payment of fines for any violation of those rights.[77] In this particular securitas, a man named Gisadus pays Anianus and Teudoteus ten gold solidi. Gisadus also mentions a pig more than once. We will never know the whole story behind this document. One possibility is that Gisadus had stolen a pig—from the sty? on its ramblings?—and was paying a hefty fine for it. Another possibility is that Gisadus owned this pig (the phrase *porcum meum* appears in the text) and it had been grazing or rooting in land to which Gisadus was not entitled.[78]

In Galicia, in northwestern Spain, the monastery of Celanova forced two families to surrender half their properties in the year 1000, because they had both given falsified evidence to the court in an earlier trial that had concerned the pig of a certain Santio. We don't know what *this* pig had done, either. We might speculate, based on what we know about pigs and about early medieval legal culture, that Santio's pig had violated the monastery's property, and the two families (Maria and her son Ruderico, and Olidus and his wife, Gota) had defended Santio untruthfully. But this is only a guess. All we can be sure of is that, like its analogue some 350 years earlier, this pig had catalyzed a court appearance—and in this case, small-scale peasant farmers lost precious resources in the process.[79]

Extrajudicial violence was also a problem. Lombard lawmakers under King Rothari assumed that at some point or another, swineherds were going to get into fights with one another, and so they drew up regulations for how to penalize them. No other herders or farmworkers were singled out in the same way. The king also alluded to the fact that incidents such as pig biting and other animal-inflicted injuries were not always put to rest after the requisite fines had been paid, even though settling the matter was precisely what the monetary penalty was supposed to do: "The animal's owner should pay compensation for the injury or death, bringing the feud or hostility in this matter to an end, because a mute thing was to blame, and there was no human intention involved."[80] Rothari's second rationale here—that a feud is all the more indefensible if it is catalyzed by a nonhuman creature—was an attempt to rebut a different kind of understanding. In this alternate ethic, farmers were holding one another personally accountable for their animals' actions and expected humans and animals to collaborate closely. And the failure to do so, according to this view, warranted retaliation.

In the course of these confrontations and debates, pigs became a formative influence not only on medieval communities' sense of proper farm management but also on their definitions of social order more generally. And that was because the value of pork in the early Middle Ages was profoundly dependent upon the characteristics that pigs exhibited as living things. The animals' brains and bodies accommodated a huge range of environments and reliably produced the flesh that humans wanted. At the same time, pigs required accommodation. They were both a flexible species and a demanding one that trotted and jumped and swam right through the boundaries that humans had set for them. So in the process of (very imperfectly) exploiting animals for food, humans' own bodies and perspectives were transformed as well. In the next chapter I show how this sensibility—this attention to dynamic interdependence as a fact of life—was connected to a Christian view of the physical world that was rigorously ecological, rather than absolutely hierarchical, as it is often assumed to be.

2 • From the Mud to the Cosmos

Pointing out the complexities of a seemingly simple animal like "the pig" is in many ways a premodern move. In the early Middle Ages, the subtle features of the physical world mattered. Farmers thought so, but they were not the only ones. Early medieval intellectuals—writers whose work blended philosophy, theology, and science—were also riveted by their environments because in their eyes even the smallest details of life on the ground could reveal insights about the larger universe. This chapter is about that way of seeing and thinking. Pigs will make some appearances in the course of it, but my larger goal here is to explore early medieval notions of environmental scale and connectivity, because even at a distance pigs were seen to be embedded in an epistemology and ethics of the physical world that connected the mud to the cosmos.

To late antique and early medieval observers, the universe was a vast, sparkling puzzle. Cosmographers described its farther reaches—the crystalline quiet of the upper air, the complex clockwork of the stars, the icy mass of Saturn—while self-consciously mapping the limits of their knowledge. The human eye could see so distantly and yet overlook so much as its vision stretched out to the celestial bodies! Outer space was not the only zone where secrets were hidden. The orb of the earth that was somehow fixed at the heart of the cosmos had its own elusive dimensions, from the mysterious creatures of the deep, to the respiratory system of an insect, to the infinitesimal mechanics of a body's decomposition.[1] Some of the most mundane features of life on earth were, on closer inspection, astonishingly complex.

But the Christian intellectuals who thought about these problems were tantalized rather than discouraged by what they did not know. There was a seduction and a joy to discovering new features of the world, of making the familiar unfamiliar and vice versa. There were also larger implications to their discoveries: each fraction of the cosmos was part of creation, and understanding a part could help elucidate the whole. It was impossible to know everything about God, but it was at least possible to learn more about him through his masterwork. The study of the physical world was in that sense a branch of theology. Science and religion were mutual inspirations. Christianity was not only an "answer" to the universe but also an imperative to learn more about it.

And so, contrary to what we might expect, the Christian Bible was not a "scientific textbook" that early medieval readers consulted to the exclusion of all else. Although they believed that the biblical narratives of creation were historically, literally true, they were also quick to point out that the accounts were often cryptic, and that in any case they were not exhaustive. Genesis raised as many questions as it answered. As Remigius of Auxerre put it in his commentary on Genesis in the late ninth century, "This book is enveloped by many depths in every word."[2] So interpreters turned to other sources and informants to explicate Genesis and more fundamentally to better grasp the architecture of the divine order. Depending on the researcher, those sources might include other exegetical works, poetry, philosophy, natural histories, encyclopedic compendia or handbooks, expert knowledge, or direct observations or experiences of physical phenomena. Even farmlands were fair game.

Early medieval analysis of the physical world would not satisfy today's criteria for what counts as science. How could it, when the concept of "the" scientific method itself was born of circumstances specific to the nineteenth and early twentieth centuries? In Late Antiquity and the early Middle Ages, examinations of the physical world blended what today we would differentiate as humanistic and scientific impulses. They involved some combination of natural history (inquiries about remarkable things in nature), natural philosophy (examinations of the reasons or causes of natural things), and exegesis (explanations of scriptural texts). Early medieval research did not insist on controlled experiments, and researchers were not obsessed with the virtue of objectivity. So it is anachronistic to see their work as science, if by *science* we mean the ways researchers today study, say, astrophysics or plant biology.[3]

But it was nevertheless the case that late antique and early medieval intellectuals wanted to learn more about the physical world and how it worked, even though they had read and respected the work of many analysts who had come before them. Their studies show a mix of curiosity, skepticism, predictive confidence, and provisionality. They believed that knowledge was inescapably situational—both because an observer's perspective is limited and because the thing observed can never be truly excised from its context—but they also saw this limitation as a reason to keep the research tradition going. Such an attitude was even unexpectedly characteristic of a genre known as hexameral literature, that is, exegetical commentaries on the Bible's first account of creation. Or perhaps it was not so unexpected, because this was a millennium that could be fairly characterized as an age of "exegetical cultures," when commentary on canonical texts was one of the favored modes of critical thinking.[4] And in the commentators' vision of a universe encoded with divine significance, even the everyday pig had a celestial tinge to it.

Exploring Creation: The Late Antique Framework

The Christian preachers and philosophers of Late Antiquity set the tone here, above all Basil of Caesarea, Ambrose of Milan, and Augustine of Hippo.[5] Far from being the archetypal (and mythical) Christians who did not concern themselves with the physical world, these men, whom later generations would come to count among the "church fathers," were obviously fascinated by it. *Cosmos* most basically meant "ornament," and the stunning shape that God had given the universe could challenge the mind and, in the process, remake the soul. Basil, Ambrose, and Augustine made these arguments in what are today called hexameral commentaries—explanations of the story of the six days of creation in Genesis. Their texts revealed distinct personalities and distinct visions of the earth, the cosmos, and humans' place within that magnificent divine order. But they all had a hand in shaping the early medieval tradition of taking nature seriously.

In antiquity, Jewish and Christian thinkers had not extensively analyzed the creation story in Genesis 1. Basil was more or less the first person to do so, and he structured his commentary as a series of eleven sermons, which he delivered as a bishop in the 370s. During his time as bishop of Caesarea—the capital of Cappadocia, a mountainous region of the Roman Empire in eastern Anatolia—the city suffered from imperial initiatives that reduced its tax base, its elite population, and its relative status among cities. But Basil's congregation would still have included some municipal elites, as well as artisans, farmers, and ranchers, and their interests and interactions with their bishop left their mark on his sermons about creation.[6]

Throughout the week it took to preach them, Basil was overtly dismissive of many intellectual traditions besides his own. He called philosophy that was not concerned with God "busywork" and mocked its practitioners for failing to reach a consensus about anything. He accused Christians who interpreted the Bible figuratively of bending scripture to suit their purposes, even though *water* simply meant "water" (a barb he liked so much he used it again a couple days later).[7] But despite the sermons' bluster, they do engage deeply with philosophical and scientific traditions, and they build on that knowledge as frequently as they reject it. Basil's many unnamed interlocutors include Plato, Aristotle, and philosophers of the Stoic and Neoplatonic traditions that mediated them; Philo of Alexandria, a Jewish scholar who in the mid-first century wrote the first Greek commentary on Genesis; and Origen, a Christian exegete (also from Alexandria) whose allegorical interpretations Basil ridiculed but who nevertheless asked questions about creation that exegetes would continue to contemplate for centuries. Basil's mixed feelings about this earlier work showed that he was both curious about the world—he stresses that there is still a lot to learn about plants, for example, and about the size and distance of the sun and moon— and also closed off to investigations whose spiritual benefits were not obvious to him. The shape of the earth, or the way eclipses worked: these subjects seemed irrelevant to Basil, even though Christian authors after him would explore them unapologetically.[8]

But when Basil *was* interested in something, his preaching glowed. He saw creation as an opportunity to approach the sacred. Humans could not see or fully know God, but learning about God's work through scripture and nature was at least a way to demonstrate that humans were *trying* to know him. And what scripture and nature made plain to Basil was the extent of God's power and foresight, which in turn pointed to the sublime eternity beyond what he could see. This theme would also pulse through the work of writers who read his sermons. One of his favorite exercises was to evoke the dizzying instantaneousness of creation. He asked his congregation to imagine the sudden bright beauty that came with the first appearance of the light, or the earth suddenly cloaked in a green robe of plants and fruit, the plains suddenly wavy with grain, the mountains suddenly shaggy with mature forests, the waters suddenly teeming with creatures. These tableaux were expected to impress an audience full of farmers and craftspeople, men and women who would have known exactly how much labor the business of agriculture and manufacturing usually required. Caesarea was also home to an imperial weaving mill, and many Cappadocians worked in imperial arms factories and ranches.[9]

The only thing more stupefying than the immediacy of creation was how complexly and perfectly God had engineered it, and Basil dwelt on the details to evoke God's otherwise ineffable expertise. He pointed, for example, to the innumerable combinations of root systems, trunks, bark, and crowns of trees and to the fact that each species' structure was still able to balance its own immense weight. He suggested that although humans tried to devise different systems of classification to account for the complexity of the physical world, their work was no match for God's inventiveness. Taxonomists spoke of "shellfish," for example, but that group included animals as different as snails and oysters—not to mention that oysters themselves came in countless varieties. So when God saw that his creations were "good," he was not simply acknowledging that they were beautiful (though they were). He was also affirming the integrity of a complex whole. The goodness of the waters upon the earth, for example, derived from their systematicity: what had started as one mass of water was, by the third day of creation, a network of visible and invisible channels that crisscrossed the entire earth, saturating and leeching from the soil, flowing from place to place, evaporating, and condensing. (Basil and his congregation knew about the waters underground thanks to construction workers with experience digging ditches.)[10]

Like the earth's hydrology, every dynamic in the universe was propelled by the motion of God's initial creative commandments, like a ball that rolls down a slope when someone pushes it, until it eventually comes to a stop on level ground. Basil saw animals as an especially lively example of that first divine push. But unlike a ball, an animal was perceptive. And even though some animals did not (according to Basil) have highly functional cognition—he thought aquatic animals were much less intelligent than land animals—Basil argued that the soul in land animals, at least, governed them and made them capable not only of sense perception but of memory and emotion as well.[11] But he was less interested in their actual cognitive capacities than he was in the rhetorical premise that animals were putting humans to shame. Animal souls were not equivalent to human souls, most fundamentally because they did not outlive their animal bodies, but Basil argued that animals were doing a much better job of sticking to the trajectories God had originally established for them, whereas humans were ignoring their own souls' instincts to make beneficial choices.[12]

Basil's approach to Genesis and the cosmos, his linking of past and present through a cross-consultation of scripture and nature, was an inspiration to many generations of readers, so much so that the works of his biggest fans are typically dismissed as derivative, in particular that of Ambrose of Milan.[13] Ambrose read Basil's work carefully, and when he wrote his own *Exameron* about a decade after Basil had written his *Hexaemeron*, he structured it like Basil's, too, as a set of sermons that he preached to his congregation at Milan in the spring of 387. Also like Basil, Ambrose saw himself as a tour guide, not of a foreign country but of his congregation's own homeland. But Ambrose departed from Basil in a number of ways. His audience was different from Basil's, and so were many of his messages. Ambrose spoke to a city of midlevel imperial bureaucrats and the merchant and service classes that had sprung up to profit from them; and to Ambrose's mind, their fixation on wealth and prestige had distracted them from the unparalleled riches of the natural world. He wanted his congregants to see their own "backyards"—and here he was thinking specifically of the vistas from their country estates—with fresh eyes.[14] In this vision, Late Roman villas were not only centers of agricultural production or elite retreats. They were also springboards to the stars.

It was a tough crowd for nine days of sermons about creation, or at least Ambrose liked to imply that it was. The first three sermons were poorly attended. By the ninth and final sermon, Ambrose was addressing complaints that he had not talked about humans for eight days straight! His response was that "we cannot know ourselves more fully unless we first come to know what the nature of all living creatures is."[15] Nature, in other words, was something to be understood both mechanically and figuratively: *natura* was both a physical thing and a divine logic. For Ambrose the story of creation was not just an account of the origins of the world but also a guide to human salvation, and so his commentary is infused with both literal and figural explanations for the state of the universe.

But Ambrose's strongest defense for nine days of natural history was his own delight in the diversity of creation and his energetic efforts to make the feeling mutual. He assumed that his audience was already interested in birds, for example, and yet the very word *bird* (*avis*) dulled a Latin speaker's sense of differences that mattered. All birds might have legs and wings, but enormous variation could be found in their diets, social behavior, migration patterns, and songs—not to mention their more abstract qualities, such as their attitude toward humans, love of freedom, and other personality traits.[16] And in order to properly evoke the diversity of the natural world, Ambrose explicitly acknowledged the expertise of people who had direct knowledge of its particulars, which often meant laborers rather than elites.

Ambrose's rhetoric here may have been deliberately edgy, in insisting to his urban congregation that they stood to learn something from the agrarian classes. But from a methodological point of view, his deference to people whom he saw as the real experts was crucial to his case. They helped Ambrose gauge the extent of God's power and love with increasing specificity. The way hydraulic engineers built canals to manage water flow fostered an appreciation for God's even greater feat of inventing fluid mechanics in the first place. Arborists discovered by working with date palms that trees, not just animals, are sexed. It was fishermen who could best identify the diversity of animals in their waters—a point Basil had made as well, although Ambrose suggested that his congregants should talk to fishermen in different locations because fish populations varied and no single person could grasp everything that God had created. Ambrose himself had asked peasants to teach him about the habits of various birds.[17]

He may have had more than one reason for mentioning this last group. Traditionally, it was diviners who had been the leading experts on bird behavior in the ancient world. The appearance of a certain species in a particular place, the feeding movements of a bird of prey, or the features of a particular flock's flight patterns or calls communicated specific portents to the bird interpreters (ornithoskopoi) who were skilled enough to read them.[18] So Ambrose's praise for his peasant informants may have been an attempt to replace one form of expertise with another that was more compatible with his understanding of Christianity—even though his rabbinic contemporaries were cautiously endorsing bird divination on the understanding, shared by Jews and Christians, that God actively communicated to humanity through his creations.[19] Regardless of his reasons, Ambrose was presenting farmers to his congregation as a credible authority on the complex subject of ornithology in the same way that he was suggesting that other nonelites could be experts in their own specialized fields.

Such capacious knowledge of the physical world heightened humans' sense of the craftsmanship of which God was capable. It also articulated the wonderful provisions God had made for their protection and pleasure—a theme that Basil had established and which Ambrose amplified with enthusiastic variations. The cedar was perfect for roofing, honey for medicine, the grape leaf for beauty and shade. God had anticipated humans' spiritual needs, too, and had encoded the physical world with countless messages about Christian morality. Bats seemed to hang together in clusters to teach humans about the importance of mutually supportive love. The withering of grasses foretold the mortality of all flesh. Even the process of creation itself had taken place gradually because God had wanted to demonstrate to his creatures that tasks needed to be accomplished in stages.[20]

As part of this physical and moral kaleidoscope, Ambrose thought about "animals" less as a single category than as an array of species with different traits and capacities. The concept of pigs as a stable "species" might not have cracked so easily under early medieval scrutiny if exegetes like Ambrose had not already been prepared to pry apart larger animal categories. The concept of "birds" was a case in point. Ambrose suggested that although all species of birds seemed to order themselves according to "a certain natural political and military order" (*politia quaedam et militia naturalis*), each "polity" had its own pronounced features. Cranes kept a night watch without needing a commander to enforce the rotation because each crane acted out of natural loyalty (*devotio naturalis*) and unconstrained choice (*voluntas libera*). Storks exhibited moral traits—above all devotion (*pietas*) to their parents. Crows were greatly concerned for their young. And anyone who watched a swallow build a nest could see that they were models of productivity (*industria*), persistence (*sedulitas*), and knowledge (*intellectus, cognitio, quaedam peritia*).[21]

Ambrose's animal kingdom, like Basil's, often provided a platform for unsubtle social critiques. He praised crows for their child care, for example, partly to shame his congregation for condoning abortion, infant exposure, and stingy inheritance bequests. The humiliating premise behind such a comparison was that humans were supposed to be morally and intellectually superior to other animals, and yet animals more perfectly enacted rationality—not because they themselves were rational but because God had "poured" his rational commands into them, and they obeyed. But even if Ambrose was certain that animals did not possess rationality, he struggled to describe their cognitive and ethical capacities in terms that rigorously maintained this distinction. The issue vexed him more than it had Basil. Basil had discussed cranes, storks, crows, and sparrows, too, but his accounts are sparser, and he was less transfixed by the idea that animal abilities seemed to shadow human ones. Basil simply said that the swallow was hardworking, for example, before describing how it used mud as a mortar for its nest. Likewise his account of the cranes' night watch is brief and includes nothing about loyalty or choice.[22]

So although Ambrose followed Basil in characterizing animals as obeying a kind of unwritten law (*quaedam lex*) of their species, Ambrose was less certain that their compliance was innate. Sometimes he implied that animals were unable to conceive of breaking the law. But other times he seemed to praise them for consistently choosing to act within their moral guidelines, as if they had the ability to do otherwise. Besides praising cranes for choosing to be obedient, for example, Ambrose likewise described bees as exercising the agency to appoint their own king and submit to him as free subjects—a "political culture" that Basil had more conservatively characterized as a function of natural law.[23]

Ambrose also cited cases for which "law" seemed to be too rigid a metaphor to explain why animals did what they did. Vultures, for example, could make accurate predictions about when humans were going to die—predictions that, according to Ambrose, "they undoubtedly seem to deduce by a kind of reasoning resembling human learning."[24] It was high praise to acknowledge that an animal could evaluate new situations as they arose and anticipate the likeliest outcome. But Ambrose's language betrays his ambivalence: the vultures "seem" (*videntur*) to exhibit "a kind of reasoning" (*quadam ratio*) that took the "guise" (*ex specie*) of human patterns of thought. Dogs were an equally slippery case—and here Ambrose and Basil were in agreement. Dogs do not possess reason per se, yet their astute acts of perception give them, as Ambrose put it, the "force of reason," *vis rationis*.[25] To illustrate his point, Ambrose imagined the thought process of a hunting dog. As the dog tracks an animal, he makes decisions just as a logician would, a comparison Ambrose owed to Basil: "'Either it turned off in this direction,' [the dog] says, 'or that one; or it certainly took off down this bend. But [as the dog sniffs out the three options] it didn't go down this path right here or that one. Therefore the remaining option is, without a doubt, that it would have taken off in this direction here.'"[26] This is the only instance in all nine sermons in which Ambrose slipped into the focal point of an animal (or any other part of creation, for that matter). It was not difficult to think like a dog when dogs seemed to think so much like people. This is probably why the vignette of dog-as-syllogist had been evoked by many ancient philosophers before Basil and Ambrose, though different writers drew different conclusions from the comparison about whether dogs were capable of reasoning.[27] But Ambrose did not tax his congregation's patience by delving more systematically into the possibilities and limits of animals' intelligence. He was giving a guided tour, and his point was to capture the magnificence of the universe in glimpses.

Things were different with Augustine's literal interpretation of Genesis, which was less a genial tour than a forensic investigation. *De Genesi ad litteram* (*On Genesis, Word for Word*) was a tenacious commentary that Augustine wrote later in his life as bishop of Hippo, a couple of decades after Ambrose had delivered his hexameral sermons (so at some point between 401 and 415).[28] Like Ambrose, Augustine treated the physical world as a body of evidence for better understanding the one who had created it. But unlike Ambrose, Augustine pointed his research resolutely toward the past, with the goal of reconstructing God's creative process step by step: he was reading Genesis exclusively as a history of actions and events (*gesta*) that had really happened. It was not that he rejected nonliteral readings of the sort we find in Basil and Ambrose. Augustine had already written a commentary on Genesis that interpreted the text's figurative meanings. But to his mind a literal interpretation was the greater challenge. The difficulties were obvious right from "In the beginning": how could there be a literal beginning with God?[29]

Fortunately, he reasoned, the present universe was full of evidence for even the earliest phases of creation, because the physical world in Augustine's time represented the logical unfolding (*explicare*) of a plan that God had first folded together (*plicare*) in the days of Genesis. Every created thing was propelled by a guiding force—its *ratio, causa, causalis ratio,* or *vis potentiaque causalis*—that God had planted at the start.[30] In the first six days of creation, God generated the ideas for everything that would ever exist on earth. But in order to acquire a clear form, each created thing—each idea of a thing—would have to be acknowledged as different from God, despite originating in him. (For Augustine this differentiation was made possible by God's very first creation, the light, which was, literally speaking, conceptualization or recognition itself.) Only after that dialectical, boomerang motion of identifying something apart from God was it possible for this conceptual thing to emerge into physical existence (*in sua natura*). Material reality was a punctuation to that whole intellectual process: even when a creature did not yet exist physically, it *had* existed, from the moment it was abstractly recognizable as a divine idea. That included pigs, which Augustine figured fell under the category of what his version of Genesis called *pecora*, or livestock (and which the Vulgate would call *iumenta*), one of the categories of land animals that came into being on the sixth day of creation. Before they materialized, pigs would have had to be differentiated or illuminated apart from the creator who thought of them. They also needed to be become conceptually distinct from other livestock, a process that was predicated on livestock becoming distinct from other land animals, and land animals from the land itself.[31]

This is why the universe seemed to Augustine to unfold itself over time—and why everything in creation, even lowly pigs, were vital clues to that process. Not only had God's creative ideas seemed to cascade or branch out from one another in the first six days, as when the undivided heavens became split by the firmament, and the waters below the firmament became the land and seas, and portions of the seas became birds and aquatic animals while parts of the land became livestock, pigs included.[32] But by the start of the seventh day, when the earth and heavens had become full of every kind of thing that God would ever create, each distinct species (*genus*) would still move and change according to the parameters that God had first imagined for it. There was always an inherent flexibility to this system. As we saw in the previous chapter, Augustine believed that although every animal in a species had the same set of limitations and possibilities, he reasoned that a lot of latitude existed for individual variations and individual decision making. The *rationes causales* or guiding logics that moved God's creations did not make them automata; it made them archives.

And so Augustine marshaled philosophical and scientific research, along with personal experiences and interviews with acquaintances, in order to illuminate features of the present, unfolded world that might help him determine retroactively what had happened in the very first days of creation.

To take one case in detail: Augustine wanted to know what it meant for Genesis to say that the first animals that came into being were aquatic animals and birds, and that both groups of animals were drawn from the earth's waters. He supposed that the answers must have something to do with the way the elements—earth, fire, water, and air—needed to work mechanically. Although he knew that there was an ongoing debate about how one element changed into another, he suggested that water-based animals were made first, in order to allow some of the primordial waters that remained to evaporate and "plump up" (*pinguescere*) into an air that was dense enough to enable birds to fly and breathe.[33]

From there Augustine delved deeper into natural philosophies of the elements, because he knew that the chemistry was complicated. Even a single being, such as a bird, made from water contained at least trace elements of fire, air, and earth as well. And he expressed a real respect for the research that had systematically determined that the four elements corresponded to the five senses: this was important for his purposes, because humans can only detect the presence of this or that element through the respective sense-acts that are capable of perceiving them. So the only way that we can know the elemental composition of a thing is by drawing ourselves increasingly closer to it, moving through the progression of all forms of sensing. The verb Augustine favored for "sensing" was *pervenire*, "to get through or arrive" somewhere: to his mind and to the philosophers on whom he was drawing (most probably Plotinus, Galen, and Porphyry), the senses were not passive but active, reaching gestures.[34]

This seeming detour into the elements and sense perception helped Augustine reconcile the watery origins of birds with the prosaic observation that birds were still in extensive contact with the world of land, as they fed and rested and reared their young there. Not only birds but every kind of animal reached beyond whatever element predominated in its body to participate in the other elemental domains. Augustine concluded that this is why Genesis variously treats birds as land animals, animals of the water, and animals of the lower regions of the air: its taxonomies had to be flexible, because the structure and movement of life forms are profoundly complex.[35]

There was another reason why Augustine incorporated cutting-edge discoveries into his interpretation of Genesis. He looked to elementary theory (or to medical studies of brain functioning, or to the stories that people told him about their dreams) in part to help him decode the historical sequences of creation and, by extension, the divine order. But they also helped him argue that modern research did not render the Bible obsolete. When Augustine imagined an audience for his work, he hoped that his fusion of exegesis and natural philosophy would rebut two groups in particular: educated philosophers who mocked Christian texts for their ostensible errors and Christians who made unfounded and overconfident interpretations of their own scriptures. Their combined ignorance was incredibly annoying (*molestus*).[36]

In contrast to the confidence of these imagined audiences, Augustine's conclusions were frequently tentative, provisional, or frankly indecisive. Many questions, including issues that Christians debated hotly among themselves, were impossible to answer with certainty, or at least they needed more research (of scripture or nature or both). Augustine did not want to decide prematurely whether the celestial bodies had some kind of governing life force (*rectores quosdam spiritos suos*), and if so, whether that force moved through them like the breath of animals or was instead entirely separate from their bodies. And he wondered whether insects had been created along with the land and water animals or whether God had made them earlier, to be a supplement to the environment that the animals would inhabit. He was also not sure if souls descended from a single ratio causalis, generated successively from the first soul, or whether God had made souls individually, each with its own ratio, to be joined to their respective bodies at the appropriate time. Augustine therefore described his approach to Genesis as *multipliciter*, a many-folded view of his unfolding universe. He examined a problem from different angles and floated several possible answers, without always choosing any of them as definitive.[37]

In writing a treatise with open ends, Augustine was not trying to discourage his readers but rather to reactivate their curiosity. The physical world seemed simple only because humans had mistaken their own perspectives for something more panoramic. Things were not always what they seemed. Our sense-based perceptions offer a useful but restricted vantage point, not a panoptic view. The moon is always round, even if it appears to wax and wane. Night at one moment is daytime somewhere else on the globe. And the narratives we use to tell a story, although they are essential to making sense of things, can nevertheless deceive us about time and causation. God accomplishes things simultaneously, for example, but narrative cannot adequately convey this. That is why, Augustine suggested, it was crucial for humans to understand the limitations of their knowledge in order to consider counterintuitive possibilities.[38]

Fish were a case in point. "Some people" (including Basil, although Augustine does not name him) thought that aquatic animals were not fully living, sensate creatures (*animae vivae*) because they seemed to lack any capacity for memory or other cognitive functions. Augustine disagreed. He pointed out that people who paid close attention to fishponds had learned amazing things about the animals—studies that unfortunately he did not summarize. But he did add his own observations as "extremely reliable" evidence (*certissmum*) that fish had memories and used them. There was a huge fountain in the city of Bulla Regia (near the northern coast of modern Tunisia) that Augustine had visited, a hangout where people gazed into the pool and tossed pieces of food to the fish stocked there. Those fish *must* be able to remember and think about things, Augustine figured, because they did not wait to swim up whenever crumbs hit the surface of the water. Instead they observed the way humans behaved around their fountain and learned to anticipate them: they would swim in groups to track the movements of people who passed by, waiting for the food that they had not even seen yet.[39]

Animals were technically inferior to humans in the universal scheme of things, or so Augustine thought, because they did not have rational souls. Unlike humans and angels, they were incapable of the perceptive and cognitive processes that Augustine called *visio intellectualis*. They could sense things physically and form mental images based on their senses and memories, but they could not move from those observations toward an understanding of truths which were not attached to any images at all, such as numbers or virtues or God himself.[40] Put another way: many animals could remember, think, and make decisions, but they did not have judgment (*arbitrium, iudicium*), so for Augustine they could not act with reference to an abstract value. Animals therefore ranked lower than humans in the hierarchy of creation, and humans were entitled to have power over them, because it was their ability to exercise rational judgment that gave humans a resemblance to God.[41]

That said, Augustine did not stress dominion as the most important dynamic between animals and humans. (And few Jewish and Christian commentators in antiquity and the Middle Ages were any more interested than Augustine was in the biblical imperative to "master" the earth.)[42] Instead, as we have seen, Augustine characterized the relationship between Christians and creation as fundamentally an educational process. It might consequently seem that nature was only instrumental to him, given that his goal was to better understand divinity rather than to learn more about the universe for its own sake. But a fascination with nature and an interest in ultimate causes did not have to be mutually exclusive. For Augustine the world was not a veil between humans and God but rather an extensive network that linked them together. Christians needed to read and observe as much as they could of the physical world, because *that* was the evidence they had for the divine order that encompassed it. And the more Augustine considered each analytical problem that he confronted in Genesis, the more respect he gained not only for God but for his creation, too, animals included. "There is a certain honor in everything," he said, "that is specific to the nature of each species."[43]

The Early Medieval World in Motion

Looking to the great late antique commentaries on Genesis, later Latin writers took it for granted that the universe was a linking of physical and divine realms and a portal to the deep history of creation. They read and recopied the late antique hexameral texts, and some of those copies survive.[44] We can also see the influence of these texts winding through the work of later writers and compilers. And although analysts returned to motifs and themes that would have seemed traditional in the centuries after Augustine, they continued to explore new ground and piece together new vistas of the world they inhabited. By the eighth century, it was not unusual to hear exegetes saying that too much had been written about the subject for most people to read! Claudius of Turin, a bishop and exegete who wrote a commentary on Genesis just before 811 for Louis the Pious, compared the vastness of this literature to hoards of treasure, to a meadow full of flowers, and—following Isaiah—to the waters of the sea.[45] This did not stop him from adding his own compilation to the pile. He and other exegetes thought that creating selective anthologies of previous scholarship would help readers tackle this material, start new conversations about it, and draw new insights about their own times in a process of applied learning. A decade or two before Claudius wrote his commentary for Louis the Pious, for example, another Carolingian exegete named Wigbod compiled a massive commentary on the first eight books of the Bible for Louis's father, Charlemagne, and he began that hefty work by insisting that the king should put what he read there into practice.[46]

But in the rest of this chapter I focus more on the common quandaries that early medieval analysts of the physical world faced, instead of highlighting their discoveries or new developments, because nearly every serious student of creation in Late Antiquity and the early Middle Ages took seriously a conceptual and methodological dilemma that can sharpen our sense of how the universe appeared to them. The basic problem was this: the world was so profoundly complex and dynamic that it was hard to pinpoint any causes or forces as constant, and thus, although individuals could be experts in localized bodies of knowledge, it would always be impossible to fully know the physical world, let alone the cosmic order that it both embodied and reflected. These observers were not simply noticing that their ecologies were complicated (and we will see in the next chapter how true that was across the post-imperial West). They were also drawn to the very concept of complexity, which widened their vision while also making them aware of their own limitations. What did this epistemology mean for early medieval cultures of nature?

Obstacles to knowledge were a source of concern, but they were not debilitating. The fact that the world was in constant motion—for it was accepted as a fact that any material thing (even rock)[47] was inherently impermanent—could be an impetus to learn more about it. Even rulers of the post-imperial kingdoms of the West took notice. Nowadays barbarian kings do not have a reputation for being bookish, but some of them certainly were, and when Sisebut became the king of Visigothic Spain in March 612, he asked Isidore of Seville to write him a text "about natural phenomena and their causes." The king and the bishop shared many intellectual interests, but in this case the "causes" they were thinking about were cosmic. The book that Isidore presented to Sisebut in the spring of 613—De natura rerum, or On the Nature of Things—was an analysis of astronomy, meteorology, and time. Its goal was to explicate the intricate workings of the heavens in order to interpret celestial occurrences accurately. There had been many dubious attempts to draw conclusions from what happened in the skies, but "in fact," Isidore insisted, "knowing the nature of such things is not a superstitious form of knowledge, as long as they are analyzed using sound and serious learning."[48]

So the book was a constructive critique, not a destructive one. Although Isidore tersely dismissed the idea that planets influenced human affairs—the Roman pagans had believed this, he said, and they were "ridiculous"—he was still eager to chart what *could* be known about its many motions. The winds, for instance: Isidore mapped the seasonal changes that attended the shifts in winds, from the cold and snowy bluster of the north wind (known as Septentrio) to the humid heat and lightning that blew in from the south (Auster/Notus). All these patterns were cyclical and predictable. Isidore also argued that winds were the reason dolphins could forecast a storm at sea. When the winds changed, the water's waves and currents shifted, and to avoid being swept ashore or flipped backward in the sudden switch, dolphins would leap out of the water. An observant human could read the position of their bodies to anticipate where the winds would come from, not because dolphins were inexplicably wondrous but because the earth's forces followed legible patterns.[49]

After reading Isidore's treatise, Sisebut responded with a poem in sixty-one hexameters. He began by contrasting the leisurely pleasures of Isidore's scholarly life with the preoccupations of a king burdened by lawmaking, judicial procedures, and warfare. But Sisebut undercut this dichotomy almost immediately. After all, the king had commissioned Isidore's treatise. But equally, his own poem was saturated with references to Latin poetry (above all, Lucretius's *De rerum natura*), and it dove into the subject of lunar eclipses—a topic that Isidore had addressed, too, but more briefly.[50] The king had ironically suggested that such a writing project was totally improbable:

Quin mage pernices aquilas uis pigra elephantum
Praecurret, uolucremque pigens testudo molossum,
Quam nos rorifluam sectemur carmine lunam.

No, really: the sluggish force of the elephants would sooner outrun
The agile eagles, and the slow tortoise the swift hound,
Than we would chase after the dewy moon with a poem.[51]

And yet here he was, doing exactly that, enjoying his own kind of upset victory.

Sisebut did not explain his choice of a racing metaphor, or what was victorious about a study of astronomic and atmospheric sciences. But it is likely that both he and Isidore saw the subject as a vital complement to the affairs of the state. Early medieval historians regularly scrutinized natural phenomena to try to make sense of the events they chronicled on earth. A disease, an earthquake, or a strangely colored sky might be a coincidence, a divine verdict, or an omen. Historians often left it to their readers to draw connections between certain occurrences. A chronicle might criticize a certain royal initiative, for example, then switch the subject without segue to describe a disastrous flood. The implication was that although the natural world was ambiguous, it rarely seemed random. To a king, these would have been unsettling insinuations. An effort like Isidore's to analyze the cosmos more systemically could forestall speculative attempts to link natural philosophy and politics—or at least discredit the worst of them. As a result of his research, Isidore did not discount the possibility that the skies could foretell human history, but he was not sure about it, either. Could a comet really presage a regime change? Some people thought so, Isidore noted, but that was all *he* was willing to say.[52]

Isidore's *De natura rerum* was therefore composed with a specific audience in mind—as every text was—but its wide-ranging and critical explorations of a universe in motion make it similar to many others from Late Antiquity and the early Middle Ages. And its influences ran deep. Isidore had definitely read his Ambrose and Augustine. He also looked to the ancient poets as his patron had, and to excerpted works of other natural philosophers. In his later work Isidore would be indebted, as many writers were, to Pliny the Elder and his *Natural History*. It is worth highlighting some elements of that famous text, particularly Pliny's interest in diversity and dynamism, to see what his later readers made of it.

Pliny completed the *Historia naturalis* in 77–78 CE, but his work would never be more popular than it was in the Middle Ages, even though his readers did not always agree with him.[53] It had been an enormous undertaking. Its thirty-seven books survey the regions, peoples, organisms, landforms, and culture of the known world—especially the terrains that Rome had conquered. But despite the work's colossal size, its vision was disarmingly particularized. As the classicist Aude Doody put it: "In the *Natural History*, knowing about nature does not mean engaging in debates about Stoic versus Epicurean philosophy; it means knowing that there are six European trees that produce pitch, that there are three kinds of lettuce, that the best kind of emeralds come from Scythia, and that rocket [arugula] is an excellent aphrodisiac. . . . In the *Natural History*, nature becomes exactly the sum of its parts, a catalogue of details that anyone can grasp, but that only Pliny has contained and organized."[54] There is a striking similarity between Pliny's perspective here and the late antique exegetes' view of the universe as an irreducible system, even if the exegetes saw that complexity as an expression of the immeasurable inventiveness of God (rather than of Nature per se). But the affinity went deeper. Pliny's interest in particulars made him alert to the fact that nature had a history, that nature was the sum total not only of its individual components but of the dynamic relationships among them. Frogs on the island of Serifos do not croak, but when they are brought to other places they do. A fish called the *scarus*, native to the Carpathian Sea (in the southern Aegean), never existed in Italy until a naval officer introduced it to the southwest coasts of the peninsula: a few decades later, in Pliny's day, it was flourishing as "the new resident" of this part of the Mediterranean. Plants and animals of all kinds might flourish in one spot but fail in another. And birds that the ancient Etruscans had described seem to have vanished entirely. Why had more animals not become extinct, Pliny wondered. At the rate humans consumed things, it was astounding that they hadn't.[55]

By Late Antiquity and the early Middle Ages, it was not so radical to suggest that the nonhuman world was not only complex but also kinetic and contingent. As far as Basil of Caesarea had seen it, change was partly a function of time and partly a function of materiality: everything in the physical world was either growing or being depleted. This was obviously true of living things, but Basil emphasized that it was true of everything, down to the elements themselves. His standout example in favor of his argument was the primordial waters, whose volume (Basil said) far exceeded the volume of the earth in the beginning, because God wanted there to be enough water to last the lifetime of the world. Water was naturally engaged in a perpetual battle with the element of fire, and God knew that it would eventually be consumed by fire, little by little, through evaporation. That is why God created a preponderant mass of water, and it is also why he made the sun rise and set, moved it along the ecliptic, and placed it at just the right distance from earth: he did not want everything to burn up immediately.[56]

Ambrose, after poring over Basil's sermons, would compound this sense of global flux. Ambrose's interest in cosmic diversity, and his respect for God's meticulous work, led him to appreciate that the world's many features were interrelated. The idiosyncratic aspects of a single organism or landform were not isolated traits but were instead affected by other variables. As a result, even a single entity that seemed entirely familiar was subject to dramatic alteration, depending on its contexts. Ambrose pointed out, for example, that water will change its color, form, taste, surface, and weight—and also its functional relationships with different species—depending on circumstances. And for that reason it was nearly impossible to reach general conclusions about the physical world while still doing justice to its significant variations: "It is an impossibly tangled task [*inexplicabile*] to investigate the properties of individual things and at the same time to distinguish their differences on the basis of clear evidence, or to uncover their unknown and hidden causes [*causae*, their ultimate origins] with infallible proof. Obviously water is one and the same thing, and yet it frequently changes itself into different forms."[57]

Ambrose counted humans as another transformative variable, though not always in a positive sense. He criticized the practice of building oyster tanks and fishponds, along with land reclamations that encroached on the Mediterranean coasts. These practices, he insinuated, damaged fish habits and habitats. (Pliny himself had disparaged the oyster and fish farms of elite villas three hundred years earlier, but his primary concern was that they were extravagant.) Although Ambrose recognized that the nonhuman world was susceptible to changes that went beyond the predictable cycles of seasonality and mortality, he saw those changes as flaws rather than as necessary features of the system. He complained about humans' effects on fish in order to underline a fundamental difference between humans and everything else: whereas humans were always striving for change, the natural preference of all other creatures was perfect order and stability. Or as Basil had put it, even sea monsters respected boundaries![58]

Pliny too had implied that humans were often responsible for the changes he chronicled in the natural world. When he spoke of animals being "conveyed" (using the passive voice, *traduntur*) to new locations, for example, the implication was that humans were usually the ones doing the conveying. But some Christian authors faulted humans more deeply. It was the Fall of Adam and Eve, they insisted, that had destabilized the physical world. The first sin had not only merited the punishments of agriculture, childbirth, and mortality (and possibly the thorns on plants). For the anonymous Irish author of the *Liber de ordine creaturarum* (*Book on the Order of Created Things*), writing in the late seventh century, the entire universe experienced dramatic mutations after the Fall. The moon and sun dimmed, environments became harsher and less fruitful, and the seasons started their cycle for the first time (whereas it had always been spring in paradise). Change was a form of mourning: after humankind sinned, the universe grieved and fell into flux. So for this author, to envision the end of time was to imagine a state of perfect immobility. Not only would humans and their bodies become immortal, but the sun and moon themselves would freeze in their orbits, never to rise or set again.[59]

But other Christians pointed to other catalysts for the tumultuous movements of the universe. Isidore suggested that flux was bound to happen since
God had set so many things in motion in the first place. Like Augustine, he
thought that the many movements of creation were part of the original physics
of the universe, not a consequence of the Fall. But Isidore was less interested
in how creation had first unfolded than in the end result—a cosmos where
many systems overlapped. So he argued, for example, that although some people attributed the outbreak of disease epidemics to the Fall, other causes were
also at play. Epidemics were the result of air whose elemental balance had
been destabilized by some kind of excess of aridity, heat, or rain. It was also
possible, he added, that disease outbreaks were catalyzed when pestilential
airborne "seeds" had been scattered widely by winds or clouds.[60]

Some manuscripts reinforced Isidore's multivariable model visually by including diagrams of select systems in his cosmology: the months and days
comprising a year, the seasons, the five circles or latitudes of earth, the elements, the phases of the moon, the orbits of the planets, the winds, and a
schematic map of the world. Most of these diagrams are represented as cosmic
wheels or spheres, a shape that conjured both the universe and time at once.
Some codices include wheels with a human head at the center. This was the
microcosmos of the cosmos, in Isidore's reading: the properties of the earth
(such as its four elements) had a symmetry or correspondence with the human body (which consisted of four humors).[61] Each wheel individually attests
to Isidore's idea that every physical transformation in the world is the result
of an interactive set of cosmic systems. In a manuscript produced in Salzburg
around 800, for example, the wheel of the five circles of the earth indicates
each zone's corresponding temperatures and habitability while also setting
out its relation to the ecliptic (the sun's annual arc along the sky; fig. 2.1). In
the same manuscript, the wheel for the seven seasons indicates their corresponding weather conditions and dominant elemental properties (fig. 2.2). Or
the wheel of the solar, lunar, and planetary orbits indicates the length of time
it takes for each celestial body to complete a revolution (fig. 2.3). Although this
image is not as visually complex as the others, Isidore's readers would have
supplemented it with the text's discussion of phenomena that hinged on these
orbital patterns, such as eclipses and moonlight.

The images that wind through some manuscript traditions inspired medieval readers to bestow another name on Isidore's book, the *Liber rotarum*, or
Book of Wheels. But the title suits Isidore's text, too, not just the images that
sometimes accompany it. By aggregating information about the many moving pieces of the universe, Isidore was arguing that to truly understand the

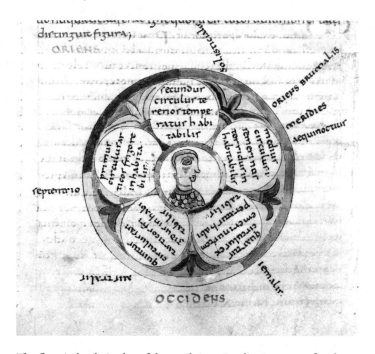

Fig. 2.1. The five circles/latitudes of the earth in a Carolingian copy of Isidore's *De natura rerum,* made in Salzburg around 800. (Bayerische Staatsbibliothek München, Clm 14300, fol. 6v.)

world or even individual pieces within it, it was necessary to consider all its interlocking systems simultaneously, from its elemental building blocks to its stellar circuits. Careful readers could visualize similar "wheels" in Isidore's writing even without an artist's help, but the painted wheels magnify the multilayered-ness of his vision, as the successive images of spheres and their human centers stack up into an increasingly complex cosmos. They are a powerful visual mnemonic for a concept that structures the entirety of Isidore's treatise.[62] And they may also explain why Isidore was ambivalent about the connection between atmospheric events and politics: there were too many variables and complex chains of causation to make definitive pronouncements.

In northern England in the eighth century, Bede was also struck by the multiplicity of movements that characterized the physical world. He had read Basil, Ambrose, Augustine, Isidore, Pliny, and the *Liber de ordine creaturarum.* But his exploration of Genesis through the testimony of creation (which he probably started in 717 and finished in 731) betrays the monk's own unmistakable interests—above all, his personal study of astronomical computation.

Bede unlocked the oblique chronological cues in the Genesis account of the Flood, for example, to figure out that it had lasted exactly one solar year. He did this by squaring the narrative's references to the lunar calendar with his own deep familiarity with historical calendars and with the lunar-solar calculations that were essential for determining the dates for Easter. The science of computation also gave depth and dimension to the present, literally. Bede marveled at how profoundly humans owed their sense of time and navigation to the celestial bodies: days, seasons, years, journeys, the daily rounds of ritual prayers, and of course Easter were all emplotted within the cycles of the sun, moon, and stars. God had created the very grid by which humans organized their lives. So to chart the heavens more precisely was not only to measure yet another facet of God's consideration for humankind (as Basil and Ambrose would have appreciated); it also synced human life to that knowledge, day in and day out.[63]

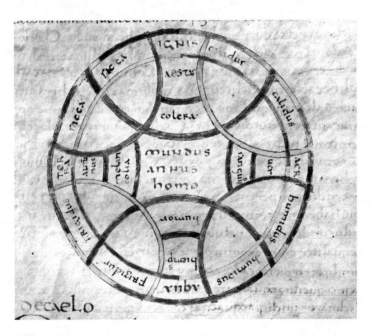

Fig. 2.2. A Carolingian diagram accompanying the same manuscript of Isidore's *De natura rerum* overlays the properties of hot, cold, dry, and wet—in the four seasons, the four elements, and the four humors. The center of this wheel reads "World/Year/ Man," a nod to the symmetries between space and time on a macrocosmic scale and in the microcosmic experience of humanity. (Bayerische Staatsbibliothek München, Clm 14300, fol. 8r.)

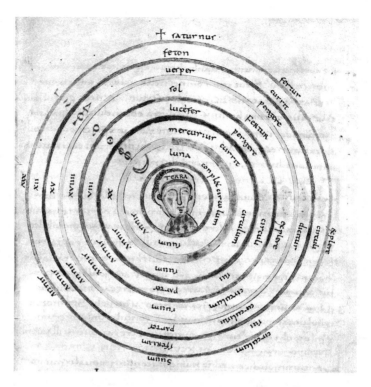

Fig. 2.3. The orbits of the celestial bodies closest to Earth (Terra), in the same Caro-lingian manuscript of *De natura rerum*. (Bayerische Staatsbibliothek München, Clm 14300, fol. 14r.)

Across the Irish Sea, about half a century before Bede, an author known to us as Augustinus Hibernicus, or "Irish Augustine," had expressed his own ad-miration for the solar and lunar cycles. He was especially impressed that even during the great Flood, when most of creation was turned upside down, the sun and moon had risen and fallen in the same mathematical relationship to each other—because if they had not done so, the ability to measure the dura-tion of the Flood itself would have been thrown into confusion. The stability of these cycles, even in times of great instability, struck Augustinus as singular, for most physical phenomena engendered a range of possible outcomes. This principle sits at the center of his *De mirabilibus sacrae scripturae libri tres* (*Three Books on the Miracles of Sacred Scripture*). Augustinus wrote it to argue that miracles were in fact instances of the countless directions nature could take. And the miracle that preoccupied Augustinus the most was the subsiding of the waters of the Flood.[64] What happened to them? Did they just evaporate, or did they kickstart the tumultuous weather system that we know today? And what about the waters that had originally flowed from underground springs: did the land reabsorb them, the way land sometimes does with water, or did some of the water stay above the land and result in a net increase in the volume of surface waters?

Augustinus looked to his homeland for help in elucidating these questions, and in a kind of reverse-Galápagos moment he noticed that the wild animals of Ireland, including its wild pigs, were not unique to the island. Why? The recent past seemed inadequate to explain it: it was unlikely that humans had managed to transport wolves and wild boars and other untamed animals from elsewhere unless the animals had previously been domesticated. And even if they had been, how could *all* these ostensibly tamed animals have escaped from their masters? Such a scenario was not wholly implausible for pigs (as we have seen), but Augustinus thought a more satisfying answer lay in the deeper history of hydrology: animals that had once lived on the same continent must have become separated by rising waters that eventually became the Channel and the Irish Sea. After all, old men in Augustinus's day could confirm that sea levels had changed even over their lifetimes, leaving formerly exposed areas submerged. (Like his late antique models, Augustinus enthusiastically looked to a range of experts to assist his investigations. Besides speaking with old men about the historic hydrology of Ireland, he had learned from the Achaemenid emperor Cyrus—via Herodotus, Seneca, and Orosius—how it was possible to divert rivers to alter their volume and flow. Physicians taught him about the saltwater in tears. Distillers understood how a small amount of matter could be transformed into a whole lot of liquid.)[65]

In the end, Augustinus was still unsure whether the receding of the Flood was the same hydraulic movement that had precipitated the formation of Ireland. The question of where the Flood waters went remained a "knotty investigation" (*nodosa quaestio*) because a single natural event entailed many movements and variables. The sky's receptivity to water, the land's saturability, the double water sources of rainwater and natural springs, and the prior existence (or not) of storm systems all figured into the Flood's potential trajectory. The results were sobering: "All the things we possess, we hardly know a fraction of them."[66]

But for Augustinus that lack of knowledge was all the more reason to investigate further. After all, he was trying to demystify the miraculous by explaining how miracles were only more powerful versions of everyday natural motion. God might speed up a natural process or intervene in one to produce a specific outcome, but these still remained amplifications of entirely routine transformations. Jesus's multiplication of fish and loaves of bread, for example, were instantaneous actions that condensed the developments that, for lesser beings, come about through the work of reproduction (in the case of fish) and agriculture and baking (in the case of humans and their bread).[67]

In the seventh century, when Augustinus was puzzling through these issues, many Christians in Europe, Byzantium, and the Middle East were thinking skeptically about miracles. Even Christians who believed that they had witnessed something miraculous needed to defend their positions fairly rigorously in order to rule out other possible causes before concluding that what they had seen was a sign of divine intervention.[68] Augustinus's own verdict was that miracles were definitely divinely activated, but they were not supernatural. Even God's most wondrous accomplishments happened firmly within the physics that he had established from the beginning. If anything was genuinely irregular, it was the original act of creation itself. So even if Augustinus had written his book in response to these larger cross-Mediterranean debates, the challenge that appealed to him most was not determining whether a given incident was miraculous (which for Augustinus was a fairly uninteresting heuristic), but rather identifying the interplay of natural forces that were at work within it.

Two centuries later, at the Carolingian court of Charles the Bald in the 860s, the philosopher John Scottus (the Irishman) Eriugena would ponder a similar idea—that nature was both regular and seemingly extraordinary; or, as he put it, that the physical world was habitually uncustomary. "Many things often tend to happen against the customary course of nature, to demonstrate to us that divine providence can govern everything, not in just one way, but in multiple and even infinite ways." That is what made thinking about the motions of nature (such as the growth of an animal or a plant) so difficult: "natural" processes, which were already extremely complicated, occurred in countless permutations. But paying close attention to those variable movements was not a pointless pursuit. For Eriugena, it amounted to the study of ethics. In contrast to physics/*physica*, which concentrated on the inherent properties of created things (which Eriugena called *substantiales naturae rationes*), ethics/*ethica* looked to nature in motion, whether it involved the "irrational" motions of (say) rivers or plants, or the rational motions of human beings. This was an expanded definition of what "ethics" was typically understood to mean. In the conventional usage of medieval rhetoric, ethics was the interpretation and application of moral principles to particular situations.[69]

Eriugena saw an analogous procedure at work throughout the universe, in which originating principles (*principia*) manifested themselves in different specific guises.[70] He argued throughout his monumental *Periphyseon* (*About Nature*) that the physical world was a kind of cascading emanation of divine forces, in which Creation began with what he called the "primordial causes" (*primordiales causae*) and branched farther into species or kinds of things, and again into individual specimens in their specific contexts. So, like human ethics, a physical ethics moved to connect the universal to its particular iterations by scrutinizing a cosmos in motion in order to know its interconnected forces more deeply. Eriugena was unusual in dubbing this mode of inquiry an ethics, but late antique and early medieval philosophers of nature shared his sense of responsibility to practice it—to seek out the links between the transcendent and the material, the absolute and the local, the eternal and a world that constantly changed.[71]

What Humans Learn, What Angels Know

All of creation was in motion, and even when it was possible to discern systemic patterns, like so many rotating wheels, within that dynamism there were enough variables operating to ensure that even careful observers would continually encounter things they could not easily explain. The life and physical sciences—which late ancient and medieval philosophers understood as physica, the study of the perceptible world—were therefore as much about identifying uncertainty as they were about discovery.[72]

Human accounts of this universe could only try to approximate its complexity, rather than fully encapsulate it, because as the exegetes often pointed out, our view of the world was not "the" view of the world. Animals were a useful reminder of this. A person did not even have to leave the farm to see the world in entirely different ways. Basil pointed to the ability of ewes to pick their lambs' bleats, colors, and scents out of a flock of a thousand sheep: the very sensory-scape of a farm seemed different to a mother sheep from the way it did to a herder, or to any other animal for that matter. Bede and Remigius of Auxerre noted that nighttime was an opportunity for humans to rest their exhausted bodies, but for animals that could not bear the sun, it was a good time to look for food. Eriugena pointed out that camels had better memories than humans did, and eagles had better vision, so a species' view of the past and even of the sun could differ from what humans saw.[73] Ambrose's attempt to think like a dog was also an acknowledgement that to *be* something else was also to *perceive* something else—even if, in the dog's case at least, that something else's sense perception and cognition at times seemed nearly analogous to our own.

In thinking about animals this way, the exegetes had radically departed from the ancient view that humans constituted a "negative exception" among all living things. In this view, as the classicist Brooke Holmes has characterized it, Greek and Latin philosophers had suggested that humans were uniquely ignorant of their environments. Unlike all other living things, which know how to take care of themselves, humans had to *learn* how to survive. Pliny had suggested that this exceptional ignorance could be rectified if humans shared knowledge about nature rather than jealously guarding it as the preserve of professionals.[74] But although late antique and early medieval writers obviously appreciated Pliny's efforts to make the wide world accessible, they did not see ignorance as a cultural or biological deficiency, at least not exclusively. When they observed animals at work in the world, what struck them most was not that humans were standout failures (or standout observers for that matter). Instead they were drawn to the idea that life itself was inescapably incomplete. *Every creature* had a perspective and a knowledge specific to it.

And there were advantages to considering a problem from an animal's point of view. The Carolingian poet and prose writer Walahfrid Strabo, for instance, would report in the ninth century that the (dead) patron saint of the monastery of Saint Gall led the monks' pigs to a secret cache of acorn-rich woods during an unusually barren autumn at a time when even wild animals were having a hard time finding food. And when the pigs were full and fat, Gallus also made sure that they returned to the monks in orderly formation. The pigs' swineherd had been completely baffled by their behavior. His pigs had initially bolted with no apparent provocation. He had had to track them down to a place more remote than any pasture he had ever known, and he was not sure how they would all find their way home, until Gallus told him in a dream to give the head sow a good smack, and she would know what to do.[75] This story might seem like a hagiographical snapshot of "everyday life," but the whole point of telling it was that almost none of what happened was typical. It was the swineherd's and monks' careful attention to woodland ecology and pigs' normal behaviors that helped them recognize a miracle when they saw one. Thinking about things from the vantage point of a pig was part of the work of clarifying the cosmos.

Early medieval "naturalists" were also well aware that even among the human species, ways of measuring and explaining natural phenomena were geographically and culturally distinct. Exegetes liked to repeat Basil's suggestion that the phrase in Genesis 1:2 as it was rendered in Greek and Latin—with the meaning "the spirit of God was carried above the waters"—lacked the pungency of the Hebrew and Syriac versions, which describe the spirit of God as "incubating" the waters. (Basil had gotten his information from a learned "Syrian" he did not name.) By alluding to the way a chicken broods, the Semitic languages implied that an analogous process was taking place on the very first day of creation, and it helped make sense of a difficult passage: God's tender warming of the waters formed the creatures to come.[76]

Language was one obvious indication that different cultures had developed different forms of understanding, but there were other systems of reckoning that pointed readers to the same conclusion. Isidore was fascinated by contrasting analytical models of measurement and computation, for example in determining the start of a day, the length of a week, the position of intercalary days (like our Leap Day), or clusters of years (like our decades). He did not reject any of these scientific cultures—Chaldean, Egyptian, Hebrew, Greek, Roman—as less accurate than the others. He was keener to point out that there were different forms of evaluation and practice that rendered the same material world intelligible in different ways.[77]

But there was no overlooking the vastness of that world. The inhabitants of Europe and the Mediterranean knew that the skies and terrains and animals that were both familiar and cryptic to them were not the same landscapes and creatures other people knew. They were literate in the localized sensibility that the natural historians and philosophers advocated—such as Pliny's and Ambrose's attention to fish habitats—and they were also avid readers of texts that conjured up the wildlife of faraway lands, such as the *Physiologus* (a late antique Alexandrian cycle of animal allegories that readers around the Mediterranean and Europe translated, excerpted, and elaborated), the English *Book of Monsters,* and the legendary narratives about Alexander the Great's adventures in the eastern Mediterranean and the Middle East, which were popular in Latin, Greek, Syriac, Arabic, Hebrew, and Old English.[78]

Readers knew that some of the stories they heard and read were fantastical. The library at the monastery of Bobbio in northern Italy, for example, catalogued this sort of literature separately from its more straightforwardly historical, exegetical, and scientific works. They were not even considered real travelogues.[79] But even in self-consciously fictional narratives, monsters were not alien life forms. They were only distortions of more familiar things, born like everything else in the first six days of the universe and somehow logically imbricated in the divine order. That did not make them any less weird: the really unsettling thing about these "disturbing hybrids" was that it was so difficult to pin them down. Their uncanniness derived special force from the late antique and early medieval conviction that although the physical world was incredibly complex, it also hung together in a coherent if elusive taxonomy. Monsters had things to show (*monstrare*) to humans, even if the knowledge that they had the potential to illuminate could be frustratingly difficult to grasp.[80]

In the early Middle Ages, monsters tended to congregate at the edges of the known world. It was not until the fourteenth and fifteenth centuries that Europeans would keep their eyes peeled for aberrant creatures that inhabited their own homelands. But early medieval observers were not content to leave monsters alone at the periphery. Carolingian missionaries, whose work took them deeper into the North, were fully prepared to encounter people with the heads of dogs—the Cynocephali, a monstrous race that Augustine, Isidore, and many other writers had warned them about. But they were also eager to learn more about these dog-headed creatures so they could situate them more precisely into the order of creation. The monk Ratramnus of Corbie concluded, after consulting his missionizing friend Rimbert as well as his books, that the Cynocephali were in fact capable of reason. They felt emotions. They even kept domesticated animals. Consequently, they were capable of conversion to Christianity.[81]

This analytical approach to the cosmos was widely enough shared to be satirized by contemporaries. The risk that came with seeing the world this way—as vast and variable, but also potentially legible—was that even the most bizarre reports of distant realms might have a ring of plausibility. In that spirit, a text written around 730 titled the *Cosmographia* tested its readers' hermeneutics in the structure of a hybrid cosmography and travelogue that critiqued these same genres relentlessly. As in any early medieval text, the author of this one drew from other sources to develop his own views, and in this case, he seems to have had the great library of Bobbio at his disposal in addition to books that he had collected in the British Isles and Gaul. But the composite view that the *Cosmographia* pulls together from its sources is deliberately slippery. The author poses as Saint Jerome, pretending to report from the fourth century what he has learned from a work he has "found" by an ancient philosopher named Aethicus Ister. The tension between these two voices—one patristic, one pagan—draws attention to some of the weak spots in the processes of learning and knowing. For one thing, it was hard to tell whether a given source of information was reliable, because the boundaries between "my" knowledge and "your" knowledge could be disconcertingly hard to disentangle. Such an operation seems nearly impossible in the *Cosmographia*. On one hand Jerome's voice and values are distinct from Aethicus Ister's, and the *Cosmographia*'s readers would have seen Jerome as the more authoritative of the two personas. But on the other, Jerome's discourse is saturated with what Aethicus has taught him. He knows what Aethicus knows, so their knowledge blurs together despite their seemingly separate identities. And Jerome's (and our) dependence on Aethicus leads to additional problems. Although Jerome is sometimes critical of Aethicus, he does not catch all of his errors. Aethicus suggests that the world is flat, for example, but this was a theory that had been criticized when it appeared in the eastern Mediterranean in the sixth century, and no exegetes or cosmographers in the Latin world endorsed it. Aethicus-via-Jerome also added to the stories of Alexander his own conspicuously original legend, about an adventure in a submarine that could crawl along the ocean floor while lighting its path with a mirrored solar device. And he was blatantly anachronistic. Besides quoting or alluding to texts that postdate his hypothetical character (as well as the historical Jerome), Aethicus also narrates events that occurred in the actual author's lifetime, hundreds of years in the "future!"[82] From the perspective of the *Cosmographia*, then, it was not only the complexity of the universe that strained humans' capacity to think critically. The referential density of the cosmographical genres was also a challenge, and so was the recursive nature of knowledge itself.

In this epistemological culture, which was generally characteristic of the early medieval Latin West, the concept of an objective researcher, or of a universal constant, would have been totally inappropriate. Being part of the physical world, witnessing some ecologies and not others, meant that perception and understanding were inescapably partial—all the more so because the universe was constantly changing and was expressive of a God who was incompletely knowable.

But early medieval writers who thought about the created world still fantasized about the possibility of disembodied and dislocated knowledge. This is one of the reasons they were fascinated with angels. Their interest might at first seem irrelevant. Neither of the two creation narratives that begin the book of Genesis mentions angels.[83] And angels were imperceptible to the senses—so why would Christians who were trying to make sense of the physical and divine realms introduce another complicating factor into their considerations? The simplest answer is that they were sure that angels existed. Both the Old and New Testaments mentioned them, even if the first three chapters of Genesis did not. And because God did not create anything new after those first six days, the exegetes reasoned, he must have created angels as part of that initial sequence. So they needed to be accounted for. But another answer to the question "Why discuss angels as part of the cosmos?" is that they helped Christian philosophers make sense of how knowing things worked.

Angels, to the mind of a seventh-century Iberian commentator on Genesis, were the best part of creation. Other Christians would have understood the sentiment. It was based on a shared conviction that no other part of creation came as close to understanding the cosmos, and understanding God, as the angels did. Like humans, angels were rational creatures. But unlike humans, angels consisted entirely of "a certain brilliant feeling of reason," as one Carolingian exegete put it.[84] They could know and understand things instantly, even invisible things, because they were pure intellects who did not have bodies to restrict them.[85] Not only were bodies bound to particular positions in space and time. Not only did bodies die. Every human body was also born with the legacy of Adam and Eve, born with the impulse to act against the soul's better judgment, just as its ancestors had done. Without bodies to limit the mind in these ways, angels could know everything there was to know. There were no "knotty investigations" among them. The exegetes envisioned this wistfully.

But knowing things still required effort, even for angels, because in late antique and early medieval epistemology, knowledge was always an active process. And more unexpectedly from our vantage point, it was a *two-way* process. Knowledge was not a passive object to be retrieved; knowledge was God himself, who, as Augustine put it, was constantly speaking to his intellectual creations, constantly reaching out to them through some "hidden inspiration" and asking them to know his work and recognize their origins. Eriugena spoke to would-be researchers in a similarly optimistic spirit: God *encourages* investigation into the properties of his creations. If it seemed as if there was not any information to go on—as might be the case, for instance, when it came to estimating the size of the sun—a person should *not* take it as God's way of suggesting that a thing should not be known.[86] To know something was to answer a divine summons, to peer deep into a created thing and retrace its path backward to the Total Knowledge that had generated it. Even angels had to do this, and they did it continuously. There were only a handful of exceptions. At the beginning of the world a few angels had chosen to focus on themselves instead of on God's complete and eternal wisdom. The damage was irreparable. They were transformed into demons and, by some accounts, hurtled into the lower air—the part of the atmosphere where birds flew.[87] As for the angels who *had* stayed focused on wisdom: they would spend a happy eternity alternating between the act of perceiving creation and the act of praising the creator for what he had done.

For humans who were thinking about the physical world, this angelic procedure was the ideal model.[88] The angels' cyclical motion between observation and reflection was what advanced true understanding. A seventh-century Visigothic commentary nicknamed *Intexuimus* (after its opening line), which was a highly popular consideration of Genesis well into the Carolingian period, put it this way:

> After all, that is what a day was: when the nature of the angels contemplated the very creation that God had made, it then became evening in a certain way. But because [the nature of the angels] did not stay in a permanent state of beholding his creation, and instead brought its praise back to God, it could better examine things through divine reason, and then suddenly it was as if it was morning. For if it had stayed in a permanent state of viewing creation while neglecting the Creator, it undoubtedly would not have become evening, but night.[89]

The world's first six days, in other words, were delineated not by the rise and fall of the sun or any other celestial body but by the progression of angelic knowledge as it moved from creation (day) to concept (evening) to acknowledgment (morning) and back to creation again. So although humans were not the smartest or most observant members of the universe, and although their bodies would inevitably constrain them, it was through this same cycle that they could learn more about the universe in its physical and divine orders, as they moved back and forth between the small and big pictures and between the things they sensed and the things they thought. From pigs to God, from the farm to the mind, and back again.

Only Moses was singled out as having become the equal of angels through the deep thinking he had done on earth. But even if Moses had not been so formidable an example, the human mind could be terribly disappointing. The Lombard king Liutprand called attention to human inadequacy when he judged a case involving an accidental death in Italy in 733. A landowner had had a well on his property that seems to have been constructed like a shadoof, or counterpoise lift, consisting of a weighted lever (*tolenus*) set on a forked post (*furca*). A second man who was drawing water carelessly discharged the lever, and its weight crushed a third man standing underneath it. Who was liable? Liutprand and his judges decided that the man operating the well was responsible for a third of the penalties, but the remaining responsibility lay with the dead man: "Because he was not an animal and was capable of rational perception (*sensum rationalem*), as a human should be, he should have looked out to see what kind of place he was about to stand in, and what sort of weight was above him."[90] Liutprand's view of rational thought here aligns neatly with the philosophical and exegetical understanding that unlike animals, humans could use sense perception or *sensus* to develop judgments about the physical world. But it was one thing to have that capacity, and another to use it. People did not always live up to their taxonomical distinctions.

Halfway between angels and irrational animals, humans faced a universe that was both alluring and evasive, and they reconciled themselves to the work of knowing the nature of things through the restless dialectic between the universal and the situational. Some of the features of natural philosophy and exegesis I have highlighted in this chapter were a strategy to address that challenge. By considering phenomena across vast geographies, hunting for patterns among interlocking physical systems, or exploring variations among seemingly straightforward groups, these "naturalists" worked to discern logical connections that were invisible at the local level. They also appealed to the expert and intimate knowledge of specialists and informants, some of whom might not have known anything about the cosmos writ large but who could speak to the profound complexity of its corners.

These were not the efforts of a culture that saw itself as separate from nature. (Even God was part of nature, Eriugena insisted.)[91] They were the efforts of a culture that considered itself to be ontologically continuous with the environment it was scrutinizing. Humans were "creatures" or "created things," *creaturae,* and so was everything else. And every bit of that created world had implications—in the folded sense of Augustine's cosmos—for something beyond itself. The analysts who wanted to trace these implications found themselves mapping the complexity of the cosmic system as a basis for their provisional answers. But if every discovery was frustrating because of the new complications it introduced, it was also exhilarating, for each revelation was more precious testimony to the capacities and designs of the creator.

I have focused on writers who thought about the physical world (and who thought about *thinking* about the physical world) to make clear that even "intellectual" culture in Late Antiquity and the early Middle Ages was concerned with things literally on the ground. These authors—who are sometimes flatly mischaracterized as mouthpieces of "official dogma" or "high culture"—had a more inquisitive, supple view of the universe than is usually acknowledged, not least because they developed their ideas in conversation with many interlocu-tors and audiences.[92] The exegetes and natural philosophers only occasionally spoke of pigs to make their points, but the animals were part of a landscape that was cosmically resonant, part of an animal world whose complexity was palpable, and part of ecological dynamics that these authors deeply appreci-ated. These Christian visions of nature were not only compatible with agrarian ethics (and its attention to species flexibility, localized and linked ecologies, environmental dynamism, and interspecies engagement). They also enlarged its scale, to reach up to the heavens and beyond everything to eternity. When pigs pointed their owners toward the intricacy of the universe and humans' constrained position within it, their value as property was not the only reason to pay attention. The farm and its physics were fused to the divine order. So although in the next chapter I turn to the specific worlds in which pigs moved, the sense of descending from the intellectual stratosphere and plunging into the everyday is partly an illusion—a failure, as the Latin naturalists would see it, of our own limited perspective.

3 • Salvaged Lands

In the early Middle Ages, pigs inhabited a landscape that was as complex as they were. What historians today call the post-imperial "West" is and was a matrix of different local environments. And yet, regardless of where you were, you were likely to find pigs there. Whether it was a farm in the High Tell of northwestern Tunisia, a cave dwelling in a rocky outcropping on the island of Mallorca, a village planted on a windy and nutrient-poor plain of southern Italy, wetland forests outside a trading town in the Low Countries, or a hillfort in southern Wales, pigs were a ubiquitous part of the landscape. Their omnipresence was made possible by the flexibility of their appetites and behaviors: it was possible to raise a pig almost anywhere, as long as an adequate supply of water was available.[1] This made pigs a good investment, because in almost any ecology, the animals could reliably transform resources that humans would not otherwise use (acorns, grubs, household garbage; the list goes on) into energy they *could* use. By some calculations, over 80 percent of a pig's weight amounted to edible, meaty energy—so even the leaner, active pigs of Late Antiquity and the early Middle Ages could have produced approximately 100–175 pounds (or 50–80 kg) of pork and lard.[2]

All domesticated livestock were technically "walking larders," to crib the title of a classic book. But the pig seemed to be an especially perfect vessel to "store" resources for the future. Ancient authors liked to repeat what the Greek Stoic Chrysippus had said about pigs in the third century BCE: they had been given breath instead of salt! The Stoics were suggesting by this that the universe had been made for humans as well as gods, and that in this case (as Brooke Holmes summed up their point) the pig's sole purpose was "keeping the bacon fresh until it was ready to eat."[3] Christians would argue in Late

Antiquity and the early Middle Ages that the world had not been designed solely for human benefit—Claudius of Turin, among many others, pointed out that some things that were toxic to humans were actually beneficial to other species—but they obviously appreciated the perks of pig keeping, too.[4] It was unusual in Late Antiquity and the early Middle Ages for a community to focus on pig husbandry as a primary source of food or income, but it was a rare Christian community that did not eat any pork at all. Most people chose to work with pigs in these centuries, despite the problems of raising them.

They took on the onerous task because pig husbandry was a valuable form of "salvage accumulation." This term was coined by Anna Lowenhaupt Tsing to describe the acquisition of commodities whose production humans exploit but do not tightly control. She was referring to the matsutake mushroom in particular, which requires growing conditions that are impossible to simulate on farms or in labs. Mushroom collectors have to harvest them wherever they happen to grow.[5] But it makes even more sense to think of early medieval pig husbandry as a form of salvage accumulation because producers and their "products" alike practiced it. Pigs salvaged the landscapes they found, taking advantage of whatever foods their environments had serendipitously brought into being, and they produced meat that their owners in turn salvaged.

But early medieval communities' use of this form of resource extraction differed from the modern habit that Tsing criticizes. Industrial and global capitalist operations today, she argues, overextend the productive capacities of salvage accumulation by failing to recognize that materials and labor depend on environments and communities that cannot be easily replicated, and in so doing they intensively harvest the fruits of a system without ensuring that the system is sustainable. By contrast, in early medieval agrarian economies, pork production was manifestly more variable than "scalable." Farmers, landowners, and entire settlements developed diverse systems of production, exchange, and consumption, because the wide social spectrum of the post-imperial West was refracted through an equally heterogeneous landscape. In the early Middle Ages, ways of living and working with the land proliferated.

In this chapter I consider the landscapes in which pigs and pig husbandry were embedded through my own kind of salvaging. Thanks to settlement archaeology and the bioarchaeological sciences, it is now possible to reconstruct, if only very partially, some of the natural-cultural spaces that humans built in conjunction with other organisms and forces. But although this material offers precious evidence for the ways in which many people in the early medieval West would have spent their days, it is crucial not to overstate it as representative of the experience of "the average person." There was no average experience in this world. Such a concept would have made no sense at a time when the future sciences of public polling and actuarial predictions had not yet instilled the impression that human lives and outlooks could be averaged.[6]

It is also important not to mistake the picture we get from material culture as something more real than the planetary perspectives of the previous chapter. The exegetes who were interested in the physical world emphasized their knowledge as an ongoing dialectic between different perspectives within nature and their reflections on the universe as a whole. For them, theology and philosophy were always anchored in "real" things outside themselves. And their views of the early medieval landscape as a variegated and interactive environment seem to have been shared by the people who worked in it every day. We should not find this surprising. These writers lived in the same places as the farmers did and derived their incomes from the same agrarian expertise. They also wrote in conversation with the wider audiences of their friends, congregations, and courts; and they assumed matter-of-factly that anyone who had worked intimately with the physical world had something to contribute to their understanding of the universe. So although texts and bones are very different kinds of evidence, the people who left them behind shared living spaces and even some sensibilities in common.

In any case, the perspectives of people who worked with pigs could be as complex and surprising as the views of their contemporaries who wrote about the cosmos. When we think about pigs as commodities within an agricultural system, it is easy to assume that their role was purely instrumental. But treating pigs as mere objects that humans manipulated overlooks their own attributes and actions that enabled these economies to tick, and sometimes to suffer. It is more faithful to early medieval perspectives to think multidirectionally, and to ask how pig husbandry was both product and participant in the opportunities and constraints of local ecologies. Even as part of agrarian economies, pigs were instrumental *and* influential. The micro-conditions of "salvage" had broader consequences.

Micro-Ecologies

We know that people living in different places eat different things, and people in antiquity and the Middle Ages knew it, too. Jonas of Bobbio, for example, who had grown up at the edge of the Italian Alps but had ended up in northern Gaul by the middle of the seventh century, treated beer as a drink in need of explanation. He referred to dates and pepper as precious exotics, and chestnuts and Irish butter as more familiar treats.[7] And it is possible to say, in general terms, that meat eating and geography were correlated. Based on the bones that early medieval eaters threw away after their meals or cast off in the butchery process, osteoarchaeologists can discern what kinds of animal were most important in a given place. There are different ways to measure a species' predominance, but it can be possible to synthesize these metrics and make some generalizations.[8]

The bone records suggest that in Ireland cattle were the predominant livestock. Deep in the North, the Scandinavian settlements on Iceland raised cattle and sheep especially, though their diet was often dominated by fish. Greenlanders did not raise pigs, presumably because it was not seen to be worth penning them up for nine months a year (it was too cold to pasture livestock except in summer). But although they did raise cattle, it was migratory harp and hooded seals that provided the key meats there, along with walrus, which the few thousand inhabitants of Greenland hunted every summer in order to trade their ivory tusks and pelts. Farmers in England concentrated on cattle or sheep, in central Europe cattle or pigs, and in Gaul all three main domesticates. The Polish lands preferred pigs in the region of the Oder in the west but cattle around the Vistula and beyond in the east. The Italian peninsula favored pigs until the eleventh century or so, then changed its emphasis to sheep and goats—also known to osteoarchaeologists as ovicaprids or caprovines or caprines, because it can be difficult to distinguish the bones of the two species. Iberia overwhelmingly opted for sheep and goats, both in the Suevic and Visigothic kingdoms from the fifth into the early eighth century, and even more so once the Berbers and Arabs conquered the Visigoths and the Umayyads set up their emirate over most of the peninsula. The Maghreb also concentrated on ovicaprids, as did Libya, Egypt, the Levant, Anatolia, and Greece.[9]

From about 3500 BCE on, coinciding more or less with the start of the Bronze Age, Europe's biotic communities and climates have consisted, in very rough terms, of the zones of the Mediterranean, the Great European Plain, the Atlantic Maritime, and the taiga. South of the Loire and the Alps, the terrain is characterized by scrubland and sclerophyll forests, moving north to glacial soils and deep deciduous forests, to marshes and moderately fertile soil at the Atlantic coasts, and then, north of the Baltic, to the boreal forests of spruce and pine (a coniferous combo that also appears in the highest elevations of the Alps). Around the Mediterranean the summers tend to be hot and dry and the winters mild and wet; throughout the Plain the summers are warm, the winters are cold, and rainfall is more regular year-round; in the oceanic climate of the Atlantic both the summers and winters are cool and wet; and in the taiga the summers are short, the winters very cold, and the precipitation low. In North Africa for the past five thousand years the Maghreb has been home to the zones of the Mediterranean coast, the Tell Atlas Mountains, and the pre-desert and desert zones of the Sahara. These too are studies in contrasts: the mountains tend to be cooler in the summers and winters compared to the coast, and they are (and were) home to arid steppes, scrub, riverine woodlands, and high-altitude forests. The pre-desert is a semi-arid transitional zone between the coasts and the Sahara, characterized by grasslands and scrub that are (and were) capable of sustaining intensive agriculture, owing to the autumn floods. And in the hyper-arid desert, summers are very hot and dry, winters are warm with occasional nighttime frosts, and plant life tends to congregate at springs and aquifers along the wadis—though the groundwater may have been more accessible in antiquity and the early Middle Ages than it is now.[10]

It may be tempting, looking at livestock husbandry in view of these schematics, to suggest that sheep and goats (for example) were the quintessentially "Mediterranean" species, in contrast to the pigs and cattle that became increasingly frequent farther north. But generalizations like that will not get us very far—whether concerning animals or ecology. As the zooarchaeologist Philippe Columeau has pointed out in a case study of the animal remains at Larina—an elite center perched on a plateau in east-central Gaul—the causal relationship between geography on one hand, and production and consumption on the other, is not predictable. Although mountainous regions are often characterized as sheep-and-goat country, for example, the Merovingian inhabitants of Larina ate less meat from sheep and goats (which provided 20 percent of the site's meat) than pigs (25 percent) and cows (nearly 50 percent). People in the sea-level city of Marseille ate a higher proportion of sheep-and-goat meat than did inhabitants of Larina.[11]

The closer we zoom in, the more variations appear. In Ireland, for example, the preeminence of cattle began to drop in certain regions after 800: while Meath/Dublin continued to emphasize cattle, settlements in the north and west turned increasingly to ovicaprids and pigs. Or in Gaul, Lyon preferred goats and sheep, then pigs, then cattle; whereas Alsace-Lorraine preferred pigs, and the Île-de-France preferred cattle. Likewise the city of Algeciras/Iulia Traducta, on the strait of Gibraltar, bucked Iberian trends and consumed a lot more cattle than the peninsular average, in both its Visigothic-Byzantine phase and under the Umayyad emirate. Residents in different neighborhoods of the city were getting good cuts of beef from specialized cattle producers, a relationship that seems to have lasted for hundreds of years.[12]

One key reason for "deviations" like these is that some of the most important factors in determining what can live and thrive in a particular place (factors such as soils, rainfall, rates of evaporation, temperatures, and species assemblages) can vary substantially within conventional geographical or topographical boundaries. Geomorphology and biogeography too have their scales, a point that historians and archaeologists have increasingly come to appreciate. Micro-ecology matters.[13]

Take the ribāt (fortified settlement) of Guardamar on the Valencian coast. Generally speaking this was a "Mediterranean" environment, but in the ninth and tenth centuries it was home to several contrasting biotopes that were crucial to the settlement's character. The ribāt sat at the delta of the Seguna and was surrounded by salt marshes. Beyond that was maquis dominated by Aleppo pine, with an understory of mastic, which probably stretched to the foothills—and the presence of heather suggests that these woods were interspersed with pockets of cultivated spaces. There were also riverine woodlands of willow, elm, and tamarisk, plus wooded coastal ranges farther to the north and south. (We know all of this thanks to the early medieval bivalves, animal bones, pollen, and charcoal that have been preserved there.)[14]

The people who lived in places like these had correspondingly localized forms of farming. In Tuscany many early medieval villages were established on hilltops, but besides some of their structural similarities, the texture of their inhabitants' lives varied from site to site. At Montarrenti, the residents in the Carolingian period focused on cereal cultivation, along with various legumes and grapes. They also grew or gathered tree fruits (fig, pear, apple) and elderberries. Pigs were their most common livestock, a preference that was typical of Tuscany, but they also raised ovicaprids for wool and milk, and cattle, probably for labor.[15] Only twelve miles away, in the same centuries the hinterlands of the fortified estate of Miranduolo were blanketed in woods of chestnut and oak, with subdominant species of hop hornbeam, maple, *Populus*, elm, and walnut. The residents focused especially on growing legumes, but they also grew grains (wheat, barley, rye, spelt, millet, oats), grapes, hemp, flax, and stone fruits—and they would have cared for at least some of the chestnut trees farther afield. Pigs predominated among the livestock here, as well.[16]

Across the Alps, in the Jura mountains near modern Courtedoux, in Switzerland, villagers could find carp, perch, trout, toads, badger, fox, wild boar, and wildcat in its local woods and waters. The community of Delle sur le Marais (in Calvados, in northwest France) might catch and eat red deer, roe deer, hare, thrushes, blackbirds, cranes, mallard ducks, magpies, frogs, and bears. Some well-fed residents of Carthage (near modern Tunis) were managing to procure wildlife from a diverse range of neighboring ecological zones: local ostriches, migrant graylag and white-fronted geese, Barbary partridges from dry rocky areas, quail from greener fields and meadows, cranes and brilliant purple gallinules from marshes; and a ream of fish, bivalves, gastropods, cuttlefish, and crabs from freshwaters, estuaries and coastal lagoons, and rocky coasts and midwaters of the Mediterranean. Fifteen hundred miles north of Carthage, residents on the estate of Flixborough (at the northern edge of Lincolnshire in northern England) opportunistically hunted the waterfowl that roosted in its grasslands, including barnacle geese, pink-footed geese, plovers, curlews, woodcocks, and ducks. The residents also had a regular supply of bottlenose dolphins to eat. The animals were probably caught in the Humber estuary to the north of the estate. These dolphins were a genetically distinct breed that were specific to the area, and the species is also known to swim in shallow waters and approach boats out of curiosity, so hunters probably found that it was easy to catch them. On the island of Sandoy in the Faroes, the Norse settlers caught puffins and cod; fewer than 10 percent of all their animal bones belonged to domesticated animals. And along the shores of Lake Mývatn in northern Iceland, Icelanders harvested eggs from the nests of migratory waterfowl that bred there in the spring—a practice that both birds and humans have kept up to this day.[17]

Early medieval lawmakers knew that their kingdoms comprised different physical environments and forms of exploitation, and they adjusted their sense of value accordingly. In Visigothic Iberia, for example, stealing water from irrigation canals in arid zones entailed a higher penalty than the same crime in wetter regions. And one of Charlemagne's capitularies (issued for the Saxons in 797) valued grains more highly if they were paid from the northern areas of Saxon territory, presumably because cerealiculture was less extensive in the wetlands. Honey, on the flip side, was worth more in the South.[18]

Within the array of micro-ecologies that constituted the post-imperial West, there is no single environmental variable that can reliably predict the importance of pigs to a local community. Woodland comes the closest, not only because both deciduous and coniferous woodlands are full of things pigs like to eat, but more specifically because it was common practice in early medieval Europe to let pigs graze in oak and beech woods during the autumn. This suited the pigs, because they loved tree nuts. It suited humans, too, because although they did not generally eat acorns themselves (even though they are edible), they believed that acorns and beechnuts made pigs' flesh especially delicious. When the animals were slaughtered in the winter, their bodies would have by that time become perfectly flavored, thanks to the trees' bounty and the animals' own preferences. As Irish speakers liked to say in the early Middle Ages, a missed opportunity was like "a pig that dies before the acorn crop" (*mucc remi-thuit mess*).[19]

The landscapes of the West had become increasingly open since the late Neolithic or early Bronze Age, but forests were cleared at different rates and in some places even rebounded or changed their species composition. In Late Antiquity and the Early Middle Ages, northern central Europe in particular (what is now Germany, Poland, the Czech Republic, Denmark, and southern Sweden) was substantially cloaked in forests, about 40 percent of it, as far as we can tell from the pollen samples analyzed to date. And in some areas, people began to raise and eat more pigs where woodland increased. In the fertile zones of the Low Countries, woods of oak, beech, hazel, alder, birch, hornbeam, cherry, pine, lime, and elm recolonized formerly open areas; and in the process pork came to constitute more than half the meat these northern Gallic communities ate. This was all the more impressive considering that it took something like three to five pigs to produce the meat equivalent of what a single cow would yield. As for the pigs themselves in that area, they were enjoying good nutrition and low stress levels. Their teeth show a low incidence of linear enamel hypoplasia, or signs of physical stress on the tooth enamel that correspond to their living circumstances.[20]

Conversely, some farmers who lived in more open environments of grassland or scrub did not raise many pigs. This was the case with the Visigothic-era villages of Prado de los Galápagos, La Huelga, and Gózquez, lying along the Jarama river in the lowlands of the Spanish Central System, and with La Quebrada II, a mid-altitude settlement west of Toledo in the same mountain belt. In these communities, pigs were a small minority of the total livestock (10 percent, 2 percent, 2–7 percent, and 0.34 percent of the total remains on-site, respectively). At Gózquez, where archaeologists have a good sense of the size of the local population, those figures translate to the consumption of one or two pigs per family per year.[21]

But although there was a tendency in the early Middle Ages to raise more pigs when substantial woodland was nearby, not all communities chose to use their woodland resources in the service of a robust pig husbandry operation. Among the properties owned by the monastery of Santa Giulia di Brescia that were located near oak woods capable of feeding pigs (also in the monastery's possession), eight farms (23 percent) raised no pigs at all. Yet 62 percent of its estates that were *not* near woodland, twenty-five farms altogether, raised from one to fifty pigs.[22] In the high plains of the Tunisian Tell, which were intensively farmed in Late Antiquity and the early Middle Ages, pork consumption was noticeably high, even without substantial woodlands close by. At the small town of Althiburos during its Vandal phase (the 430s to the 530s), for example, pigs made up 30.1 percent of the total animal remains, even though the paleobotanical evidence points to widespread land clearance and erosion in the same century—in the service of oleoculture especially, but also for other fruit and nut trees, along with cereals, legumes, and grapes.[23] By contrast the village of Zaballa, at the edge of the foothills of the Cantabrian Mountains in northwest Iberia, in what is now Basque country, had access to woodlands of cypress, pine, oak, and beech, and yet there the villagers concentrated on raising sheep and goats for both wool and meat; for every pig, there were more than two ovicaprids.[24] Or at Larina, the elite center in central Gaul on its little island of a plateau, pig consumption moved in an inverse relation to the presence of woodland. In the Roman period, when the villa's inhabitants cleared wooded spaces to grow walnut and chestnut trees (which bore nuts that humans *would* eat), the pig population peaked at 40 percent of the site's animals. But as oak, pine, and spruce rebounded in the early Middle Ages, the proportion of pigs relative to other livestock actually decreased, dropping to 32 percent in the sixth century and 22 percent in the seventh.[25]

Woods, in short, were not always evidence of a lot of pigs and pigs were not always evidence of woods, because woods and pigs were part of complex ecological systems, in which any given farming practice was the product of interlocking variables, not a linear relationship between two quotas. Archaeologists who have tried to explain the declining rates of pig husbandry in some Italian cities have therefore floated a number of different hypotheses, all of which point to the multiple ways pigs were linked to other resources and subject to multiple forces. Perhaps the decline went hand in hand with the end of the imperial *annona* system, which (as we will see) involved the collection of foodstuffs, including pork, and their distribution to armies and cities. Perhaps it was the result of increased land clearance and field agriculture around urban areas—or, conversely, perhaps it meant the increase of *pasture* (and with it, an uptick in grazing animals). Or possibly towns had decided to focus on sheep and goats with an eye to the wool trade.[26] All these hypothetical scenarios point to the fact that pig husbandry was contingent on a number of environmental and economic calculations.

Early medieval farmers would have sympathized with our difficulty in determining causation here, because like their contemporaries who contemplated natural history writ large, they viewed the worlds they inhabited as systems of interdependent and fluctuating resources. Large-scale landowners, for example—monasteries in particular—understood that the array of properties in their possession had different assets. They paid attention to the productive features of each of their estates and tenancies and developed networks between them. The monastery of Bobbio, in northern Italy, made sure to send regular shipments of salt from its property in Comacchio, on the Adriatic coast, to its fishery on Lake Garda, about 125 miles northeast of Comacchio. The monastery of Saint-Germain-des-Prés in Paris owned a cluster of properties on the Île-de-France, where its tenants dedicated a fair part of their labor to viticulture at home and on their landlord's farms, while some of its tenants over 100 miles to the west, in the forested areas of the Perche region (whose flinty and waterlogged soils were tougher to farm), built most of the barrels for all that wine. Once it was barreled—in an average year, the total volume was roughly equivalent to 6,500 hectoliters (about 172,000 gals.), or more than 850,000 of today's wine bottles—it would be shipped to Paris, again propelled by tenant labor. In these arrangements, a landowner operated as a "center of centers," managing local ecologies as part of a larger coordinated economy.[27]

We are mostly reliant on monastic property inventories from the ninth and early tenth centuries for this picture, and these records are concentrated in the Carolingian empire. They are restricted to a particular swath of Europe (northern Francia and northern Italy) at a particular time in the early Middle Ages, and they are the product of some of the largest landholders in the early medieval West. The picture they offer is partial. But a more widespread indication that early medieval communities were thinking about their lived environments as systemic and contingent spaces is the pervasiveness of an agrarian approach in this period that historians and archaeologists sometimes call agro-pastoralism. Rather than concentrate on one agricultural or extractive activity, many rural communities farmed a wide array of crops (cereals, legumes, fruits, fibers, and to a lesser extent vegetables) in tandem with placing a heightened emphasis on livestock husbandry. It was also typical for early medieval settlements to practice some mix of fishing, foraging, hunting, textile production, mining, metallurgy, ceramics manufacturing, and bone working. As a general strategy this concert of agricultural and economic work was structured to accommodate local environments that were susceptible to change and to help make communities less vulnerable to shortages or failures, which were predictably unpredictable. The result was that in the early

Middle Ages, animal products tended to be a more significant part of humans' diets compared to both the imperial period and the high Middle Ages.[28]

And animals, unlike most crops, offered more flexibility when it came to "harvesting" their resources. Pastoralists in Iberia, for example, manipulated their flocks to suit their changing priorities. A farmer raising goats and sheep might slaughter most of his lambs before they reached the age of two months, in order to take advantage of their mothers' milk. Alternatively, he might choose to wait until they were six months old, in order to have some meat in addition to a milk supply. Or if he was like most farmers in Muslim Iberia, he would have slaughtered his animals on a curve, as the zooarchaeologist Marta Moreno García has pointed out: the favored strategy in the ninth to thirteenth centuries was to raise and kill ovicaprids for a mix of purposes, the rough equivalent of diversifying a portfolio.[29]

The Merovingian rural settlement of Develier-Courtételle offers an example of how livestock production fit into a larger scheme of agrarian life—and how it could be affected by, and affect, highly localized environmental conditions (fig. 3.1). The settlement hugged the banks of the river Pran on the Jura plateau in what is today northwest Switzerland.[30] The Pran is as straight as an arrow today, but in the early Middle Ages it was curvy and full, and between 650 and 850 it often overflowed its banks because this was a particularly wet period for southeastern Gaul. As a result, the village was surrounded by secondary watercourses, marshes, and floodplains. But the residents were undeterred by all the water. They built their houses a mere 5 to 10 meters (16–33 ft.) from the riverbank, on top of a clay-and-limestone surface that was naturally water resistant. They also built a series of artificial pools and bank reinforcements, and they took advantage of the water for their textile workshops (hemp and flax were the main fibers here) and for an extensive metallurgical operation.

When the settlement was founded in the second half of the sixth century, the marshes were forested with white fir, beech, oaks, alder, and ash, and they were surrounded by lower-density woods (or savannahs)[31] that were good for pasturing livestock. In the next century and a half, significant portions of those woods were gradually cleared in order to feed the iron furnaces, to cultivate more cereals and textile fibers, and to provide more prairieland for cattle, whose meat was fairly skillfully butchered and then exported. Grazing also had the effect of changing the composition of the woodland: the cattle seem to have feasted on fir saplings, which encouraged the growth of beeches and oaks that would otherwise compete with fir (fig. 3.2).

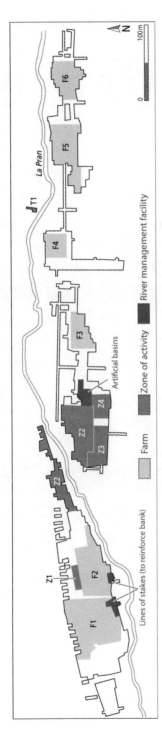

Fig. 3.1. The site of Develier-Courtételle. (From Guélat et al., *Develier-Courtételle*, p. 12, fig. 5. Reprinted with permission from the Office de la culture, Section d'archéologie et de paléontologie and the Société jurassienne d'Émulation. Key translated from the French original.)

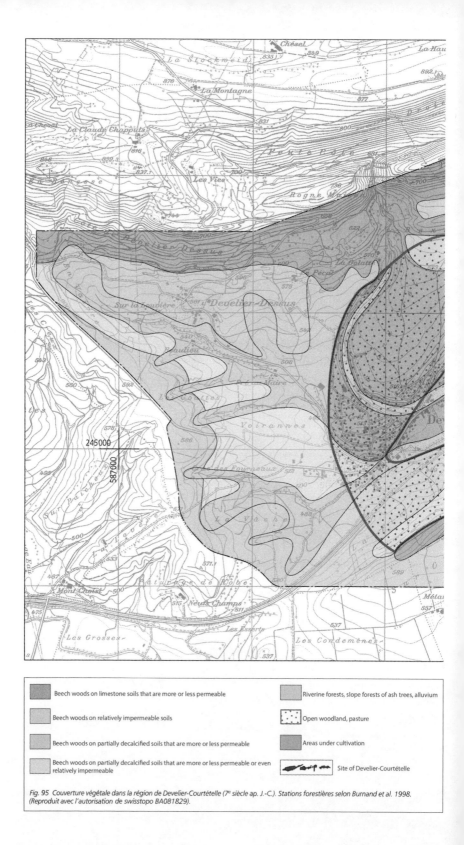

Fig. 95 Couverture végétale dans la région de Develier-Courtételle (7ᵉ siècle ap. J.-C.). Stations forestières selon Burnand et al. 1998. (Reproduit avec l'autorisation de swisstopo BA081829).

Beech woods on limestone soils that are more or less permeable

Beech woods on relatively impermeable soils

Beech woods on partially decalcified soils that are more or less permeable

Beech woods on partially decalcified soils that are more or less permeable or even relatively impermeable

Riverine forests, slope forests of ash trees, alluvium

Open woodland, pasture

Areas under cultivation

Site of Develier-Courtételle

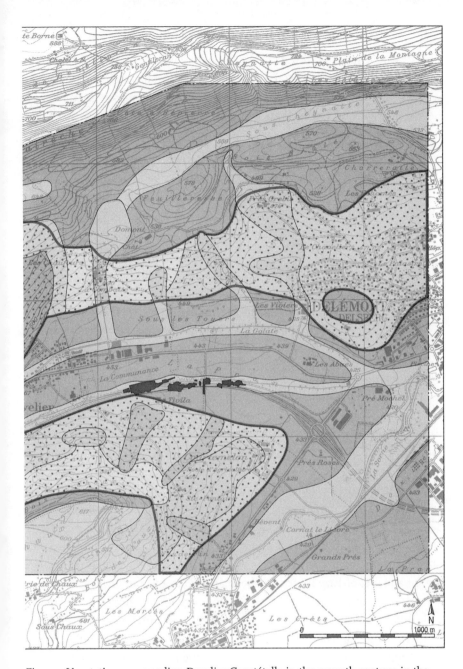

Fig. 3.2. Vegetation surrounding Develier-Courtételle in the seventh century, in the course of woodland thinning and clearance that would continue into the eighth century. (From Guélat et al., *Develier-Courtételle*, pp. 152–53, fig. 95. Reprinted with permission from the Office de la culture, Section d'archéologie et de paléontologie and the Société jurassienne d'Émulation. Key translated from the French original.)

Pigs would have loved the beech- and oak-filled woods, but they make up considerably fewer of the total number of animal remains than cattle (about 20 percent versus 40 percent). And unlike cattle they mostly seem to have been eaten on-site, rather than being raised for export in ways that had a demonstrable impact on the landscape. Such a practice makes sense for a settlement that found beef production and export highly compatible with other elements of its environmental, artisanal, and agrarian framework: forest clearance generated fuels for industries that were built upon the swollen river, and the resulting grasslands and savannahs were good for cows. Pigs fit in to Develier-Courtételle's ecology, as they fit in to nearly every niche we have seen in this chapter, but their lives and roles in this wet woody space would have been distinct from the lives of pigs elsewhere.

Variable Economies

As the case of Develier-Courtételle also suggests, local environments did not determine absolutely how communities lived. Instead they presented various possibilities that humans responded to, and those choices in turn affected what was possible, in an ongoing feedback loop that is characteristic of any ecology. This is what made it possible for the Garamantian kingdom in Fazzān, which controlled vast stretches of oases networks along the wadis of the Libyan Sahara, to raise pigs in its vibrant capital city of Garama. In this hyper-arid environment, the Garamantes cultivated oases where water collected near the surface at the edges of sand seas and massifs. With the help of an extensive irrigation system, they grew a diverse range of crops including date palms, grapevines, fig trees, pomegranates, cereals, legumes, melons, barley, wheat, sorghum, pearl millet, flax, and cotton. There were also wild plants growing along the wet zones of these farms and water channels, where the inhabitants of Fazzān grazed sheep and goats and cattle. There was even enough water to raise pigs. And all this agrarian activity developed in concert with robust trade networks that the kingdom maintained between the Mediterranean and sub-Saharan Africa, from the first century CE into the sixth—and at reduced but similar forms, including the pigs, for several more centuries, until the 1000s.[32]

Although Garama's situation was strikingly stable, a settlement's profile and relationship to its habitat could change considerably, and this was the commoner situation. Ecologies changed over time, not just across space, and pig husbandry was enmeshed in those trajectories. A good example of such

Fig. 3.3. Reconstruction of the fourth-century dining room at Faragola, 31.5 × 55 ft. (9.63 × 16.82 m). Much of the stone *stibadium,* marble flooring, and opus sectile were still in place when the structure was excavated, even though three centuries after this *cenatio* was built it would be transformed into a workspace (fig. 3.4). (From Volpe and Turchiano, *Faragola 1,* pl. 1. Image provided by Giuliano Volpe.)

change is the site of Faragola, in northern Apulia in the valley of the Cara-pelle.[33] Faragola sat at the juncture of several ecosystems. In addition to the valley corridor, it was linked to the Tavoliere plain, the foothills of the Monti Dauni, the promontory of Gargano, and the high plain of Morgia. Under the Roman Empire, both the state and many prominent senatorial families had invested heavily in this area, which resulted in an excellent road infrastructure, thriving towns to the north and south, and many villa complexes. Faragola itself had begun as a villa in the second or third century, and in the fourth century the residents scaled up: they built a bath complex and an opulent summer dining room replete with a carved stone dining couch (or *stibadium*), inlaid stone "rugs" that were probably imported from Egypt, and floors covered in polychrome marbles (fig. 3.3).

During this late antique phase, when the villa was an elite residence and expansive agricultural complex, the occupants were not particularly invested in raising sheep and goats, even though northern Apulia was a center of trans-humant pastoralism (that is, the seasonal herding of flocks to different pastures). But at Faragola, pigs were by far the most prominent livestock in the fourth and fifth centuries, constituting over 70 percent of the livestock remains found there.[34]

The villa was continuously occupied into the sixth century, but by 600 or so there had been dramatic changes to the structure and function of the property. Most strikingly, the great dining room was turned into an artisanal area where animals were stalled, grain was stored, and metallurgy and ceramics were manufactured (fig. 3.4). We also know that at this time Faragola was surrounded by woodland that was dominated by deciduous oaks and mastic. Both these species were perfect for the metallurgical and ceramic work that was happening there: oak burns hot and long, and mastic is great for kindling. But the site as a whole does not seem to have housed any residents; instead, by the seventh century it was functioning as a center not only for the furnace but also for field agriculture, boneworking, and sheep and goat husbandry. Whoever was working at Faragola in this period, the inhabitants were at least eating their lunches on-site, and the meat they ate came mostly from their flocks, along with a good deal of chicken, fish from the nearby river, a little bit of pork, and occasionally beef from old draft animals.

Fig. 3.4. The seventh-century transformation of the dining room at Faragola into an agricultural and artisanal zone. (From Volpe and Turchiano, *Faragola 1*, pl. 8. Image provided by Giuliano Volpe.)

Things changed again in the eighth century. Now there were residents living at Faragola (in huts they had built inside the residential rooms of the former villa!). They were raising more pigs than the farmers before them had done—in this period, ovicaprid and pig remains are equally represented—but it seems that they were exporting the best cuts of pork off-site, because it is the bones from pigs' heads and feet that overwhelmingly dominate the remains. The site also seems to have shifted away from artisanal work, and the amount of oak on-site also drops, a decrease that could indicate either that the woodland had been substantially reduced compared to the previous century (thus giving us another example that bucks the pigs-and-woods trend) or that the community had chosen to cut back on its timber usage for the sake of the oaks' acorn crop, in order to fatten the pig herds in the fall. Regardless of what might have happened to the woodland, the aggregate picture is that this single site had recalibrated its relationship to the landscape several times over.[35]

It may seem counterintuitive to suggest that pigs were not always a choice element of an agro-pastoralist package. The animals have been characterized as a nearly cost-free commodity, requiring almost no labor or feed "inputs" and constrained only by their need for plentiful water.[36] They are also fertile reproducers. According to ancient and later medieval estate manuals, a good adult sow could produce two litters a year, or around sixteen piglets annually. It was even possible for her to produce a third litter in a year, or five litters every two years. Piglets take four months to gestate, so if owners intensively managed the reproductive process and kept the sow on a continuous fertilization and birthing schedule, she could theoretically be pregnant almost year-round.[37]

This was not necessarily the most productive system. The ancient agronomists insisted that high-frequency farrowing would compromise a sow's overall strength and fertility. In general they advised one litter per year and recommended that the sow be allowed to nurse no more than eight piglets from that litter. In Late Antiquity, Palladius (whose work enjoyed a good readership in the early Middle Ages) would further lower this number to six.[38] And if we look at our first opportunity to measure medieval livestock populations down to the animal—thanks to the livestock tallies that English manors began to take of their herds in the later thirteenth century—it is evident that a third litter would not necessarily have tripled the total piglet output. The manor of Hinderclay, for example, which was a possession of Bury Saint Edmunds in Suffolk, tried to farrow its sows three times in a year. But as a result of that practice the size of their litters fell well below average, so much so that the total number of piglets that were born from three issues did not exceed the

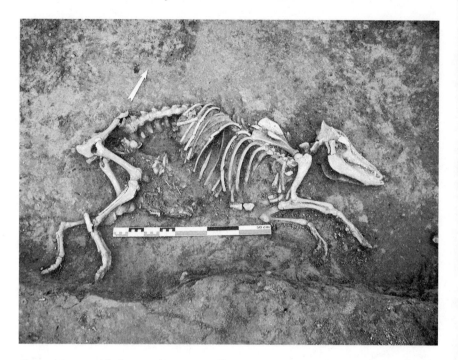

Fig. 3.5. A sow with three piglets in utero found in a hut that was converted to a disposal area at Hintere Buen (Sermersheim) in the tenth century. (Photo: Édith Peytremann, Institut national de recherches archéologiques préventives [INRAP], Paris, France. © RMN-Grand Palais / Art Resource, NY.)

number that two litters would typically have produced.[39] There were limits to what even flourishing farms could ask of their animals.

Sometimes farmers pushed these limits incautiously. In a very rare find from the village of Hintere Buen on the lower Rhine, excavators found the complete skeleton of a female pig and three fetal piglets (fig. 3.5). The sow was sixteen months old and had been pregnant for nearly four months; she may have died in labor, based on the position of one of her piglets near the birth canal. If it was not the delivery that killed her, it was probably the pregnancy, since she shows no other signs of illness or injury. She would have become pregnant just as she was turning a year old, and although the ancient agronomists agreed that sows were fertile between the ages of one and seven, Varro (who was writing in the Late Republic) cautioned that it would be better to wait until a sow was twenty months old at the earliest before breeding her. So this sow was probably bred at a vulnerable age. We obviously cannot know whether her owner learned anything from the loss of her, but we do know that this person took one last opportunity to profit from her: there are knife marks on the sow's bones that tell us she was skinned before she was buried.[40]

For many early medieval farmers, the costs of raising a whole herd of pigs on their own may have outweighed the benefits. If they wanted to feed their pigs in woodland that they did not own personally, they would have had to pay one-tenth of their pigs for the privilege, either to government officials or to the owner of the woods. (More on this later.) Piglet mortality was another cost. Some were likely to die of illness or by accident, maybe 20 percent of them if the mortality rates of free-range pigs today can provide a rough basis for comparison. Subadults (pigs under two years old) could also die unexpectedly, as could breeding boars and sows, even when they were carefully tended. Caring for the breeding sow entailed other optional expenses. She could be fed special mixtures of grains or legumes (which ancient manuals recommended and which appear in English manorial accounts as an annual expenditure in the high Middle Ages), and she and her piglets may have been housed in their own sty, although so far it has been impossible to identify any such structures on early medieval sites.[41] Surveillance of the entire herd was a more necessary investment, for obvious reasons, but that too was an expense: most swineherds who show up in the written record are unfree adult men, as we will see in Chapter 4. If a farmer did not have a swineherd, someone else in the household could herd pigs instead. But small children could not do it on their own, since pigs were capable of harming them and were in any case not easy to manage; and older children or adults who were capable of guarding and herding pigs would be using labor that they might otherwise dedicate to agricultural or artisanal work.

None of those operating costs was prohibitive, but a farming community that shared breeding animals and divided the offspring would have substantially mitigated the expenses and potential losses. The Merovingian law codes assumed that a swineherd and his assistant were capable of herding forty pigs, or even as many as seventy; and pigs were either branded or "painted," so it would have been possible to keep track of an individual household's pigs within a larger herd. But there were risks to this strategy. The Visigothic kings and legal advisers who compiled the *Liber iudiciorum* assumed that having a herd of animals belong to several owners could lead to confusion about who owned which animals, and they worried that this situation could be exploited by a herder intent on fraud.[42]

Such an attitude probably stemmed in part from an ancient suspicion of herders. But it was also indicative of early medieval lawmakers' apprehension about entrusting one's animals to another person under any circumstances. It was as likely to cause problems as it was to solve them. To take an extreme example: when one married couple living in the kingdom of León were given charge of another couple's livestock, including "countless" pigs, they damaged them so badly (*damnavit*, meaning that they mistreated, injured, or killed them) that they had to hand over a vineyard in order to rectify the situation. That was in 995. For centuries before that, lawmakers had regularly expressed concern that injury, overwork, or death could befall an animal when it was not in its owner's possession, and that animals could damage the property in which they were impounded—and if that happened, it created a host of complications when it came to assigning blame. The legal liabilities of taking possession of animals one did not own were apparently so unpalatable that in 643 the Lombard king Rothari added an additional layer of bureaucracy to the process of pawning animals, to discourage debtors from handing over living things as a surety. And if a lender wanted to take an entire herd of horses or pigs in the name of an unpaid debt, he would have to get royal permission first.[43]

Despite these liabilities, some people did share ownership of their pigs. Farmers were sharing pigs in Ireland, as the Old Irish laws make clear, and various provisions covered the legal complications of doing so. The evidence from the continent is sparser (and the evidence from North Africa nonexistent), but what we have does show individuals pooling their pigs occasionally. When two brothers exchanged properties with a church in the diocese of Lucca in the early ninth century, they specifically excluded their pigs from the transaction, because they owned them jointly (*in societate*) with "their men." Fifteen years later, the same church would acquire half the shares of a stable of pigs (*porcile*) in joint ownership with a different group of brothers.[44] These examples from Lucca are only an accident of survival; we happen to have an unusually high number of original charters from that diocese. But given the financial and logistical benefits of this sort of corporate investment, it is likely that many communities practiced it. Based on pigs' fertility rates, if a group of households shared six sows and a boar—a unit that appears in the *Lex Ribuaria,* a seventh-century code created in Gaul during the reign of King Dagobert—they could have slaughtered and consumed twenty-five to seventy adult pigs a year, with an equal number of subadults remaining. The penalty for stealing that sort of productive capital ran to six hundred solidi plus costs for replacing or returning the animals and losses incurred while they were missing. To put this fine into perspective, six hundred solidi was also the rate of compensation for stealing twelve mares and a stallion, stealing twelve cows and a bull, or murdering a man in the king's entourage.[45]

These are very rough estimates that represent the upper limit of pork production that was possible in fortunate years of fertile sows, healthy pigs, and labor-intensive management. It is likely that many communities kept smaller herds—closer to the law codes' figures of 40 to 70 pigs, which is what the writers assumed a swineherd could handle. But the only firm figures we have for herds come from charters of donation, and from a type of document known as a polyptych, an inventory that large-scale landowners conducted of the scattered farms they owned. Unsurprisingly, these herds vary in size. Pope Hadrian (r. 772–795), for example, expected that on one of his properties the tenants would be able to slaughter 100 pigs after every acorn season. By contrast, a property on the Torío river (which was part of the Duero system in northwest Spain) had only 9 pigs when a priest donated it to a monastery in 993. A farm owned by the monastery of Saint-Remi in Reims in the late ninth or early tenth century was noted as having 35 adult pigs and 20 piglets. On the demesnes owned by the monastery of Lobbes (that is, on the properties that the monastery owned and oversaw), herd sizes ranged from 2 to 30 pigs when a polyptych was drawn up in 868–869; the median was 15. And a decade or two or three later, the estates belonging to the monastery of Santa Giulia di Brescia kept between 0 and 180 pigs, with a mean herd size of 27 pigs, and a median of 17.5.[46]

In aggregate these herds amounted to hundreds and even thousands of pigs among the assets of wealthier landowners. It was by owning a range of properties and herds near the most extensive woodland in England—the Weald, in Kent—that an ealdorman named Ælfred had accumulated over twenty-four hundred pigs by the 870s or 880s, which he then bequeathed in his will in groups of a hundred or more. Ælfred and his wife, Wærburh, are better known for having ransomed a set of gospel books from the Danish (Viking) army that had stolen them. An inscription in the manuscript proclaims that the couple "acquired these books from the heathen host with pure money, that was with pure gold": this gold and these gospels were at least tangentially connected to the ecology of those twenty-four-hundred-plus pigs.[47]

The differences in pig husbandry across time and space were influenced by other factors besides individual resources and micro-ecologies. Herds were also linked to ecologies and economies farther afield. In the early Middle Ages, it was typical to see a certain amount of gardening and livestock husbandry happening within urban centers—as was the case, to name just a few places, in London, Dorestad (in the Netherlands), Verona, Rome, Naples, Sétif (in

Tunisia), Mérida, and Madīnat Ilbīrah (near Granada). But towns still needed their hinterlands to provide them with food and fuel. Connectivity was also a feature of rural communities, because although they produced much of what they needed to survive, they were not autarchic. Most rural communities, even the ones that did not supply cities, were acquiring at least a few products regionally for themselves, even though transregional and long-distance trade was more typical of cities and emporia.[48]

For example, in southern Apulia, in the center of Italy's heel, inhabitants of the five-acre village of Apigliano were producing a diverse array of crops in the eighth to eleventh centuries (fava beans, lentils, wheat, barley, olives, plums, apples, carob), raising sheep for both meat and wool, making their own textiles, and managing the surrounding terrain so that some of the garrigue, or low-growing shrubland, had a chance to grow into more mature scrub. This was a community that was locally sufficient and attentive to its balance of resources. But the residents of Apigliano, who lived under the jurisdiction of the Byzantine Empire in this period, also participated in a regional ceramics culture and kept abreast of styles that were current in the wider Mediterranean world. They even imported a few things from the eastern Mediterranean, including at least one piece of Glazed White Ware II: this was a decorative style, manufactured in Constantinople, which appealed to aspirational consumers who could not afford tableware made of glass or metal but who nevertheless wanted something that resembled it.[49]

Simply by virtue of being part of a settlement's ecological and economic calculus, pig husbandry was tied to these larger scales of influence. But most pigs were probably raised and eaten locally. In the late Roman Empire, herds of pigs had been driven to the city of Rome as part of the annona, or food-supply tax, from the southern Italian provinces of Campania, Lucania, Brutii, and Samnium. In the early Middle Ages, however, they were probably only infrequently transported significant distances because (as we will see) the old tax system had evolved, pigs were difficult to herd, and pigs could be raised almost anywhere in the West.[50] Some pigs did make medium- and possibly long-distance trips. In the late ninth century the monastery of Prüm required some of its tenants to deliver pigs from almost 125 miles (200 km) away, directly to its doorstep. And a few centuries earlier, some of the pig teeth that were found at the well-connected settlement of Oegstgeest, on the Rhine delta in what is now the Netherlands, show strontium isotope ratios that differ significantly from those that are characteristic of the local geology, so they must have come from farther afield—the eastern Netherlands, or even Germany,

France, Scotland, or England. The likeliest scenario is that they were shipped up the Rhine from western Germany, since the settlement was also getting a lot of its pottery from Germany, and pigs were easier to ship than to herd.[51] But it will take more data of this kind to gauge how frequently pigs were actually moved these distances—let alone to discern any patterns in the economic and ecological profiles of the settlements that ended up with them.

The restricted ranges of most pigs may have been one reason why the animals so rarely suffered from disease outbreaks in these centuries. Herds of cattle were much likelier to succumb to epizootics in the early Middle Ages, and as the historian Tim Newfield has argued, the pathogens that infected European cattle had probably originated farther east. Trading centers in northeastern Europe imported their cattle, and these newcomers could have introduced opportunistic organisms to the established "disease landscape" of western Europe.[52] So it is possible that another way pigs helped communities reduce risk was by being relatively easy to raise anywhere, thus keeping microorganisms "local"—although the humans who raised them would not have known that.

But pigs did make local circuits—sometimes as live animals, and sometimes as pork—between the farmers who raised them and the people who ate them. In the city of Tours, in the northwest corner of the late antique city core, one residential trash pit survives from the later sixth century, and it points to a commercial relationship between the town and countryside (fig. 3.6). Pigs are best represented among the animal remains (36 percent), followed by cattle and ovicaprids, plus a great deal of poultry (19 percent) and fish and oysters (7 percent). The deposit is not necessarily representative of the average diet of the household that occupied this residence, let alone representative of what the rest of the residents of Tours were eating. But even on the basis of a single pit, this urban household evidently had access to suppliers, presumably in the western agrarian suburbs, who were carefully culling herds and providing the choicest cuts of meat to their customers: cattle at prime ages (rather than old draft animals), piglets and lambs, and the premium, meaty parts of pigs—pork shoulders and thighs.[53]

Pork was also circulating in Tuscany, as the zooarchaeologist Frank Salvadori has noticed, and the diagnostic for this is the anatomical distribution of animals' bodies on a site. Typically, when it comes to pigs, a disproportionately high number of cranial and foot fragments is taken to indicate that the animals were being slaughtered and butchered on-site, and that their choicer parts, especially the shoulder-and-arm cuts and the pelvic-and-leg cuts, were being exported elsewhere. One of the clearest examples of this situation is

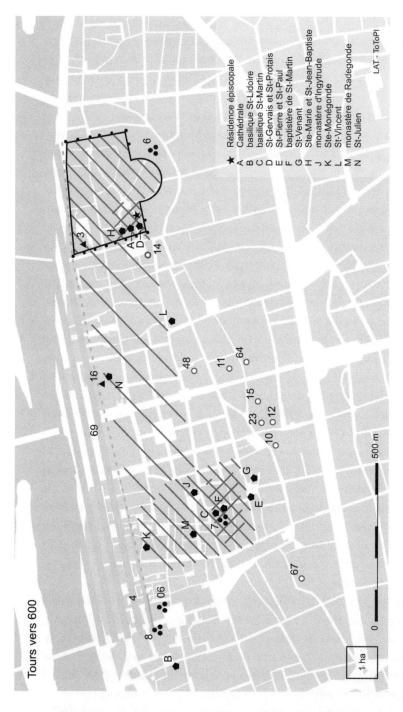

Tours vers 600

★ Résidence épiscopale
A Cathédrale
B basilique St-Lidoire
C basilique St-Martin
D St-Gervais et St-Protais
E St-Pierre et St-Paul
F baptistère de St-Martin
G St-Venant
H Ste-Marie et St-Jean-Baptiste
J monastère d'Ingytrude
K Ste-Monégonde
L St-Vincent
M monastère de Radegonde
N St-Julien

LAT - ToToPI

Fig. 3.6. Tours and the Loire river, ca. 600. The residence with its oysters and good meats is site 3 on the map, in the northwest corner of the walled city, just north of where Gregory of Tours would have lived until his death in 594. (From *Tours antique et médiéval: Lieux de vie, temps de la ville*, ed. Henri Galinié, Revue archéologique du Centre de la France, Supplement 30 [Tours: FERACF, 2007], p. 365, fig. 47. Reprinted with permission.)

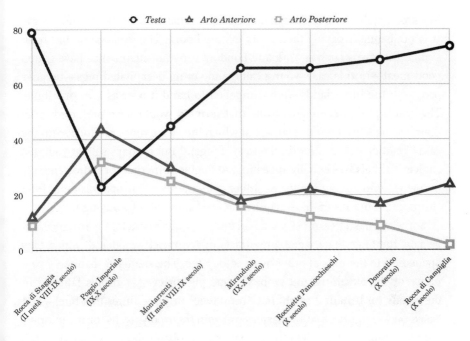

Fig. 3.7. The anatomical distribution of pigs' bodies on settlements in early medieval Tuscany, expressed as a percentage of total pig remains. Circles are cranial elements, triangles are forelimbs, squares are hind limbs. The elite estate of Poggio Imperiale is the outlier here: it was probably importing cuts of pork rather than slaughtering its own pigs exclusively. (Image courtesy of Frank Salvadori.)

the settlement of Poggio Imperiale, which began as a small and probably un-hierarchical village in late antiquity but by the ninth and tenth centuries had become an elite estate that was probably run by a proprietor and worked by dependents. Pork was not the commonest meat there, but unlike almost every other early medieval site in Tuscany, this one contains an usually low representation of cranial bones; instead the forelimbs dominate the sample (fig. 3.7).[54]

It is impossible to tell from bones alone what political or financial mechanisms brought them to a particular place. The usual explanation for a skewed anatomical distribution such as that found in Poggio Imperiale is that rural estates that imported their pork were getting it as a form of tenurial obligation. Archaeologists who work in Tuscany, for example, often suggest that we are seeing the evidence for what in the tenth century would be called the *amiscere* tax, an obligation of tenants to render a pork shoulder to their landlord as part of the rents and labors they owed annually. And even before the tenth century, inventories, charters, and customaries show tenants in northern and central Italy occasionally paying their rents in cured pork. The explanation has been similar for towns such as York and London: urban residents may have gotten good meat—in this case, young cattle and young decapitated pigs—because people in the hinterlands were compelled to hand it over as rent or tribute. The assumption here seems to be that farmers would have preferred to let their livestock live longer, to an age at which they were more productive (in the case of cattle) and meatier (in the case of pigs).[55] But perhaps selling younger, choicer animals was equally appealing. At Poggio Imperiale, or more generally in towns, emporia, and other wealthier settlements in Europe, residents who "imported" pork might have acquired at least some of it by buying it.

Some monasteries must have had seasonal pig markets, for instance, especially the ones that owned large tracts of acorn-rich woodland, which they opened up to the pigs of other owners for a fee. The standard "pannage" payment for the autumnal nut crop was one pig for every ten pigs fattened in the woods (in Britain it might have been twice or three times that rate)—and based on the figures that monasteries give in their polyptychs, or inventories, the monks and nuns of wealthy monasteries probably did not eat all the pork their revenues generated. Bobbio might have collected 400 to 500 pigs or more in pannage revenue over a good season, and the nuns at Santa Giulia di Brescia reported or projected that their aggregate woodland could have fed 6,940 pigs (amounting to 694 pigs as a maximum pannage income), plus the pigs they had either collected or expected to collect through rents (165), the pigs they owned outright on their various satellite properties (1,601, though the polyptych is incomplete), and whatever pigs they kept at the monastery proper (a figure we do not have). And the Rhineland monastery of Wissembourg counted its woodland capacities at 1,650 pigs (thus a maximum yield of 165 pigs in fees)—but the monks also collected almost 60 pigs and 800 piglets in annual rent payments.[56] So in a good year, some large-scale landowners would have collected many more pigs than they would have consumed, and they were probably selling them—especially the premium, acorn-fed animals—at local or regional markets.

But the monasteries did not view their massive annual influx of pigs as a fixed income. And this takes us back to the ways that pig husbandry fostered multi-vectored views of agrarian ecologies. The farm managers and administrators who drew up the polyptychs treated their holdings as diverse, fluctuating, and contingent lands, and they developed correspondingly flexible approaches to their resources. The polyptychs' accountants would observe, for example, that harsh winters might make it impossible to obtain fish from

Plate 1. Getty Gospel Lectionary (England, ca. 1000). (Los Angeles, J. Paul Getty
Museum, Ms. 9, fol. 1v. Digital image courtesy of the Getty's Open Content program.)

Plate 2. Stuttgart Psalter (Saint-Germain-des-Prés, Paris, 820–830). (Stuttgart, Württembergische Landesbibliothek, Cod. bibl. 23, fol. 96v.)

Plate 3. Mosaic of the Small Hunt at the Villa del Casale at Piazza Armerina, Sicily, fourth century (detail). (Photo: LaurPhil on flickr, CC BY 2.0, https://www.flickr.com/photos/51417107@N03/11748447616/.)

Plate 4. Mosaic of the Small Hunt at the Villa del Casale (detail). (Photo: Herbert Frank on flickr, CC BY 2.0, https://www.flickr.com/photos/liakadaweb/24465893287/.)

Plate 5. Adonis mosaic in the *oecus* of the villa of Carranque, near Toledo, late fourth century. (Photo: Samuel López Iglesias.)

Plate 6. Gellone Sacramentary (Gaul, 780–800). (Paris, Bibliothèque nationale de France, Ms. Lat. 12048, fols. 38v and 91r.)

Plate 7. November and December in the "Calendar of Salzburg" (818 CE). (Copyright
© Österreichische Nationalbibliothek Vienna, Cod. 387, fol. 90v.)

Plate 8. Utrecht Psalter (Reims, 816–823). See fig. 1.8 for a detail. (Utrecht University Library, Ms. 32, fol. 82v.)

Plate 9. The eastern half of the village of Gózquez (Spain, 525/40–750). (Reproduced by permission of Alfonso Vigil-Escalera Guirado.)

Stone structure
Excavated feature
Non excavated
Main boundaries

planting plot

planting plot

planting plot

planting plot

Well

animals trail

animals trail

animals trail

modern quarry

E15

E6

E7-8

N

0   25   50 m

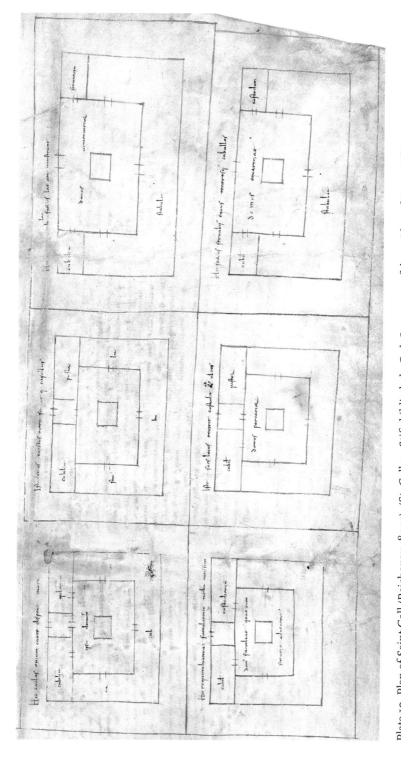

Plate 10. Plan of Saint Gall (Reichenau, 820s). (St. Gallen, Stiftsbibliothek, Cod. Sang. 1092, fol. 1r.—Plan of Saint Gall.)

Plate 11. Copy of Isidore, *De natura rerum* (Salzburg, ca. 800). (Bayerische Staatsbibliothek München, Clm 14300, fol. 6v.)

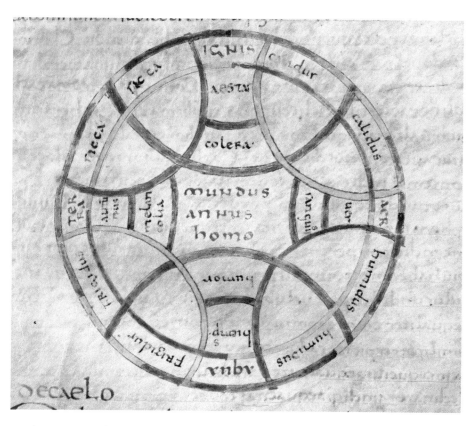

Plate 12. Copy of Isidore, *De natura rerum*. (Bayerische Staatsbibliothek München, Clm 14300, fol. 8r.)

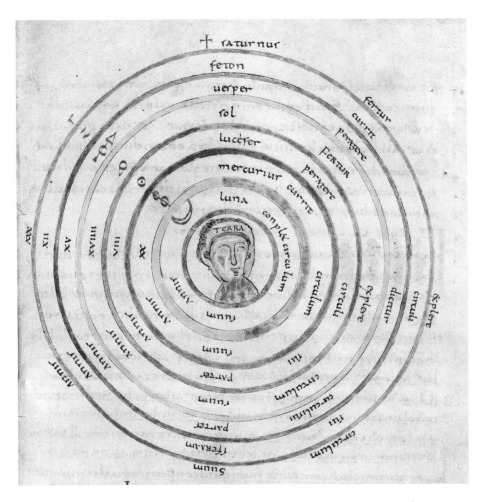

Plate 13. Copy of Isidore, *De natura rerum*. (Bayerische Staatsbibliothek München, Clm 14300, fol. 14r.)

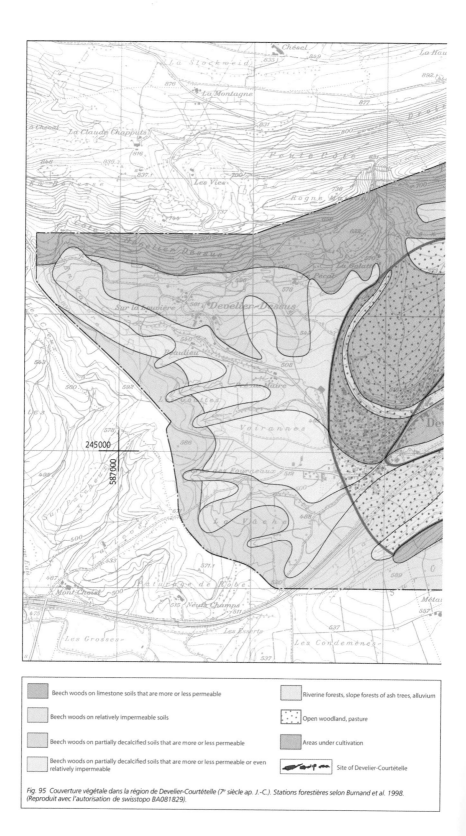

Beech woods on limestone soils that are more or less permeable

Beech woods on relatively impermeable soils

Beech woods on partially decalcified soils that are more or less permeable

Beech woods on partially decalcified soils that are more or less permeable or even relatively impermeable

Riverine forests, slope forests of ash trees, alluvium

Open woodland, pasture

Areas under cultivation

Site of Develier-Courtételle

Fig. 95 Couverture végétale dans la région de Develier-Courtételle (7ᵉ siècle ap. J.-C.). Stations forestières selon Burnand et al. 1998. (Reproduit avec l'autorisation de swisstopo BA081829).

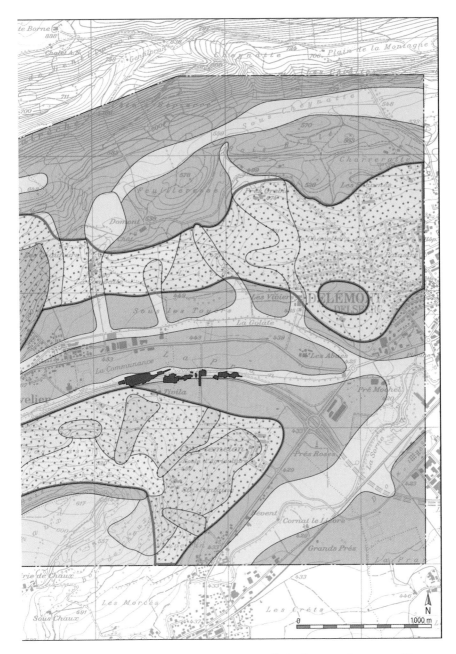

Plate 14. Vegetation surrounding Develier-Courtételle in the seventh century. (From Guélat et al., *Develier-Courtételle*, pp. 152–53, fig. 95. Reprinted with permission from the Office de la culture, Section d'archéologie et de paléontologie and the Société jurassienne d'Émulation. Key translated from the French original.)

Plate 15. Reconstruction of the fourth-century dining room of the villa of Faragola, Italy. (From Volpe and Turchiano, *Faragola 1*, pl 1. Image provided by Giuliano Volpe.)

Plate 16. Faragola's dining room transformed in the seventh century. (From Volpe and Turchiano, *Faragola 1*, pl. 8. Image provided by Giuliano Volpe.)

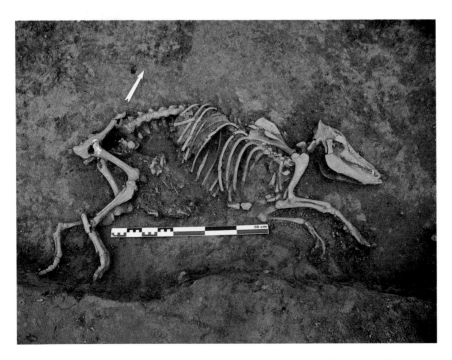

Plate 17. Sow with three piglets in utero, Hintere Buen (Sermersheim), tenth century. (Photo: Édith Peytremann, Institut national de recherches archéologiques préventives [INRAP], Paris, France. © RMN-Grand Palais / Art Resource, NY.)

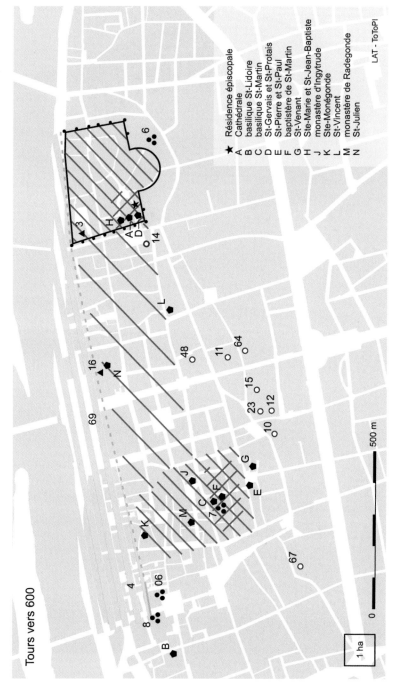

Tours vers 600

★	Résidence épiscopale
A	Cathédrale
B	basilique St-Lidoire
C	basilique St-Martin
D	St-Gervais et St-Protais
E	St-Pierre et St-Paul
F	baptistère de St-Martin
G	St-Venant
H	Ste-Marie et St-Jean-Baptiste
J	monastère d'Ingytrude
K	Ste-Monégonde
L	St-Vincent
M	monastère de Radegonde
N	St-Julien

LAT : ToToPI

Plate 18. Tours and the Loire river ca. 600. (From *Tours antique et médiéval: Lieux de vie, temps de la ville*, ed. Henri Galinié. Revue archéologique du Centre de la France, Supplement 30 [Tours: FERACF, 2007], p. 365, fig. 47. Reprinted with permission.)

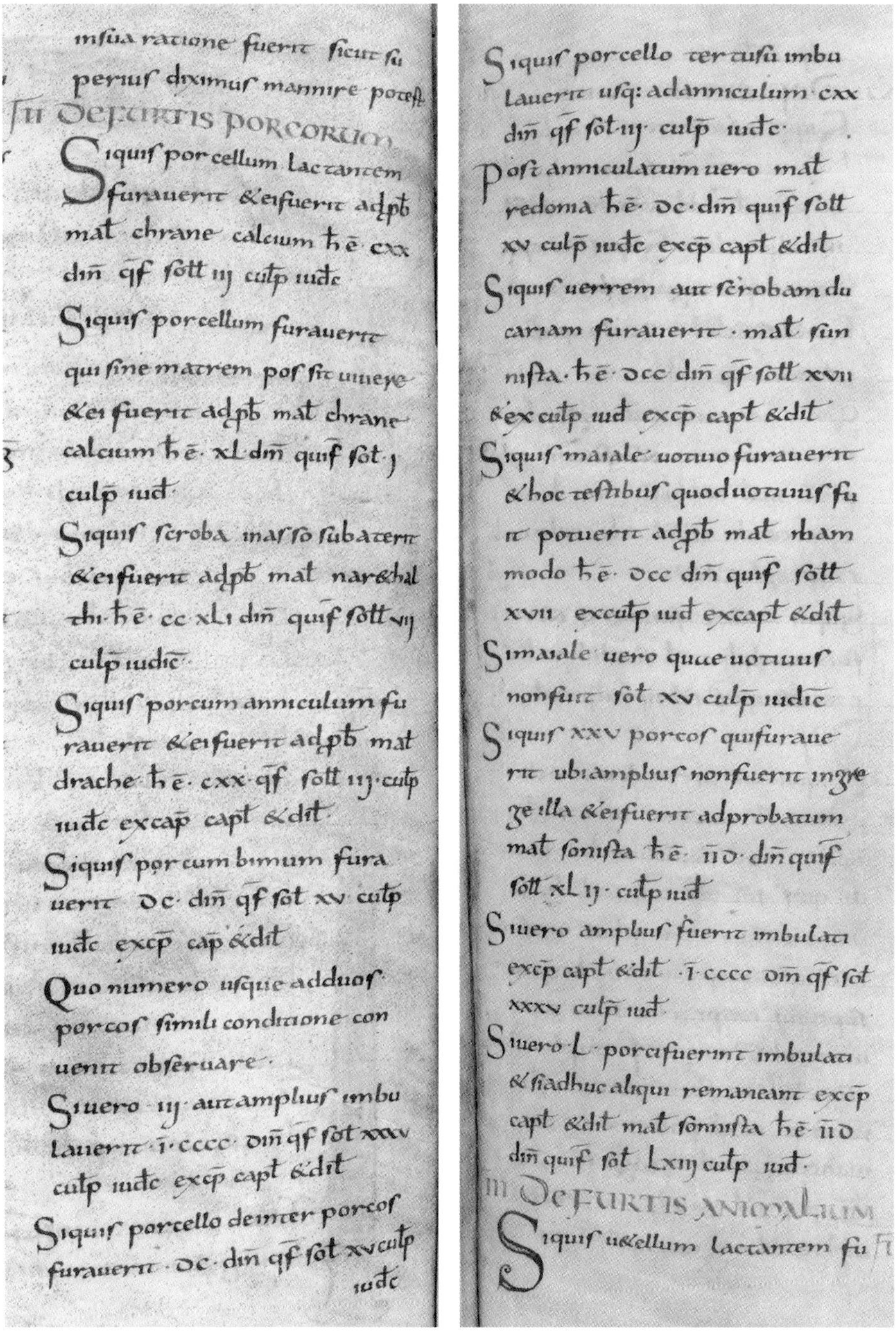

in sua ratione fuerit sicut su
perius diximus mannire potest.

Tit. DE FURTIS PORCORUM

Siquis porcellum lactantem
furauerit & ei fuerit adpb
mat chrane calcium h̄ ē cxx
din qf soll iij culp iudc

Siquis porcellum furauerit
qui sine matrem pos sit uiuere
& ei fuerit adpb mat chrane
calcium h̄ ē xl din quis sot j
culp iud

Siquis scroba marso subaterit
& ei fuerit adpb mat narshal
thi h̄ ē cc xli din quis soll vij
culp iudic

Siquis porcum anniculum fu
rauerit & ei fuerit adpb mat
drache h̄ ē cxx qf soll iij culp
iudc excap capt & dit

Siquis porcum bimum fura
uerit oc din qf sot xv culp
iudc excp cap & dit

Quo numero usque ad duos
porcos simili condicione con
uenit obseruare

Si uero iij aut amplius imbu
lauerit i cccc din qf sot xxxv
culp iudc excp capt & dit

Siquis porcello deinter porcos
furauerit oc din qf sot xv culp
iudc

Siquis porcello tertiusu imbu
lauerit usq: ad anniculum cxx
din qf sot iij culp iudc

Post anniculatum uero mat
redoma h̄ ē oc din quis sot
xv culp iudc excp capt & dit

Siquis uerrem aut scrobam du
cariam furauerit mat sun
nista h̄ ē occ din qf sot xvii
& ex culp iud excp capt & dit

Siquis maiale uotiuo furauerit
& hoc testibus quod uotiuus fu
it potuerit adpb mat iham
modo h̄ ē occ din quis sot
xvii excul iud excapt & dit

Si maiale uero quae uotiuus
nonfuit sot xv culp iudc

Siquis xxv porcos qui furaue
rit ubi amplius nonfuerit in gre
ge illa & ei fuerit adprobatum
mat sonista h̄ ē iio din quis
sot xl ij culp iud

Si uero amplius fuerit imbulati
excp capt & dit i cccc din qf sot
xxxv culp iud

Si uero L porci fuerint imbulati
& si adhuc aliqui remaneant excp
capt & dit mat sonista h̄ ē iio
din quis sot Lxiij culp iud

Tit. DE FURTIS ANIMALIUM

Siquis uicellum lactantem fu

Plate 19. *De furtis porcorum,* "Thefts of Pigs," in a copy of *Lex Salica* (early ninth century, probably Tours). (Paris, Bibliothèque nationale de France, Ms. Lat. 4404, ff. 180v–181r.)

Plate 20. Gadarene swine mosaic in Sant'Apollinare Nuovo (Ravenna, 475–526).
(Photo: Bridgeman Images.)

Plate 21. Gadarene swine, ivory, early fifth century, probably Roman. (Musée du Louvre, Paris [OA 7878]. Photo: Daniel Arnaudet. © RMN-Grand Palais/Art Resource, NY.)

Plate 22. Gadarene swine, ivory, Carolingian
(Aachen, ca. 800). (Oxford, Bodleian Library,
Ms. Douce 176. Photo: Bodleian Libraries.)

Plate 23. Gadarene swine, now with Legion, ivory antependium panel for the cathedral of Magdeburg (made in Milan, 962–973). (Hessisches Landesmuseum Darmstadt, Inv. no. Kg 52:101. Photo: Wolfgang Fuhrmannek.)

Plate 24. Gadarene swine, fresco at Saint George in Oberzell (Reichenau, ca. 985–987). (Photo: Bridgeman Images.)

Plate 25. Gospels of Otto III (r. 983–1002), painted at Reichenau. (Bayerische Staatsbibliothek München, Clm 4453, fol. 103v.)

Plate 26. Gadarene swine in an eleventh-century gospel from Constantinople. (Paris, Bibliothèque nationale de France, Ms. Gr. 74, fol. 72v.)

Plate 27. Gadarene swine, Ripoll Bible (Catalonia, 1015–1020). (Copyright © 2020 Biblioteca Apostolica Vaticana, lat. 5729, fol. 367r. By permission of Biblioteca Apostolica Vaticana, with all rights reserved.)

Plate 28. Fresco cycle at Santa Maria Immacolata in Ceri (Lazio, 1100–1130). (Photo: Bibliotheca Hertziana—Max-Planck-Institut für Kunstgeschichte, Rome.)

Plate 29. Cooking scene from the Ceri fresco. (Photo: Bibliotheca Hertziana—Max-Planck-Institut für Kunstgeschichte, Rome.)

Plate 30. Nicholas of Myra, John the Evangelist, John the Baptist with the Lamb of God, Martin of Tours, and Leonard of Noblat/Noblac/Limoges in the Ceri fresco. (Photo: Bibliotheca Hertziana—Max-Planck-Institut für Kunstgeschichte, Rome.)

Plate 31. Panel in the Ceri fresco of Potiphar's wife and Joseph. (Photo: Bibliotheca Hertziana—Max-Planck-Institut für Kunstgeschichte, Rome.)

Plate 32. Adam and Eve in the fresco at Ceri. (Photo: Bibliotheca Hertziana—Max-Planck-Institut für Kunstgeschichte, Rome.)

their lakes (because of the ice), and they made clear that their projections for the pig-tenth assumed a "good season" (*bonum tempus*) for acorns.[57] They were well aware that acorn yields were (and are) unpredictable and highly variable. A single white oak might produce from a handful to ten thousand acorns in a season, but it might also not produce any in half of the years of its lifetime. In some years a whole stand of oaks might not fruit. The reasons for this seem to be as varied as the environments the trees inhabit: genetics, water availability, the timing of frosts, crown size, pollination efficiency, acorn maturation cycles, and the presence of other oak species have all been demonstrated to make a difference. Beech trees are more reliable, but their production is still periodic: they tend to produce mast every two years in consistently large crops, but sometimes the interval between crops might be eight years or even longer.[58]

The unstable nature of nature prompted some large-scale landowners to take a somewhat improvisational approach to their revenue. Sometimes they modified a tenant's rent if the acorn crop had been negligible. A rental contract drawn up between the church of Pistoia and a man named Martin, who was a *libellarius*, or tenant, with the right of usufruct, stipulated a pig worth four tremisses as part of Martin's annual payment; but in years with negligible (*menime*) acorn crops, the payment was reduced to an animal of any kind worth just one tremissis.[59] And one group of tenants of the monastery of Lobbes did not have to pay pigs as part of their rent at all if there was no pannage. But other landlords worked to protect themselves rather than their tenants against the uncertainties of their environments. The monastery of Wissembourg required some of its tenants to care for its pigs over the winter if there was no pannage (which was still a more lenient arrangement compared to *other* tenants' obligations to feed the landlord's pigs regardless of what the trees produced that year).[60] And at the estate of Migliarina, which was located in an ideal area for pig husbandry—by the farm's reckoning, its woods were capable of feeding four thousand pigs in a good year—the *massarii*, dependent tenants, were asked to convert their customary payments of pigs into cash if the acorn crop did not materialize that year.[61] This may have been a bad deal for the massarii, having to pay something in equivalent value even though acorn fodder was not available. On the other hand, pigs may have been worth more in years of low acorn yields, and paying in cash might have given tenants the option of selling their pigs at a profit if there was local demand. In yet other cases, some landowners gave tenants the choice of what kind of animals or types of grain to render as rent, according those farmers even more leeway in managing their own household economies.[62] Whether the flexibility of these arrangements represented the landlords' spontaneous initiatives, or whether

it was the hard-won fruit of tenants' negotiations, it spoke to the widely acknowledged fact that animal husbandry was never a consistent enterprise.

For a similar reason few landowners calculated pannage in terms of their
predicted revenues (with the exception of southeast England). Rather than
state how many pigs they expected to *collect* in a good year, they counted how
many pigs they expected their woods to *feed*. This was a more flexible unit of
account, and there are probably several reasons why landowners in Italy, Francia, and England used it. First, it is possible that some tenants paid for pannage in currency other than pigs. The monasteries of Saint-Germain-des-Prés,
Saint-Maur-des-Fossés, and Montier-en-Der collected fees for *pastio*—pannage
or pasture—in cash, wine, sheep, and barley.[63] A second reason to measure
woodlands not in renders but in capacities is that landowners did not always
own the woods they documented in their inventories. Some major landowners
(including the monasteries of Saint-Remi at Reims, Wissembourg, Lobbes,
and Prüm) kept track of the pig capacities not only of the woodlands they
owned outright but also of *communal* woodland or *silva communis;* they would
not have received pannage fees from these properties but merely had access to
their woods like any other farmer.[64] Finally, landowners who owned woodland
might have been feeding their own pigs in the woods, in addition to allowing
other farmers to graze their pigs in them for a fee, and so whatever pigs the
landowner was feeding there would not have counted as "taxable income."

The case of Santa Giulia di Brescia can highlight the virtues of this metric,
because its polyptych inventoried both its woodlands and its livestock holdings on the farms the monastery managed itself, rather than rented. (These
farms are conventionally called demesnes, after the Latin *curtes dominicae*.)
The monastery owned a property called Insula, for example, which included a
woodland capable of feeding seventy pigs. But the estate at Insula also owned
fifty-three pigs, so depending on whether Insula's manager decided to feed the
estate's pigs in the woods in a given year, pannage revenues could fluctuate
between two pigs (if all fifty-three pigs were fed in the woods, leaving room for
about twenty other pigs belonging to someone else) to seven (if none of the
demesne pigs were fed there). Or if another property belonging to the monastery, one that was "in vico Porzano," fed *its* pigs in woods adjacent to it, there
would have been no pannage revenue at all; there was not enough of a nut
supply there to feed all the estate's pigs. So if we consider its woodland and pig
holdings overall, the monastery's total pannage revenue could have varied by
as much as 20 percent, depending on whether the institution's assorted pigs
were also being fed in the woods it owned (see table).[65]

Properties in Santa Giulia's Possession That Owned Both Acorn-Bearing Woodlands and Pigs

Property in Santa Giulia's Possession	Pig Capacity of the Property's Woodland (w)	Pigs Already Owned by Each Property (p)
Miliarina (*curtis*)	2,000	180
Barbada (*curtis*)	800	70
Alfiano	700	100
Riveriola	560	92
Gatariolo	300	76
Nuvolento	300	16
Castelluna (*curtis*)	250	67
Cigonaria	200	51
Novelaria	200	28
Bissarissu (*curtis*)	150	43
Tontolfi	100	50
Mariano	100	35
Marcharegia	100	25
Insula	70	53
Ecclesia S. Petri	60	24
Bersigo	50	20
Bogonago	50	7
Rivalta (*curtis*)	40	50
Miliarina (*capella*)	40	35
Basilica S. Salvatoris de Umbrusolo	40	17
Obeningus	40	10
Capella S. Margarite	40	4
Laureto	30	17
Isis	30	15
Capadello	20	35
property "in vico Porzano"	20	24
Barbada	20	13
Cinctura	20	13
Vuassaningus	20	8
Bissurissu (*capella*)	18	3
Magonivico	15	30
Gutus	10	6
Castelluna (*capella*)	6	5
Rivalta (*capella*)	6	4
Total	6,405	1,226

Note: Data are according to an inventory drawn up ca. 879–906. If all these properties fed their pigs in monastic woodland, the monastery might expect to collect approximately 123 fewer pigs per year, if total pannage revenues amounted to $\frac{w_i - p_i}{10}$ as opposed to $\frac{w_i}{10}$. The nuns may have collected even more pigs than the maximum total here: although this is the longest surviving polyptych from early medieval Italy, it is incomplete. Santa Giulia di Brescia had other properties that are not accounted for in the extant document.

The bottom line is that this simple accounting device offered an elegant solution for landowners who wanted to measure and anticipate their assets without defining profit too narrowly. Calculating woodland in terms of the pigs it could feed gave the monastery and its demesne estates room to manage their resources in different ways over time, whether by leaving the woods clear for "customers," feeding all estate-owned pigs in the woods, or a mixture of the two. And it also accommodated the fact that pig populations on any given farm would fluctuate—not least because, as we have seen, early medieval settlements repeatedly adjusted their agrarian regimes in response to a cluster of ecological and economic circumstances.

In any case, the nuns of Santa Giulia and their property managers were yet another group of people who appreciated that the physical world was in flux, and that changes to one part of a system would have ramifications elsewhere. But the efforts of farmers and landowners across early medieval Europe are also a reminder that the differences between their settlements are partly a result of the diverse environments they inhabited, and partly the result of the choices communities made (under constraint or not) to focus on different combinations of agrarian, artisanal, and commercial work.

Pannage

If we follow pigs deeper into the woods during acorn season, we can see more clearly how they made an imprint on policies that humans developed from the local to the royal level. The practice of pannage was special, because it was lucrative enough to attract the attention of local landowners as well as kings and their courts. It was only one of several occasions at which environments, animals, and human culture interlocked as mutually influential forces, but its documentary footprint helps us see that pigs were more than consummate salvagers in a kaleidoscopic landscape. They also altered the lives and perspectives of the communities that engaged with them. This may sound like a uniquely modern, post-humanist perspective, but early medieval observers were the ones to suggest it—though in other ways their views were very unlike ours.

Disparate references to pannage occur in various sorts of early medieval sources throughout the post-imperial West with the exception of North Africa, where the written evidence that survives is much sparser compared to that of its neighbors across the Mediterranean.[66] But the most striking appearance is a piece of legislation issued in the Merovingian kingdom in 614, when lawmakers drew explicit attention to some nonhuman forces that affected their kingdom and called for an elastic approach to handling them. In this year, pigs appeared as a part of royal policy in a major royal decree that is now called the Edict of Clothar II (614).

When Clothar issued the edict, he had only recently become the sole ruler of a kingdom his family had governed for about a century and a half. In the previous decades, a rotating cast of royal relatives had been waging sporadic aggressions against one another. *Bella civilia* was the term that contemporary historians applied to those conflicts, but they do not necessarily match our expectations of what civil wars involve. They were not usually elaborate battles. Instead, rulers and small bands of elite warriors would make targeted raids on the territories of their opponents. They would destroy whole fields of crops, dismantle entire buildings, and loot farms and villages. Their field of action was small, but they would empty those zones of their resources.[67]

That destructive cycle ended in 613, when Clothar killed his last serious competitor, his aunt Brunhild. The real reason for his success was not Brunhild's execution as much as it was the coalition that Clothar had built with elites who were based all around the kingdom. Their support came with concerns that *how* the government operated was as critical as *who* operated it. Clothar addressed these concerns in his edict, and he made clear that any violation of it would count as a capital offense because this "deliberation" (as he put it) had been carefully worked out between himself and his bishops, magnates, palace officials, and subjects who had sworn an oath of loyalty to him.[68]

Pigs were integral to their plans: "State swineherds (*porcarii fiscales*) may not presume to enter woods belonging to churches or private owners without the permission of the one who possesses them. . . . And whenever there is no pannage for pigs to be fattened on, the *cellarinsis* tax will not be collected for the fisc [treasury]."[69]

This was not the only document in which Clothar would discuss pigs and pannage. He had also addressed them in a decree directed specifically to the southern subkingdom of Burgundy. In this decree, known as the Precept of Clothar, the king granted to the Burgundian churches, in exchange for their continued loyalty, immunities from crop, pasture, and pig taxes, called the *agraria, pascuaria,* and *decimae porcorum*.[70] A grant of immunity did not mean that those taxes ceased to be collected. Farmers still had to pay them, but to a different beneficiary. After the takeover of Clothar II, tax exemptions such as these, along with judicial immunities, became a valuable instrument in Merovingian political culture. Kings granted immunities in order to strengthen ties of loyalty between themselves and their beneficiaries, and, according to the rationales they gave in their charters, they also made these gifts for the health of their souls and the stability of the kingdom. These were forms of profit that the crown understood to exceed, in certain cases, the short-term gains of taxes on pannage, crops, and property.[71]

The court's sense of woodland was equally multifaceted. Not only were there different kinds of forest that formed part of the kingdom's mosaic of micro-ecologies.[72] Within these zones, even within a single woodland, count-less variations were possible, owing not only to microclimatic and topo-graphical variations but also to historical changes. All woodlands experience "disturbances"—events such as wind, fire, drought, and animal and human exploitation—and woodlands respond to these disturbances in transformative ways. Different tree species will rebound at different rates, non-arboreal nitro-gen fixers will take advantage of gaps in the tree canopy, grasses will thrive in savannahs where livestock frequently browse the trees, and so on.[73]

The Merovingians would have had plenty of reasons to pay attention to woodland in all its complexity. The nature of these environments had political implications. One of the distinctive features of early medieval political culture is that power was measured in terms of rights more than in terms of territo-rial sovereignty. And because woodland was biotically dense and regenerative, early medieval law before and after the edict treated it as a unique legal space where different rights to its many resources overlapped.[74] Woods tied many incomes and interests together.

There were also different categories of woods, legally speaking, but all of them still involved clusters of distinct rights. A wood could be private property, it could belong to the king or the fisc, or it could be public woodland, a silva communis. It is hard to be certain how public woodland worked, but from the few references we have to it, it seems to have been supervised by the crown, and its resources were apparently open to all without restriction. (The right to timber was an exception and was more carefully controlled, probably in the in-terests of monumental architecture and shipbuilding.)[75] Legal sources outside Gaul also patchily attest to the existence of public woodland in England, Ibe-ria, and Italy, though they only tend to turn up in the documents when their use was disputed, or their legal status was being altered. Irish law recognized common rights in unowned woodland, but most Irish woodland was privately owned and more strictly regulated than it was elsewhere.[76]

As for privately owned woods and royal woodland, anyone who lived nearby was entitled to collect fallen branches in them for firewood and to mark trees to fell for timber after a one-year waiting period.[77] And anyone could harvest wood in a private woodland for fires or smaller woodworking projects, and even for timber, if the trees were not already claimed. But there were limits to these basic allowances. Or, perhaps more accurately, the owners of woodland resented the fact that the limits were too generous. It seems to have been technically legal under Lombard and Visigothic law for anyone to take away wood by the cartful, for example, but to the woodland proprietors who happened upon these oxcarts, such a haul seemed excessive. They at least expected to be asked for permission![78]

Woodlands harbored many resources besides scrap wood and timber. They were grazing grounds for livestock. They were good places to raise bees and domesticated deer. And they were full of food that humans ate, which in Gaul included berries, nuts, mushrooms, herbs, fish, frogs, waterfowl and other birds, red and roe deer, ibex, chamois, fox, wildcat, bear, and of course wild boar. They were even a place to find pets: foxes could be taken in as companion animals, and songbirds could be taught to fly around the grounds of woodland estates and sing for their "noble" audiences. (Woods-loving birds could use estates to their own advantage, too. At the great villa of San Giovanni di Ruoti in the mountains of Lucania, thrushes gorged on the cherry trees that were cultivated nearby, and at least one pair of flycatchers nested on the property for multiple breeding seasons.)[79]

Some people understood the density of woodland rights and interests well enough to manipulate them. The Lex Salica, the oldest law code of the Merovingian kingdom, assigns a fairly steep fine to hunters for killing a deer that is domesticated, branded, and obviously too easy to hunt. The same section also penalizes hunters who kill a wild deer or wild boar that has already been pursued and exhausted by another hunter's dogs. The laws drawn up in the Merovingian duchy of the Alamans dealt with similar crimes; so did the Lombard laws in Italy. And in Iberia, too, woodlands could be resource-rich locations with many intersecting claims to them. If a tree fell in the forest, any number of people and animals could be expected to hear it—or be injured by it.[80]

The rights and obligations of pannage introduced yet another legal layer to the mix. It was generally the case that pigs could be grazed in any woodland, but if the woods were not public, that entitlement came at a cost. A farmer who rented a woodland as part of a property agreement might not have any claim to the pannage revenues there, or might owe pannage revenues personally, or might be obligated to let the landlord's pigs pasture there as well. Some tenants were even obligated to collect the season's acorns by hand, a tedious job that was probably assigned to children.[81]

So it is understandable why, in the ninth century, a group of residents from a village in Italy called Flexum would see woodland and pannage as totally separable entitlements. The monastery of Nonantola had taken these villagers to court twice already for feeding their pigs in a wood the monastery owned. The farmers claimed that they were entitled to the pannage. At their third court appearance, in 824, they produced a charter from King Aistulf (749–756), which had granted them the privilege of feeding their pigs in the woods tax free. When Aistulf had made that grant to Flexum, the woodland had been part of the fisc; at some point after that, Aistulf had granted the property to Nonantola. But as far as the residents of Flexum were concerned, the transfer of ownership (which they originally tried to claim had never happened) did not nullify their rights to pannage. For the imperial agent who was adjudicating the case, however, the villagers were only entitled to feed their pigs without payment if some portion of that woodland still belonged to the royal treasury, which the court concluded was not the case. The judgment fell in favor of the monastery on the logic that when Nonantola received the woods from Aistulf it had received the pannage rights along with them. But this outcome represented only one possible reading of the law here: even with proper legal documentation on both sides, the rights to woodland were not straightforward.[82]

Back in Gaul two centuries earlier, Clothar's edict was rooted in a closely similar legal and environmental context, and it anticipated that pannage would involve three proprietary claims: rights to pannage, ownership of the woods, and possession of the pigs themselves. Although the edict does not specify how the state swineherds fit into this matrix—because its audience would have already understood the situation better than we do—the likeliest scenario is that the porcarii fiscales had the right to collect pannage revenues from privately owned woodland.

It is also not clear today—though again it would have been obvious to Clothar's subjects—whether his policies on pannage represented something new. The cellarinsis and decimae porcorum taxes did have late antique roots, but the genealogy is faint. To sketch it quickly in a paragraph: the Roman Empire had collected pigs from landowners both for the annona levy (to supplement the grain, oil, and wine that were supplied to the army, the imperial court, and the cities of Rome and Constantinople) and for food requisitions called the *cellaria*, which were part of the salary package of high-ranking civil servants and military officers. Neither collection seems to have been measured as a function of woodland, and some contemporary criticisms of the cellaria imply that they were collected unpredictably, rather than annually, as this Merovingian iteration of the tax clearly was. (In Ostrogothic Italy, the cellaria were apparently collected to provision the army in times of war—but this too may have been a modification to imperial tax policy rather than a simple continuation of it.) It is also significant that, under the Roman Empire, the provinces had to pay the annona every year as a flat obligation. There were no environmental or social leeways built into the tax policy itself, though the emperors did make occasional adjustments to the laws. As for the decimae porcorum, they had been part of a standard package of payments made by a legal class of free tenant farmers called *coloni* in the late imperial period. The coloni, rather than the landowners, would pay taxes to the state on the agrarian lands they used, as a form of rent. But by the seventh century if not earlier, this arrangement had obviously broken down. In Iberia, the Visigothic laws treat the same pannage fee (also called decimae porcorum) as a private entitlement, something that the owners of a woodland, or owners of acorn rights, collected for themselves. But in Gaul, Clothar's move to exempt Burgundian churches from paying the decimae porcorum implies that the crown had already enjoyed the rights to collect that tax for some time—though for how long, we cannot know.[83]

So as regular, annual rights in woodland held by the crown or conceded by the crown, the Merovingian pig taxes only obliquely resembled their imperial forms. The edict's approach to the cellarinsis tax might therefore represent a qualification of an earlier policy, or it might have been what the Merovingians euphemistically called a "new song," or unprecedented law.[84] But despite the gaps in our knowledge about the details of these tax policies, it is clear that whether the crown was appropriating this revenue for the first time or not Clothar was framing them as concessions. There is a concession to prohibit the porcarii fiscales from entering private woods without the owners' permission, and there is a concession to suspend the tax on pannage when there are no acorns for the pigs to eat. These were savvy measures. If a Merovingian king was going to collect taxes successfully, the cooperation of local elites was essential.[85] A state swineherd would have a better shot at doing his job if he was not dealing with landowners who were hostile or obstinate or simply hedging their bets on whether to support the king. Clothar's promise not to send his men into various woods until he had the authorization to do so attests to his interest in counterbalancing fiscal revenues with the support of the subjects he also expressly valued.

His agents also depended on locals' knowledge of the land. There is a common motif in ancient and medieval literature that swineherds and pigs were guides to miraculous discoveries: they knew the woods better than most people did.[86] Woodlands were not easy grounds to mark and measure. A landowner might specify, down to the individual tree, where his property line stood— from this maple tree to the two oaks past it and beyond them a cherry tree, and so on—but such a meticulous surveying was not feasible for larger chunks of territory, and it spoke to the real difficulty owners had in keeping track of a visually and legally complex property that was also constantly changing. In at least one documented instance the Merovingian kings could not even keep track of their own wooded territories. In 670 Childeric II reclaimed 75 percent of a property that Sigibert III, his uncle, had granted to a monastery three decades earlier. Sigibert seems to have been unaware of precisely how large a property he had given away![87]

Another problem with woods was that even though they were part and parcel of early medieval agriculture, their terrain made them easy places for subterfuge. Swineherds would try to sneak their pigs past the tax collectors, or herd them out of the woods before the end of the season to avoid paying. Joint owners of pannage rights (*consortes de glandibus*) would squabble about who was getting more pig traffic, so much so that in Iberia they were required to distribute the pigs and the revenues more evenly across their holdings. That would have been a squirrely operation, and herders could have exploited this situation, too, to complicate the question of who was owed what. We know about these problems from the Visigothic laws that penalized them in Iberia, and it is likely that farmers in Gaul tried to dodge their pannage payments in similar ways.[88]

Clothar was therefore acknowledging the interdependence of himself and the kingdom's landowners through his policies on pannage. The prevailing political ethics of the 610s, the physical and agrarian features of Gaul's wood-lands, and the preferences and pitfalls of our notorious animal were the ma-jor reasons why the king and his court structured the law according to such a relationship. And on the basis of this view, Clothar was also assuring his subjects that royal fiscal practices would be responsive to local environmental conditions by promising to collect pannage revenue (or feed the crown's pigs) only when there was actually an acorn crop. Private woodlands, he promised, would be exploited only in good times. The edict's outlines for pannage there-fore reflect how Clothar and his court saw profit as a function of multiple vari-ables. Courtiers, landowners, pigs and their owners, trees and even climates had to cooperate in order for the king to fill the fisc justly.

There is no direct evidence for what happened when the pannage fees were paid. But circumstantial and comparative evidence can help us sketch some of the calculations and complications that must have been part of this exchange. Pigs, after all, were something more than a currency. Their fleshy specificity made a difference.

It is possible to take an abstract view and suggest that the pigs rendered as pannage payments were like money. As part of a fiscal system, they served as units of account that brought seemingly irreducible and dissimilar entities (woodland, livestock appetites, social obligations) into a workable equivalence. But in other ways pigs were thoroughly unfungible. There was no consistent "conversion rate" for pigs' bodies. In Iberia, the Visigothic laws treated individual animals as having variable values, and the costs for killing one illegally were not fixed. Instead the culprit had to provide a replacement animal "of equal worth."[89] Into the early 800s, accountants and landlords tended to express these differences in terms of age or weight. A few of the rental agreements contracted with the church of Lucca stipulated the payment of a one-year-old pig (*porcus annotinus*), and the earliest of these insisted that the pig needed to be a *good* one. And the monasteries of Wissembourg and Saint-Germain-des-Prés in Paris sometimes specifically requested "fat" pigs (*porci crassi*) or pigs that had been fattened on pannage (*porci saginati*). As the ninth century progressed, the differences in pigs' values were increasingly expressed in cash. In Italy, tenants who owed a pig as part of their rent were often asked to render a pig of specific price—a pig worth two tremisses, for example, or a pig worth four. The same was true at the Rhineland monasteries of Prüm and Wissembourg.[90] Likewise the *Lex Salica* meticulously enumerated a wide range of values that were based on the animals' age and reproductive status.[91]

Children who had some sense of the various differences would have had an advantage when it came to solving this early medieval math problem:

There were two traders who had 100 solidi between them, and they bought pigs with the money. They bought them at the rate of 2 solidi for 5 pigs, intending to fatten them and sell them again to make a profit. And when they realized that it was not the time for fattening pigs, and they could not feed them over the winter, they tried to see if they could sell them at a profit anyway. But they couldn't, because they were unable to sell them for more than the price at which they had purchased them— that is, the rate of 2s. for 5 pigs. When they registered this, they said to each other: "Let's divide them up!" And in dividing them up and selling them at the same rate they had paid, they made a profit. Who is able to say how many pigs they had at the beginning, and how they divided and sold them and generated a profit that they couldn't have made by selling them all together?

The answer was to split the 250 pigs equally, but to divide them into groups of pigs in better shape (*meliores*) and worse shape (*deteriores*): the better pigs could be sold at the rate of two per solidus, and the lesser pigs could be sold at the rate of three per solidus. In other words, "grading" the animals and selling them accordingly was a better deal than buying a mixed lot at an averaged price.[92]

What all these price distinctions underscore is that even though the standard pannage rate was one pig for every ten fattened in the woods, it was nevertheless possible to manipulate that transaction in different ways, because the value of a pig differed significantly from animal to animal. Because size varied according to a pig's age and phenotype, swineherds might have tried to pay with smaller animals, or officials might have looked for larger ones. Animals could also harbor injuries or illnesses that were undetectable to a person who did not know them well, making it possible to unload sick pigs on an unsuspecting agent.[93] Even Roman emperors had wrangled with the particularity of pigs' bodies. The state had calculated annona payments by weight, but when the pigs were actually weighed, their owners would cheat (by weighing them on a full stomach), and when the tax collectors tried to eyeball them, owners complained that they underestimated. Centuries later, in the 820s, the courtier and writer Einhard (who is best known today for his glowing biography of Charlemagne) would upbraid an estate administrator for trying to dodge the revenues he owed: one of his scams was to send Einhard thirty pigs "that were not even good ones."[94]

And unlike coins or even, say, cows (which Merovingian rulers also collected as a tax on occasion),[95] transporting pigs was also a problem. They were difficult, though not impossible, to herd long distances. In the first century, Pliny had noted in his *Natural History* that anyone who fed pills made of ravens' brains to pigs would induce the pigs to follow him wherever he went: a sign that humans needed help in this department. In Late Antiquity, the transit of live pigs from the Italian countryside to the city of Rome incurred routine losses of 15 percent of the herds' original value—the result of weight loss, as other historians have suggested, but surely also the result of runaways. That is what had made Walahfrid Strabo so impressed with the regimented pig herd of Saint Gall (which we met in the previous chapter): it was something of a miracle for pigs to travel in an orderly file. So it was probably the case that rather than actually drive the pig-tenths from different corners of the kingdom to Paris or Metz or other royal residences, the kings' agents exchanged them locally for renders in gold or silver. The kingdom had an active network of local mints, and Merovingian officials would sometimes use these mints to convert taxes in kind back to the crown as cash when it seemed financially advantageous.[96]

Under the Roman administration, the western half of the empire had commuted the pig dole to cash in the fifth century to ensure that the returns were paid in gold (which was uninflated and consistently valuable), measured in prices that the state could fix, and then spent to buy pigs or cured pork locally. The military officers who received the annona as part of their salary had manipulated tax collection in the fourth century to achieve precisely this goal: the advantage of getting paid in cash was that soldiers or bureaucrats could calibrate fluctuations in market prices, population size, and supplies throughout the empire. Put more bluntly, cash enabled state employees to profiteer.[97] But it is unlikely that the Merovingian government ever converted its pig revenues entirely to cash. Such a move would have been at odds with a tax system that the historian Chris Wickham has characterized as increasingly "local." Over the course of the Merovingian period (481–751), taxation did not disappear, but it fragmented into different policies and arrangements for different regions, cities, and landowners. That process had started before the Merovingians were kings: Clovis, the "founder" of the dynasty (481–511), had built alliances with Roman and non-Roman soldiers in northern Gaul in exchange for contracting recruitment, taxes, and laws more locally than the Roman emperors had.[98]

More generally, across the early medieval West the imperial tax system was selectively adopted and modified in different ways—depending not only on the kingdom but also on the specific arrangements that different communities within these kingdoms worked out with their rulers and officials. And the Merovingians were not the only government to capitalize on pannage in the early Middle Ages. The Byzantine government was collecting pannage from the residents of Rizana (in modern Slovenia) in the middle of the eighth century, for example, and by the early ninth century this tax was called *glandaticum* by the Frankish administrators who had taken over there and continued to collect it. The landowners of Rizana clearly viewed these payments as taxes rather than rents, not only because the revenues were collected by ecclesiastical and royal officials (rather than themselves) but also because they expected about half of all those taxes to be reinvested in their town. For that reason they took the tax collectors to court in 804 to accuse them of embezzlement: the court records are the only reason we know about the pannage tax here.[99]

So the fact that early medieval communities were "localizing" Roman taxes was a structural feature of post-imperial politics. But what the Merovingian case shows with particular clarity is that many factors, including animals and ecologies, shaped the form that these fiscal arrangements took. In the culture of pannage—through the salvaging, surveying, paying, calculating, converting, and transporting that hinged on an unreliable crop—pigs were one of multiple forces that propelled certain ways of making money and thinking about value. They even prompted the Merovingian court to recognize that its resources were constrained by interlocking variables, to adjust to conditions as they changed, and to understand that profit was a matter of perspective. Fiscal revenue was not always the top priority. And the Merovingian kingdom's approach to its pig revenues was based on an understanding that the kingdom's vitality required a politics that functioned in step with its ecology.

Unexpectedly, then, the economy of salvage became profoundly scalar. It was not "scalable" in the sense we use in economics today, to mean the possibility of expanding and replicating a mode of production without disproportionately increasing the costs of doing business. As Anna Lowenhaupt Tsing pointed out, that approach is antithetical to salvage, to the economy of the hyperlocal and the serendipitous. In any case, such a view of scalability was a creation of the nineteenth century. Meat production, for instance, only became economically scalable through massive environmental and economic changes. In the United States, this process involved the destruction of the prairie through widespread ranching, the penetration of the railroads into the Midwest, the use of ice to release butchery from its dependence on the cold season, aggressive tactics on the part of Chicago meatpackers to edge out competition with butchers in the eastern United States (who acquired their meat locally and live), and the processing and marketing of byproducts to subsidize the low prices that new suppliers were pushing.[100]

The early medieval picture is a far cry from this. People *were* thinking in terms of scale, but in a different way. We have already seen the natural philosophers and theologians mischievously but also seriously inverting conventional orders of magnitude to insist that the most minuscule phenomena could illuminate the whole of the cosmos. The Merovingian configuration of its political culture took a similar view, linking the microcosms of pigs and their herders to the meso-level operations of local and regional economies and to the macro-level considerations of the royal court. In this kingdom, local conditions influenced the larger mechanics of the fisc, and they inspired a set of priorities that consciously emulated the distinctive resourcefulness of salvage. The result was counterintuitive: the kingdom hinged its prosperity on policies that scaled down rather than up.

This is not to say that pigs were the only inspiration for these developments. As we have seen, Clothar and his court were already rethinking what the entitlements and responsibilities of political engagement should be. But the pigs that people raised, thanks to their ubiquity, difficulty, and special flexibility, would make them one of the most relentless reminders of the ways an economy was—and could be—responsive. And so the animals were raised and slaughtered in the service of a principle that they had helped cultivate. Maybe more than any other "commodity," pigs showed early medieval farmers, landowners, and rulers the benefits of redefining what counted as a resource, of shifting a metabolic system to respond to the ecological, economic, and political profile of a particular place and moment.

It is important to be clear that this particular sense of resourcefulness was significantly different from the concept of sustainability that scholars and activists advocate today. The early medieval interest in the interplay of human and nonhuman forces was not coupled with an overt concern that these relationships could self-degrade. And the early medieval sense of "ecology," and the ethics that derived from that understanding, did not aim to ensure that different groups could share in the physical world more equally.[101] As I will show in the next chapter, an adaptive approach to producing, raising, and exchanging pigs was still accompanied by significant disparities in handling and eating them. This is not to say that early medieval societies were unconcerned with poverty or powerlessness. Far from it. Serious reflection and debates occurred throughout these centuries about the obligations of the rich toward the poor, rulers toward their subjects, bishops to their cities, monks to their donors and neighbors, and elites toward the lands they helped control.[102] But equalizing opportunities was not on the agenda.

4 • Partnerships

Biologists use the term "species assemblage" to describe the organisms that hang together in a habitat. It indicates interconnected rather than parallel lives. And scholars of literature and history have seized on the idea to ask how humans' own experiences and perspectives have been shaped by interspecies relationships—as, for example, by the fusion of a warrior and his horse to form "a knight," or the cross-communication between hunters and their dogs, or the cyborg-like symbiosis of humans and the bacterial creatures (or spiritual forces) in their guts.[1]

Sometimes humans notice and nurture these interactions, as medieval knights and hunters did, and sometimes they do not. I look here at assemblages of both kinds: at the exchanges that developed between humans and pigs in conscious and nonconscious ways. Anthropologists and biologists might describe such a process as coevolution or co-domestication, because close relationships between species transform the bodies and behaviors of all involved.[2] The early medieval engagements between humans and pigs also show that humans' *concepts* and *evaluations* of themselves and others could change through these relationships. Certain identities and institutions became defined by the interactions between pigs and people, and these social profiles would have been significantly different without pigs in the picture.

The groups highlighted here became assemblages in the course of humans' raising, acquiring, and eating pigs, and in examining such moments we will find additional reasons to see pigs as more than economic resources in the early Middle Ages. As creatures that both facilitated and thwarted their handlers, they helped *make* the humans who exploited them, by guiding the paths they walked, the days they worked, the ways they learned, the prestige they won, the military bases they established, the legal cultures they created, and the bodies they transformed. And humans were aware of this interdependency more often than we might expect. They saw that the social groups they invested with meaning were altered and enriched by interspecies engagement at the individual and local levels, and so in this way, too, they were thinking ecologically.

Swineherds

The swineherd—usually called *porcarius* and occasionally *subulcus* or *custos porcorum* in Latin, or some variant of *swan* in Old English and *muccid* in Old Irish—had a kind of double status in the early Middle Ages that owed its complexity to the pigs under his care. Professional (that is, full-time) swineherds were nearly always enslaved or unfree, and their partnership with a species that was caricatured as muddy and greedy made them a sometime symbol of degradation. Saint Martin of Tours once noticed a swineherd shivering in the cold and thought immediately of Adam after his exile from paradise. Adam had been a swineherd after the Fall, Martin insisted, and this contemporary swineherd was both the symbol and the substance of the "old Adam," the ancestral Adam whose misery and sin every human being had inherited.[3] But such a view is only half the story. Although they could be condescended to, swineherds were also respected as highly skilled workers, precisely because the work of breeding, feeding, monitoring, herding, and healing pigs was a real challenge.

We know only a few names of the swineherds who did the tough work of tending pigs in the early Middle Ages, even though there would have been thousands of them working in the West at any given time. In Iberia: Aulfus and Petro Aquilion. In Italy: Barulo and his brother Aurulus. Adoald. Maurulo. Gratiolus. Amulo. In Gaul: Melloricus and his wife, Pascasiola. Agnechild and Baccio. Idoldo. Eusebius, his wife, Beroild, and their adult son Bernard. Frotgius and his wife, Ragambolda, and *their* adult son Ontbold. Bertlinus and his wife, Lantsida. Gisleuold and Adalind, and Gisloin and Dominica. Gundilanis. In England: Eadstan. Byrnstan. Brihtelm. In Ireland: Dub, Dorm, and Dorchae.[4]

Swineherding was sometimes a family profession, as the case of the brothers Barulo and Aurulus implies (though another brother of theirs was *not* a swineherd, and we do not know what their father did).[5] Byrnstan may have herded pigs with his younger son. Eadstan's son, whose name we do not know, definitely became a swineherd. Some of the married couples who are identified as the caretakers of their landlords' pigs did this work as a form of rent payment, so they may have passed on the obligation to their children. Gundilanis is the only example I have found of a female swineherd working on her own.

Being an adult, or at least a teenager, was a more fixed requirement than being male when it came to swineherding. Pigs could have easily harmed children, and, in any case, the work was too difficult for them when dealing with herds of almost any size. Saint Brigit of Ireland, who was born to a Druid father and an enslaved mother captured in warfare, is sometimes said to have been a swineherd as young girl. But the hagiographer who mentions this, writing in the ninth century, makes clear that swineherding was not her usual occupation. Her father had asked her to herd his pigs for the day, and she did a terrible job: two of the boars were stolen. The only reason the incident was worth narrating was because God replenished the herd for her.[6]

We know about Brigit because she became a saint, but we know the names of other swineherds only because they were unfree and under someone else's control. The vocabulary of social statuses was notoriously imprecise in the early Middle Ages. There were plenty of terms to describe unfree people (*servus, ancilla, puer, famulus, colonus, originarius, manicipium, litus, libertus, haldius, tabularius, censualis, tributarius, massaricius, libellus, þeow, man, þegn, scealc, þræl, mug, cumal, fuidir, bothach, senchléithe*), and the reality was even more complicated: a single term could be applied to very different legal and economic circumstances.[7] But swineherds often appear in contexts that suggest that they were slaves or dependent tenants who were seen to be part of a package deal with the pigs they supervised. A wealthy woman named Æthelgifu, who drew up her will around 990, even seems to have seen swineherding as incompatible with free status. In one case she freed the son and wife of one of her swineherds but not the herder himself; and in another case she freed a swineherd (Eadstan, mentioned above) and his entire family *except* his son, who assumed control of the pigs his father had supervised.[8] So it is not surprising that most people had no interest in naming their children Porcarius, or Swineherd. Only elite couples did this, and they probably did it ironically. One of the main characters in a seventh-century hagiographical text was an elite landowner named Porcarius, and we first encounter him hunting wild boar on his property, rather than herding domesticated pigs.[9]

People who were *actually* swineherds typically appear in documents only when their owners or lords were recording the work they owed, splitting their labor with another landowner, or gifting them, along with the pigs they tended, to new proprietors. In narrative texts, the swineherds are usually not introduced. The nameless swineherd in Sulpicius Severus's story about Martin is typical. Or to take another case: Gregory of Tours tells a story about a swineherd who was struck blind and eventually cured by Saint Martin. He was even manumitted by his owner in acknowledgement of the miracle. But Gregory never gives the man's name. Instead he tells us that the owner's name was Theudulf and that Theudulf was a citizen of Tours.[10]

We do not know how these swineherds became unfree. The situation would have been different for each of them because, as the historian Alice Rio in particular has demonstrated, unfree persons in the early medieval West had many different backstories. There were enslaved captives of war, enslaved persons who had inherited their status from their parents, and individuals who had sold themselves into servitude. The Visigothic kings advocated the enslavement of free persons as a punishment for certain crimes (such as rape, poisoning, and abortion), and the Bavarian duchy within the Merovingian kingdom prescribed temporary enslavement to enable poor criminals to pay off their penalties. And it is also impossible to say what the "usual" rights and obligations of swineherds would have been, because the arrangements that were struck or coerced between unfree individuals and their owners and lords varied widely. When the monastery of Saint-Germain-des-Prés in Paris drew up an inventory of its estates and tenancies between 825 and 828, it recorded different situations for each of the families who served as swineherds. One family possessed no land but still owed swineherding to the monastery (and they might have been household slaves), two others paid the rents for their land almost entirely through swineherding, and two additional families who shared a small tenancy owed swineherding in addition to *other* labors, as well as payments of chickens and eggs.[11]

We can surmise, on the basis of the law codes, what legal handicaps swineherds could have experienced as slaves or dependent workers—such as restrictions on their personal property or on their sexual relationships and marriages—but these laws only represent the limits of the possible. This was a world in which status was continually contested and reappraised, and these restrictions would not necessarily have been permanent. Indeed, masters and lords often chose *not* to exploit these possibilities to the fullest. It was more advantageous for them to stop short of their maximum lawful entitlements and grant their unfree dependents a certain leniency: this bound their subordinates to them more tightly out of a sense of obligation—and also out of fear that the "charity" of restraint could be revoked at any time.[12]

It was also possible, especially when it came to property law (which included the laws of servitude), to modify or even circumvent the parameters established in a kingdom's legislation by drawing up documentation that set up an alternate legal framework for the parties involved. Using a contract of this kind, a farmer might arrange to pay off a loan by working as a servile laborer a few days a week while remaining free the rest of the time. Or an enslaved man who "ran off with" (that is, married) a free woman could turn to a similar procedure to avoid execution, and the woman and her children could remain free.[13]

Not every swineherd was enslaved or unfree. A Visigothic law dealing with the logistics of pannage payments suggested that when a swineherd first brought his herd into a woodland, the owner of the woods should take a token deposit from him and pass it on either to the swineherd's lord (*dominus*) or to his relatives (*parentes*). Presumably the choice depended on whether the swineherd was tending a landlord's pigs or his own. In Lombard Italy, King Rothari wanted to be clear in one of his laws that "the herders we are talking about are ones who serve free men and who set off [with the herds] from their [lords'] own property." The implication was that there were free animal herders or unfree herders who cared for their own personal animals who would be treated differently. And a tenth-century outline of obligations to an estate in southwest England, known as the *Rectitudines singularum personarum* (roughly, *The Obligations of Different Groups of People*), is careful to specify swineherds who are unfree (*ðeow swan* or *æhteswane*), in contrast to those who are not (*swan, inswane*): the landlord employed both types. There were also farmers for whom swineherding was only a part-time responsibility. In the ninth century the Rhineland monasteries of Prüm, Wissembourg, and Lorsch obligated some of their tenants to care for their pigs on a periodic basis. Sometimes that meant taking them to the woods, and sometimes it meant bringing a few of the monks' pigs to their own farms and feeding them over the winter.[14]

But it is rare to catch glimpses of free or part-time swineherds working on behalf of their families or farming communities. The *Rectitudines* mentions an arrangement in which free peasants sent their pigs off with the landlord's swineherd for the acorn season and paid him six loaves of bread each for the favor—but we do not know who cared for their animals the rest of the year. Or to take another ambiguous example to stand for many others: a farm called Bagarris in the subalpine zone of Provence was run by a young widow named Deidona who had a five-year-old girl and two unmarried daughters aged at least fourteen. Deidona also had a son, but he was not on the property when the document was drawn up, so we know nothing about him, including whether he was coming back. This small family owed one pig and one piglet every year to the monastery of Saint-Victor of Marseille, which drew up a polyptych in 813 or 814. Were Deidona and her daughters caring for a small herd of pigs themselves, in addition to their other farmwork? Or were they pooling their pigs with other farmers nearby?[15]

This is hard to answer because landlords and lawmakers, who were responsible for much of the documentation that survives today, were more interested in the lives of full-time, unfree swineherds. Two laws from Italy, for instance, were dedicated to sorting out penalties for injuring swineherds—but only because those injuries were "damaging" to the free persons who owned them. These laws were originally issued by King Rothari in 643, and in the ninth century a legal compiler grouped them into a section about violence against free persons—assuming, as Rothari had, that the "victims" of violence were the swineherds' masters.[16]

But even when swineherds were unfree, they were treated as a special and differentiated group. The laws recognized that unfree swineherds had statuses among themselves, and they were considered more valuable than other farmworkers, a sign of the early medieval respect for their craft knowledge. Merovingian and Carolingian editions of the *Lex Salica* considered swineherds to be specialized unfree workers, a group that also included, depending on which version of the law one consulted, vintners, hunters, carpenters, millers, grooms, blacksmiths, goldsmiths, and other artisans. All these workers were as costly to lose as higher-priced slaves. In the early sixth century, the Merovingians' Burgundian neighbors in the Rhône valley were not willing to rate swineherds that highly, but they still put them on par with plowmen as a fairly valuable class of subordinate. In Italy, Rothari's edict of 643 ranked its swineherds: a master swineherd (*porcarius magister*) was assumed to have two or more apprentices (*discipuli*), and his death incurred a penalty of fifty gold solidi, whereas the deaths of lower-ranking swineherds (*inferiores porcarii*) incurred only half that penalty. What exactly made them "lesser" is not clear—probably they handled smaller herds without helpers—but even these swineherds were valued more highly than the other rural laborers included in this edict, including ox drivers, farmers, and goatherds, shepherds, and cowherds, even the master herders among them.[17]

These were the complex societies in which swineherds operated, in a legal and economic culture of multiple and mutable forms of unfreedom. We can only occasionally catch a glimpse of what their opportunities and restrictions were, but what *is* clear is that the individual herders' situations would not have been as rigid as the surviving documentation makes it seem. A swine-herd named Adoald is a case in point. Adoald appears in a dispute involving the Lazian monastery of Farfa in 747, in which he introduces himself to the court as a former head swineherd—"Ego adoald tempore illo, dum essem archiporcarius"—and although he was not serving in that capacity anymore, he explained that as an archiporcarius he had owned property in a contested woodland and was willing to swear an oath to prove it. It is extremely unusual to find a swineherd speaking on record in the first person (albeit mediated through the court). But Adoald's story shows that it was possible for some swineherds to hold a rank of some importance, to own property, and even to quit the job.[18]

The physical and intellectual work of swineherding was as variable as the stature that went along with it. We have already seen how communities kept pigs in countless ways: the size of herds, their environmental contexts, and their economic functions varied across the West and even within a single site over time. And the husbandry that swineherds practiced would have been adapted to local conditions of salvage. In northern Iceland, for example, in the basin of Lake Mývatn in the tenth and eleventh centuries, different farms within about six miles of one another were feeding their pigs different things and probably raising them differently, too. At the farm of Hrísheimar, the pigs were eating plants that had not grown on manured fields: these were free-range animals. But the pigs at the farms of Sveigakot and Hofstaðir—one a small farmstead, the other a great feasting hall—were also getting food from nearby freshwaters and possibly even from the Atlantic, including fish guts and bones (trout and char were especially important to the humans at Hofstaðir) and maybe bird eggs, too. These fish-fed pigs may have been mostly confined to stalls and therefore more in need of monitoring than herding, but they might also have occasionally been led to the scrubby birch woodlands that still survived around Hofstaðir after the Norse first colonized the area.[19]

If we take seriously the view of the natural philosophers and exegetes that expertise was not restricted to intellectuals alone, the reserves of specialized knowledge that the swineherds developed theoretically had the potential to unlock cosmic connections between physical and divine orders. But today it is hard for us to assess what they knew. A master swineherd (such as the magister porcorum mentioned in the Lombard laws, or the archiporcarius Adoald) would have passed along his expertise by talking to his apprentices (his discipuli or *iuniores,* as the laws called them) and by training his dog, not by writing it down.[20] There are no surviving texts from the Middle Ages about the theory or practice of swineherding. We can only scrounge for hints about the tacit knowledge their work would have required. They were probably the people responsible for giving their animals medical treatments, for example, but we can only infer this from the osteological record, from broken bones that had been healed through human care. At a large pig farm in southern Italy—San Giovanni di Ruoti—we have evidence of a pig successfully recovering from a fractured foot. Or to take another example based on patchy material: the *Rectitudines* drawn up for one English estate asserts that the swineherds there were in charge of debristling and curing pigs' carcasses after they were slaughtered. This responsibility could have been specific to this estate, or it might have been fairly common. From the documentation there is, we cannot say.[21]

The ancient and late antique agronomy manuals give us other indications of what swineherds needed to know, and although these texts were written by aristocratic landowners with large-scale operations in Roman Italy, they point to the breadth and depth of expertise that some swineherds would or could have developed in their work. According to Varro, the head herder of each species should ideally be literate, at least to a degree, in order to keep track of animals' illnesses and the herd's demography. Some eight hundred years later, Charlemagne would also emphasize the importance of keeping accounts, or *rationes,* on his royal estates, and in the thirteenth century English manors would commit to this practice with stunning regularity. On most early medieval farms, keeping records was probably not a priority.[22] But it *was* likely that swineherds were involved in breeding the animals, which entailed knowing their sows' fertility cycles, being able to tell when they were pregnant (in order to separate them from the rest of the herd), castrating most of the male pigs, and offering advice on the purchase of new breeding animals should an owner ever opt to do that. And according to the agronomists, a good swineherd kept track of which piglets belonged to which sows, in order to make sure that the milk was getting evenly distributed (rather than having the inevitable stray piglet take more than its fair share). They made sure that piglets were not crushed by their mothers. They trained pigs to respond to a horn or a bell—first on the farm, when the pigs were little, then in the fields and woods, when the pigs were older.[23] And they were supposed to keep the pigsty tidy, because the pigs themselves insisted upon it! As Columella put it in the first century CE, "No matter how much filth this animal rolls around in while feeding, it longs for an extremely clean place to sleep."[24]

Columella seems to have recognized that swineherds would not have just learned from one another; they would have also learned from their pigs: swineherds would have been in constant consultation with them. Alexandra Horowitz, a specialist in dog behavior and cognition, has pointed to the communication that has to happen between dogs and human co-workers to enable the dogs to hunt for the things that humans want them to find. Sniffing out a truffle, for instance, depends on the dog, but it also depends on a human collaborator who can motivate the dog, interpret the signals the dog is sending, and help the animal reach the prize. The obvious differences between truffle-hunting dogs and food-foraging pigs aside, swineherds must have been alert to the invisible landscapes their animals were sensing—a geomagnetic field line, for example, or a scent—that humans were incapable of registering on their own.[25] A swineherd who paid attention to the ways pigs learned and navigated would have known when a seemingly errant pig was actually following clues to a sweet (and ideally legal) payload. But however swineherds interacted with their animals, they were evidently respected for it. Several law codes in Gaul made spooking or scattering pigs as they were being herded a punishable offense, even when no physical damage was done: the infraction was disrupting the swineherding process.[26]

A few references in the law codes suggest that swineherds in at least some agricultural regimes lived in the woods with their pigs—probably throughout pannage season and perhaps also in the spring and summer, since pigs love many things that woods have to offer. This meant learning to live in a different kind of agrarian environment, making do with basic shelters or shacks, and living apart from their families and friends, accompanied only by their assistants.[27] In the great oak forest of Kent, known as the Weald, most swineherds traveled a considerable distance every pannage season, as the historian K. P. Witney has shown in a fine history of this forest. Because the Weald was roughly in the center of Kent, the swineherds and their pigs would have set out from farms on its periphery, closer to the coasts, then passed through the outer boundaries of the forest that was owned by the king (and therefore off-limits), and plunged finally into the common grazing grounds they *were* permitted to use. In pannage season the swineherds would have been living far from home for about seven weeks, which were "among the wettest of the year, when the sun was losing its power, the leaves were falling, and the clay droves coming more and more to be churned into morass."[28]

As it happened, these radial droves or herding paths converging on the Weald even came to structure the modern road system in Kent, including a couple of highways to London. Some of the droves were based on old Roman trails that had been carved out for the iron industry, but most originated through centuries of swineherding, and they came to shape the forest in ways that left their imprint on modern infrastructure.[29] Farther north, in the North Atlantic, the topography on the Faroe Islands is still imprinted with the old haunts of swineherds and their pigs, in the form of place names that the Norse colonists would have become accustomed to using. On the southern island of Sandoy alone, for example, we find *Svínadalur* (Swine Valley), *Svíndaliður* (Swine Gate), *Svíngeil* (Swine Passage), *Niðari* and *Ovari Svínstíggjur* (Lower and Upper Swine Path), *Svínstíggjaheygjar* (Swine Path Mounds), *Svínstígamýra* (Swine Path Bog)—and this is only a partial list.[30]

Besides these modern hoofprints, the Weald also attests to pigs and swineherds working together in ways that early medieval landowners and lawmakers recognized and accommodated, practices we know thanks to the rich charter evidence from Kent and Canterbury, especially. Starting in the seventh century, the kings of Kent began to carve out pieces of woodland that was commonly shared to make as private gifts. These zones of land were called "pig pasture" or "dens" (*pastus porcorum, denbær,* or *denn*). As a result of that process, the swineherds had to learn where the jagged boundaries of the dens lay, to ensure that their lords' pigs were eating only in their lords' lands. But although the property lines could be complicated, both the kings and their beneficiaries tried to ensure that the individual dens they transacted were plotted in a way that was conducive to how pigs were pastured. The main concern, when swineherds first entered the Weald with their herds, was to let pigs start feeding as soon as possible. The alternative would involve restraining an entire herd of pigs from eating any of the acorns they passed until they got deeper into the woods to a place where they were legally allowed to feed. So landowners usually arranged to set up their newly private holdings either as a long continuous slice of woodland or as a successive series of lands that were positioned strategically along the droves, ensuring that the pigs would not need to travel for long stretches without a chance to glut.[31] Legal boundaries were plotted with pigs and swineherds very much in mind.

Besides knowing about landscapes and boundaries, and counterbalancing that information with what their pigs were actually doing, swineherds also needed to sense where the dangers lurked, to think like their animals in order to anticipate what their pigs could *not* perceive. Wild animals could pick off pigs, even in towns. Lawmakers were also concerned about the hazards that logging and hunting posed to humans and livestock, especially when they were traveling through woodland. Tree cutters could accidentally kill a human or an animal with a felled tree. And although a hunter and his dogs were expected to be skilled enough to keep their prey from harming bystanders, their traps—trip wires, catapults, snares—were a tougher matter. A hunter might set a trap so badly that whatever wild animal it captured would still be mobile enough to tear around doing damage, and even a good trap could ensnare livestock or even humans by mistake. Hunters were only obligated to publicize the location of their traps to neighbors who lived in areas that were heavily cultivated. When it came to traps they had set in remote places, they were absolved of most or all of their liability if a person or animal was accidentally ensnared. But no matter who was liable, the laws were predicated on the idea that "a quadruped cannot avoid [traps] by itself."[32]

Working with animals was also a distinctive form of labor at a time in which Christians were debating the protocol for working on Sundays. The seven days of the week were said to mirror the seven days of creation: God had created everything in the universe in six "days" or creative phases, and on the seventh day he "rested"—not because he had gotten tired or gave up on the world, exegetes assured their readers, but because he had simply finished making everything.[33] So every seventh day, Christians were supposed to honor *Dominica*, the Lord's Day. In the early Middle Ages some Christian leaders argued that this made most agricultural labor off-limits on Sundays and feast days. But many Christians across the social spectrum objected to this policy or ignored it. Some critics (including Gregory the Great, who was arguing with his own congregation) considered such a restriction to be uncomfortably similar to Jewish observations of the Sabbath. Other Christians took a different tack, and suggested that working through the holidays was the true Christian thing to do. One farmer in Orléans, for example, felt entitled to work in his vineyard on the feast day of Avitus of Orléans, on the logic that Avitus too had been "a working man."[34] But even when the stricter view of Sunday work gained the upper hand in the Christian West, and rulers began to endorse it, no farmer would have had to make the argument about tending his livestock, because the Sunday prohibitions did not include animal husbandry. When Charlemagne enumerated all the work that had to wait until Monday—viticulture, plowing, harvesting, drying hay, fence building, assarting, tree felling, masonry, carpentry, gardening, adjudicating, clothmaking, sewing—the care of animals was conspicuously absent. And in an Icelandic legal compilation from the thirteenth century (*Grágás*, or *Grey Goose*, which probably incorporated older traditions within it), herding and milking were expressly *permitted* on Sundays.[35] In short: swineherds worked all week long, and this was because unlike crops or construction projects, pigs needed continuous care.

For all these reasons, the things that swineherds knew made their employers and owners dependent on *them* and their expertise, even when they were dependents themselves. The most direct evidence we have for this is the suspicion, evident in more than one source, that masters were colluding with their slaves to commit crimes. Once again it is the laws that attest to this. Some of them—in Lombard Italy, the Alamannic duchy of Francia, and Carolingian Saxony—distinguished between a servus who committed a crime voluntarily and a servus who was acting on the orders of his owner. If a slave had distorted property markers of his own volition, for example, it was his responsibility to pay the penalty, but if his owner had told him to do it, only the owner was culpable. And when it came to graver crimes, lawmakers (in Italy, Bavaria, and Iberia) assumed from the start that slaves were following orders or acting with their owner's tacit approbation: this included poisoning, counterfeiting coinage or minting without authorization, setting fire to a church, or committing despoliation as if it were an act of legitimate warfare. In these cases, both the owner and the enslaved person he had coerced were held liable. For the slave this meant torture, disfigurement, or execution; for the owner it meant a monetary penalty and damages. From the perspective of early medieval lawmakers, these cases involved a criminal abuse of power. And that abuse seems to have stemmed from slave owners' interest in exploiting skills and knowledge that they did not always possess themselves. For example, when swineherds were caught pasturing their pigs in places where they did not belong, or dodging pannage payments by sneaking their pigs out of the woods before collection time, their owners were suspected of having told them to do it.[36]

It is not very likely that slave owners were asking their slaves to commit these crimes in an attempt to avoid suspicion themselves, because the laws almost automatically took the view that an owner was involved if one of his slaves was discovered to have done something illegal. And some owners were unwilling to lie to exculpate themselves or their slaves. One Lombard law, for instance, envisioned a scenario in which a pig owner would be unwilling to take an oath about the intentions of his swineherd (whose status here is unspecified), and this reluctance would cost him a penalty in pork.[37] But the question of whether owners were coercing their slaves to commit crimes as a way of deflecting guilt is somewhat beside the point: some of these crimes— the ones involving pigs especially—would have been impossible for owners to commit without the help of their dependent laborers. A free person with no experience in herding pigs would have done a poor job of it regardless, let alone been able to graze them surreptitiously or feed them in a private woodland for nearly an entire season and yet manage to herd them out of the woods covertly to avoid paying the fees they owed. Anyone who employed a swineherd was dependent on the herder's knowledge. What was different about lords who forced their swineherds into illegal situations was that they were making this dependency more explicit.

The swineherds may have turned this to their advantage, as other sub-altern groups would do in later centuries; the Ottoman state, for example, would rely heavily on Egyptian peasants as their primary "ecological experts" in constructing a new irrigation infrastructure for the Nile in the eighteenth century. Consequently those peasants could steer the attention and resources of the empire when they pursued their property claims in court, as long as they appealed to the state's interests that intertwined with theirs.[38] If early medieval swineherds did anything similar, the evidence does not survive, but given the fragmentary nature of the evidence for swineherding in general, we should not rule out the possibility that herders sometimes leveraged their expertise.

In any case the movement of knowledge between different social levels— and between humans and other elements of the physical world—suggests that the mode of research that the natural philosophers were idealizing in the same centuries may not have been all that radical. Only the motives were different: the philosophers were focused on tapping into any available information that could help them map the created world into an intricate divine schema, whereas landowners who talked to their swineherds about herding strategies were looking for a bargain.

It was *not* expected in this ecology of knowledge that herders would in turn meditate on the architecture of the cosmos. But at least one of them did any-way: Bede tells a celebrated story of a cowherd named Cædmon who was di-vinely inspired to compose a beautiful song about the start of creation. This accomplishment made him extraordinary, but to Bede's mind the act was not miraculous. Cædmon was gifted or graced, but on the whole he worked as any good monk would, ruminating on his knowledge and in the end making something new. And Bede suggests that the stable was an apt place for com-positions of this kind, given that Cædmon's ruminating first took place *among his ruminants.*[39] So although the story of Cædmon was singular, it was part of a world in which many ways of working treated knowledge as a process that was fluid and collaborative and shaped by the objects under scrutiny.

Swineherds, after all, were not just acting in concert with their bosses. They were also learning from their pigs, whose escaping, jumping, swimming, and rooting—magnified by the animals' capacity to learn and share information with one another—created ongoing challenges and legal liabilities that the swineherds and their teams worked hard to mitigate. Sometimes this earned swineherds a degree of respect, whether that entailed valuing them as highly skilled laborers or taking advantage of their knowledge for illegal ventures. But for the most part this collaboration, like the swineherds themselves, went mostly unrecorded.

By contrast, the mutual influence of a second assemblage—pigs and state institutions—is much more visible in the surviving evidence, though some of our informants viewed it as an unholy alliance.

Soldiers and States

The gospels of Matthew, Mark, and Luke all tell the story about Jesus sending an exorcised demon into a herd of pigs, and Mark's and Luke's versions add the joke that the demon called itself Legion. In the early centuries of the Roman Empire, the legions were its foundational military units. They mostly comprised Roman citizens who received rigorous military training, and they manned permanent garrisons that formed the skeletal structure of the military's presence across the empire. This was in contrast to the more flexible auxiliary units whose recruits often came from the imperial frontiers.[40] So in the gospels of Mark and Luke, a herd of pigs is the perfect host—unclean and rapacious—for an aggressively parasitic empire that many of its Jewish subjects resented. In Late Antiquity the rabbis were still picturing the Roman Empire in similar guises: "When the swine is lying down it puts out its hoofs, as if to say, 'I am clean'; so does this wicked State rob and oppress, yet pretend to be executing justice."[41]

Roman Jews drew on a rich exegetical tradition for this imperial–pig partnership, but they were also playing on common knowledge. The Tenth Legion, based in Jerusalem, displayed the wild boar as its favored avatar. The emperors Vespasian and Titus, the father and son who had crushed the Judean revolt and plundered the Temple of Jerusalem in 70 CE, minted coins that featured a sow and three piglets on their reverse. The imagery was a traditional homage to the white sow and thirty piglets that Aeneas had discovered in fulfillment of a prophecy about the founding of Rome. But it was also a reference to the Jerusalem legion and its recent victory (fig. 4.1).[42] And besides these totemic

Fig. 4.1. Silver denarius minted in Rome, 77–78 CE, less than a decade after the fall of Jerusalem to Roman forces. On the obverse is Vespasian (CAESAR VESPASIANVS AVG[VSTVS]); on the reverse is a sow with three piglets and the phrase IMP XIX, indicating that Vespasian had received nineteen imperial acclamations by the time the coin was struck. (18 mm, 3.47 g. British Museum, R. 10436. © The Trustees of the British Museum.)

signals, most Romans loved to *eat* pigs, so much so that modern historians used to think that pigs were providing the empire with most of its meat, because the written sources fixated on their flesh. Pliny insisted that unlike other meats, pork had fifty different flavors to tantalize the connoisseur, and a cookbook compiled around 400 focused overwhelmingly on the many possibilities of preparing a pig, with only a cursory glance at other domesticated mammals. In English we say, "The grass is always greener on the other side of the fence," but if we wanted to translate this into ancient Latin, we would also have to change our metaphor: "Tu si aliubi fueris," says a character in the *Satyricon* of Petronius, "dices hic porcos coctos ambulare." "If you were somewhere else, you'd say that *here* the pigs walk around already roasted."[43]

But in reality, the Romans talked about pork more often than they actually ate it, and we have zooarchaeologists to thank for noticing the discrepancy. The meat they ate, more often than not, was beef. On the Italian peninsula, where the faunal remains have been intensively studied, most people ate much more beef than pork, with the exception of central Italy, where pork and beef consumption were more equal. This was not because Italians preferred beef—their enthusiasm for pork suggests that they did not—but because beef was effectively a secondary product of the dairy and oxen industries. They were mostly eating cows that had given them cheese, and oxen that had pulled their plows and carts.[44] The story was similar in the provinces. Beef was the commonest meat eaten in Britain and Gaul, and in the frontier regions along the Rhine and Danube rivers. On the Iberian peninsula, pork was outranked by beef, and more dramatically by mutton and goat. In North Africa, although pork may have become more popular in some places after the Roman conquests than it had been in the Punic period, the meat of ovicaprids and cattle usually still outweighed it. Likewise in Egypt, the Levant, Anatolia, and Greece, sheep and goats provided most of the meat on Romans' tables.[45]

But as we have come to expect, variations arose within those general patterns, and Roman soldiers often ate more pork than was typical of wherever they were stationed. This tendency was especially pronounced, as the authors of the Gospels may have known, among Roman legions. So it seemed only fitting that Marcus Grunnius Corocotta Porcellus—Mark Grunter Roasted Squealing Piglet, whom fourth-century Roman schoolboys and scholars knew as the "author" of a will satirizing Roman legal and military culture—would speak in the gutsy slang of a Roman soldier.[46]

Archaeologists have debated why Roman military units frequently favored pork more than their neighbors. Local agrarian structures and the soldiers' own backgrounds and preferences did play a part in what those stationed at each fort ate; the "military diet" was still a strikingly heterogeneous thing. But the logistics of early settlement may have been a common denominator. Pigs' ability to fatten quickly, and their undiscriminating appetites, made them a key food for pioneers and invaders. When soldiers first colonized a territory, before they had set up long-distance and local food-supply chains, pigs could provide a vital stopgap in the early phases of their settlement. Sometimes this arrangement is characterized as "self-sufficiency," but that term undercuts the role that animals would have played in a community's survival.[47]

Even after a military contingent had integrated itself into local economies, pork remained part of its provisioning, thanks to the annona tax. In the imperial period, the annona helped provide free or discounted food to select residents of the capital cities, supplies to the imperial court, and provisions to the military: grain (later bread), wine, olive oil, and, starting in the third century, pork.[48] But it is unclear where that pork came from, how it was financed, and how it reached the soldiers it was supposed to feed. We have already seen that when it came to the annona destined for Rome, the supplies arrived on their own four feet, having been herded up to the city from different parts of Italy. But there is less evidence for the logistics of the military annona compared to what we know about the annona slated for the cities. It is improbable, knowing what we do about the difficulties and costs of herding pigs, that the pigs were driven long distances to the borderlands of the empire—to Hadrian's Wall, to the Rhine, the Danube, the Caucasus mountains, the Euphrates, the Arabian desert, and the Sahara—or to the large contingents of field armies on the move in Late Antiquity. If pigs were making long-distance trips, they probably did so dead rather than alive. Only one ancient shipwreck to date has included a large amount of pork in its cargo (and in any case it was wrecked in 100 BCE, long before the pork annona existed), but we know from Egyptian and Byzantine sources that imperial soldiers were supplied with cured pork. The meat could be packed in brine, pickled in wine, preserved in honey, salted and smoked, or turned into sausages.[49]

More often than not, the Roman military probably purchased or requisitioned its pork, or its pigs, closer to its bases. Archaeologists have found that the military forts in northern Europe, once they were better established, relied on local cattle ranches for their beef, and that some of these farms were specialized operations in terms of their breeding, culling, and butchery practices. Likewise troops on the Arabian border, in particular at the legionary fort of El-Lejjūn, were slaughtering livestock that had grown up in the area, focusing especially on sheep and goats. The soldiers there may even have been raising the animals themselves. But not everything that the empire's soldiers ate originated locally. Many forts imported the fish sauce known as *garum* (a beloved condiment mostly manufactured in Spain and North Africa), as well as olive oil, wine, and nonnative vegetables, fruits, and nuts. Some of their grain was imported, too; we know this because the bits of cereals that still survive are sometimes mixed with plants and pests that are not indigenous to the places where they ended up. The ceramics found at the imperial borders also show a mix of supply setups. In Late Antiquity the lower Danube was getting amphorae (shipping jars, usually for oil or wine) from the Aegean; Roman-Gothic soldiers stationed in Thrace (Bulgaria today) were receiving deliveries from the Vandal kingdom in North Africa; and armies at the Rhine were using a bit of olive oil from Iberia. But along the Euphrates, the military was getting its wine regionally, from Syrian producers. And from the third century on soldiers in Britain stopped importing olive oil almost completely, and perhaps wine too, and turned to the island itself for supplies, even though grapes and olives did not grow well there.[50]

As for pigs: because they could be raised almost anywhere, most were probably locals. It seems likely, for example, that the large pig farms in Pannonia (today the northwest Balkans), where "an enormously large number of juvenile individuals are missing," were exporting these animals to the soldiers stationed nearby. And in the second and third centuries CE, the Roman provinces that stretched across what is now modern Switzerland served as a supplier to the frontier zones farther north along the Rhine. Those provisions included cured meat. Every Roman settlement but one that has been excavated in these provinces included smoking ovens and pottery for meat storage, probably for brining pork.[51] There was no single system for military provisioning in the empire, and supply systems changed over time; even when we do have material evidence this good, it is still unclear what kind of fiscal arrangement was moving the meat along. Most of the time we cannot distinguish when the soldiers were collecting pigs or pork as a tax in kind, buying pigs through government contracts, purchasing them on the free market, or raising the animals themselves together with their families.

When imperial authority fractured in the western provinces in the fifth century, the link between pigs and the state did not dissolve; it evolved, like so many other political arrangements. We have already seen that in the sixth and seventh centuries, the Merovingians were including pigs among their fiscal calculations, possibly as an offshoot of the old annona or cellaria systems, and in Iberia hundreds of slate accounting tablets found in the central plateau of the peninsula indicate that the Visigoths were collecting taxes in both cash and kind—though given the low incidence of pig husbandry there, they were probably not collecting many pigs. In Italy the pork annona continued to be collected for the city of Rome at a reduced rate during the short century of Ostrogothic administration (from the late fourth to the mid-fifth century), and the kingdom was also advancing cash to government contractors to procure food, including pork, for the military.[52]

Archaeologists may have even hit upon one of the Ostrogothic state's suppliers, at the expansive villa complex of San Giovanni di Ruoti. This estate was located in the mountainous interior of Lucania, a province which the fourth-century *Expositio totius mundi et gentium* (*An Explanation of the Whole World and Its Peoples,* an overview of the iconic features of various places within and beyond the empire) highlighted for its hefty exports of bacon or *laridum*. Lucania was one of the few provinces in the empire whose obligation to pay the pig annona was prioritized above other tax payments. And its pork was honored in the name of a particular kind of sausage, the *lucanica*.[53]

The villa at Ruoti is unusual for a number of reasons. In the fifth century, at a time when few elites were building villas in the western provinces, the old structures on-site were demolished and an expansive residential complex was built to replace them; it was restored and enlarged *again* after an earthquake in 460. The owners splurged on glass windows, mosaics, and a top-notch stable for horses. The number of pigs vastly outnumbered other animals: from roughly 460 to 540, they constituted about 70 percent of the villa's domesticated mammals. There may have been 100 pigs in the herd there at any given time, or possibly two or three times that many. And based on the particular pig parts that were left behind, it seems that they were being exported from the estate in the form of preserved pork, most likely as cured hams (bone-in, cut from the femur and pelvis) and pork slices brined off the bone.[54]

The residents at San Giovanni were also eating and dressing in cutting-edge style. They sat at a table in their dining room instead of reclining on couches (like the one at Faragola shown in fig. 3.3), and they wore fashionable, even exoticized jewelry. In doing these things they may have been presenting themselves as aspirational or actual members of the Ostrogothic administrative or military elite. But we cannot say whether they were recent immigrants, second-generation Italian-Goths, or Italians with deep roots in the peninsula. In Late Antiquity elites of various backgrounds would seize on the same trends to present themselves as powerful cognoscenti.[55]

Not many coins turned up among the finds at the villa. But the pig bones do point to an operation whose scale seems overtly commercial. And in this region, which was obligated to supply the state with pork, or (in more recent centuries) with cash to purchase pork, it is plausible that the villa was doing brisk business as a state supplier. Rather than owing the tax themselves, its owners would have been selling pork to Ostrogothic officials. The head of the household might have been a civilian whose family had lived in Italy for one or more generations. Or he might have been a military officer who had served the Ostrogothic kingdom and received the villa as a retirement package. (The late Roman state had rewarded retired veterans with land, and so did the Ostrogothic administration.) Soldiers paid no taxes, but they were well placed to be provisioners. Someone with intimate knowledge of the logistics of military supply could take advantage of his military and state contacts to secure some kind of provisioning contract to sell pork to the state officials who were collecting taxes for that very purpose in the province's cities.[56]

North of the Alps, the empire's investment in pork, and the military's taste for it, may also help explain one of the most bizarre features of the early post-imperial law code known as the *Lex Salica*: it is inordinately preoccupied with pigs. And this is a particularly striking example of how, yet again, the animals contributed to the functioning of a state. The *Lex Salica* survives in eighty-eight manuscripts, more than any other early medieval book of law by far, and the manuscript tradition indicates that many more copies were produced that do not survive today. Karl Ubl, the leading analyst of this code and its legacy, has shown that the *Lex Salica* would become a legal touchstone in the Merovingian kingdom, centered on what are now France, Belgium, and Switzerland, and also in the successor kingdom of the Carolingians, which pulled the equivalent of today's Netherlands, Germany, and substantial parts of Italy into its orbit. But the code itself was created before there was a Carolingian or even a Merovingian kingdom to speak of. It was probably drawn up in the 470s or 480s (at the same time that San Giovanni's pork production was flourishing much farther south), and issued by a king for the benefit of a small society of farmers and soldiers in a militarized corner of the empire.[57]

Although the *Lex Salica* does not name this king and only gives trace indications of him, credit is due either to a general named Childeric or to his son Clovis. Their family called themselves Franks, which by the fifth century was the most prominent ethnic identity in northern Gaul. But they had also lived in the Roman Empire for four generations at least. Childeric had served as a military officer on the imperial payroll, and Clovis may have done the same, although eventually he became an ally, rather than an employee, of the emperor. Childeric and Clovis worked with the empire at a time when its influence in Gaul had become tenuous. When Childeric died, probably in 481, Clovis gave him a magnificent funeral that he thought was fitting to his own status as a successor to his father. He buried Childeric with weapons, hundreds of gold and silver coins, a throng of slaughtered horses, and jewelry that included a brooch signaling his service to the Roman military and a signet ring inscribed with *Childirici regis*, "[property] of King Childeric." Although the ring identified Childeric as *rex*, the title was even more apt for the son who staged his funerary ceremonies. "King" was a term that the Roman emperors in this period applied to leaders whose authority had a bifurcated, chiasmal personality: *reges* were fixers for the imperial government, but the people they governed were basically independent of the empire. Their authority among their subjects derived in part from the privileged relationship they maintained with Rome, and their authority in the eyes of the emperor derived from the loyalty and power they elicited from their people. Like other kings of his age, Clovis sometimes distanced himself from an imperial framework, and sometimes he was invested in it. But by the time he died in 511, Clovis had created a kingdom that was recognizably post-imperial. Although his descendants would keep in contact with the imperial court in Constantinople, and their subjects would remain connected in their own vital ways to a cross-Mediterranean culture, the realm was built through conquests, laws, alliances, and agreements that Clovis had negotiated as an alternative to imperial command.[58]

The *Lex Salica* was one step in this direction, whether it was Childeric or Clovis who had engineered it. Its title roughly means (according to the most convincing interpretation) "The Law of Landowning": it is a Latin lawbook, emanating from a region and a group that had served the empire. But unlike other early law codes drawn up by other early post-imperial successor states, it marks a conspicuous turn away from Roman law.[59] Probably its most striking departure is the absence of corporal and capital punishment of free persons. Another difference is that the *Lex Salica* addressed the subject of livestock in much more detail than any Roman laws had ever done. Most notoriously, the second law in the code consists of a lengthy and highly specific series of policies regarding the theft of pigs (fig. 4.2).

No other theft or crime in the code includes so many provisions. There are about sixteen permutations of pig theft (depending on the manuscript witnesses to the oldest version), spelling out how the penalties would vary according to the pigs' age, sex, function, and herd size. Stealing a one-year-old pig, for instance, entailed a fine of 3 gold solidi (or 120 silver denarii); stealing a two-year-old pig cost the perpetrator five times as much. Stealing a stud boar or breeding sow was fined at 17 solidi (or 700 denarii), stealing twenty-five pigs at 35 solidi (or 1,400 denarii), or nearly twice that much if the theft had completely depleted the herd, and so on.[60]

Although this bafflingly long list with its fixed fines would not have struck a jurist as Roman, the pigs themselves may have done so, because pig husbandry had been important in Roman Gaul, not only in the militarized borderlands in the northeast but also in the Gallic provinces more generally. When Varro wrote his guide to running a profitable farm in the Late Republic, he could not resist repeating a few tall tales about the size of the pigs that were responsible for Gaul's large, tasty flitches. The mosaics and sculptures around the Roman Empire that began to celebrate seasonal agricultural work in the imperial period never included pigs in their cycles—except in Gaul (fig. 4.3). Even into the Merovingian period a Byzantine physician named Anthimus would repeat the old claim to fame, remarking to one of the sons of Clovis, King Theuderic I, that he knew how the Franks loved their bacon.[61] And because northern Gaul in particular had been providing supplies to the armies along the lower Rhine, it is possible that the pigs in the *Lex Salica* were the

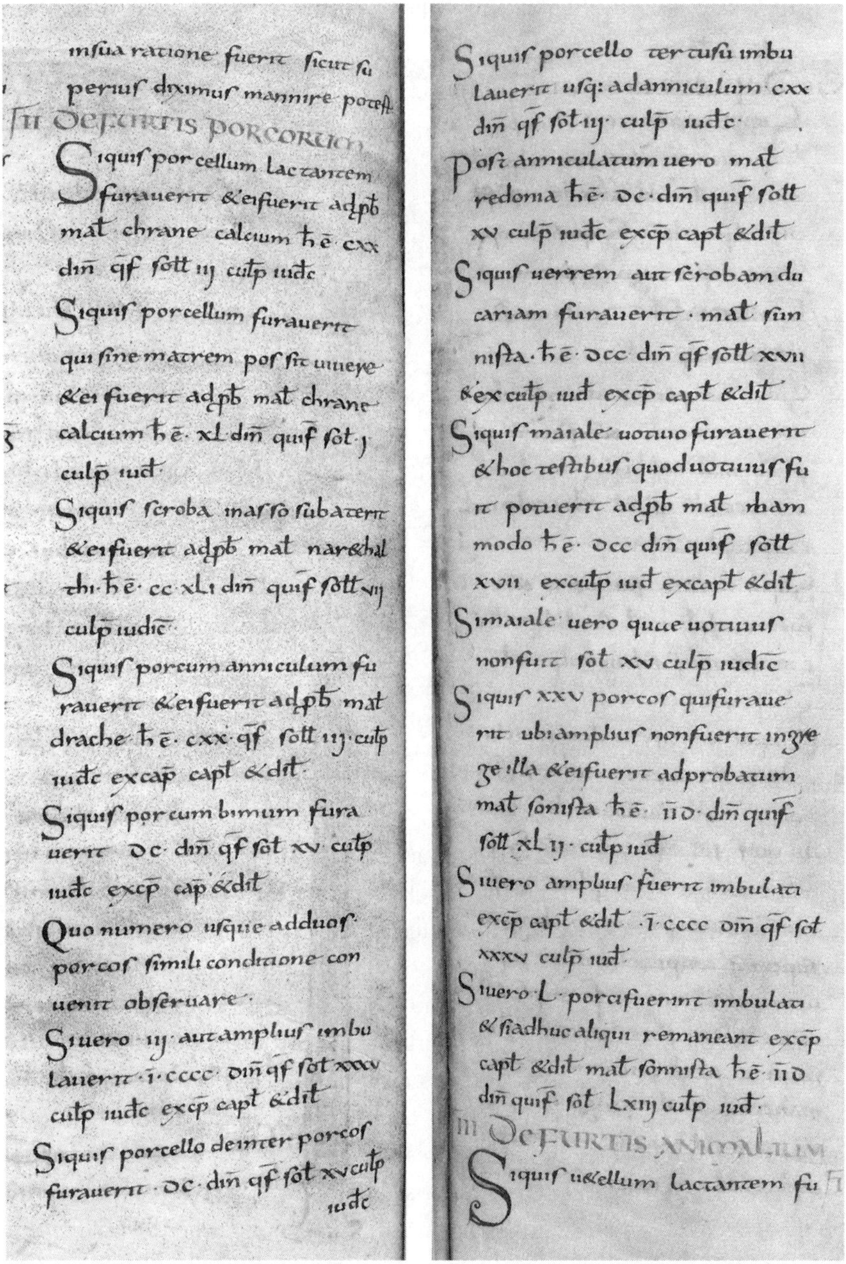

Fig. 4.2. *De furtis porcorum*, "Thefts of Pigs." This manuscript, and its early version of the *Lex Salica*'s pig list, was in the possession of Charlemagne's legal team when they researched different versions of the code and drew up their own edition at the start of the ninth century. It was probably produced in Tours. (Paris, Bibliothèque nationale de France, Ms. Lat. 4404, ff. 180v–181r.)

Fig. 4.3. Detail of pig butchery (November) from the Porte de Mars in Reims, built in the last decades of the second century. The arcade has not survived, so we are reliant on drawings done in the seventeenth and eighteenth centuries, including this one by Jacques Martine Silvestre Bence. (From Alexandre de Laborde, *Les monumens* [sic] *de la France, classés chronologiquement*, vol. 1 [Paris: Didot L'Aîné, 1816], [pl. CXIII]. Photo by John Blazejewski/Princeton University. Courtesy of Marquand Library of Art and Archaeology, Princeton University.)

descendants of annona pigs, memories of a state supply chain. Or maybe the pigs in the law code, like the code itself, represented a deliberate alternative to Roman infrastructure and constituted a new system of provisioning—one which nevertheless was shaped in response to a Roman pork economy.[62]

For a society in which pig husbandry was so conspicuous a part of economic life, the *Lex Salica* used these animals to establish a template for what constituted threats to the community and even the kingdom as a whole. The code was concerned with more than compensation, since a fine had to be paid in addition to damages and interest. As Karl Ubl has argued, these fines measured a crime's larger implications. The point was to represent private, individual losses as consequential for an entire public order. A pig-herding bell was not actually worth the fifteen solidi that were attached to the crime of stealing one; instead the penalty was a measure of how serious a problem stray pigs, and an act of intentional malice, could be.[63]

The pig list was also pointedly departing from the Roman laws of livestock rustling. The section is introduced in manuscripts as *De furtis porcorum*, "Thefts of Pigs," which would have struck many jurists as a surprising choice.

In a Roman legal framework, thefts of a certain number of animals would amount to rustling (*abigeatus*) rather than theft (*furtum*). And unlike theft, rustling was classed as an act of banditry, a form of organized violence that rattled the authority of the state and was punishable by death. Driving off five pigs was enough to count as rustling according to the North African juristic work known as the *Sentences of Paul,* and this was echoed by the Ostrogothic *Edict* of Theoderic when it was drawn up a few decades after the *Lex Salica,* at some point between 500 and 512. In the 530s, the *Digest* (a massive legal compendium drawn up by the eastern Roman emperor Justinian) quoted the third-century jurist Callistratus at four or five pigs.[64] But the *Lex Salica* rejected the concept of rustling entirely. Its enumeration of fines for stealing two pigs, three or more pigs, twenty-five pigs, or fifty pigs makes clear that all these crimes were *thefts* (*furta*), not rustling. The point was to methodically decouple capital punishment from these violations and forecast the code's rejection of penal torture and execution more generally.[65]

So the pig list had both mundane and radical implications. Pragmatically, it provided a scale for measuring the severity of other crimes. From just one suckling piglet among its many siblings to a herd of fifty pigs, a community's sensitivity to the value of these animals would have provided a proxy for loss and indemnity. Coinage could not have done this on its own; it had to be paired with crimes whose consequences were clear. And in creating this system of measurement, the codification of these seemingly minuscule details of rural life were what made the *Lex Salica*'s political theory so high-minded. Public interest extended to even the littlest piglet.

After the *Lex Salica* had first been issued, subsequent kings and legal communities interpreted and modified its laws and occasionally released new "editions" of the code. Already by the middle of the sixth century, the *Lex* had ceased to work in the way we might expect, as a list of laws that were consulted and enforced in their particulars. Instead it became a reference book for the kings of the Franks, a document they consulted (and updated) when they were seeking inspiration or guidance for their own policies and laws. It had a touch of the mystical about it.[66]

But it is striking that even as the code was acquiring its status as an ancient touchstone, lawmakers were still interested in tinkering with its pig list to accord with their own agrarian understanding. As the code was scaled *up* out of consideration for what had become a large kingdom that encompassed different identities, legal traditions, and environments, the pig provisions were also expanded and, in a sense, scaled *down* to become even more specific.

Roughly a century after the *Lex* was originally issued, for example, one of the grandsons of Clovis, King Chilperic I (r. 561–584), developed what is known as version *C* of the *Lex*.[67] This updated version added a couple of additional types of pig theft and elaborated some of the laws that were already in place. For the first time, the *Lex* now considered the category of birth order (alongside the categories of sex, age, and herd size) as a significant criterion for gauging the stakes of a crime: its editors modified the first pig law of the list, which dealt with the theft of a suckling piglet, to pertain to suckling piglets from the first or second litter specifically, and added an additional law about third-litter piglets. (They were worth more.) The editors of version *C* of the *Lex Salica* also added provisions for piglets stolen from a locked pen, piglets stolen while the swineherd was present, and piglets stolen together with their mother. And they specified that the original code's law regarding a theft of three or more pigs only applied to up to a maximum of six stolen pigs.[68] This was hardly the last time the code was changed. When Pippin, the first Carolingian king, overhauled the code in the 760s, he cut the pig list down to half its original length, but he also added an additional penalty for the theft of a herd of fifteen pigs, while keeping the provisions for thefts of twenty-five and fifty pigs.[69] And in Charlemagne's version of the *Lex Salica,* whose drafters had consulted all the editions in circulation, the pig list was expanded to include twenty laws, with some minor modifications for the sake of clarity. For example: because Chilperic's *C* version (which Charlemagne treated as the most authoritative edition) had added a provision about stealing piglets from a locked pen, Charlemagne's editors modified the *A* version's provision about stealing piglets to apply specifically to a herd out at pasture.[70]

We are almost out of the fine print, but a final set of examples gives another angle on how lawmakers and legal scholars were thinking about the microrealities of pigs as part of their statecraft. These have to do with language. The code is in Latin, but in the Merovingian redactions of the *Lex Salica,* most varieties of pig theft are glossed with words in an older dialect of Frankish that probably even struck Frankish speakers at the time as archaic. The code would introduce these words with the phrase *in mallobergo* ("in legal terminology"), and so today they are called the "Malberg glosses." The point of including them may have been to give the code an aura of ancient legitimacy by employing an arcane linguistic register. Because the Carolingians mostly got rid of them in their own editions, and because even Chilperic's version cuts back on them, they probably represent the earliest layer of Merovingian legal activity—though we must keep in mind that the copyists of the oldest editions, which continued to circulate alongside the new ones, still retained the glosses and occasionally even changed them![71] The fit between these glossed words and the Latin is inexact. A law against causing a pregnant sow to abort, for example, glosses the animal as *narechalti*, which technically meant a nursing sow. Or "pigsty" (*sutis cum porcis*) is glossed in some manuscripts as "barn" (*sundeba*) while others call it a shelter or stall (*leodeba*). Some of these discrepancies between the Latin and the glosses might simply indicate a patchy knowledge of the older Frankish language, but some suggest more clearly that copyists were also reinterpreting the code in light of the agrarian situations they were more familiar with. In particular, the theft of a dedicatory boar—a *maialis votivus*, in the original—was variously glossed as "offering of a castrated boar" (*barcho bagine*), "castrated boar dedicated to the watch-house" (*chuc cham rham modo*), "property of the village" (*baragameo amitheotho*), or in the cryptic Latin emendation of Chilperic's *C* version, some kind of specially designated (*sacrivus*) boar.[72] Whether the original castrated boar had religious significance or not (and it is hard for us to tell one way or the other today), it is clear that later interpreters were working to reevaluate the law in light of their own agricultural and cultural worlds.

All these shifts over the centuries might seem insignificant to us now, but they point to variations in the ways pigs were raised and valued, and they indicate that legal experts were interested in adjusting an important legal code to better fit circumstances that made more sense to them. And that elaborate matrix helped them focus the kingdom's many corners on the center. Not only in its pig list but throughout its laws, this was a code that was stretched to straddle both central authority and the local perspectives that the Merovingian kingdom and, later, the Carolingian empire comprised.[73] So the redactors of the *Lex Salica* were trying to link the particular to the public, and to implicate singular organisms and incidents in the whole. Their efforts were based on an understanding that a realm's fate was tied to smaller-scale communities, and that the political order was intertwined with the material culture of farms and fences as much as it was tied to the courts. The changes they made to the code, however subtle they seem—in fact, *because* of their subtlety—offer a long-term view of pigs' modest influence upon that scalar sensibility. Pigs were still integral to the state, but in this new state they were more than a tax. They had become a hinge between local and royal political economies.

Tastes

If swineherds and pigs formed a rough partnership in the process of raising pigs, and if states and pigs shaped each other through the annona and the laws, a third sort of assemblage converged in the act of consumption. For eaters of different sorts, pork helped define their experiences and even their identities apart from what other people were eating and tasting. But pigs were not just an instrument of difference. They also generated their own force. Even in death, they could push people around.

That "pushiness" was possible because the act of eating was seen to be a vital link between humans and the world outside them. In late antique and early medieval epistemology, taste and smell were good guides to the truth. Unlike the eyes, which were the most important sense organs but also the most fallible, the nose and tongue encountered and transmitted information that was less likely to deceive. Sensory inputs were not interchangeable—you could not learn the same thing from your ears as you could with your skin—but what you learned from tasting and smelling was more reliable. Taste was special for another reason, too. Although all the senses were believed to involve physical contact between the self and the world, taste went farther. Taste internalized and absorbed what it was perceiving and learning to know. It collapsed the boundary between subject and object.[74] This theory of taste was especially pronounced in discussions of Eucharistic eating. But even the pigs that humans raised would eventually become them, transform them, give them a surefire sense of a piece of the universe.

So it mattered all the more what pigs had done in their lifetimes, because those actions had ramifications for their flesh, and for the flesh of the people who consumed them. Had a pig eaten a dead animal, tasted human blood, or chewed on a human corpse? Some Christians refused to eat it if it had. Had it gorged itself on figs? This was supposed to make a delicious foie gras. Had it munched on roots in the woods? Pliny thought this made its fat all the more valuable as a medicine, because roots themselves were medically useful.[75] And although ancient and medieval eaters would not have known this, their animals would make atomic imprints on their very skeletons, which are visible to osteoarchaeologists today. The analysis of stable isotopes present in bone collagen can show the transfer of chemical elements down the food chain. Cattle eating sugarcane scraps in late medieval Valencia, for example, acquired a C_4 isotopic signature that they passed on to the Christians and Muslims who ate *them*.[76]

The possibilities for a dead pig were, well, legion. They could be killed very young, or raised to subadulthood, at which point their lips, shoulders, bellies, udders, haunches, loins, feet, tails, entrails, and sweetbreads could be baked, boiled, simmered, poached, fried, roasted, grilled, or turned on a rotisserie.

Their skin could be pickled in honey mustard. ("*Miraberis!* It will wow you!" the recipe raves.) Their intestines could be used as sausage casings. Their lard could be spread on bread. Leftover bacon fat could be drizzled on vegetables. Their brains could flavor a fish stew. Their unusually greasy bones could make a stock or be thrown to lucky dogs. And the porcine uterus was a prize delicacy that connoisseurs graded based on the age of the sow, the number of litters she had birthed, and when she had been killed relative to her most recent delivery—which made this food an easy target for Ambrose when he wanted to complain about rich people and their appetites.[7] There were extra-culinary ways to use pigs' bodies, too. Their skins were rarely used for book production before the late Middle Ages. But shoemakers used their bristles for shoes. Their lard could be used to grease machinery—"axle grease" was the literal meaning of the word for "lard," *axungia*—or to polish and waterproof boots. It could also be used as lamp fuel, but it was seen as an inferior product, used only when olive oil was unavailable. Their bladders might be inflated and used as balloons or toy balls for children. The long bones of their feet, or metapodials, could be hollowed out and turned into "buzz bones": think miniature kazoos, minus the membrane (fig. 4.4). And according to ancient and early medieval medical theories, pigs' organs and effluvia had great curative potential. Depending on the medical authority, their brains or blood or a concoction of both was a possible remedy for boils, warts, and sexually transmitted infections. Their brains could also soothe the gums of a teething baby, not to mention several other applications. Their bellies, in the form of bacon, could be boiled and wrapped around a broken bone to help it set; and the Franks were reputed to use it raw as a panacea. Their spleens were good for human spleens. Their marrow could be applied to inflamed eyes—or taken as an aphrodisiac. Their lungs, when roasted and eaten, were supposed

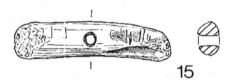

Fig. 4.4. This 2.4-inch (61 mm) "buzz bone" was carved from a pig metapodial in the tenth or eleventh century, on the late Saxon settlement of West Cotton, in the Nene Valley in England. (From Chapman, *West Cotton, Raunds*, fig. 11.40, no. 15. Drawing by Lesley Collett. Reproduced with permission from Andy Chapman for Northamptonshire Archaeology, Northamptonshire City Council.)

to keep a heavy drinker from getting drunk. Their livers were said to reduce the frequency of urinating or defecating. Their hooves, when cremated, could treat dental, urinary, and podiatric problems. One late antique medical writer named Marcellus also glowingly recommended this product as a toothpaste: "They make your teeth sparkling white!" Pigs' testicles alleviated epilepsy, and the genitals of both sexes were medically useful for the genitals of humans of the opposite sex. Their semen was said to cure earaches. Their milk could induce labor or encourage a healthy production of milk in nursing mothers. Their urine could be mixed with other ingredients then poured in the ear to combat hearing loss. Their feces (sometimes fresh, sometimes desiccated or burnt) could be applied as a topical ointment for a surprising array of issues, most commonly for skin and joint problems. This apparently disgusted some late antique readers, because one medical writer repeatedly urged them not to be embarrassed. And pigs' gall—the most effective of animal-based medicines, Pliny insists—was a potent potion for all sorts of internal and external sicknesses. Pig fat was a close second, and in late antique and early medieval medical texts, one of the commonest base ingredients in healing remedies was *adeps porcina* or axungia: lard.[78]

These myriad suggestions come from a limited number of sources: Pliny's *Natural History*, which was itself based on other materials; late antique and early medieval spinoffs of Pliny and other medical texts, whose authors and compilers were not simply repeating ancient wisdom but adding their own insights to the mix; the satirical fourth-century *Will of a Piglet*, in which the testator bequeaths various parts of his body as legacies; a collection of recipes and medicines attributed to a gourmet named Apicius that was compiled in its final form around 400 CE; a cookbook that the Apicius collection inspired written by one Vindarius, perhaps in the fifth or sixth century; Anthimus's text on food and health, which the Byzantine physician had written for Theuderic in the sixth century; and passing references to meals in narrative and poetic texts. Besides the fact that this list is fairly short, it points to another problem: almost nobody in the post-imperial West wrote down recipes except Vindarius, the people who copied his cookbook, and Apicius (or whoever wrote the book attributed to him). If we were to count the pork preparations recommended in the medical texts as early medieval recipes, we might add Anthimus to this list, because he lived in Italy for a time, and certainly the compilers who copied and updated Pliny and assorted late antique medical texts such as Serenus's *Liber medicinalis*, the *Medicina Plinii*, the *Alphabetum Galieni*, Marcellus's *De medicamentis liber*, and the *Physica Plinii*.[79] But the cookbook as we think of it was not considered an important genre in the early medieval West. (In the eastern Mediterranean, many chefs, physicians, poets, and even caliphs wrote cookbooks for the 'Abbāsid courts, and countless other men and women jotted down or explained recipes that went into circulation. These no longer survive in their original form, but some of them were anthologized in the oldest Arabic cookbook that does survive, written by al-Warrāq in the 940s or 950s. There are no pigs in these pages.)[80] For the most part, like swineherding, cooking was an art that one had to learn in person. But although this absence of written material is especially hard to understand today, when we are swimming in recipes and food photography, we should not take it as a sign that cooking was considered unimportant.

The ceramic evidence is another potential clue—and an underutilized one—when it comes to culinary culture. As styles of cooking change, so does cookware. At the winery of Villa Magna southeast of Rome, the residents replaced their pans with deep casserole dishes in the sixth and seventh centuries, and they also used more lidded jars and mortars than had residents in the settlement's earlier days as an imperial villa. So it seems likely that cooking methods and preferences had changed: this generation was apparently eating more stews, soups, and sauces. Ceramics can also point to cuisine at a microscopic level. Unglazed pottery can absorb the lipids, or fatty acids, of animal products and preserve them for thousands of years; the carbon isotope values of those residues can point to the specific animal products that people were using. At the estate of Flixborough (the estate in northern England that was catching dolphins and many wild birds), the lipid residues from eighth- and ninth-century vessels show that the residents were cooking with the fat or marrow or bones or milk of ruminants, and with the fat of pigs, geese, and chickens. And of course, we have the bones themselves, which can point to features of food preparation, too. At Wroxeter in Britain, the early medieval meat market moved away from late Roman butchery techniques, in which cleavers were used to chop straight through joints and bones, toward fileting meat off the bone with knives before sale.[81] The butchers may have been responding to a change in tastes as much as anything else.

Although pigs' bodies presented an almost limitless array of possibilities, certain ways of cooking and eating were intertwined with social groups as much as the meat itself was. Food has a "morphology" and a "syntax," as the historian Massimo Montanari has put it: the ways it is prepared and the contexts in which it is eaten can completely change its character.[82] A pig's head in the Late Republic, for example, could be prepared in a way that distinguished it as a delicacy known as *siniciput*. But the head could also be cured and brought aboard ships to feed sailors on their voyages (as one shipwreck attests, also from the Late Republic), or it could be turned into sausages, which is probably what early medieval eaters who got stuck with all those heads did with them.[83]

In the grammar of pork, the recipes that survive were often speaking in an elite register, with their talk of pork-liver patties cooked three ways—roasted, then smoked in laurel-leaf packages, then finished on the grill—or of uterus dumplings (mixed with cumin, leeks, rue, garum, and nuts) poached in an oily and fishy broth with a bouquet garni of leeks and dill. But some of their recommendations are much simpler, such as a dish of mushrooms seasoned with salt, or snails simmered in milk and flour, or chopped meat fried in fish sauce and glazed with honey.[84] We do not know much about the meals that most early medieval cooks made, but we should not underestimate their options or their talents, given the wide range of ingredients that paleobotanists have found in their settlements. The farmers of Develier-Courtételle were growing, among other things, dill, cilantro, celery, and mustard greens—each of which, according to the Apicius recipes, made a delicious accompaniment to peas or fava beans (which the farmers at Develier-Courtételle also cultivated).[85]

So middling farmers may have eaten very well, and they may have sought some of the same flavor profiles as the cooks who worked for elite diners. But they were probably eating less meat. One metric for this is the presence of nitrogen isotopes in human bone collagen: a greater value of $\delta^{15}N‰$ points to a greater share of animal protein relative to plant protein in a diet. When it is possible to determine the relative social status of the subjects who are tested, the elites usually show signs of having eaten more meat. Besides the stable isotope analysis of human skeletons (which is becoming increasingly common but is still expensive to do), animal remains offer more indirect metrics for gauging the quantity of meat consumption among early medieval communities. Scorch marks on animal bones are infrequent, which suggests that most households were preserving their meat to make it last through the year by smoking or dry salting or brining it. And a common way to make that meat last would have been to add a few pieces to a stew simmered with grain, vegetables, and a heaping of fresh herbs. This dish was called pottage, and it has left traces at the bottoms of ceramic cooking vessels found around Europe.[86] Wealthier eaters, on the other hand, were able to eat fresh meat more frequently and to feature it as a main course or entrée, rather than restrict themselves to charcuterie. In our age, when a barbecue seems to be a democratic meal, it is easy to overlook how cooking fresh pork and eating it on the spot can be an ostentatious use of resources. Even in the American South, folksy mythology about "traditional" cooking has obscured the fact that before the mid-twentieth century "a chance to eat barbecue was typically a treat provided by others": by white slaveholders at their plantation parties, by politicians at their rallies, and by churches at their fundraisers.[87]

More generally, landed elites throughout the West (if they were Christian) often ate a higher percentage of pork, relative to other meats, than the regional averages. This had already been true in the imperial period, during which the inhabitants of villas often ate more pork than their neighbors. And in the early Middle Ages, we can find other clues. The Old Irish saga *Scéla mucce Meic Dathó* (*The Tale of the Pig of Mac Dathó*), which was written around 800 and retold for many more centuries after that, centers on a feast that the king of Leinster has thrown for the warriors of the kingdoms of Ulster and Connaught. The centerpiece is an enormous pig. In good saga style, subtle matters of etiquette and status have serious consequences: there is competition over who gets to carve the pig, and the winner is so stingy in apportioning the meat to the elite warriors from Connaught that the banquet ends in war. Outside literature, when archaeologists are able to confirm the elevated status of a settlement through certain clues—the presence of riding gear, for example, or glassware, coinage, weapons, and jewelry—the inhabitants will also tend to betray an appetite for pork.[88]

So for example when the gymnasium complex of the Roman-British town of Wroxeter evolved into a marketplace and then into an elite or episcopal residence in the sixth and seventh centuries, its pork consumption increased, and so did its consumption of younger cattle. The residents were also tapping into long-distance markets: they had pottery from the Levant, and, more unexpectedly, a Barbary macaque, which had been imported from its home in North Africa. The Carolingian palace of Paderborn ate significantly more pork than the nearby settlements of Soest and Höxter, which ate primarily beef. At the settlement of Karlburg in northern Bavaria, both the occupants of the fortress and the inhabitants of the valley below ate a great deal of pork—but the elites in the fortress, who had more resources than their neighbors, ate even more of it: it was the predominant meat in their diets. We also have the spectacular example of an estate in the Parisian basin called Serris "Les Ruelles," a site that included an elite complex of four stone buildings flanked to the east and northeast by peasant settlements, along with a church and cemetery to the northeast (fig. 4.5). The elite center features an extremely high proportion of pig remains compared to other animals (pigs are about 75 percent of the total),

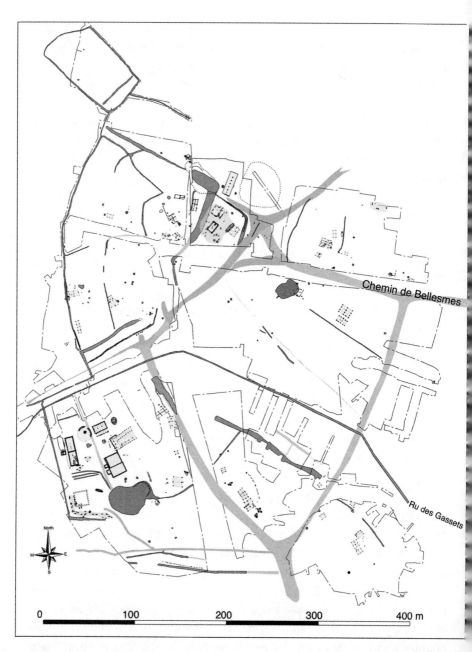

Fig. 4.5. Serris "Les Ruelles" in the eighth century. Pork consumption there concentrated on the elite complex in the southwest zone of the settlement. (Courtesy of François Gentili [INRAP].)

as well as luxury foods that included peacock, sturgeon, and oysters. In the nonelite zones, the presence of pig drops and the proportion of cattle rises.[89]

This elite preference for pork was a tendency, not a rule. For one thing, early medieval societies were not split unambiguously between elite and nonelite classes. Social status was as finely variegated as geography was: it was a spectrum, rather than a fixed point.[90] Households and settlements could therefore eat a combination of ordinary and sumptuous meals. The thriving village at Delle sur le Marais, for example, in Calvados on the plain of Caen, lacked the standard telltale forms of prestige but butchered an astonishingly high number of piglets, 17 percent of all its pigs.[91] Most farmers preferred to treat piglets as a low-cost investment in future meat, rather than waste them while they were little, but eaters who could afford the extravagance were happy to eat as many as they could. The abbot of Prüm, for example, insisted that his tenants at Rhein-Gönheim personally deliver piglets to him whenever he was in the area, and several of the same monastery's tenants closer to its home base were required to send young pigs to Prüm whenever the king came to visit.[92]

But some people with means opted for other meats instead of pork. At the hilltop village of Miranduolo in eighth-century Tuscany, the workshop of the blacksmith, who may have been a prominent figure in the village, seems to have had unusually steady access to the hind-limbs of cows, ovicaprids, and pigs, and the consumers there were eating more beef and more mutton or goat than their neighbors.[93] The elite-pork connection is also unverifiable in many places, because there are few settlements that show an obvious "elite" presence almost anywhere in the post-imperial West of the later fifth and sixth centuries. This does not mean elites did not exist—the textual record makes clear that they did—but they are hard to locate in the built environment. This is partly because elites were generally less rich than their counterparts in Late Antiquity. And it is partly because people who had wealth were using it in different ways. They were no longer building villas or civic monuments (though North Africans offer a partial exception to this trend). Instead they were giving it to churches. They were building walls for towns and other settlements. They were burying their dead with precious objects. They may have even been founding or taking ownership of villages in order to invest in local agriculture. Starting in the seventh century, sites in Francia, England, Ireland, and Scandinavia begin to show a greater range of statuses, and this in turn makes it possible for archaeologists to recognize that in these regions an above-average consumption of pork was often one of the perks of being wealthy. But in Iberia, Italy, eastern Europe, and rural North Africa these distinctions are harder to make, because here the wealthy or politically powerful are for the most part not identifiable archaeologically until the ninth and tenth centuries.[94]

The pork-leaning tendencies of early medieval elites whom we *can* identify persisted into the age of *incastellamento*. In the tenth and eleventh centuries, different sorts of fortified settlements were becoming a more regular feature of the western landscape, and with the construction of walled habitations, mottes, towers, and castles, we often see a concomitant uptick in pork consumption when those sites are Christian. The proportion of pigs at the settlement of Goltho, in Lincolnshire, jumped from 8 percent of the total animal remains to 31 percent when the site transformed from a village into a fortified elite residence in the late ninth century. Pigs also dominated at the motte of Haus Meer, a settlement that rose out of the Rhine wetlands (whose warrior inhabitants also seem to have had an appetite for kirschwein). At the castle of Mur, located in the militarized frontier zone of the Montsec range in Catalonia, the counts of Pallars Jussà enjoyed luxuries like windows and washbasins, and they also kept more pigs than any other animal. And pork was the favored meat at the lakeside fortification of Colletière, which for forty years at the start of the eleventh century was an unambiguously prestigious residence on the shores of the Lac de Paladru in southeast France, with masterfully engineered timber frames, a knife-manufacturing business, musical instruments, games, riding equipment, jewelry, weaponry, coinage, and imported ceramics, glass, almonds, and figs. But in this period, too, there were exceptions to the pattern. To take just one example: inhabitants of the mining village of Rochette Pannocchieschi in the Colline Metallifere of Tuscany ate a markedly high amount of pork in the eighth to tenth centuries (over 60 percent of the animal remains here came from pigs), but in the eleventh century, as the village was transforming into a stone castle, its share of pig bones dropped to the frequency of sheep and goats and was later surpassed by ovicaprids in the 1100s.[95]

It would also be presumptuous to reverse the logic and suggest that the presence of an unusually high proportion of pig bones at a settlement automatically indicates privilege. Pigs were not a luxury animal per se. Other animals had a more consistently elevated pedigree. In Greenland, walrus bacula (penis bones) were treated as trophies because the walrus hunt constituted the precious core of the island's economy. Or in Gaul and England, the presence of certain animals—such as peacocks, dolphins, porpoises, and sturgeon—indicate what the archaeologist Christopher Loveluck has referred to as "feasting kits": they are giveaway signs that we are dealing with gourmet consumption. Oysters could go either way. The household in the city center of Tours that we met briefly in the previous chapter may have eaten them because the Loire estuary was not far away. But at the villa of San Giovanni di Ruoti, folded into the mountainous interior of Lucania, the staggering quantity of saltwater oysters uncovered was an unmistakable luxury. For an estate that was as far inland on the Italian peninsula as it could be, the oysters had probably been acquired at five times their cost on the coast. For similar reasons, the *absence* of fish at the tenth-century site of Bir Ftouha, outside Carthage, may be a sign that elite eaters lived there. In addition to importing all their pottery (a truly unusual situation), and eating young, meaty livestock, they might have also snubbed marine resources because they were all too common on the coast![96]

Domesticated pigs were not coded as prestige animals in the same way that peacocks or walruses were, or even in the sliding-scale way that oysters and fish were, and this had a lot to do with the pigs themselves: they could flourish almost anywhere, and despite their obstinacy and cleverness they were easily accessible because they were domesticated. But a pork-rich diet was often political, in the sense that it depended on and generated forms of personal and state power. The higher rate of pork consumption among wealthier eaters reflected more than the constraints of environments and economies that developed in dovetail with pig husbandry. It also reflected their entitlements as landowners, because (as we have seen) some farmers would have owed pigs to landowners as pannage payments, and others paid pigs as part of their tenancies. Some of these tenants were free, and some were not, and sometimes pig payments of free tenants were described as "gifts." (This was a way of expressing a relationship of reciprocity, even though it was a highly imbalanced one.)[97] And so the differences in higher and lower pork consumption were causally related: elites were eating more pork because they were getting it from people who were obligated to provide it to them.

This is not to say that consumption patterns were fixed by class. Food was a discourse that eaters used strategically, and archaeologists are increasingly coming to appreciate this.[98] One of the best studied cases concerns the traders who operated in the North and Baltic Seas. Christopher Loveluck and Dries Tys have shown that these merchants—and the artisans who worked with them—used foods and goods to manipulate cultural codes, rather than to simply reflect the status they already had. They were not landed elites. They worked out of Gaul's northern estuaries and the English and Scandinavian coasts. And yet they had ready access to products that were otherwise only available to wealthy landowners. The trading communities living in England's ports, for example, feasted on whale meat, walnuts, grape seeds, and cilantro.

All of these were luxury foods in the North, or at least they would have been to settlements that were not close neighbors to international emporia.[99]

And so the inhabitants of Delle sur le Marais, the village in Calvados with a high percentage of piglet bones among its trash, may have been eating in a similarly aspirational spirit. But piglets were not the only animals that gave them a taste of power. This village is also one of four places in Gaul known to have possessed a four-horned sheep (fig. 4.6), though archaeologists have found others in Britain, Scandinavia, the Low Countries, and Egypt. In most livestock, polyceracy (having more than two horns) is usually a random accident of birth. But among sheep it is a genetic mutation that can be encouraged through selective breeding, and Gaul's specimens had probably been imported as exotics from breeders across the North Sea, where the animals were somewhat commoner.[100] One of Gaul's other polycerate sheep was found at a Merovingian palace outside Sens, but Delle sur le Marais, about two hundred miles to the northwest of the palace, was a very different kind of site. The village enjoyed some forms of elite consumption (such as its piglets) and long-distance connectivity, but in other respects it was a fairly unassuming community. And yet here was this four-horned foreigner, fit for a royal residence,

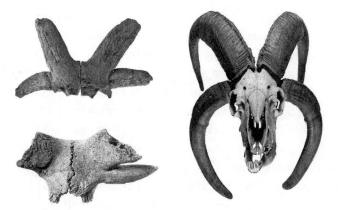

Fig. 4.6. Skulls of male polycerate sheep. The top left skull was found at the Merovingian palace outside Sens (at Malay-le-Grand) and dates to the sixth or seventh century. The bottom left skull is from Delle sur le Marais. The skull on the right is a modern specimen for comparison, now at the Muséum d'Histoire naturelle de Genève. (From O. Putelat, "Des littoraux nordiques à la Bourgogne?" [2007]. Photographs by Olivier Putelat [Archéologie Alsace] and Jean-Hervé Yvinec [INRAP].)

an alluring testimony to the world's dizzying array of creatures. Its "uncanny" presence among the other livestock might have given a surreal tinge to the farm and made it something special.[101]

Today we tend to assume that the most obvious fault line of pork consumption was religious difference, but in the early Middle Ages the situation was not so sharply defined. Early medieval religious culture was as internally differentiated and dynamic as elite culture was, and the practices of eating or avoiding pork among religious communities are another example of how diet was an active force in material and social ecologies as well as an expression of them. As we will see, the pig became an increasingly complex Christian symbol in the early Middle Ages—but it could also be fairly said that pigs participated in the process of Christianization because they were never simply symbols. They were flesh-and-blood animals that altered lives and institutions while they lived, and bodies and identities when they were dead. Even recent converts to Christianity were soberly aware of this, as we learn from a group of "Hebrew" citizens of Toledo. They were called this because they were Jews who had converted to Catholicism, and in 654 they sent a letter to King Recceswinth to bring him up to date about their religious commitment since their conversion a few decades previously.[102]

This community assured the king that they were still Christians, that they believed fully in Christ, and that they had abandoned practices that would have suggested any residual affiliation with Judaism. They would not socialize with people who were unbaptized. They would obey Christian rules of consanguinity when it came to contracting lawful marriages. They would not practice circumcision, or celebrate Passover or the Sabbath. But they hedged a bit when it came to pork. They agreed that no distinctions should made among foods (because Christians were not supposed to consider certain foods unclean). But even though they recognized that pork was now a licit meat, the most they would promise was that they would be willing to eat food that had been cooked with a little pork, rather than say more sweepingly that they would eat pork in any form. It was well established in rabbinic tradition that to eat pork was to become "the Other," to defect to the side of non-Jews both symbolically and physically. But these Christian converts could not bring themselves to do it.[103]

Their reluctance was not for lack of trying. Throughout this letter the Toledan community strongly implied that all these concessions represented difficult adjustments for them because they departed from the customs that their families had practiced for generations. They knew that tasting pork was socially and historically conditioned, because they were trying, with great difficulty, to counteract the "nausea and horror" (*fastidio et orrore*) they had once felt at the thought of eating a forbidden meat. Their visceral reactions were rooted in the antiquity (*vetustas*) of their traditions.[104] And in saying these things to the king, they were pointing out that changing one's tastes required a conversion of the innermost kind, not of the mind on its own, but more profoundly the turning of a body away from itself and from the foodways that had sculpted it. Not all Christians thought that the changing of identity required the eating and absorption of pork, as we will see. But it was a widely shared conviction that eating was a transformative process on somatic, cognitive, and cultural levels. And it was another way in which pigs were remaking human lives and identities.

5 • The Christianization of the Pig

In the Christian cosmos, everything was designed and brought into being by God, and every part of that creative masterwork had the potential to reveal something significant about the whole. But certain components of the universe seemed to be especially revealing. They appeared to work like hotspots (to use a modern metaphor), or like "commonplaces" (to use a medieval one), which connected the mind and memory to the world beyond. Christians turned to certain images again and again, and layered them with increasingly dense ideas to make sense of larger complex systems.[1] In the course of the early Middle Ages, the pig became one of these interpretive tools. It became a concept that helped Christians think through how the world worked, physically and metaphysically, and what their obligations within that world were.

The pig's Christianization might seem inevitable to us. Because Christians eat pork, and Muslims and Jews do not, we might assume that the pig had been a symbol of religious identity since those religions came into being. But we do not have the same expectations for frogs (which are also harām in Islam) or rabbits or shrimp (which orthodox Jews will not eat). The reason the pig seems to us to be an obviously meaningful boundary between the monotheistic traditions is because it *did* eventually become one—but only over the course of the early Middle Ages.

Pigs became Christian in other ways, beyond their role as a signature ingredient that insiders and outsiders highlighted as a mark of their difference from one another. In Late Antiquity and the early Middle Ages, Christians also began using pigs as a means of better understanding and defining their own religion—but again, this was centuries after they had condoned the eating of pork in the first place. In Latin Christendom, pigs came to represent the flesh.

The word for "flesh," *carnis,* was also the word for "meat." And because pigs were seen to embody meatiness so completely, they also gradually acquired the attributes that Christian commentators ascribed to flesh as a powerfully corrosive and redemptive force. Pigs became symbols of the ways that human bodies faltered in pleasure and selfishness. But as representatives of carnis they also came to stand for something transcendent. They stood for the salvation that God had made possible by taking his own fleshy body and sacrificing it.

Historians are more familiar with the negative side of pigs' split symbolism, because after 1100 or so, it took on an increasingly sinister aspect. The historian Michel Pastoureau has shown that the Capetian dynasty in France waged a publicity war against pigs after a pig caused the death of the junior king Philip in 1131. Philip had been crowned as the designated successor to his father, Philip VI, but a loose pig in the suburbs of Paris got under the foot of the horse Philip was riding, and the young co-king was mortally injured in the fall. The tragedy exposed the vulnerability of a royal family whose legitimacy was somewhat insecure at the time. The response of the Capetians and their supporters was to dub the culprit a *porcus diabolicus,* a "diabolical pig," and to cultivate a new alliance with the Virgin Mary and her personal color (blue) and flower (the lily or fleur-de-lis). In that way, we owe the lilies and blue pigments that flooded the interior of Sainte-Chapelle a century later to a pig![2] But there were uglier consequences. This porcus diabolicus was the start of increasingly vicious portraits and associations. The historian Isaiah Shachar and the anthropologist Claudine Fabre-Vassas have each examined the intensely anti-Semitic imagery that piled up in the figure of the pig in the late Middle Ages and early modern period, imagery that included the acidic figure known as the *Judensau* (an image of Jews sucking at the teats of a sow), and the twinning of Jews and pigs as leprous, bloody, castrated, odorous, and anti-Christian.[3]

What is less well known is that, even in the high Middle Ages, the figural pig was as positively Christian as it was counter-Christian.[4] The seeds of this seeming contradiction were sown centuries earlier. But despite this evolutionary link, the pigs of the early Middle Ages were not styled in the same way they would be in 1100 or 1400 or 1800, because like any culture or ecology, Christianity has changed.

The Roman Animal

Before the pig was Christian, it was Roman. We have seen throughout this book that the species inspired many complex judgments about its capacities, and that several different identities coalesced in the process of engaging with the animals. Romanness was only one of the pig's attributes in Late Antiquity and the early Middle Ages. But it was pervasive.

Latin writers sang the praises of pork, the empire made pork a part of its civic and military supply chains, and military forts and aristocratic villas were often (but not always) greater consumers of pork than their neighbors. In some places, pig husbandry and pork eating even increased significantly as an effect of Roman occupation. This was not true everywhere, and the extent to which the Romans transformed local foodways varied regionally and locally. The most dramatic instances have come from excavations in Tunisia, at sites with unusually long lifetimes. The small town of Althiburos, for example, in the High Tell of Numidia (near modern Médéïna, in northwest Tunisia) left a continuous record of animal bones from the start of settlement there in the late tenth–early ninth century BCE all the way into the sixth century CE. In the tenth to second centuries BCE, Althiburos was in the orbit of Phoenician Carthage, and over those eight hundred years or so, pig bones vacillated between about a twentieth to a quarter of the total remains of the main domesticates (in comparison to beef and ovicaprids). When the Romans came to town and began monumentalizing the urban spaces and scaling up cereal and olive agriculture, pork consumption also changed: pig bones shot up to 38.5 percent of the triad of domesticates. The numbers for Carthage itself are virtually identical: Romans were pushing out older pastoral systems in favor of more arable agriculture and more pigs.[5]

When Jews living in the Roman Empire thought about the pig, they too were struck by its imperial resonance.[6] Take the psalm about the boar ravaging the vine of Israel, number 80 in the Hebrew Bible. Before Pompey had conquered Judea in the first century BCE, Jewish readers (including the authors of Maccabees and the book of Enoch) had interpreted the psalm as an account of the profanation and destruction of the First Temple in 586. Later, rabbinic commentators reactivated these readings in light of the violence of Roman colonization. After Vespasian and Titus suppressed the Judean revolt and leveled the Second Temple in the first century CE, and then again after the enormously destructive Jewish-Roman war following the Bar Kokhba Revolt in the 130s, the imagery of the psalm became intensely and newly significant. Now it looked as if the vine of the people of Israel had been ravaged by the boar *of the Roman Empire*.[7] (Hebrew did not distinguish between domesticated and wild pigs: *ḥazir* was the term for both.) And the rabbis working in Late Antiquity saw the psalm's boar as homologous to the fourth beast that appeared in the dream of the prophet Daniel (chaps. 7–8). This fourth beast—which the rabbis saw as assimilating the figures of Edom, Rome, and pig—foretold the rise of a kingdom that would devour the whole world.[8]

The presence of Edom in this equation points to another association the rabbis made. They intertwined the figures of the pig and the Roman Empire with Esau, the twin brother of Jacob and the son of the patriarch Isaac. It was a rich elision of several lines of thinking, as the historian Misgav Har-Peled has pointed out. Whereas Jacob would father the nation of Israel, Esau was the progenitor of Edom, and because Edom was taken to be the evil empire that prefigured Rome, Esau was connected to pigs by way of Edom and Rome. But the late antique rabbis also saw Esau personally as a "sow." Esau had slept with non-Jewish women (Hittites specifically), which violated a prohibition that was often understood in the same category as pork avoidance. Both were rules about everyday behaviors that made Jews distinctive in the act of following them, and by breaking one Esau came to stand for the violation of both. As the rabbis also knew, Esau had been linked to the wild boar of Psalm 80 in the book of Enoch (1 Enoch 89:66–67), which was written well before Rome colonized Judea. In Enoch's reading of the psalm, the destruction of the vine was an account of the destruction of the First Temple, and Esau's descendants had been the ones responsible for its ruin. The cherry on top of this layer cake of associations between Esau and pigs was a delicious interlingual pun: Esau/ sow is an accidental pun in English but a very purposeful one in Hebrew, in which Esau's name (עֵשָׂו) plays on the Greek *sous*. Rather than mention this Greek word explicitly, however, the midrashim only hint at it through their Hebrew. (In one instance they even use the term *ḥazirah,* an unusual feminine form of the more typical *ḥazir* and the equivalent of the Greek *sous*.) This extra degree of allusiveness would have made the joke even better to an audience that would have known both Greek and Hebrew/Aramaic (and other languages). There are puns of this class throughout the Midrash and the Palestinian Talmud.[9]

There is yet another element to the Rome-Edom-Esau-pig connection, and it concerns the problem of lawbreaking. According to *Genesis Rabbah,* which was compiled in the fourth or fifth century CE, Esau "used to ensnare married women and violate them," and when he finally married at the age of forty, he had the audacity to compare himself to his father in a perverse attempt to manufacture legitimacy (because he was not marrying Jewish women). And in the *Midrash Psalms,* Esau is likened to the corrupt judges of Rome because he "displays himself so openly on the seats of justice that the legal tricks whereby he robs, steals, and plunders appear to be just proceedings."[10]

Pigs were still part of the picture here, though it might not be obvious to us why the midrashic commentators saw the species, along with Esau and Edom-Rome, as a cipher for deception and false justice. The issue for the rabbis was that the physical world did not always reflect with crystalline clarity the laws and ethics that ordered it. They said more than once that pigs *seemed* to be clean, even though Moses had established unambiguously that that they were not: "The swine who is cloven-hoofed but does not chew the cud [is unclean to you]" (Leviticus 11:7). And yet—to quote a passage we have seen before—commentators noted that "when the swine is lying down it puts out its hoofs, as if to say, 'I am clean.'"[11] A pig tries to pass as a ruminant, in other words, and so it commits the same gesture of misrepresenting itself that Esau and the Roman Empire were guilty of.

The vignette of a prone pig was partly a reminder that Jewish dietary restrictions were based on non-absolute taxonomies (not *all* cloven-hoofed animals or *all* ruminants are lawful to eat), and so any kind of shortcut for distinguishing clean from unclean animals was going to be insufficient. But the image also underscored a point that other rabbinic commentaries on Leviticus were making in Late Antiquity: the designation of this animal as unclean was essentially arbitrary. The avoidance of pork was not "natural," not rooted in any particular feature of the pig or its relationship to human beings. It was, essentially, a rule that Jews followed because God had instituted it. The point was to maintain the distinctions he had drawn without asking why they were there. In the high Middle Ages, some rabbis—most notably Maimonides, who wrote in the twelfth century—would change their tack and begin to *give reasons* for why pork was prohibited. These rationales were naturalist, in the sense that they explained the uncleanness of the pig as both ritually and literally true, as rooted in the animal's physical properties. According to these later explanations, pigs were dirty, disgusting, and bad for one's health.[12] But in the rabbinic culture of Late Antiquity and the early Middle Ages, nature was not so transparent a guide. Pigs, like Esau and Rome, seemed inoffensive to those who were ignorant of the law.

Many of these rabbinic commentaries were written or at least compiled in a post-Constantinian world; the evil empire of which they spoke was now governed by Christian emperors. But the rabbis did not stress the empire's Christianness—or even mention it. In part this omission would have been because some of the commentaries they were working with predated Constantine's conversion and the gradual Christianization of the Roman aristocracy. But it is striking how thoroughly the Rome of the Midrash and the Talmuds lacks a religious profile. Pigs, by extension, are not Christian either. The empire and the pig were only negations of the law, rather than representatives of something substantive.

Christian exegetes carried the association of Rome and pigs into their own biblical commentaries, and in their hands the Romanized pigs were equally bereft of Christian signification. This is surprising only if we assume that Romanness and Christianness were fused like bone in the late empire, at least among imperial subjects who saw both identities as positive values. But this was not the case. It is true that some Christians saw the Christianization of the empire as a triumph, and they paired the polity and the religion as victorious complements. Other Christians were more skeptical, however. Augustine of Hippo was one of them, and he argued that the success of the empire could not be so plainly expressive of Christianity's legitimacy because everything on earth—even a thousand-year-old empire—was inherently transitory, and Christianity was not. Augustine died in 430, at a time when the western half of the empire was just beginning to fracture and develop new forms of political order. Sometimes Romanness was excised from these models. We have seen, for example, that the *Lex Salica* was created as a deliberate alterative to Roman law in the later fifth century. But more often than not, the *idea* of Rome was still a captivating one, not only in Gaul but across the West, and it was coopted and reinvented in many different ways for centuries to come.[13]

And in these innovative centuries, the Roman pig remained resolutely non-Christian. Some Christian commentators interpreted the psalm about the boar with clear debts to the rabbinic tradition, and some even intensified the animal's Romanness—but this boar was never Christianized. To take two influential exegetes as examples: Eucherius of Lyon, who wrote a couple of interpretive handbooks in the fifth century after years of conversations with his friends and students, suggested that Psalm 79 (the Vulgate's numbering for Psalm 80) might have even been speaking *specifically* about Vespasian and Titus. Figurally the boar represented the devil, but historically it may have stood for the way the two emperors had wasted and consumed the Jews and Jerusalem in their military assaults. A century later, in the mid-500s, Cassiodorus, who was an exegete and former administrator in the Ostrogothic government, also tentatively suggested that the boar and the singular beast referred to the imperial duo. (It is worth remembering that the "singular beast" that appeared in Eucherius's and Casssiodorus's Latin Bibles was not present in the original Hebrew passage. The boar's two names here lent themselves nicely to the double personification of the emperors.) In Cassiodorus's reading, the excessive strength and savagery of the wild animal mirrored the way the two emperors devastated and ate up the people and the city as if they were fodder.[14]

In describing the boar's strength as excessive, *fortitudo nimia*, Cassiodorus may have been thinking of the passage in Daniel 7:7 that describes the fourth beast of the prophet's vision as excessively strong, *fortis nimis*. This was the same passage that the midrashic commentaries had linked to the Psalms through the common denominator of Rome, the empire that took the form of both beast and boar. So Cassiodorus might have been following Jewish exegesis here. There were thriving Jewish communities in places where he had lived and worked for years, including southern Italy, Rome, Constantinople, and possibly Ravenna. Alternatively he might have been taking a cue from a commentary on Daniel that Jerome had written about 150 years earlier. But in that commentary, Jerome had rejected the rabbinic equation of Daniel's fourth beast with the boar of Psalm 79/80. While Jerome agreed that this beast signaled the Roman Empire in the prophet's vision, he noted that Daniel himself had not identified what its animal avatar was—either because the beast did not resemble any actual wild animal, or because it was too terrifying to name—and that readers would picture whatever intimidating animal came to mind.[15]

Whatever the influences to be found in the work of Eucherius and Cassiodorus, their vision of the Roman boar is striking because it amplified the rabbinic position. They sharpened the animal's imperial identity without celebrating its Romanness. Eucherius and Cassiodorus are unambiguous in their judgments of Vespasian and Titus. They used verbs like *vastare* (to lay waste), *consumere* (to eat up), *conterere* (to obliterate) to underline the Romans' extreme violence. The excessive strength of the boar mirrored the excess of the emperors. And so the Roman animal never became a Christian one in the early Middle Ages. On the contrary: the church, like the people of Israel, was associated with the vine that the evil boar destroys.[16] In order for the pig to become Christian among Christians, it would have to shed its attachment to the empire.

The Romanness of the pig was legible to early Muslims, too. There are signs of it among the reports of the sayings of the Prophet Muhammad and his Companions—narratives known as the hadith—in a rich set of apocalyptic traditions from the Umayyad period (661–750). Some of these accounts prophesized that Jesus would be resurrected as a messianic guide to right wrongs in a new millennial age, and that one of his first acts would be to destroy all the crosses and pigs on earth.[17]

To a modern reader, these crosses and pigs seem to be Christian targets. But to a late antique person they would have been just as obviously Roman. The hadith were written down in the 'Abbāsid period, a century or more after the earliest informants had spoken them. But the coherence of certain apocalyptic materials suggests that they stemmed from events that had taken place in the first century of Islam, during the Arab and Umayyad conquests of territory that the eastern Roman Empire controlled, the Levant in particular. Muslims in Syria who experienced the wars with the eastern empire (or what Arabic speakers simply called *Rūm*)—the treaties made and broken, the Muslims' failure to capture Constantinople, the persistent threat of Roman reconquest until the 690s—were interpreting them as signals that heralded the end of the world, or at least as the start of a new apocalyptic cycle.[18]

Some Umayyad leaders made a point of exploiting that messianic mood in their ongoing campaigns. Christian chroniclers reported that the Umayyad caliph 'Abd al-Malik (685–705) ordered all the pigs in different conquered regions to be killed. One chronicler added that the caliph had all the crosses taken down, as well. Muslim historians reported that one of the caliph's sons, the prince and general Maslama ibn 'Abd al-Malik, ordered that a treacherous general named Yazīd ibn Muhallab be crucified, and that a pig be crucified next to him. More generally the Umayyads strategically deployed crucifixion not only for its fearsome apocalyptic overtones but also because it had been used in the Roman and Sasanian Empires—the very states that the Umayyads were supplanting from the Iranian plateau to the western Mediterranean.[19]

What the Umayyads were *not* attempting to conjure through this form of execution was any sort of reference to Christianity: to them, crucifixion was a predominantly imperial symbol. The late Roman and Umayyad governments did both recognize that the cross, unlike other crucifixion apparatuses, was indelibly associated with Jesus. And Muslim apocalyptic narratives took many opportunities to denigrate the cross as a Christian symbol.[20] But although crosses and pigs were things that Christians valued in contrast to Muslims, the political context in which the apocalyptic traditions arose suggests that the sacred significance of Jesus's prophesized acts of destruction were only partly about the fall of a Christian world order and the triumph of a Muslim one. They were also about the end of Rome—the very empire that had killed him.

As it turned out, the Roman Empire would not die (to borrow a phrase from the historian John Haldon). Byzantium survived for another thousand years after the loss of the western provinces, and another eight hundred years after the Muslim conquests lopped off North Africa, Egypt, and the Levant from its possession. There were also elements of Rome that endured in the imagination, and ideas about the pig were one of these cases, at least in the early post-imperial years. Historians of Late Antiquity are accustomed to seeing the Mediterranean world as an "echo chamber," in which societies that were in some ways worlds apart from one another were also reflecting on shared traditions and conversations.[21] But it is still surprising to see that this cultural convergence was even characteristic of an animal that we would expect to be polarizing. Across these centuries, from roughly the 300s to the early 700s, Jewish, Christian, and early Muslim cultures shared a concept of pigs that was especially enduring because a formerly polytheist empire had so happily eaten them (and because pigs themselves had enabled that appetite).

And yet, although everyone saw pigs as "Roman" animals, not everyone ate them. Diets could differ even when symbols were shared. The Umayyads had reportedly killed actual pigs in Mesopotamia and the Levant in the service of their apocalypticism, and they were only able to do this because the animals were part of the life of Christian settlements they had conquered. So at the hinge between the Roman and post-Roman worlds, pigs were both a point of alignment and a marker of difference. And gradually, over time, the Roman-ness of the animals faded and gave way to a more unambiguously Christian profile. Or, more precisely, the Roman features of the living pig surrendered to the Christian features of the dead one in the early medieval imagination, because the newly "religious" character of pigs was mostly defined by diet.

In the western Mediterranean, scattered conflicts involving licit foods arose in the early Middle Ages, though our best evidence here is not about Christian versus non-Christian views but instead involves Christians' debates with one another. That is partly because, in the western areas that came to be governed by Muslims after the Umayyad conquests—namely, North Africa and Iberia—the written evidence that survives is scarce until the ninth and tenth centuries. It is hard to know how western Muslims viewed the foods of their Christian subjects and neighbors. And Hebrew texts from the West are nonexistent until the ninth century (in Iberia) or the tenth and eleventh centuries (elsewhere in Europe), despite the fact that Jewish communities were part of the post-imperial kingdoms.[22] But there may not have been much to document: it is possible that pork was not particularly entangled in interfaith relations in the first millennium CE. What we *can* see is that in the early medieval West, some people did come to identify pigs as representative of Christian praxis more than as the Roman animals that Jews, Christians, and Muslims had invoked for centuries, but this happened only in a slow and staggered way.

The Suspect Meat

Dietary norms in the early Middle Ages were diverse, fluctuating, and at times indeterminate: similar to the ecology of pork itself. And even when the rules for eating were fairly fixed, the rationales behind them were varied and sometimes uncertain. This is worth keeping in mind when it comes to the elusive search for the "origins" of the pork prohibition. The reasons why the Judaic and Islamic traditions originally forbade the consumption of pork are mostly a mystery to us. Researchers continue to propose new explanations, but many of these are materialist and unconvincing. The best-known hypothesis in recent decades has been that the ecologies of the Middle East were not ideal conditions for pig husbandry, and so the communities who lived there came to see the meat as untouchable—which is basically an argument that Jerome made over sixteen hundred years ago.[23]

The problem with reasoning of this sort is not only that it treats religious culture, especially the religious culture of outsiders, as something determined almost totally by the environment external to it. It is also undermined by the archaeological record. In the Late Bronze Age, settlements throughout the Levant consumed small quantities of pork, and in the first half of the Iron Age (roughly 1200 to 1000 BCE), Philistine towns ate quite a lot of it—in contrast to their Israelite and Canaanite neighbors in the countryside. Clearly, one *could* raise pigs in hot arid climates. The interplay between ecology and culture was subtler than these explanations assume.[24]

What is more interesting from the vantage point of the early Middle Ages is that whatever rationales God and his believers had originally had for taking pigs off the menu, those reasons were not fully legible to early medieval observers, either. Jewish, Muslim, and Christian exegetes continued to develop new interpretations over the years about why some groups did not eat pork and why others did. The late antique rabbis, as we saw, deliberately rejected the question of why pork was a forbidden meat, in contrast to their counterparts in the high Middle Ages. And the celebrated Abbāsid writer al-Jāḥiẓ, working in Baghdad in the ninth century, figured that Muslims refrained from pork in part because pigs ate feces—which made it all the more bizarre to him that the emperors of Persia and Rome had loved this meat most of all. A century later, as part of a compendious collection that would quickly make its way to Iberia, a group of esoteric Muslim philosophers in Basra imagined what the pig's grievances against humanity would be. Their pig accused Muslims of treating him as accursed and disgusting. He accused Jews of hating him for historical reasons, "just because of the enmity between them and the Romans and Christians." (Note the authors' separation of these identities here.) And he accused everybody of stranding him between different zoological and cultural taxa, which left him totally bewildered. Should he litigate against the people who despised him or against the humans who avidly exploited his body for food, medicine, magic, and manufacturing? Their infatuation seemed to be its own kind of injustice. Alternatively, a genre of Christian biographies of Muhammad that became popular in Europe in the eleventh century had a more reductive and inflammatory explanation of why Muslims did not eat pork. According to these legends, a pack of wild boars had eaten Muhammad alive.[25] These were just a few of many theories.

But religious difference was not always as polarizing as it is often assumed to have been. For one thing, the Muslim conquests of the western Mediterranean only gradually changed the foodways of local populations—or at least, the rates of change differed significantly from place to place. Among the new settlements that Muslims established in newly conquered territories, pigs were never present. This was the case in the Córdoban suburb of Šaqunda, for instance, which was a planned development built on the bank of the Guadalquivir River opposite the city core, in the earliest days of the Umayyad emirate. But for communities whose roots stretched back farther than the conquests, diets were slower to shift. This is in part because the Umayyads had not been interested in converting their subjects to Islam, and even in later regimes that did encourage non-Muslims to convert, the process took centuries. Meanwhile the Christian, Zoroastrian, and Garamantian members of their polity (among others) continued to raise pigs and eat pork, though in some cases at increasingly reduced rates. In one of the few settlements in the western Muslim world whose chronological sequences have been carefully studied, the neighborhood of Cercadilla in the capital city of Córdoba, pork consumption declined between the eighth and tenth centuries, when pigs dropped from 17 percent of all animal remains to 10 percent: a substantial change, but a slow and partial one. Cercadilla was also somewhat unusual because its residents were eating more pork than was typical of Iberia (especially the interior meseta) and North Africa (especially the Libyan desert and pre-desert). In these areas, people had eaten only small amounts of pork *before* the Umayyads had taken over. That continued to be the case after these regions were conquered for at least a few centuries, sometimes longer.[26]

Occasionally pigs were even a *major* source of meat for Christians well into the age of Al-Andalus (the eighth to fifteenth centuries)—a possibility that is evident from another phase in Cercadilla's surprising history. Later residents of this neighborhood, who lived there in the twelfth century when Córdoba was the capital of the Almohad caliphate, were consuming proportionally more pork than in most places in Europe. The pig bones from this period are about 64 percent of the main domesticates, or, measured differently, about 60 percent of the minimum number of animals that are present among the trash. They were also unusually large specimens, which probably means that they were stall fed or specially bred, even though this is hardly the place one might expect to find an abundance of big pigs. Cercadilla was evidently a Christian neighborhood, but the evidence is also a reminder that social and religious change was piecemeal and locally variable.[27]

It is also possible that new converts to Islam did not necessarily give up pork as soon as they became Muslim, because the narrative and legal traditions of Islam are not always a reliable guide for the norms that Muslims actually practiced. We know, for example, that Muslims throughout the Middle Ages hunted for sport, even though many hadith relate that Muhammad prohibited it. In the great Mamluk court of late medieval Egypt, which fostered a highly sophisticated culture of veterinary medicine, pork was recommended as a nutritious supplement to a hunting dog's diet (along with cumin, dates, lentils, and salt), even though technically both dogs and pigs were unclean. And in the seventeenth century the Mughal Emperor Jahangir was even proud to say that he had killed ninety wild boars before he was fifty years old. So the situation may have been similar in the early Middle Ages. At a fortified settlement in Valencia known as El Molón, for example, the residents who settled the site starting in the middle of the eighth century were Muslim: they buried their dead to face the qibla (the direction of Mecca), and in a pair of their buildings each one was outfitted with a miḥrāb (or niche indicating the qibla). But there are also a few pig remains there—not enough to point to pig husbandry, but large enough in size to be the bones of young wild boar.[28]

The problem is that, because the written evidence from Muslim Iberia and North Africa in the first century and a half after the Umayyad conquests (between roughly 700 and 850) is virtually nonexistent, it is impossible to know what the dietary rationales of Muslims and their subjects were in these regions at this time—or more generally to know who was leaving pig bones behind and why. When the documentary record picks up in the later ninth century, the opinions of Iberian and North African jurists indicate that pig husbandry and pork eating did sometimes trigger the need for legal clarification. Could Muslim husbands sleep with or even kiss their Christian wives if those wives had eaten pork? Could a pork-eating Christian wet nurse feed a Muslim baby? Could Christians pay their taxes in pigs? If a Christian man converted to Islam, could his Christian wife keep the pigs that he had given her as a dowry? Could a Christian debtor pay a Muslim lender with money he had obtained from selling his pigs? The jurists thought the answers to all these questions should be "no," with the exception of the last one, which a line of Andalusian and Maghribi jurists figured was perfectly acceptable. But other Muslims may have seen things differently, and even the jurists themselves assumed that some of these things (like sex between a Muslim man and his pork-eating wife) would happen in spite of their opinions on the matter. The core premise that Muslims were prohibited from eating pork, however, was not considered negotiable. In the tenth century, the chief of police of Córdoba compiled a long dossier of accusations against a man named Abu al-Khayr (for which he was ultimately executed). One of these offenses was asking a Christian for some pork. Abu al-Khayr may have been a political partisan or a religious radical, and we cannot judge whether the testimonies assembled against him were true. But his alleged desire to eat pork was presented as unobjectionably bad, not to say weird: even the Christian was said to have been taken aback by his request! And yet a hint also appears that this particular offense would not have been considered as awful if Abu al-Khayr had not voluntarily told the Christian, by way of explanation for his appetite, that he did not believe in the religion of Muhammad.[29]

The food boundaries in the Christian kingdoms were not any sharper. Bishops in Gaul especially complained at their councils about Christians being guests at Jewish dinner parties, or at meals hosted by "heretical" Christians, or at feasts that were allegedly polytheist. Their concerns were that these meals ostensibly involved ritual prayers, sacrificial meat, or associations with holidays that some critics considered un-Christian, such as the old Roman new year's holiday of the Kalends. The bishops also objected to clerics and laypersons dining with Jews because, they argued, it was an imbalanced relationship. Jews thought the foods that Christians ate were unclean, and so Christians should convey the same level of condescension by rejecting the dinner invitations they received from Jews.[30]

This normative evidence does not give us much to go on. But it does suggest that the bishops' efforts to draw these distinctions is a sign that other people were blurring them, and Christians would continue to disagree about the issue for centuries. In the ninth century, for example, Agobard of Lyon cited some of the old conciliar pronouncements to protest the fact that imperial officials were willingly sharing meals with Jews on his home turf. But this was only one way to see things. It is likely that some Christians who *were* dining with people of different faiths did not actually see their dining companions or the meal itself primarily in religious terms—and that others may have even understood the meal to be ethically defensible within the contours of Christianity, in contrast to the opinion of their bishops. As the historians Éric Rebillard and Lisa Bailey have shown vividly for late antique North Africa and Gaul, respectively, Christians not only had many identities besides a religious one. They also treated the norms of their religion as a subject for debate, rather than as a settled matter.[31]

That included reappraising their own diets over the centuries. Some Christians were concerned, for example, that meat eating was the result of a historical failure. In the Genesis narratives, humans did not eat meat of any kind until after the Flood. Adam and Eve had been vegetarians. God had said to them, "See, I have given you every plant yielding seed that is upon the face of the earth, and every tree with seed in its fruit; you shall have them for food" (Gen 1:29, NRSV). He only made animals available to humanity to eat after the receding of the Flood he sent to punish the earth. Just before Noah and his family disembarked from the ark, God told them, "Every moving thing that lives shall be food for you; and just as I gave you the green plants, I give you everything" (Gen. 9:3, NRSV).

Most Christians did not take this to mean that eating animals was a bad thing. But early medieval commentators did see these passages as evidence of environmental and physiological decline. They argued that Adam and Eve and their early descendants had lived on plants because the earth had been more fruitful in its earliest days. The Flood seemed to have sapped the vitality of all living things—not only the fertility of the land but also the strength of human beings. God told the ark's passengers that they could start eating meat because their former diet would have been inadequate under the circumstances. And this was still true, the exegetes believed, of the present. Meat eating was a legacy of that ancient punishment and transformation.[32]

But even if animal meat was edible, it was still dispensable. What today we call vegetarianism and veganism were widely admired in mainstream Christianity as a core part of ascetic practice. If there was a celebrity diet in Late Antiquity and the early Middle Ages, it was this one, the regimen modeled by the late antique desert elders of Egypt and Palestine. The holy hermits had used fasting and selective ingredient selection in order to make the body "the discreet mentor of the proud soul," as Peter Brown put it. By withholding immediate gratification from the body's most fundamental appetite of all—not sex, but *eating*—the mind and soul could be trained in the course of disciplining the body.[33]

Any Christian could live ascetically, and in the early Middle Ages many ascetic men and women lived alone or even at home with their families, without any formal conversion to a monastic life.[34] Some of them took the "desert diet" to extremes: pork was out of the question, but so was almost everything else. Germanus of Auxerre ate only barley bread and water. He even refused to eat salt, which was more than Saint Antony himself had done! Likewise the poet Venantius Fortunatus mentioned repeatedly that his friend Radegund of Poitiers only ever ate barley bread, lentils, and greens—even while she was still a queen. (Radegund was married to Clothar I, one of the sons of Clovis.) Fortunatus was especially impressed because Radegund often ate like this, or ate nothing at all, while she was seated in plain view of the generous banquets she served to her guests: they feasted on three-course meals while she "filled up on fasting," he joked.[35]

But a bare-bones diet was not the only ascetic option. Late antique and early medieval monastic communities adopted diets that were strikingly diverse—as we can tell from their institutional guidelines and also their garbage—even though they were all inspired by the same somatic psychology that the desert fathers had embodied. There was only one point on which all monastic models agreed, and this was the principle of moderation: do not eat so much that you become stuffed—or even sated. This was also a guiding principle in contemporary medicine, and physicians recommended dietary restraint in exactly the same terms. But monks were looking after their minds as well as their bodies, and in this way of life the body was not supposed to call the shots.[36]

Beyond this consensus there were many interpretations of what an ascetic diet entailed, in part because of the diversity of monastic systems in the early Middle Ages.[37] But that variability was also by design, because eating was a very personal thing, as many monastic planners observed. Individual bodies had different needs and abilities—or as the sixth-century *Rule of Benedict* put it, quoting Paul, they had received different gifts from God. A strict and spare diet might be easy for one monk but impossible for another. Culture and class were partly responsible for these differences, which is why Augustine of Hippo made allowances for elite converts to the monastic life: he figured that they would have a harder time adjusting to monastic dietary rules. Other monastic theorists were more concerned about monks going too far. John Cassian, whose work in the fifth century would become highly influential in early medieval monastic culture, had made a point of *not* specifying how or what monks should eat, because he was afraid that they would take on more than their bodies could handle. He figured that as long as the liturgical fasting calendar was respected, the portions were small, and the ingredients were cheap, an eater could effectively keep the body's desires in check, which was, after all, the ultimate goal—not ascetic brinkmanship. It was probably some combination of these sociological and psychological concerns that motivated the early-sixth-century *Rule of the Master* to let individual monks modulate their own fasting at Lent. This slack policy stands out in a Rule whose recommendations more often resembled a tightly executed choreography. At mealtimes, for instance, the monks were expected to lower a basket of bread onto the abbot's table with an engineered pulley system, "so that it seemed to descend from heaven"! But how they should eat this bread, or anything else, was a more decentralized balancing act.[38]

Many monastic planners treated meat as a problem, but in the medical world, pork in particular was thought to be good for you. In the late second or early third century the imperial physician Galen had described pork as a kind of superfood: it was more nutritious than anything else a person could eat and was therefore ideal for people who needed a lot of energy, like athletes and hard laborers. Early medieval physicians and pharmacologists also praised its benefits, but for different reasons. (Although medical writers in the West liked to mention Galen as an authority, their work was often substantially different from his.) They tended to describe pork as light, *levis,* meaning that it was easily digestible in contrast to foods that were bitter, or *acer,* like bread, which tended to catalyze powerful transformations in the body.[39]

Monks knew their medicine, but their primary concerns lay elsewhere. They assumed that meat was something that most people wanted and enjoyed, that it was more pleasurable to eat than the foods and wine or beer that *were* permitted, and that eating something this enjoyable and potent could destabilize the delicate balance between mind and body that they worked so hard to cultivate. For these reasons the author of the *Rule of the Master* treated meat as a strictly celebratory food. Birds and "quadrupeds" could be eaten only during the holiday seasons of Christmas to Epiphany and Easter to Pentecost.

These meats were thus rarer treats than sweets (*dulciores*), which the *Rule* permitted on any feast day, Sunday, or day when guests were present. But the author still insisted that it was better for a monk to skip meat even when he was allowed to eat it. The monks who did decide to eat meat on special occasions would have to sit at a different table and eat from different serving dishes from their other brothers, "so that the diners may recognize how great a distance there is between the people who are slaves to their desires, and the people who have control over their belly."[40]

In contrast to the *Rule of the Master,* most early monastic theorists decided that the dilemma of whether to eat meat should not be left up to an individual. Instead the corporate body of the monastery would be regulated as a whole. So the *Rule of Benedict,* in its characteristically austere fashion, prohibited the flesh of birds and mammals (literally, "quadrupeds") to everyone at all times, unless a person was seriously ill. An anonymous *Rule for Virgins* (*Regula cuiusdam ad virgines*), which was probably written by Jonas of Bobbio in the middle of the seventh century for his community of nuns at Marchiennes (in what is now northern France), recommended daily meals that sound like vegetarian stews or braises: dishes of legumes or vegetables prepared with a sprinkling of flour. Fruit was fine on the side, but there is not a word about meat. These were a few among many models. The questions of whether monks could have any meat, and what constituted "meat" in the first place, were debated throughout the early Middle Ages.[41]

Even among monasteries that all adhered to the same Rule, interpretations and diets varied. When the archaeologist Enrico Cirelli canvassed the material evidence for Benedictine monasteries in Europe in the ninth and tenth centuries, he found that some institutions did not eat any four-footed animals at all, in keeping with the advice of the *Rule of Benedict.* But others did eat those meats, which could be interpreted either as a violation of the Rule or simply as one of many customized adaptations of it. It was probably also reflective of the early medieval tendency to structure settlements in line with their micro-ecologies. And because monastic diets were so variable, and settlement morphologies can be similar, it can be difficult sometimes for archaeologists to tell whether a site they are dealing with is an early medieval monastery or a lay estate. In the ninth-century phase of the settlement at Flixborough in northern England, the material evidence could point in both directions: either this was a monastic community, or it was a partially literate lay community that was specializing in textile production. No matter who the inhabitants were, they were still eating bottlenose dolphins![42]

Bishops were also expected to exercise dietary discipline. They were not supposed to hunt. They were also technically supposed to eat their own medio-cre cooking, but it is apparent (from a council in Tours that says so) that many bishops were hiring women to be their chefs instead, which bothered some of their colleagues. The evidence that archaeology provides about ecclesiasti-cal eating has slightly different stories to tell. Generally speaking, religious settlements tend to feature little to no wild game and a higher proportion of poultry, fish, and shellfish among the total animal assemblages. And yet some ecclesiastical sites, such as the clerical complex of Saint-Julien in Tours, betray diets that were almost as meat heavy as the diets of their lay counterparts. At San Pietro at Canosa in Apulia, an impressive cult site to Saint Peter that included an episcopal residence, the bishop's household was eating chicken from its extensive chicken farm, but it was also eating very young cows, which was highly unusual in Italy.[43]

As for the place of the pig in *lay* diets, Christians had different opinions about the ethics of eating pork. The most striking example is that, in the same century that the Visigothic kings were insisting that their Jewish sub-jects should not think of certain foods as unclean, King Erwig acknowledged that some Christians in his realm were also refusing to eat pork. His conclu-sion was that this was permissible as long as those eaters seemed straight-forwardly Christian in every other regard. "It really seems unfair," he said in 681, "for people who are ennobled by an obvious faith in Christ's works to be singled out just because they have rejected one particular food."[44] We cannot say whether Erwig was trying to convince his subjects that this dietary aber-ration was acceptable, or whether he was explaining his own change of heart. Either way, there was a disagreement about what a "Christian" diet could be. His law also shows us that the Visigoths were wrangling with how to define a Christian independent of the pig, precisely because pigs otherwise seemed to them to be an important part of what constituted Christian identity—even though early medieval Iberians were not eating much pork, and many ascetics never ate it. In this corner of the early medieval West, at least, the relationship between pigs and Christianness had tightened, but at the same time, some Christians were working to relax it.

Other Christians were anxious about what the Old Testament meant when it spoke of some animals as *mundus*, or clean, and others (including the pig) as *non mundus/immundus*, or unclean. This taxonomy of purity was put into place the moment Noah began boarding pairs of animals onto the ark, well before the legal discussions in Leviticus. For Carolingian commentators in particular, writing in the eighth to tenth centuries, this conceptual framework was disconcerting, because it called their own practices into question. They suggested, following Alcuin's proposal in the eighth century, that *mundus* and *immundus* were only figures of speech. "Clean" meant "useful," they insisted, and an animal was unclean if it was not particularly advantageous in meeting the needs of human beings. That is why God told Noah to stock more clean animals on the ark (seven of each species), compared to the number of unclean animals that he welcomed aboard (two of each species). If unclean animals were actually abhorrent, rather than merely less useful, they would not have been admitted at all.[45]

This line of reasoning swept aside—or was unaware of—the Palestinian and Babylonian rabbis' own arguments that unclean animals were not inherently bad, only off-limits. But it was often the case in the early medieval debates about meat (in the West, at least) that Christian exegetes were not so much arguing with Jews or Muslims; they were arguing with other Christians. And the scrutiny of the pre- and postdiluvian moment in biblical history was probably instigated by the court of Louis the German (r. 843–876). In the middle of the ninth century, the elites of East Francia were keenly interested in the parameters of eating meat, and the historian Eric Goldberg has discovered this concern running through their hunting treatises. The king and his intellectual circle wanted to pin down what made an animal unclean, and to clarify the restrictions on certain forms of flesh (in particular, blood, suffocated or strangulated animals, and carrion). They also wanted to determine whether there were any mitigating circumstances. Could a famine suspend the regular rules? And did the game animals that had been killed by hunting dogs and birds of prey count as licit meat? There was no consensus about the answers.[46] This may explain why most of the exegetes who discussed the status of unclean meat, and meat eating after the Flood, tended to concentrate in the later Carolingian period. Their commentaries were speaking to live questions.

A low-key kind of Christianization was under way in which pigs were becoming a somewhat more meaningful part of Christian diets in the early Middle Ages. Christians were not necessarily eating more pork—some were, and some were not—but they were thinking about pork in their conversations about dietary protocols, and Jews and Muslims were starting to draw attention to pigs as a salient part of Christianity. But there was another kind of Christianization developing at this time, too. Pigs were becoming theologically useful by coming to serve as an organizing concept for thinking through Christian ethics more generally. And unlike the debates about diet, the engagement with the pig as a mental-philosophical device was substantially defined by the animals' particular features, and by the ecological sensibility they had fostered among the communities that lived with them.

Selfishness and Sacrifice

The most striking feature of this deeper form of Christianization is that pigs became entwined within several contrasting strands of thinking. Early medieval Christians would have seen the multiplicity of meanings not as a contradiction but rather as a crucial key for unlocking a complex divine order. This was, for example, the opinion of the prolific ninth-century writer Hrabanus Maurus. Hrabanus had been a monk since his childhood, but like many monks and nuns of the early Middle Ages, his horizons extended far past his monastery (Fulda, in what is now central Germany). We have already seen that some monasteries managed extensive properties and economic networks. They were also politically engaged, and many chronicles and histories were the work of monastic writers who kept a close eye on current affairs. Their libraries were the best in the Latinate world. So as part of his upbringing at Fulda, Hrabanus came to appreciate, like many readers before him, that there was a vast and even overwhelming amount of information about the world to be found in books. And also like many writers before him, he wanted to contribute something to that knowledge. He dubbed his project *De rerum naturis, The Natures of Things,* which pluralized a title that Lucretius, Isidore, and Bede had all used for their works of natural philosophy, *De rerum natura (The Nature of Things).* Later copyists would spot Hrabanus's ambition here and more bluntly call the work *De universo: About Everything.* Fortunately, Hrabanus was between jobs when he wrote it, after leaving his position as abbot of Fulda in 841–842, before becoming archbishop of Mainz in 847.[47]

What Hrabanus thought was lacking in his predecessors' consideration of the cosmos was that they treated its meanings too compartmentally.[48] It was crucial to him that when someone looked out upon the physical world, that person could see that every single piece of it was saturated with significance, or what Hrabanus called force and consequence, *vis* and *effectus.* He knew that excellent studies had been written on the literal or historical views of the physical world, and that equally excellent work existed on what Hrabanus and others variously called the figural, mystical, allegorical, or spiritual meanings of things. What Hrabanus aimed to do was fuse these two ways of seeing back together. He wanted to reassemble all the world's knowledge so that its multiple natures could be joined into one universe, as they were supposed to be experienced.

De rerum naturis seems lighter on the literal material than Hrabanus advertised. This was partly a sign of snobbery. Hrabanus thought that only "quicker" thinkers could appreciate allegory and that the "masses" (*turba populi*) would be unable to follow his arguments. But Hrabanus also thought that humans' failure to conjoin these two perspectives—the literal and the figurative, or human learning and Christian morality (*scientia* and *moralis vitae fidelis institutio*)—was mostly a problem of habit. They had to get used to seeing the physical and the spiritual simultaneously.[49] That is where *De rerum naturis* came in. Hrabanus did not have to convince his readers to care about the world they lived in. Instead he offered a microscope of meaning to deepen their sense of the world they could already see and to intensify their engagement with it. As he said to his two dedicatees—Louis the German, who had recently become the king of East Francia, and Bishop Haimo of Halberstadt—he hoped that his book would help them rule wisely.[50]

De rerum naturis is a very long book, not only because of Hrabanus's encyclopedic interests but also because (as Hrabanus repeatedly observed) a single object carried a ream of meanings, all of which needed to be recorded. Those meanings could be positive or negative, depending on the context, and as so many medieval commentators pointed out, the contexts of things were vastly variable. In the case of meat, for example, the Bible might use it to mean the body of the Lord or, conversely, a human's outer self. It could call to mind gluttony, luxury, and a lack of reflection, or it could mean spiritual food. It all depended on the situation. Hrabanus collected some of these meanings of meat/carnis from other sources.[51] But for the most part, the materials about meat—like so many of the collections in *De rerum naturis*—were mostly curated by Hrabanus himself. This was the real work of his book, the dense collation of physical things and their many overtones to do justice to a world that hummed with divine communications. The result was a universe whose symbolic environment was as complex as its physical environment. There was no easy formula for knowing it.

We should take Hrabanus's argument seriously in thinking about the Christian meanings of pigs. Everything in the cosmos had layered and contrapuntal meanings, as Hrabanus exhaustively demonstrated, but pigs were an unusually strong magnet for paradoxical associations. Their intensely polysemic condition was a result of the mixed legacies of antiquity and of the many permutations of pig-human relationships that we have surveyed across the early medieval West. It was also a result of the complex Christian theology of the flesh, which implicated pigs by virtue of their position as *the* quintessential meat makers. But it was only in the course of the early and high Middle Ages that this connection would become a conspicuous part of Christian culture.

One cluster of associations tied the pig to matter and pleasure. It was part of a prominent strand in Christian thinking that subordinated the world of meat-flesh (*carnis*) to the loftier life of the mind and soul. In this semantic mode, late antique and early medieval Christians concentrated on the physicality of pigs—their meatiness—and linked them to selfish and hedonistic impulses that interfered with more intellectually and ethically demanding ways of living. That is how Isidore of Seville caricatured Epicureanism in the seventh century: "The Epicureans are so called from a certain philosopher Epicurus, a lover of vanity, not of wisdom, whom the philosophers themselves named 'the Pig,' as if he were wallowing in carnal filth by asserting that bodily pleasure is the highest good." Hrabanus considered the jab worth repeating in *De rerum naturis*.[52]

There was a bit of truth to Isidore's snide comment. Epicureans really were compared to pigs in antiquity, and the philosophers reappropriated the comparison as a kind of mascot for themselves: a fat happy pig was the very picture of pleasure. The Epicureans who used the Villa of the Papyri in Herculaneum as a headquarters even kept a bronze pig in the house; today it resides at the Museo Nazionale Archeologico in Naples. (It may not come as a surprise that this particular token of contentment was styled more like a member of the free-ranging breed than as the stall-fed, sacrificial type that was also bred in Italy at the time.) But Isidore was off the mark in other ways. His association of pigs with pleasure reduces the Epicurean ideal to "bodily pleasure" (*voluptas carnis*), even though Epicureans had always included calmness of mind as an essential part of pleasure. And they were sure that human happiness and pig happiness were not the same. Pigs and humans were constrained by different forces, and they possessed different physical and mental capacities, so their experiences of pain, discomfort, and pleasure were activated and alleviated in different ways. Above all, pigs' pleasure had nothing to do with mental states; Epicureans argued that animals did not possess rationality.[53] So although pigs were an icon of pleasure for a philosophical school in which pleasure was the ultimate good, the pleasures particular to their species were still inferior and strictly fleshy.

In late antique and early medieval Christianity, the pleasure that pigs were made to represent most often was adultery. In the fourth century Sulpicius

Severus compared the ground that pigs rooted up to the "disfigured image of fornication" (which in Christian culture meant any sort of sex outside marriage). Likewise the bishops who gathered together in the Burgundian city of Mâcon in 585 likened Christians who committed incest—according to the bishops' very broadly defined notion of it—to "completely repulsive pigs rolling around in shit." And Isidore's etymological connection between pig/porcus and illegitimate children/spurii (singular, spurius) would give this metaphor a long life in the Middle Ages.[54]

This line of thinking might have owed something to pigs' actual reproductive traits. Female pigs, both wild and domesticated, can mate with multiple males to produce piglets with different fathers in a single litter.[55] There is no explicit evidence that early medieval farmers or writers knew this, but they might have, given that they paid close attention to their animals in so many other respects. In any case, they were well aware that pigs were polytocous (they gave birth to multiple offspring in a single litter) and iteroparous (they reproduced more than once in a lifetime) because these abilities made them an asset on early medieval farms. It was even common knowledge among children. A math problem given to early medieval students asked them to imagine a landowner who sets up a new pigpen. He puts a sow in the center who gives birth to seven female piglets, then these eight pigs each give birth to seven more (female) piglets in one corner of the sty. This happens in the other three corners, too: each successively larger group of (all-female) pigs gives birth to seven more piglets three more times. Finally all *these* pigs give birth in the middle of the sty, each to seven piglets. How many pigs were there in the end? (The answer key scrambles the solution because it assumes the sows were birthing litters of eight rather than the litters of seven stated in the setup—and on top of that, the final sum varies in the different surviving manuscripts. The fertility of pigs was a daunting thing.)[56]

And yet Sulpicius, the bishops at Mâcon, and Isidore did not equate sexually transgressive Christians with sexually active sows. Instead their analogies turned on pigs' affinity for mud—their love of rooting and wallowing in particular. This choice is all the more striking because in antiquity, and again in the high Middle Ages, it would be the *femininity* of pigs, rather than dirt, that governed their use as sexual metaphors. So one finds imagery ranging from a scene in Apuleius's second-century novel, *The Golden Ass*—where Lucius the narrator watches the hypnotically bouncy body of an enslaved woman as she chops and stirs minced pork—to a fourteenth-century sign in France advertising a brothel that featured a pig performing oral sex on a half-woman, half-pig.[57] These are two among countless instances in which pigs and women were tied together as symbols of excessive sexuality. But although this was clearly an ancient tradition with a long future ahead of it, there are few signs of it (literal or otherwise) in the early medieval West. It is possible that our surviving sources simply do not reflect what was a continuous thread in Western culture, but it seems likelier that this discourse lay dormant in the early Middle Ages. In any case, polemicists and policy makers chose not to activate it.

Another motif with an ancient pedigree that gained traction in the high Middle Ages was the association of pigs and demons—and in this case, early medieval writers did make a few contributions to that theme. The Capetians did not pull the porcus diabolicus out of thin air. In 642, Jonas of Bobbio told a story about an elite young woman who had joined a monastery but had started to steal food because the devil had made her gluttonous. God punished the nun by depriving her of an appetite, and for a year she could only stomach bran and leaves and wild plants. One day as she was eating this stuff, she saw the likeness (speciem) of a huge wild boar eating next to her and tossing things around with its snout. When she asked the boar what was going on, he told her that every time she had stolen food and eaten it, he had been there too, eating alongside her. The nun (or Jonas) saw this as confirmation that that devil had been involved and that God was punishing her appropriately.[58]

When he connected pigs to the idea of demonic influence, Jonas may have been thinking of the story of the Gadarene/Gerasene swine—that story in the Synoptic Gospels about Jesus exorcising a possessed man (or men) in Gadara or Gerasa and sending the exorcised demons (Legion) into a herd of pigs, which then ran off a cliff into the sea.[59] More than half a century after Jonas was writing, Bede took that biblical incident to mean that demons can only seize control of people who live like pigs, which according to Bede basically meant prioritizing oneself or other idols over God.[60] He was drawing on a long exegetical tradition for this interpretation. In the fourth century a spate of commentaries by Hilary of Poitiers, Chromatius of Aquileia, Ambrose of Milan, and Augustine of Hippo had all suggested that the demons targeted pigs because of the way they lived (though depending on the author, piggishness meant various things: focusing on physical desires, being unclean, living sinfully, being governed by pride, and/or worshipping idols). Ambrose in particular had insisted that an important lesson to be drawn from the story was that "a human is his own source of distress: unless you live like a pig, the devil will never have power over you."[61]

These commentators were not speaking literally, because they did not believe that a pig or any other created thing was naturally or inherently bad.
The pigs they were talking about were figural animals, *figurae,* which signified
(*significare*) or pointed to (*indicare*) a deeper, ethical interpretation of the narratives. Even Jonas had been talking about his wild boar as a superficial image: it was a disguise for the devil. But a few exegetes who thought about the
Gadarene swine—Jerome in particular—were also interested in anchoring the
spiritual reading in the literal story, since it was supposed to have actually happened. If the pigs only served as conduits of *symbolic* sin, why would a legion
of demons enter a real herd of them?

Jerome's answer in 398, which Bede reiterated just over three hundred
years later and which Charlemagne's official commentator singled out a century after *that,* was that the pigs had presented an opportunity for salvation
(*occasio salutis*). The death of the animals had made it possible for the possessed man or men to be saved. Jerome argued that this tradeoff worked only
because the souls of pigs were unequal to the souls of humans, even though
God had created them both: "If the souls of humans and beasts consist of the
same substance and came from the same maker, how could two thousand pigs
be drowned in order to save one person?"[62]

On the surface this is a dismissive statement about the value of animal life.
It was also a polemical one. Jerome took this episode as a proof text against
Manichaeanism, a religion in the late antique Mediterranean and Persia (and
eventually central Asia) that had counted Augustine among its members for
almost a decade and which was conversant in the religious cultures of Christianity, Zoroastrianism, and (later) Buddhism. Its elite practitioners adopted
a strict form of vegetarianism, possibly even veganism, on the conviction that
animal and human souls alike were imprisoned pieces of the divine substance
or Light that coursed through everything in the cosmos. In this system, if an
animal (human or otherwise) ate something, the divine properties contained
in its food would become enfleshed when the eater went on to reproduce
young.[63] Many Christians rejected the Manichaean sense that the divine was
subject to material forces. But the Manichaeans' fluid model of organisms and
essences still seems to have prompted Jerome to think about alternate kinds
of embodied exchanges between animals and humans. And although he unambiguously ranks the life of a single human above the lives of two thousand
pigs, his literal reading of the Gospel story still treats the pigs as real animals
in a way that other Christian exegetes before him did not. The very effort to

think about the death of a herd of historical pigs was not just a rhetorical shift (from Christians to Manichaeans, from metaphors to actual animals); it was an ethical one. And in asking why these pigs died, Jerome and his readers ended up according them a positive place in the Christian drama of redemption. Their death set in motion a survival, and in doing so it prefigured the ultimate *occasio salutis* that Jesus would open up through his own self-sacrifice.

So although pigs-as-flesh represented the obstacles to salvation, they could also be the vehicle for it. They were similes for sin, but they were also members of a Christian ecology with positive and even salvific potential.

The pigs that were actually trotting around in the early medieval West made their own contributions to the system of salvation, though not in the same way their Gadarene cousins had. Above all, they offered their flesh as food, and thus kept worthy humans alive, which Christians themselves saw as both physiologically and spiritually significant. Occasionally God would be the one to kick this exchange into gear. In the fifth century, for example, Saint Patrick recounted a miracle in which God delivered a herd of pigs to a starving group of travelers (Patrick included) and their dogs. But usually it was humans who decided to incorporate pigs into their spiritual economies. By the later eighth century in many parts of Europe, Christians were expected to pay one-tenth of their agricultural revenues to their local churches, which bishops could in turn allocate as they saw fit. So pigs were at least a fraction of their capital. It is also fairly common to see pigs and other livestock made as spontaneous gifts to charitable medical centers (*xenodochia*), priests, churches, or monasteries, on the understanding that the clergy would either feed the neediest members of society from those resources or feed themselves and in the process maintain their vitality as professionals in the social work of prayer. Many donors also expected that, besides creating social ties while they lived, their gifts would also eventually benefit their souls, or even the souls of other people, because they had sacrificed something material as proof of their priorities.[64]

A few examples from many: in 720, a man named Petruald returned from a pilgrimage to Rome and decided to donate several properties to the monastery of Saint Michael the Archangel in Lucca, as well as 10 percent of all his horses, cattle, sheep, and pigs that were born that year. He expected these gifts to support widows, orphans, the needy, the poor or powerless (*pauperes*), and travelers and pilgrims like him. In 838, a donor in the Rhineland named Gebolt gave a quarter of the woodland he owned to the monastery of Wissembourg. He hoped that the gift, including the revenues that the monastery could expect from fattening (or collecting pannage taxes on) two hundred pigs every year, would work toward forgiving a different kind of debt, namely "the permanent forgiveness of my sins." About thirty years after that, a man named Rosselmus together with his unnamed brother built an oratory in the diocese of Lucca on behalf of their mother, "because she lived far away from any church." In order to enable the priest they installed there to do his work for her, the brothers endowed the church with lands, along with a small group of pigs, goats, and sheep, twelve animals in all. Another sixty years later, in 927, an Iberian widow named Adosinda granted various properties and assets—including ten pigs—to a church that she had founded with her husband. In exchange she asked the priests there to make a eucharistic offering on behalf of herself, her husband, and her children: every Christmas, every person present in the church would receive bread and wine. And in the later tenth century, an English testator named Æthelflæd asked that half of all her livestock be distributed to the tenants of her estates for the benefit of her soul.[65]

In the ninth century, donors in England also began to make gifts of annual food subsidies that would be paid out of their estates even after they died. One annual gift to Saint Augustine's at Canterbury included cured pork or lard (*spic*); in return the donor asked the community to sing Psalm 20 every day for herself and the soul of a named person who was probably her late husband. A food subsidy to Christ Church Canterbury, also including spic, was made by a woman who hoped the gift would benefit not only her own soul but also the souls of her friends and relatives who had helped her secure her property claims.[66] Christians also made annual payments of food to religious institutions in the German-speaking territories east of the Rhine. But here the payments tended to be part of what were often called precarial grants, in which a donor signed over ownership of a property to a church or monastery but retained usufruct—sometimes until his or her death, and sometimes in perpetuity, as long as the heirs continued to make the annual gifts. Most conspicuously, the monastery of Saint Gall (in today's northeast Switzerland) drew up dozens of usufruct arrangements between the 760s and 860s, which still survive as original charters, that involved annual and sometimes biannual payments of a piglet or young pig (*friskinga*).[67]

Not everyone made these payments happily. One nobleman named Herefrid found himself in court for unlawfully seizing land that had been donated to the monastery of Stavelot-Malmedy (in what is now eastern Belgium). He was allowed to retain usufruct of the property, but he had to pay for it, presumably as the original gift had stipulated, in linen and pigs. The heirs of generous donors sometimes resented their ancestors' choices. But for the donors who had initiated these special exchanges, the giving of pigs and other forms of property in return for spiritual nourishment and even eternal peace was a dizzying transformation. It was a bit like converting "pork into porcelain," as a trustee of the Metropolitan Museum of Art put it to philanthropists in the Gilded Age: it was something more public and enduring than the everyday economic magic of turning one kind of commodity into another. But there was more to it than this. No mere mortal could ensure that the donation of a pig helped save a soul. The expert communications system of the liturgy could catalyze the process. The ritual prayers that clerics and monks offered daily relied on their own physical and cognitive discipline in order to reach God. Even then it was not certain how God would respond: he was not obligated to make a counter gift. But the possibility that he *could* transform the material of land or livestock ("down to the smallest chicken," as the Iberian charters often said) into the treasure of heaven was electrifying. This linking of seemingly distant realms through localized acts of generosity was yet another way that a pig's meaning and its body could reverberate from the small to a cosmic scale.[68]

Many kinds of matter, not just pigs, circulated in the Christian system of salvation. As their charters attest, Christians figured that any animal they donated had the potential to sustain human life in specially designated ways and in the process shape an eternity. Pigs were not the only species with this power. Other livestock also seemed to sacrifice themselves on a regular basis. In the early fifth century, Sulpicius Severus noted several occasions on which his late friend Saint Martin had shown sensitivity to the perspectives of animals, and he was impressed by what Martin had once said about a sheep that had just been shorn: "She has fulfilled the command in the Gospel: she had two cloaks and gave one of them to someone who had nothing, and so you should do the same thing." Although Sulpicius did not mention it at the time, Martin was also alluding to his own most celebrated deed. The saint had once cut his own coat in half to share with a beggar—who turned out to be Christ.[69]

The ewe is more than a symbol of charity in this small scene. She is also the very fabric of it. Although her offering is not exactly equivalent to Martin's, it is nevertheless a precondition for his, because her wool makes the gift of a cloak possible. So, regardless of the sheep's entrenchment in an industry that humans engineered, her contribution struck Martin and Sulpicius as a fundamentally generous gesture. In a similar way, poets and monks and other writers in the high Middle Ages would observe that their work would have been impossible without sheep and the other animals that supplied them with skins. Not everyone took the production of parchment this seriously, which was part of the point of drawing attention to it. The Bible itself, these arguments went, needed sheep to constitute it (a few hundred of them per pandect). Ideas and words, including the Word, were kept alive by animals that were dead but also enduring. In human time, parchment seemed to last forever, and so did the culture that parchment preserved.[70]

What distinguished pigs' contribution to Christianity against the gifts of other animals was their flesh, which was itself derived from their omnivorous and adaptive engagement with the physical world. And because pigs were *the* metonym for meat, they were slowly drawn to the center of Christian culture as a blend of both metaphor and matter. Over the medieval millennium, the bifurcated nature of meat that had been present in the late antique and early medieval theology of the flesh intensified, and so did the conflicted nature of the species and its body.

An early hint of this crescendo can be found in artwork of the "central" Middle Ages (roughly 900 to 1100), when the Gadarene swine episode became a fixture in visual cycles of the life of Jesus. A couple of earlier examples of this scene have survived. The most prominent of these appears in the basilica of Sant'Apollinare Nuovo in Ravenna (fig. 5.1), which was built in the capital city during the reign of the Ostrogothic king Theoderic the Great (475–526). This shimmering mosaic portrays the opening and closing events in Mark's version of the story. The possessed man at the center of the frame beseeches Jesus, who is accompanied by an apostle, while, to the right, the pigs that became the new hosts of the exorcised Legion have already plunged into the sea. Two ivory panels, one made in the early fifth century and another made for Charlemagne that was closely based on it, also focus on these two phases of the narrative (figs. 5.2 and 5.3).[71]

But the story as it appears in objects and paintings shifted a few decades before the year 1000, most conspicuously within the networks of the Ottonian kings, who ruled what is now Germany and northern Italy and campaigned to extend their reach farther east and south. The Ottonians styled themselves as Roman emperors in the spirit of Charlemagne, and the Holy Roman Emperor Otto III (r. 996–1002) had the grander ambition of extending his title to encompass Constantinople and even the entire world—though his early death cut his plans short. Consequently the Ottonians were big fans and frequent recipients of Italian and Byzantine artworks, and representations of the Gadarene swine from the tenth and eleventh centuries were visibly inspired by late antique models.[72]

Fig. 5.1. The Gadarene swine mosaic in Sant'Apollinare Nuovo, built in Ravenna between 475 and 526. This mosaic appears on the upper register of the north nave wall as part of a cycle of stories about the life of Christ. A small panel, about 5 × 3 ft. (1.5 × 1 m), it sits high on the wall above the first window on the left as one enters the nave. But it represents an influential late antique tradition. Whenever the Gadarene swine later appeared in early medieval art, it would be in the context of a similar sequence of Jesus's historical life and miracles. (Photo: Bridgeman Images.)

In the mode of the Ravenna mosaic, Ottonian renditions of this scene almost always share its positioning (apostle or apostles to the left, behind Jesus, who heals with his right hand, the demoniac to Jesus's left, and the pigs on the far right). But they were not exact imitations of older iconographies. The Ottonian pieces also change the narrative focus to the moment of the exorcism itself. In contrast to the earlier scenes that survive, demons are now animating the action, catapulting out of the mouth of the demoniac and riding the pigs into the sea like rogue cowboys (figs. 5.4, 5.5, 5.6). This is also a change that appears in Byzantine manuscript painting in the eleventh century (fig. 5.7). Given the extensive contacts between the Ottonian and Macedonian dynasties it is difficult to say who was influencing whom. It is possible that artists on both sides of the Mediterranean were looking to a shared culture of older exemplars that no longer exist. A fragmentary English lectionary made around 1000, for example (fig. 5.8), may have based its own presentation of

Fig. 5.2. This representation of Gadarene swine was part of an ivory diptych of Christ's healing miracles that was made in the early fifth century, probably in Rome. It originally appeared in the bottom register of a three-scene panel measuring 19.7 × 7.9 cm (7.8 × 3 in.), which is now broken up; all three are housed together at the Musée du Louvre, Paris (OA 7878). (Photo: Daniel Arnaudet. © RMN-Grand Palais / Art Resource, NY.)

Fig. 5.3. This ivory is part of another Christological cycle, this one in the form of a book cover (21.0 × 12.5 cm [8 × 5 in.]). It was constructed at the Carolingian palace of Aachen around 800, and as the composition suggests—the three pigs sinking in the water below the long-haired demoniac who turns away from Jesus in his agony—the artist was working directly from the model of the late antique ivory in fig. 5.2. (Oxford, Bodleian Library, Ms. Douce 176. Photo: Bodleian Libraries.)

Fig. 5.4. Legion make their appearance. This ivory carving, which would originally have been backed with gilded copper plate, is one of sixteen surviving panels that were designed and made in Milan as part of an antependium, or decorative hanging, for the altar or ambo of the cathedral of Magdeburg, founded by Otto I in the tenth century. Note the presence of Saint Peter, identifiable by his keys, standing prominently behind Jesus (who appears in true profile, unlike the much commoner three-quarter view): he is yet another sign of the Ottonians' connections to Rome. One person among the crush of townspeople on the right physically restrains the possessed man: in Mark's account, the Gerasenes had tried in vain to keep the demoniac restrained. Only Jesus's treatment works. (12.8 × 11.8 cm [5.0 × 4.6 in.], Hessisches Landesmuseum Darmstadt, Inv. no. Kg 52:101. Photo: Wolfgang Fuhrmannek.)

Fig. 5.5. These Gadarene swine are part of a fresco program at the church of Saint George in Oberzell, painted ca. 985–987, which focuses on the miracles that Jesus performed publicly. Like the mosaic at Sant'Apollinare Nuovo (fig. 5.1), this panel appears on the top register of the left wall of the nave, though it is considerably larger than the scene at Ravenna, about 14 × 7.5 feet (4.24 × 2.28 m). The church was part of the monastery of Reichenau, which produced several Gospel books that featured images of the Gadarene swine, including fig. 5.6. The text below this panel concentrates on the switch between human and porcine possession: "The demon whose name was Legion is cast out, then he clings to the pigs, [and] they head for the depths of the sea." Some of the pigs have already drowned. (Photo: Bridgeman Images.)

the Gadarene swine on a late antique tradition of biblical illumination—but the Bibles that seem closest to its visual program are either missing or incomplete themselves.[73]

Yet whatever they had seen, the artists who made these scenes were not boxed in by their models. Their iconographies of the Gadarene story draw fresh attention to the relationship between humans and pigs by suspending the moment of demonic transfer between them, holding the ideas of sin and sacrifice in tension.

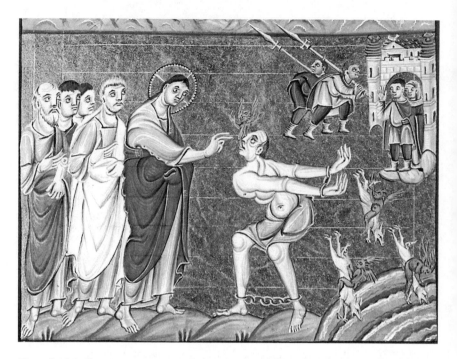

Fig. 5.6. This illumination is part of a lavish copy of the four Gospels produced at the monastery of Reichenau for Otto III (r. 983–1002). The codex was meticulously planned to coordinate the images (seven each for Matthew, Mark, and John, and eight for Luke) with their text; this image accompanies Mark's account. The contorted pose of the demoniac closely resembles the fresco at Oberzell in figure 5.5, and in contrast to the text of Mark, chains are successfully fettering him, although they have not alleviated his suffering. (Bayerische Staatsbibliothek München, Clm 4453, fol. 103v.)

Two other elements had become characteristic of this iconography by the late tenth century, and they raise the stakes of the scene: the swineherds who saw these events unfold, and the citizens of Gerasa who heard their news. According to all three of the Synoptic Gospels, when the swineherds ran to town to report the news of the exorcism, the townspeople were not glad to hear it. Instead they told Jesus to leave. And so a long line of exegetes had interpreted the town as a figuration of the Jews or heretics or philosophers, or anyone else who failed to recognize Jesus as the only source of salvation.[74]

When these two groups of witnesses appear in the visual field, the transaction between humans and pigs takes on cosmic proportions. The scene becomes something for all witnesses to accept or reject, and by extension to

accept or reject the theology it embodied. The human-pig kinetics were a dis-
tillation of Christianity itself, a complete case that Jesus made salvation possible. For a viewer, the appropriate reaction—in contrast to that of the residents
of Gerasa—was to recognize and appreciate this.

The prominence of the Gadarene swine in visual culture at the turn of the
millennium may have had something to do with the Ottonians' interest in asking what kinds of sacrifices were like or unlike Jesus's self-sacrifice, and the related question of what kinds of exchange and transformation took place in the
ritual celebration of the Eucharist.[75] But whatever their local resonances, these
themes also caught the eye of artists farther afield. About half a century after
the first Ottonian examples were made, the monastery of Ripoll in Catalonia
produced a Bible whose representation of the Gadarene swine is bracingly different from the Ottonian and Byzantine traditions (fig. 5.9).[76] And yet it shares

Fig. 5.7. This rendering of Mark's Gadarene swine appears in a Gospel codex that
was painted in Constantinople in the eleventh century, and it is one of the closest
correspondences with the mosaic at Sant'Apollinare Nuovo in fig. 5.1. In addition
to the horizontal positioning of the figures, the painter has included cave graves
among the mountains, a reference to the tombs in Mark 5:3. Even the tree is similar.
But like the Ottonian examples (such as figs. 5.5 and 5.6) and unlike the Ravenna
mosaic, the presence of demons and a swineherd shifts the action of the story to
focus on the movement of Legion into the pigs, and on the public's (or swineherd's)
choice to accept or reject that miracle. As in the Getty Gospel Lectionary (fig.5.8)
the herd here is furry and multicolored. (Paris, Bibliothèque nationale de France,
Ms. Gr. 74, fol. 72v.)

Fig. 5.8. This folio from a Gospel book made in England around 1000 represents the Gadarene swine episode as Matthew tells the story, in which Jesus heals two possessed men. The vertical orientation cleverly reimagines the mountainous landscape around Gerasa as it had been presented in late antique models, resulting in an image that reads from middle to bottom to top. Although the painting is damaged, it seems that demons were never part of the picture. But the pair of swineherds and the city of Gerasa are present, very like their Ottonian contemporaries. (Los Angeles, J. Paul Getty Museum, Ms. 9, fol. 1v. Digital image courtesy of the Getty's Open Content program.)

Fig. 5.9. The Gadarene swine in the Ripoll Bible (Catalonia, 1015–1020). This entire Bible was copied by a single monk named Guifré of Ripoll, who also drew many of its illustrations, including this one, which is part of a series of frames depicting the life of Jesus, collated from all four Gospels. Its style is very personal: Guifré was a skilled artist who favored quick, firm strokes to produce figures that were both schematic and highly expressive. Here he made the unusual choice of flipping the scene around its vertical axis, and many of the components are different, too: there are no apostles, the demons lack wings, and the demoniac is kneeling as at Sant'Apollinare Nuovo (fig. 5.1). The townspeople have the same wild hair as the demons, which together with their square jaws and outsized muscular bodies make them almost monstrous. But despite these differences, the core components of the "new" iconography are here: the demons who are leaving one victim for another and the witnesses who are confronted with the choice of accepting or rejecting this sacrificial miracle. (Copyright © 2020 Biblioteca Apostolica Vaticana, lat. 5729, fol. 367r. By permission of Biblioteca Apostolica Vaticana, with all rights reserved.)

the two key elements of demons and unbelieving witnesses that nearly all the contemporaneous cases have in common. So its pigs, too, had become both unholy and redemptive, both historically situated and universally relevant.

When the paradox of fleshiness came to preoccupy Christians from the twelfth century forward, pigs became even more of a pivot point than they had been in the Gadarene fixation of the central Middle Ages. In high and late medieval culture, scholastic texts, meditative materials, images, and devotional objects were saturated with the twinned notion that on one hand, flesh was inferior to immaterial things because it decayed and died and often obstructed the soul's best interests—and on the other, it was nonetheless the instrument of human salvation. Christians were also starting to see the material world around them as a *re*-created landscape, as matter made new through the uniquely transformative event of Jesus's execution and resurrection. The world now seemed to be not only an intellectual access point but a contact zone between humans and the divine.[77] So when preachers spoke to their congregations, they used pork to evoke both sides of this puzzle. In the fourteenth century Bernardino da Siena energetically insisted that gambling dens and their scents of roasted pork were one of Satan's proud creations. And yet, as a thirteenth-century preaching text pointed out, meat was the very stuff of Jesus's human body. It had cured in the *lardarium*—the meat cellar—of Mary's womb![78]

There were medical resonances here, too, not just theological ones. The internal anatomy of human beings was believed to find a close match in the bodies of pigs. This was one of the reasons why Galen opted to vivisect pigs in his public anatomical demonstrations in Rome. (He also thought that the pigs' tortured squealing enhanced the performances.) And a text called *Anatomia Porci*, or *The Anatomy of a Pig*, which was written at the medical school of Salerno in the twelfth century, guides its readers through the parallel universes of pigs' and humans' inner bodies. It moves briskly but congenially from the tongue to the intestines, with an unusually long disquisition on the uterus before finishing in the head. (The section on the uterus drew on a Greek medical text from Late Antiquity known as *De spermate*, which had been translated into Latin by the mid-1000s. It might have been appended to the *Anatomia* later, or it might have been incorporated into the text from the start.)[79]

The entire anatomical tour is based on a double vision of seeing humans through pigs, but that dual sensation is most intense in the uterus. The Latin writers who talked about the culinary wonders of this part of the pig almost always called it *vulva*, and occasionally *uterus, sterilis, eiecticia, porcaria,* and *abdomen*, depending on the features of the particular pig uterus in question. (It was, after all, a delicacy.) But the *Anatomia* calls it a *matrix*, a word that was otherwise strictly reserved for the human uterus, because *this* uterus is serving as a stand-in for its human counterpart. And because the subject here is always simultaneously pig and person, the text makes abrupt shifts in perspective that it sees as anatomically continuous. So the reader is told that it is fortunate to find a fetus in the specimen (pig) he or she is working with, because this gives a dissector an opportunity to study the architecture of the placenta and its various conduits—but the text then slides seamlessly into an explanation of how midwives tie off the umbilical cord of a newborn (human).[80] I have set these species distinctions in parentheses because the text does not supply them. The pig's womb was just as much a lardarium as Mary's: the life it created was both meat and model for humanity.

Christians were encouraged to internalize these meaty metaphors. The mind itself was a kind of "butcher shop," where the work of meditation dismembered the self into small pieces and offered them up to God in exchange for salvation. This was a process of learning, rather than self-destruction. Knowledge was something to cut up (in order to understand it) and to digest (in order to be nourished and transformed by it). And what needed to be understood and digested above all was the butchery of Jesus himself. It was important that Christians see how they continued to "tear the flesh of our Lord" when they sinned, as a French preacher in Amiens put it in the middle of the thirteenth century.[81] And sometimes it was the pig—that omnipresent and complicated animal—that helped them appreciate this.

The material and metaphorical uses of the pig in Christian theology are condensed most brilliantly in the frescoes of a small church about twenty miles north of Rome, Santa Maria Immacolata in Ceri (today the Chiesa della Madonna). The wall paintings were executed between 1100 and 1130, and the art historian Nino Zchomelidse has shown in her masterful analysis of the program that it was designed in part to communicate support for the moderate wing of a reform movement that had been launched by the papacy a century earlier. It was probably commissioned by Peter of Porto, the bishop of the diocese in which Ceri was located. Peter made frequent trips to Rome, because he was close to Pope Pascal II, and the fresco at Ceri shows many stylistic and iconographic similarities with churches that Peter would have seen on his travels to Rome and elsewhere, in particular the Roman churches of San Clemente and San Pietro in Vaticano.[82] But it is also a strikingly original piece, as Zchomelidse points out, and other ideas wind through its imagery in addition to its extensive argument about ecclesiastical reform.

If one faces the altar in the church at Ceri, the fresco lines the entire right wall of the central nave (fig. 5.10). It is structured as a grid. The top two rows, consisting of sixteen panels, consist of an Old Testament cycle, and the third row is a series of portraits of biblical and more recent saints. The fourth and lowest row—painted on the plinths of the nave—involves a set of images that

Fig. 5.10. The fresco cycle at Santa Maria Immacolata in Ceri (Lazio, 1100–1130), span-
ning about 50 × 20 feet (15 × 6 m) across the wall of the nave. (Photo: Bibliotheca
Hertziana—Max-Planck-Institut für Kunstgeschichte, Rome.)

Zchomelidse characterizes as a "zone of evil." One of these low-lying paintings is a cooking scene that prominently features a pig roasting on a spit,
with hams and sausages curing and a pot of more pork bubbling away in the
background. A butcher or cook keeps the pig juicy and the spit turning; the
two women to his left are probably servers (fig. 5.11).[83]

The scene stirs up a malevolent mood. On the next plinth to the right, demons battle or torture a human, and a fire-breathing chimera haunts the far
corner.[84] Through a horizontal reading of the fresco, this lowest level plays on
the longstanding association of pigs with evil. But that is not the only way to
see the pig panel. It takes on richer meanings in the context of the cycle as a
whole, especially the panel immediately above it: a portrait of five saints, with
John the Baptist in the center (fig. 5.12). John holds a lamb in his hands, en-
sconced in a eucharistic disc. This was Jesus, the Lamb of God or the Paschal
Lamb, and in the logic of this metaphor Christ was a spiritual lamb whose sacrifice would replace the Passover lamb that Jews offered to God every year in

memory of the Exodus. John holds the Lamb to underscore his own status as a bridge between these worlds: as a prophet of Jesus he represents the transition from the Old Testament to the New (which John's midlevel position in the cycle at Ceri further underscores), and as the Baptist he serves as the gateway to the eucharistic sacrament. These arguments move downward into the cooking scene below. As Zchomelidse suggests, the lavish display of pork stands in stark contrast to the food above it, the carnal pig versus the Lamb of God.[85]

More typological connections appear farther up the wall. The sensuousness of the cooking scene also echoes two narratives of seduction that are situated over the five saints: the attempt of Potiphar's wife to sleep with Joseph (fig. 5.13, based on Genesis 39), and above that scene, in the top row of the

Fig. 5.11. Cooking scene from the fresco program at Santa Maria Immacolata in Ceri, roughly 4.5 × 3 feet (1.4 × 0.9 m). The hams, sausages, bubbling pot of pork, and roasting pig offer a multisensory challenge while also pointing to the sacrifices (porcine and divine) that make human life possible. The Latin caption identifies the saints who stand above this panel (fig. 5.12). (Photo: Bibliotheca Hertziana—Max-Planck-Institut für Kunstgeschichte, Rome.)

Fig. 5.12. Five saints in the third register of the fresco at Santa Maria Immacolata in Ceri. From left to right: Nicholas of Myra, John the Evangelist, John the Baptist with the Lamb of God, Martin of Tours, and Leonard of Noblat/Noblac/Limoges. (Photo: Bibliotheca Hertziana—Max-Planck-Institut für Kunstgeschichte, Rome.)

fresco's grid, the temptation of Eve (fig. 5.14, based on Genesis 3). At the bottom of this vertical axis, the sausages and the pig perform another seduction. Very much in the mode of a medieval aesthetic that was supposed to activate the senses, the meal in progress invites the viewer to smell the pig on the spit, to hear its fat crackling and spitting as it drips in the fire, to imagine how delicious it would be.[86] This is what temptation feels like.

But not even *these* pigs were pure evil. There is a third dimension to consider, too, one that pulls the cooking scene away from its vertical and horizontal framework toward the other side of the paradox of the flesh. Moving out of the flat space of the fresco, these dead pigs faced the altar. Every mass brought them close to the liturgical offering of Jesus's body and blood that recapitulated his sacrifice. It may be that their position below the Lamb of God was not exclusively a study in contrasts. Positioned between two eucharistic moments, the pigs demonstrate sacrifice in their own way. If pork was a dangerous distraction, it was also a death that made life possible.

So ultimately this scene represented not an idea for Christians to reject completely but rather one to compare against other models of struggle and satisfaction. Meat was a seduction but also an offering, and it is an example of how (as the literary scholar Mary Carruthers put it) "medieval aesthetic experience is bound into human sensation," and how "human knowledge is sense-derived."[87] To fully understand and appreciate something, in other words, a person relied on the forms or experiences that communicated it. What that meant for the pigs at Ceri—and for the pigs in other corners of late antique and medieval Christianity—was that in the process of helping Christians think about Jesus's sacrifice, they became entangled with the concepts they served to clarify. And if the inconceivable magnitude of God's gesture could be rendered more palpable by likening and elevating it against the sacrifice of slaughter, the metaphor could move in both directions, up or down the cosmic

Fig. 5.13. In this panel from the second register of the fresco at Ceri, Potiphar's wife lifts her garment above her knees with her right hand, while grasping Joseph's coat with her left. Joseph has wriggled out of his coat but looks back as he runs away. The Latin caption here is fragmentary, and the text above the panel belongs to the temptation of Adam and Eve (fig. 5.14). (Photo: Bibliotheca Hertziana—Max-Planck-Institut für Kunstgeschichte, Rome.)

Fig. 5.14. The temptation of Adam and Eve in the top register of the fresco at Ceri, initiating a series of alluring scenes that will snake vertically down the fresco. The Latin caption reads, "Evil woman! What are you touching? Death is what the snake offers." (Photo: Bibliotheca Hertziana—Max-Planck-Institut für Kunstgeschichte, Rome.)

scale. The familiarity of the pig helped people think about something singular such as Jesus's sacrifice, and through the comparison, the pig itself appears as something precious and necessary and ultimately unrepayable.

In the course of this book I have presented various ways in which Christians were thinking about individual, actual animals as integral to their ethical systems (political, economic, religious), even though they believed that animals lacked the capacity to make ethical judgments. This may seem like a contradiction, but for late antique and medieval Christians, creatures did not have to act with reference to some moral principle in order to participate in ethics. Instead they could, through their own particular ways of being, change humans' sense of the world and their obligations to it. And they could furnish the very stuff of ethical action, by feeding or clothing or providing the reading material that helped humans thrive. What pigs in particular offered was a connective tissue that was both cognitive and literal. Their salvaging of the early medieval landscape linked humans to their environments and to the landscape of heaven, through exchanges of meat for soul.

Of all the ways in which pigs helped shape humans' evaluations of the world, it was through this most basic sense of pigs as matter that the species became Christianized, became the literal lifeblood of Christians but also a theological key to seeing the flesh in both its toxic and its salvific incarnations. The discourse of sacrifice opened up the possibility of acknowledging the contributions that pigs made to the mechanics of human salvation. It was a linking of the mud to the cosmos in a very material way. And so it offered another instance of pigs prompting an ecological ethics, or an ethics of integration and scale, because in considering the animals and their meat as an iconic case of energy transfer, Christians were noticing how small forces—being a pig, or gifting or butchering or eating a pig—could become something bigger.

But as consummately carnal beings, pigs became not only Christian but also counter-Christian, though compared to the twelfth century on this paradox floated only lightly through the post-imperial centuries. It was in the late Middle Ages and early modern period when the negative view veered into intense anti-Semitism. For the first time, pigs became emblematic of the Christian conviction that Judaism was too literal (or in the favored expression of the time, too "carnal" or "fleshy") an interpretation of scripture, whereas Christianity appreciated its truer, more elevated meaning. Pigs were represented as blood relatives or even nurses of Jews, joined by their shared baseness. And yet the species also remained quintessentially Christian, not only because Christians were the only monotheists in the western Mediterranean and Europe who ate pork, but also because pigs were a food to eat in acknowledgement of the life-saving function of flesh.[88]

So the Christianized iconicity of the pig accelerated and evolved in the high Middle Ages, but it was rooted in a bifurcated way of thinking about the animal that had been percolating since roughly the year 400. And the highly textured and even contradictory personality of the pig in Christian culture, as it came together in exegesis and book painting and precious objects and sacred places, was an outgrowth of cultural and material environments that had long taken both "the" pig and particular pigs very seriously. Pigs served as multiple symbols because there were multiple ways of knowing and living with the animals themselves. In this domain, too, pigs were adaptable and difficult and valuable, even when they were imaginary.

Epilogue

The interactions of pigs and ecologies did not come to a halt in the next millennium, but they did change character. By the eleventh century, for example, pigs had become a negligible presence among the animals of Iceland, in contrast to the early days of Norse colonization. One hypothesis for their gradual disappearance is that the environmental degradation they had caused since their introduction in the ninth century had finally outweighed the value of keeping them around. Farther south, pigs remained a vital part of agrarian life, but their habitats looked significantly different from those of the early Middle Ages. The inhabitants of Europe were clearing more and more woodlands, wetlands, and other "marginal" areas and converting them into farmland. There were many reasons for this: the population was growing, manufacturing industries were demanding larger supplies of wood for fuel, farms were increasingly focusing on cereal cultivation in contrast to earlier agro-pastoral arrangements, some settlements (like the city of Venice) needed timber to stabilize the very ground on which they stood, and a more widespread use of the moldboard plow made it easier to cut through heavy soils that had been difficult to farm previously. The woodlands that did survive these centuries were vigilantly monitored, and by the 1400s (and in some places even earlier), the regulations for pannage had become much stricter and more systematically enforced than they had been in most early medieval communities.[1]

As a result, pig husbandry became a less effective way to salvage resources in the areas where these changes were pronounced. When the British Isles suffered a sheep scab epidemic in the later thirteenth century and a bovine pestilence (probably rinderpest) in the early fourteenth century, agricultural estates came up with various strategies to mitigate the losses of their herds.

But supplementing their meat supplies by sizing up their pig herds was an ancillary strategy at best, because at this time their livestock were primarily put to the service of other industries—cerealiculture, dairying, and the wool trade.[2]

Another consequence of large-scale land clearance was that some pigs spent more time in farmyards than their ancestors had. Nonetheless, the move to intensive sty-based pig husbandry was a centuries-long transformation that was specific to local ecologies. At Dudley Castle in the West Midlands of England, a region that had worked to protect the resources of its woods, the switch took place in the mid-fourteenth century. And it would not be until the eighteenth century that European farmers began to engineer their pigs to fatten rapidly, which they did not only by making their pigs more sedentary but also by introducing Chinese pig stocks to their more established breeds. This shift too was locally variable. In some places, such as the live oak and shrub oak savannahs of Extremadura and Andalucía in southwest Spain, pigs continued to be pastured during the early modern period and even up to the present, and they were never mixed with Asian breeds. Consequently the medieval art of swineherding would not have disappeared entirely. But swineherds' identities would have changed as the nature of the job shifted, and as the early medieval legal culture of unfreedom gave way to new forms of dependency and social status.[3]

Meanwhile, although the relatively diverse diets of the early Middle Ages were becoming more focused on grains, especially for nonelite eaters, many Christian lay elites continued to eat more pork, especially piglet meat, compared to their less affluent neighbors. In the high Middle Ages, too, pigs were often more prevalent at castles and other fortified sites than was typical for their surroundings. (The fortresses that Muslim elites controlled in al-Andalus also included a few pig bones within their trash, but it was probably the Christian tenants who had discarded them.) The elites who were eating pigs were not acquiring them in the same ways they had before, however. Pannage taxes tended to be collected in cash in the high and late Middle Ages, and the obligations and rents that tenants owed their landlords were also increasingly monetized. So the people who favored pork were either pulling pigs from their own herds, or purchasing them at regional markets and fairs, which were a more conspicuous part of the landscape than they had been in the early Middle Ages. And the pork market introduced new opportunities for subjugation: every time a serf of the bishop of Worcester sold a pig, for example, he or she was obligated to pay a fine known as *tak,* literally "the take."[4]

Most farms in the high and late Middle Ages kept pigs in numbers that were close to the size of early medieval herds. The duke of Burgundy made a habit of purchasing over two hundred pigs for his household every autumn, but he had to amass them piecemeal, through several suppliers across multiple markets who sold only a few pigs each to his agents. Pig husbandry did not balloon as sheep husbandry was doing in Italy and Iberia, especially. These forms of animal husbandry may have even been inversely correlated in the high Middle Ages: some historians and archaeologists have suggested that the rise of the wool industry, coupled with woodland clearance, was "good" for sheep and "bad" for pigs.[5] But in many of Europe's micro-ecologies, the situation was different. In the Apulian village of Apigliano, for example, sheep and goats were much better represented before 900 than they were after 900, and the village's textile manufacturing never seems to have been geared toward export. Even in places where pig husbandry declined, deforestation and wool production were not always to blame. In the coastal foothills of Tuscany, Campiglia had been a hub of pig husbandry in the tenth and eleventh centuries, but by the time the village had become a fortified settlement and military garrison in the fourteenth century, sheep and goats were the favored meats. Perhaps the woodlands around Campiglia had shrunk in the intervening centuries, but we lack data about the plant life of its early phases, and by the time the charcoal samples from the high Middle Ages appear, the picture is surprising. Whatever the woods had looked like previously, Campiglia was now home to extensive and mature woodlands dominated by deciduous oaks and elm, with smaller populations of chestnut, maple, beech, cherry, willow or some species of *Populus,* and juniper. But the counts who lived here in the 1200s, and the soldiers who were stationed here in the 1300s, changed their diets anyway. They (or more precisely, their suppliers) raised sheep and goats as much for their meat as for their milk and wool, and their pork intake plummeted.[6]

Another agrarian change was bureaucratic: English landowners began keeping track of their animal herds with astonishing consistency in the middle of the thirteenth century. Thousands of surviving parchment scrolls attest to this new accountability, as reeves across the kingdom were assessing, year after year, the livestock they were breeding, feeding, buying, pannaging, slaughtering, selling, and donating. These were big pig data, and they were part of an effort of landlords and their staffs to make their farms more productive and profitable. But rather than disappear in a sea of calculations, pigs become more visible in these sources than they ever were in early medieval documents. It is even possible to follow the "life" of a dead pig from the moment it first enters a larder, to nineteen months later, when it is recorded as being essentially worthless (*nichil valentes*), and then to the following year, when it is donated to charity. The process of commodification is also an opportunity to individuate.[7]

The sort of evidence we have for natural philosophy and natural history also changed in the twelfth and thirteenth centuries, when Aristotle's work began to be translated from its Arabic versions into Latin or, less frequently, from Greek directly into Latin. Aristotle's readers seized on his taxonomic distinctions between human beings and other animals to emphasize the superiority of humans in newly elaborate ways—and in a departure from early medieval views, to suggest that living things sat on a sliding scale of increasing complexity, from plants up to humans. This amounted to a more stringent view of the dominance of the human species compared to early medieval perspectives, but other writers had different ideas. Hunters and horse riders in particular pointed out that humans had to learn from their animals in order to be successful in the chase and in war—and that their animals could in turn learn from *them*. Even if the human perspective was superior, it could not work in isolation. The concepts of hierarchy and domination were still inadequate ways of understanding the world.[8]

In other ways, the spirit of early medieval cosmology was highly compatible with what scholastics found in the Philosopher. After all, many of the late antique and early medieval writers who explored the organization of the universe had been responding either directly or indirectly to Aristotle, among other interlocutors. And the scholastics' working methods can also look strikingly similar to what exegetes were doing five hundred to a thousand years before them. When Albert the Great commented on Aristotle's zoology (specifically his *History of Animals, De historia animalium*) in the middle of the thirteenth century, he injected his own personal observations about the plants and animals of Germany and the Low Countries to set alongside Aristotle's Mediterranean biosphere, and he consulted other experts, such as hunters and whalers, for their insights. Ambrose of Milan would have approved. More generally, Albert and his peers were still animated by the early medieval conviction that the complexity of the physical world was a kind of key to the logic of God's creation, and that blending scriptural, analytical, and observational authorities was the best way to unspool those secrets.[9]

Many of these scholastics lived in the great cities of Europe. We know that they paid close attention to their surroundings, so they might have noticed that ecologies were changing there, too. Towns were becoming increasingly densely settled, and pigs were one of the most vexed signs of the shift. To many critics, pigs seemed to overrun the cities of high medieval Europe. It is likely that every faculty member who pondered the connections between the smallest creature and the largest cosmic systems would have found himself put out by a pig at some point. The problems were familiar, only magnified. Pigs were sometimes led outside the city walls to pasture—this happened in York, for instance—or were kept close and fed on kitchen or commercial food waste. But pigs did not abandon their zest for ranging and scavenging, and the problems they caused provoked litanies of public outcry.[10]

There had been some grievances about city pigs in antiquity. A character in one of Plautus's plays complains about the smell at bakeries, for example, because the bakers were feeding their pigs with leftover bran, and he also mentions in passing that pigs were roaming the city streets. But in the more lightly settled and agrarian urban spaces of the early Middle Ages, pigs had not been a standout concern, no more than they were in rural areas. In the high Middle Ages, by contrast, things escalated. Pigs began creating traffic congestion in towns. Their smell "polluted" the city air and (in keeping with contemporary medical theory) created an infectious miasma that could destabilize the humoral balance within human bodies and make them sick. They may have also been an eyesore whose very visibility could threaten human health, according to contemporary concepts of sight pollution.[11]

When the towns' human residents tackled these hazards, pigs became, once again, a formative influence not only on medieval communities' sense of proper husbandry but also on their definitions of social order more generally. In the Low Countries they sparked debates that became central to the agendas of late medieval cities. City governments decided that one of their main responsibilities was to keep waterways unclogged with waste and roads clear of obstructions, which in turn meant setting constraints on how city dwellers handled their private property. Their concept of "cleaning up" a town— to impress visitors, to keep trade flowing, to keep residents safe, to make it respectable—was deeply inspired, or provoked, by pigs. Such a sense of the city was inconceivable without pigs' intervention, even if (in some places, such as Dublin, Nuremberg, and Bologna) they were eventually banned from cities entirely, or at least raised in town less frequently (as at Novgorod).[12] This was a new spin on the early medieval spirit of accommodation: pigs were still making a dent in public policy, to the point that they were ejected from the most crowded public spaces.

Other pigs, the horrifically delinquent ones, were targeted with a different punitive measure: the animal trial. Starting in the thirteenth century and peaking in the fifteenth to seventeenth centuries, secular courts in continental

Europe occasionally put individual animals on trial—usually pigs, usually for homicide—which involved a strict adherence to legal protocol and often ended in a death penalty. The imprisonment and proceedings could take weeks. People were employed to feed these animals, act as their jailors, prosecute them, defend them, build their scaffolds, carry out their executions, and (at least once) paint a picture of the event and install it in a church.[13]

These trials would have seemed as strange to early medieval communities as they do to us now. Although it used to be thought that they were rooted in "Germanic" custom—a proposition without evidence to support it, and reflective of an older tendency to sweep all kinds of unusual practices under the "Germanic" rug—they were in fact an invention of the later Middle Ages. As soon as the trials appear in the written record, criticisms of the practice also crop up. Scholastics were often the people making the objections, because they had become riveted by the question of whether animals participated in the same moral universe as human beings. The animal trials, and the jurists who rationalized them, were responding to the same questions, except their answers leaned closer to "yes," while the philosophers tended to say "no."[14]

But although putting a pig on trial was specific to late medieval and early modern legal and intellectual cultures, the idea that pigs were simultaneously inferior and influential was not. The conceptual tensions these trials involved would have been recognizable to early medieval farmers, philosophers, and lawmakers, too. Their sense of the cosmos as an infinitely complex arrangement of forces, their attention to the systemic implications of even the smallest organisms, and their alertness to the ways that humans became *themselves* through their pigs: these ways of thinking presupposed that animals were thoroughly enmeshed in humans' understanding of causation and responsibility. It was immaterial whether animals were also rational.[15]

The collaborations between pigs and people were also crossing the Atlantic in these centuries. When Europeans set their sights on colonizing and exploiting the New World, their brutal projects might not have succeeded without the help of their pigs. The species had originated in Malaysia and been resident across Eurasia for thousands of years, but there were none to be found in the Americas or Australasia until the Columbian Exchange. When pigs did eventually reach those places, whether they were deposited on the pampas of Paraguay or the islands of the South Pacific, they took well to their new homes. They were, as the historian Alfred Crosby put it, the "weediest" of livestock. On Columbus's second voyage, he brought eight pigs to Hispaniola. It did not take long for people to describe their numbers on the island as "infinite."[16]

In an echo of late Roman and medieval practices, Spanish soldiers in Central and South America ate a pork-rich diet and made pig husbandry a central part of their agricultural-military complexes. When Spanish generals set up supply bases before beginning their campaigns, pig farms were a crucial part of their preparations. Hernán Cortés had a deputy establish a large pig operation in Veracruz before his siege of Tenochtitlán. Francisco Pizarro did the same thing on an island just off the coast of Tumbes, Peru. In other cases, armies imported their pigs from the Antilles or other colonial centers that already teemed with them. After native settlements were defeated, their conquerors quickly set about wrenching their landscapes into new agrarian regimes, and for the first decade or so, they mainly did it with pigs because pigs were an efficient source of food that could convert an "alien" environment into a familiar one. Indigenous populations were also forced to pay tribute in pigs and other produce, continuing a long European tradition of pork as an instrument of coercion and elitism. In the process, Hispaniola was not the only place to become overrun with pigs. In less than a decade after pigs came to Quito, the city set a cap on the number of pigs per resident. Three years after that, in 1541, the city was still able to supply Gonzalo Pizarro (half-brother of Francisco) with some three thousand to five thousand pigs to accompany his crew on an exploratory journey down the Amazon. And there were other, more regular customers: many a Peruvian pig ended up surrendering its fat to the miners deep in Potosí and elsewhere. The backbreaking work of the colonial silver mines was artificially lit with their lard. (And the hearts of their descendants may eventually pump in humans' chests: an immunologist's lab in Massachusetts is editing the genes of pigs from the Andes and the South American Rockies to turn them into viable organ donors for human beings. The species interplay continues.)[17]

Pigs were obviously an asset to the Europeans who muscled their way into the Americas because the animals were so adaptable and self-sufficient. But their usefulness should not overshadow the fact that they were semi-autonomous agents who were capable of major destruction—and the earliest settlers would have known this, based on their experiences in European farming communities and cities. The Pizarro brothers, for instance, had come from Trujillo, and Cortés was from Medellín. They hailed from Extremadura, in other words, where pig husbandry was a lucrative and highly regulated facet of the local economy in the late Middle Ages and early modern period.[18] Letting pigs run free in the New World was an act of willful negligence: there were costs, and some of those costs were entirely foreseeable, but colonists did not care about them until they impinged on their own enterprises.

This particular consequence of colonization has been studied best in the British colonies of New England and the Midatlantic.[19] In the seventeenth-century Chesapeake, colonists had originally intended to pen their pigs and cows. But for all their talk of human dominion (which was far more full-throated in the early modern world than it had been in the early Middle Ages, when people had been more interested in the many perspectives that organisms offered), they quickly gave up this plan in favor of letting the animals run loose to fend for themselves because it saved farmers an enormous amount of labor and food. So although their owners were unquestionably familiar with more supervisory forms of livestock management, in this new colonial situation the pigs roamed far and wide, and they quickly turned feral. European visitors who saw this state of affairs were shocked by the contrast, but their sensibilities were not the only collateral damage. The "wild gangs of the Chesapeake" devastated fields of maize, beans, and squash that indigenous farmers had planted; raided the food that had already been stored; trampled the marshes where women collected grasses and reeds for weaving; outran humans to their otherwise reliable sites for berries, nuts, and clams; and interrupted the rhythm of hunts. Pigs were as much a problem as a solution to the challenges of English colonization, and it was the Algonquian-speaking peoples who bore the brunt of the costs.

Pigs' histories have yet to be explored this deeply for their other landing spots in the Americas, but there are indications that their introduction went no more smoothly elsewhere. In the cities of Spanish America, free-ranging animals prompted the colonists to complain about some of the same things that had bothered them and their ancestors in the Old World. The pigs smelled, they drank and bathed in potable water, they defecated in waterways, and more generally their wanderings through public areas made them conduits of disease. These qualms persisted into the nineteenth century, although they were not universally shared. The Yucatán state, for example, targeted loose pigs as a sign of public-health deficiencies during cholera outbreaks. This allowed officials to fix the blame and the correctives on the Maya population, who did not necessarily endorse their medical theories. And when New York City also tried to contain its pig problems in the 1810s, some residents protested that the new ordinances would make it harder for poor people to feed themselves— and harder to clean the trash off their streets! Here, too, it was only during the cholera epidemic in 1849 that the municipal government was finally able to recast these "filth removers" as "filth producers," in order to exile the animals from the city.[20]

But the history of pigs in the New World was in other ways dramatically different from that of the late antique and medieval West, which locally specific studies could illuminate more clearly. Not only were the environments that pigs encountered totally new. The humans they met interacted with them in different ways. Indian communities in North America, for example, quickly decided to integrate pig husbandry into their preexisting agrarian practices, and they even sold pork back to colonists in Boston and Manhattan in exchange for guns. (This irritated some colonists, mostly because the Indians had adopted the European animals on their own terms and were edging out colonial pork suppliers.)[21]

There were other ways to coopt the pig. Native peoples across the Caribbean and South America were guided by a concept they called *iegue,* which referred to an animal or human who had its labor transformed into the service of the human companion who "familiarized" it. Almost any creature could be transformed into an iegue: parrots, iguanas, manatees, monkeys, sloths, deer, peccaries, and capybaras, for instance. Nonnative animals were candidates, too. But unlike European livestock, the individual animals who underwent this process could never be eaten. In the sixteenth century, for example, one Taíno man in Hispaniola trained three feral pigs to hunt and live with him. A group of Spanish soldiers later killed the animals, mistaking them for genuinely wild boar. And although the soldiers thought that the Taíno man was leading too "bestial" a lifestyle—the notion of iegue confused Europeans when it came to domesticated livestock—they also felt very sorry for having killed his pigs.[22]

In central Mexico, pigs received an entirely different reception. Although the Mesoamerican subjects of New Spain had begun to raise imported livestock not long after the conquests, a diviner named Juan Teton advised his people to give it up, because these animals were a sign that the world was ending. He warned them that people who ate the meat of European livestock would be transformed into their meals: "Those who eat the flesh of cows will be transformed into that. Those who eat the flesh of pork will be transformed into that." . . . Teton made these predictions after carefully consulting his calendars and cosmologies. He had also closely watched the lands around him at a time (in 1558) when the Mesoamerican population had dropped precipitously while the livestock population boomed. He pointed to places where the Indians who had embraced Christianity and foreign livestock were now barren. The residents there had indeed turned into the animals they had eaten.[23]

The idea that eating could dissolve the difference between eaters and their foods shared an affinity with the European epistemology of eating that had developed in Late Antiquity. And the association of domesticated meats with Christian identity, especially the pig, would also have made sense to the Spanish forces who occupied Teton's homeland. Maybe the diviner was purposely playing on these homologies. But on the whole, his response was pitched to a culture with an entirely different view of the local and cosmic forces at work in their lands. The cases of central Mexico, Hispaniola, the Chesapeake, and New England point to the fact that although some of the patterns of pigs' lives in the Americas were structured by their medieval histories, their responsivity to new environments also indicated that their early modern histories were as variable as their ancient and medieval ones. We cannot, then, sum up the afterlife of the "ecological ethic" without considering the range of material and social environments that would have conditioned it in the second millennium. Pigs continued to be prominent working partners with humans—that much is clear. But if we wanted to know precisely how they altered a culture's sense of scale or influence or value, we would have to start small.

Abbreviations

AASS   Acta Sanctorum quotquot tote orbe coluntur
CCCM   Corpus Christianorum Continuatio Medievalis
CCSL   Corpus Christianorum Series Latina
ChLA   *Chartae Latinae Antiquiores* (vols. 1–49)
ChLA2   *Chartae Latinae Antiquiores*, 2nd series (vols. 50–118)
CLA   Lowe, ed. *Codices Latini Antiquiores*
CSEL   Corpus Scriptorum Ecclesiasticorum Latinorum
Flixborough 1   Loveluck and Atkinson, *The Early Medieval Settlement Remains from Flixborough*
Flixborough 2   Evans and Loveluck, *Life and Economy at Early Medieval Flixborough*
Flixborough 3   Dobney et al., *Farmers, Monks, and Aristocrats*
Flixborough 4   Loveluck, *Rural Settlement, Lifestyles, and Social Change*
MGH   Monumenta Germaniae Historica

	Auct. ant.	Auctores antiquissimi
	Epp.	Epistolae
	LL	Leges (in Folio)
	LL nat. Germ.	Leges nationum Germanicarum
	SS rer. Germ.	Scriptores rerum Germanicarum in usum scholarum separatim editi
	SS rer. Merov.	Scriptores rerum Merovingicarum

NRSV   New Revised Standard Version
PL   Patrologia Latina
Sawyer   The Electronic Sawyer, www.esawyer.org.uk
SC   Sources Chrétiennes

NOTES

Biblical and other translations are mine unless otherwise noted.

Introduction

1. Fentress, Drine, and Holod, *An Island Through Time.*

2. Examples of appurtenance clauses for *pecudes/pecora/animales/res* described as *minores/minuta:* ChLA 13.570 (Theuderic III, 688 CE); *Traditiones Wizenburgenses,* no. 17 (739); ChLA 24.774 (S. Salvatore in Monte Amiata, 778); ChLA 29.874 (Treviso, 790); *Chartes de l'abbaye de Saint-Étienne de Dijon,* no. 1 (793); *Portugaliae Monumenta Historica,* vol. 1, nos. 6, 15, 28, 40, 55, 58, 76, 99, 114.

3. Augustine, *De Genesi ad litteram* 11.8 ("quis autem hos audiret, si dicerent: quoniam excellentior sensus est uidendi quam audiendi, quattuor oculi essent et aures non essent?").

4. In that sense, early medieval humans were already thinking about animals as being "inside ethics," to borrow a term from the moral philosopher Alice Crary (*Inside Ethics*): human decisions about what mattered were derived not only from human perspectives but also from animal lives. But for Crary, bringing animals "inside ethics" is both a normative and a disciplinary move: philosophy and literature should play a key role in sensing what is important to animals. Marcy Norton sees history and anthropology playing a similar role in ethics: Norton, "The Chicken or the *Iegue,*" 56–57.

5. Marzluff, *Welcome to Subirdia,* 101–2; for a neurochemical hypothesis of how birds, especially corvids, become "interspecific social junkies" see Marzluff and Angell, *Gifts of the Crow,* 163–68. Octopolis: Godfrey-Smith, *Other Minds,* 179–93.

6. On the vitality of "dark ages": James C. Scott, *Against the Grain,* 219–56. For challenges to the conceit that late antique and early medieval "society" was split between Roman and barbarian identities, see (among a very rich bibliography) Pohl and Reimitz, *Strategies of Distinction;* Rummel, *Habitus barbarus;* Halsall, *Cemeteries and Society*

in Merovingian Gaul; Pohl, Gantner, and Payne, *Visions of Community in the Post-Roman World;* Pohl and Heydemann, *Strategies of Identification;* Pohl and Heydemann, *Post-Roman Transitions;* Reimitz, *History, Frankish Identity and the Framing of Western Ethnicity;* Pohl, Gantner, et al., *Transformations of Romannness.* For the argument that the post-Roman world is an ideal laboratory for thinking about changes in spatial and political horizons, see Escalona and Reynolds, *Scale and Scale Change in the Early Middle Ages;* and on the necessity of thinking about scales and contexts for this period, Sessa, "The New Environmental Fall of Rome."

7. Readers who would like an introduction to late antique and early medieval political and cultural history should start with Peter Brown, *The Rise of Western Christendom;* Fowden, *Before and After Muḥammad;* Smith, *Europe After Rome;* Wickham, *Framing the Early Middle Ages; New Cambridge Medieval History,* vols. 1–3; *New Cambridge History of Islam,* vol. 1. Rabbinic culture: Fonrobert and Jaffee, *The Cambridge Companion to the Talmud and Rabbinic Literature.* Punctuation: Parkes, *Pause and Effect.* Musical notation: Thomas Forest Kelly, *Oral and Written Transmission in Chant.* Latin and proto-Romance: Roger Wright, *A Sociophilological Study of Late Latin.*

8. Nyhart, *Modern Nature,* 2.

9. See, e.g., Berkowitz, *Animals and Animality in the Babylonian Talmud;* Wasserman, *Jews, Gentiles, and Other Animals;* Schliephake, *Ecocriticism, Ecology, and the Cultures of Antiquity;* Jeffrey Jerome Cohen, *Stone;* Belser, *Power, Ethics, and Ecology in Jewish Late Antiquity;* Ellen Arnold, *Negotiating the Landscape;* Siewers, *Strange Beauty.*

10. Even the exceptions are telling: Lindberg's second edition of *The Beginnings of Western Science* includes about eighteen pages for this half-millennium (and this includes an expanded discussion of Carolingian astronomy and *computus* that the first edition lacked). And only one-tenth of the *Cambridge History of Science,* volume 2 (*Medieval Science*) is dedicated to the early medieval West, including North Africa and Iberia. Hoffmann's *Environmental History of Medieval Europe* is an outlier for its chronological balance.

11. Siracusano, "The Fauna of Leptis Magna"; Finbar McCormick and Murray, *Excavations at Knowth 3,* 73–76.

12. Tsing, *The Mushroom at the End of the World.*

13. Matthew 8:28–34; Luke 8:26–39; Mark 5:1–20. The Legion quotation that follows is Mark 5:9 (NRSV). On this pericope in ancient and early medieval culture see Chapters 4 and 5.

1. A Singular and Plural Beast

1. "Trí báis ata ferr bethaid: bás iach, bás muicce méithe, bás foglada": *Triads of Ireland,* no. 92 (second half of the ninth century).

2. Pig manure may have had its uses, although the lone passage that is sometimes cited as evidence for this is based on a weak translation of a phrase in the polyptych of

Prüm, *suo fimo,* which probably means "the manure of his own [animals]" rather than "pig dung," not only because that would be a more grammatically correct reading but also because this source prefers the terms *sualis, porcus,* and *friskinga* for pigs, rather than *sus: Prümer Urbar* 1; cf. Richard Jones, "Understanding Medieval Manure," 147. The archaeological evidence of manuring suggests that sheep and goats were more often the main fertilizers: see, e.g., Kallala and Sanmartí, *Althiburos II,* 471–74 (carpological analysis by Dani López and Francisco José Cantero).

3. This is so consistent that citing all instances of it would be excessive, but see for example Gilchrist, "A Reappraisal of Dinas Powys," 56–58; Wigh, *Animal Husbandry in the Viking Age Town of Birka,* 76–84; Catteddu, Clavel, and Ruas, "L'habitat rural mérovingien de Genlis," 90–92 (faunal analysis by Benoît Clavel); Riera Rullan, Cau Ontiveros, and Salas Burguera, *Cent anys de Son Peretó,* 30–31 (faunal analysis by Damià Ramis Bernad); Salvadori, "L'allevamento nell'Italia medievale," 130–37; Kallal and Sanmartí, *Althiburos II,* 424–30 (faunal analysis by Silvia Valenzuela-Lamas).

4. Greenland: Enghoff, *Hunting, Fishing and Animal Husbandry,* 79, with some qualifications in Arge, Church, and Brewington, "Pigs in the Faroe Islands," 23–24. On Jewish and Muslim attitudes to pork see Chapters 4 and 5. Wills: see, e.g., *Tumbos del Monasterio de Sobrado de los Monjes,* no. 1 (952 CE); *Cartulario de "Sant Cugat" del Vallés,* no. 188 (986).

5. *Vita prima sanctae Brigidae* 117; al-Jāḥiẓ, *Kitāb al-ḥayawān* 1.234, 4.40–41, 4.95, trans. Souami, *Le cadi et la mouche,* pp. 331–35.

6. Augustine, *Confessiones* 2.4. My thanks to Brent Shaw for reminding me what happens to the pears!

7. For the context in which the Stuttgart Psalter was produced, see *Polyptychon von Saint-Germain-des-Prés,* ii-vii; Elmshäuser and Hedwig, *Studien zum Polyptychon von Saint-Germain-des-Prés; Stuttgarter Bilderpsalter.* For the ways that Jews and Christians interpreted this psalm in Late Antiquity and the early Middle Ages, see Chapter 5.

8. Most recently: Essig, *Lesser Beasts;* Pastoureau, *Le cochon.*

9. Genesis 2:19–20; Isidore, *Etymologiae,* book 12, preface.

10. In early and classical Latin *porcus* itself often specifically meant "young pig," though this inflection receded in later Latin. See the debates in *In Medias Res:* Kuhner, "Porcus Does Not Mean Pig"; Gitner, "Porcus Does Not Just Mean Piglet Either"; Kuhner, "A Definitive Guide to Pig Latin."

11. My interpretation of the terms *bevralis* and *genalis* is based on the specific contexts in which they appear in the Frankish polyptychs, and so they vary from the more general definitions in DuCange's *Glossarium:* see, e.g., *Polyptyque . . . de Saint-Remi de Reims,* pp. 56, 64.

12. *Edictus Rothari* 351.

13. See Index 1 in Fergus Kelly, *Early Irish Farming;* Paul the Deacon, Epitome of Sextus Pompeus Festus, *De verborum significatu,* 30 (*cicur* appears under *bigenera*), 49, 63.

14. Augustine, *De Genesi ad litteram* 3.11; Apuleius, *Metamorphoses* 8.4 ("impetu saevo frementis oris totus fulmineus"), trans. Ruden, p. 162.

15. See, e.g., Bianchi, *Campiglia*, 2:479–82 (faunal analysis by Frank Salvadori); Iwaszczuk, "Animal Husbandry on the Polish Territory," 87–88. On the long history of wild-domesticated interbreeding, with additional methods for telling domesticated and wild pig populations apart in the archaeological record, see Albarella, Dobney, and Rowley-Conwy, "The Domestication of the Pig (*Sus scrofa*)"; Larson et al., "Current Views on *Sus* Phylogeography and Pig Domestication"; Scandura, Iacolina, and Apollonio, "Genetic Diversity in the European Wild Boar," 131–33.

16. Aurochs in Europe: Hoffmann, *Environmental History of Medieval Europe,* 191; Clavel and Yvinec, "L'archéozoologie du Moyen Âge," 81. Aurochs and Barbary sheep in North Africa: Mattingly, *The Archaeology of Fazzān*, 1:339–42; Siracusano, "The Fauna of Leptis Magna"; Veen, Grant, and Barker, "Romano-Libyan Agriculture," 241, 251–52; H. R. Hurst, *Excavations at Carthage*, vol. 2.1, p. 314 (faunal analysis by Marsha A. Levine and A. Wheeler); Vos, "The Rural Landscape of Thugga," 169.

17. See Pastoureau, *Le roi tué par un cochon,* esp. 43–65; Pastoureau, "La chasse au sanglier"; Allsen, *The Royal Hunt in Eurasian History,* 165–66 and passim.

18. Förstemann, *Altdeutsches Namenbuch,* 438–48, s.v. "EBUR"; search results of all **ebur*-lemma in the Nomen et Gens onomastic and prosopographical database, www.neg.uni-tuebingen.de/?q=de/datenbank (accessed 1 November 2015). For female names with the lemma, see the index of the names of tenants of Saint-Germain-des-Prés: *Polyptychon von Saint-Germain-des-Prés,* 294.

19. See Beck, *Das Ebersignum im Germanischen;* Janssen, "Das Tier im Spiegel der archäologischen Zeugnisse," 1304–5. An accessible introduction to the modern fiction of Germanic barbarians is Goffart, *Barbarian Tides;* and see also the essential work of Pohl, *Die Germanen,* and Pohl, "Der Germanenbegriff." On the contexts of that older historiography see *inter alia* Wood, *The Modern Origins of the Early Middle Ages;* Effros, *Uncovering the Germanic Past;* Krebs, *A Most Dangerous Book.*

20. Farnum, *The Positioning of the Roman Imperial Legions,* 15, 22, 24; Deines, "How Long?" 207–12; Har-Peled, "The Diaological Beast," 117–31 (on Legio X Fretensis, with further bibliography); Malone, *Legio XX Valeria Victrix.* See more generally Keller, *Die Antike Tierwelt,* 1:389–93.

21. See Guardia Pons, *Los mosaicos de la antigüedad tardía en Hispania,* 327–35; Ennaïfer, "La Maison des deuz chasses à Kélibia"; Balmelle, *Les demeures aristocratiques d'Aquitaine,* 300; Blázquez, *Mosaicos romanos de España,* 245–71; Fernández, *Aristocrats and Statehood,* 80–81; Andreae, *Die römischen Jagdsarkophäge,* 108–10. On Christians' use of mythological iconography in their mosaics across the Mediterranean, see Bowersock, *Mosaics as History,* 31–63.

22. Luxorius, *Liber epigrammaton* 292. See further Conant, *Staying Roman,* 53, whose reading is more persuasive than the speculations in North, "You Sexy Beast."

For the contexts of the figures reproduced here see Gino Vinicio Gentili, *La Villa Romana di Piazza Armerina*, 2:49–65; Pensabene, *Piazza Armerina*; Fernández-Galiano, "La villa de Materno"; Blázquez, "Nombres de aurigas," 960–61; Blázquez, *Mosaicos romanos de España*, 251; Andreae, *Die römischen Jagdsarkophäge*, p. 111, no. 112.

23. See Jarnut, "Die frühmittelalterliche Jagd," esp. 778–83; Wickham, "European Forests in the Early Middle Ages," 485–90; Montanari, "La foresta come spazio economico e culturale," esp. 315–19; Lorzen, "Der Königsforst (*forestis*) in den Quellen der Merowinger- und Karolingerzeit"; Sykes, "Rhetoric of Meat Apportionment." On wild game at sites that are not conspicuously elitist, see, e.g., Grau-Sologestoa, "Faunal Remains and Social Inequality," 53–54; Yvinec, "La part du gibier"; Veen, Grant, and Barker, "Romano-Libyan Agriculture"; H. R. Hurst and Rostams, *Excavations at Carthage*, vol. 1.1, pp. 229–56. For wild birds and fish in early medieval diets, see Chapter 3.

24. Goldberg, "Louis the Pious and the Hunt"; Gravel, "Of Palaces, Hunts, and Pork Roast." When speaking of hunting Carolingian writers preferred the active verbs *capere* and *caciare*, in part because they portrayed a successful hunt as the work of the hunter: see Goldberg, "'The Hunt Belongs to Man,'" 39. See Chapter 3 for more on pig taxes.

25. Charter of 1217 (Henry III): Stubbs, *Select Charters*, 346; charter of 1297 (Edward I): *Statutes of the Realm (1225–1713)*, 121; Rackham, *Ancient Woodland*, 177; Sykes, *The Norman Conquest*, 66. Eventually English elites would stock game parks with pigs they had raised in captivity: Thomas, *Animals, Economy and Status*, 49; Woolgar, *The Great Household in Late Medieval England*, 115–16.

26. Arles: Cyprianus of Toulon et al., *Vita Caesarii* 1.48 (referring to the monastery *in suburba insula civitatis* from 1.12); this section of the *vita* was written by Viventius, Messianus, and Stephanus. On the text, see Klingshirn, "Charity and Power." Shooting at eagles: *Lex Baiwariorum* 19.5. Crop damage: Jordan, "Count Robert's 'Pet' Wolf," 412–13.

27. For the late antique evidence see Stern, "Les calendriers romains illustrés," esp. the mosaic at Saint-Romain-en-Gal, the Porte de Mars in Reims, and the mosaic (III) from Carthage. Among many compendia of the high medieval visual evidence see Cate, "*Wan god mast gift*"; Baruzzi and Montanari, *Porci e porcari*; Phillips, "The Pig in Medieval Iconography"; less reliable analytically is Kearney, *The Role of Swine Symbolism*.

28. The Utrecht Psalter, for example (fig. 1.8), was a classicizing program that was pitched to the Carolingian court's interests in Roman antiquity: Horst, "The Utrecht Psalter."

29. Fergus Kelly, *Early Irish Farming*, 80; *Colección documental del Monasterio de Santa María de Otero de las Dueñas*, no. 54. The charter is unusual for mentioning a *pig* of a certain color; it was common enough in northern Iberia in the ninth and tenth centuries to sell a piece of land in exchange for *cattle* of a certain color, or for a certain kind of textile: see, e.g., *Cartulario de Alaón*, no. 29 (851 CE); *Tumbos del Monasterio de Sobrado de los Monjes*, vol. 1, no. 81 (895); *Colección documental del archivo de la Catedral*

de León, vol. 2, no. 291 (955); on similar sorts of gifting exchanges see Innes, "Rituals, Rights and Relationships."

30. Andersson, "The Molecular Basis for Phenotypic Changes," 45–49; Baruzzi and Montanari, *Porci e porcari,* 37–40. See, for example, British Library, Ms. Add. 42130 f. 19v (a spotted pig in the Luttrell Psalter, East Anglia, 1325–50); Vienna, Österreichische Nationalbibliothek, Cod. ser. n. 2644, fol. 15 r (striped pigs in a copy of the *Tacuinum sanitatis,* 1390–1400); and Ambrogio Lorenzetti's fresco known as *The Effects of Just Government in the Countryside,* on the eastern wall of the Sala dei Nove in the Palazzo Pubblico in Siena (truffle hunter with striped pig in the lower left corner, 1337–1339 CE). Although the earliest evidence for pigs used in truffle hunting dates to the late Middle Ages, the practice may have started earlier: see Pacioni, "Truffle Hunting in Italy."

31. Sykes, *The Norman Conquest,* 50.

32. Ettel, *Karlburg—Rosstal—Oberammerthal,* 306, 320–21 (faunal analysis by Katrin Vagedes and Joris Peters), for the wild mammals that indicate extensive woodland in this region, see pp. 253, 308–9, 317; Iwaszczuk, "Animal Husbandry on the Polish Territory," 87–88 and fig. 9. On forest cover in central Europe: Woodbridge, Roberts, and Fyfe, "Vegetation and Land-Use Change in Northern Europe." For smaller pigs elsewhere in the West: Salvadori, *Uomini e animali nel Medioevo,* 103–7; Doll, "'Im Essen jedoch konnte er nicht so enthaltsam sein . . . ,'" 447; Prummel, *Early Medieval Dorestad,* 214–17; Putelat, "L'homme, l'animal et L'Ajoie," 102–3; Clavel, "L'animal dans l'alimentation," 78; Wigh, *Animal Husbandry in the Viking Age Town of Birka,* 80–81. If the majority of pigs in a certain place were slaughtered as adults, rather than the more typical subadult age of under two years, it may be a sign that the farmers were raising pigs that were slower to fatten. But this hypothesis has not been fully explored: see, e.g., Grau-Sologestoa and Quirós Castillo, "Peasant Economy in Late Roman Álava," 95.

33. MacKinnon, "High on the Hog"; Colominas, Fernández Rodríguez, and Iborra Eres, "Animal Husbandry and Hunting Practices in Hispania Tarraconensis," 518–20, 524–25; Frémondeau, Nuviala, and Duval, "Pigs and Cattle in Gaul," 498; Rizzetto, Crabtree, and Albarella, "Livestock Changes at the Beginning and End of the Roman Period in Britain," 545, 547–48. Unfortunately there are not many biometric data available yet for North African pigs.

34. Valenzuela-Lamas and Albarella, "Animal Husbandry Across the Roman Empire," 406–8; on decrease in pig size see Frémondeau, Nuviala, and Duval, "Pigs and Cattle in Gaul," 498. For the interpretation that smaller livestock are a sign of a decline in economic activity and standards of living: Ward-Perkins, *The Fall of Rome,* 145.

35. Elsner, "Sacrifice in Late Roman Art," 124; Cameron, *The Last Pagans of Rome,* esp. 65–67. On the Ghirza inscription: Brogan and Smith, *Ghirza,* 262, no. 6.

36. Columella, *De re rustica* 7.9.6–9, 7.11.3; Palladius, *Opus agriculturae* 3.26.3, 14.38; Ballari and Barrios-García, "A Review of Wild Boar *Sus scrofa* Diet"; Masseti, "The Eco-

nomic Role of *Sus* in Early Human Fishing Communities," 160–67; Albarella et al., "Ethnoarchaeology of Pig Husbandry," 291–93, 303; Halstead and Isaakidou, "A Pig Fed by Hand"; Hadjikoumis, "Traditional Pig Herding Practices," 359; Redding, "The Pig and the Chicken," 341–42; Greenfield, "Bone Consumption by Pigs"; Frazier, "Hogs Wild," 73; Goursot et al., "Behavioural Lateralization in Domestic Pigs," 579 (raisins).

37. *Cartulaire de l'abbaye de Gorze*, no. 19 (770 CE); *Polyptychon von Saint-Germain-des-Prés*, nos. 9.2, 13A; *Prümer Urbar*, 180; *Liber possessionum Wizenburgensis*, no. 68; *Charters of St Augustine's Abbey Canterbury*, no. 11 (762 CE = Sawyer 25; no discussion of rent payment here, but the property includes both a mill and pig pasturing rights); Fergus Kelly, *Early Irish Farming*, 83; Arge, Church, and Brewington, "Pigs in the Faroe Islands," 28–29; Jennifer R. Jones and Mulville, "Norse Animal Husbandry in Liminal Environments," 347; Ascough et al., "Stable Isotopic (δ¹³C and δ¹⁵N) Characterization of Key Faunal Resources," 37–38.

38. Frazier, "Hogs Wild," 73. On more recent problems in Texas: Wright, "The Future Is Texas," 42, 56–57, 59.

39. On the destructive introduction of pigs to North America: Virginia DeJohn Anderson, *Creatures of Empire*, 107–40. There are also wild-pig problems in continental Europe: Warner, "Boar Wars." On situations in which wild pigs are more beneficially destructive: Sandom, Huges, and Macdonald, "Rooting for Rewilding."

40. Morelle et al., "Towards Understanding Wild Boar *Sus scrofa* Movement."

41. Drake, Fraser, and Weary, "Parent-Offspring Resource Allocation in Domestic Pigs."

42. Podgórski et al., "Spatiotemporal Behavioral Plasticity of Wild Boar."

43. Morelle et al., "Towards Understanding Wild Boar *Sus scrofa* Movement," 20; Garcia et al., "Wild Boar (*Sus scrofa*) Vocalizations." On the health benefits to piglets when they interact with their mothers and in the process learn about feeding: Oostindjer et al., "Learning from Mom How to Eat Like a Pig."

44. Walahfrid Strabo, *Vita sancti Galli* 2.18 ("leader," *ductrix*, was both the word for a breeding sow and the feminine form of the word for military commander); Focardi et al., "Cooperation."

45. Morelle et al., "Towards Understanding Wild Boar *Sus scrofa* Movement"; Kornum and Knudsen, "Cognitive Testing of Pigs."

46. Kornum and Knudsen, "Cognitive Testing of Pigs," esp. 442–45.

47. Morelle et al., "Towards Understanding Wild Boar *Sus scrofa* Movement."

48. Kornum and Knudsen, "Cognitive Testing of Pigs," 442–45; Murphy, Nordquist, and van der Staay, "A Review of Behavioural Methods," 16–17.

49. Augustine, *De civitate Dei* 19.12, p. 677.

50. On *genus* as the structural features that get reproduced: Augustine, *De Genesi ad litteram* 3.12; *Intexuimus*, lines 233–35. The generation of fertile offspring was another medieval measure for "species": Epstein, *The Medieval Discovery of Nature*, 40–77.

51. "Sus dicta, quod pascua subigat, id est terra subacta escas inquirat. Verres, quod grandes habeat vires. Porcus, quasi spurcus. Ingurgitat enim se caeno, luto inmergit, limo inlinit. Horatius (Epist. 1,2,26): Et amica luto sus. Hinc etiam spurcitiam vel spurios nuncupatos." Isidore, *Etymologiae* 12.1.25; I have modified the English translation of Barney et al.

52. Basil, *Hexaemeron* 8.1–2, 9.3–4; for the translation by Eustathius, see PL 53:945–48, 958–61.

53. Gregory the Great, *Dialogi*, vol. 3, 4.3–4; Dhuoda, *Liber manualis* 4.4; Eriugena, *Periphyseon*, vol. 3, lines 4945–5068 (= PL 122:736C–739B). On the long ancient tradition of ascribing souls to animals: Sorabji, *Animal Minds*, 97–100; French, *Ancient Natural History*, 22, 46–49, 287–88. On the context for this section of Gregory's *Dialogues*: Dal Santo, *Debating the Saints' Cult*, 85–148. For more on Basil and Eriugena, see the next chapter.

54. Boethius, *In Isagogen Porphyrii commenta*, second commentary, esp. 2.4, 3.2–6. Thanks to Julie Orlemanski for asking about the phoenix!

55. Animals acting *contra naturam*, e.g.: Jonas of Bobbio, *Vita Columbani abbatis* 1.17. Wild boars and pigs specifically: Gregory of Tours, *Liber vitae patrum* 12.2; Cogitosus, *Vita sanctae Brigidae* 21.

56. Augustine, *De Genesi ad litteram* 2.6, 6.14, 7.10.

57. Hence the methodological challenges of recovering the history of animal health: see the discussion in Newfield, "Livestock Plagues in Late Antiquity." Only two of eighty-seven references in early medieval texts to livestock pandemics involved pigs (492).

58. For example: as of March 2018, the U.S. Department of Agriculture identified the following diseases among the most immediate concerns of the swine industry: porcine epidemic diarrhea (PEDv), porcine delta coronavirus (PDCoV), various subtypes of swine influenza (H1N1, H1N2, and H3N2), pseudorabies, classical swine fever (CSF), and swine brucellosis—in addition to viral and bacterial infections that are already routinely treated with vaccinations and antibiotics. https://www.aphis.usda.gov/aphis/ourfocus/animalhealth/animal-disease-information/swine-disease-information (last modified 30 March 2018). A 2012 USDA report of the industry identified the most typical health problems (afflicting more than half of the 4,600 farms surveyed) as porcine reproductive and respiratory syndrome (PRRS), *Mycoplasma* pneumonia, and influenza in weaned and reproductive pigs, and navel infections, colibacillosis, and *Streptococcus suis* in piglets: *Swine 2012, Part II: Reference of Swine Health and Health Management in the United States* (Fort Collins: USDA, 2012), downloaded from https://www.aphis.usda.gov/aphis/ourfocus/animalhealth/monitoring-and-surveillance/nahms/nahms_swine_studies. Note that the "small" farms in this study include any operation with 100–2,000 pigs: large to colossal by early medieval standards.

59. Columella, *De re rustica* 7.10; Palladius, *Opus agriculturae* 14.36–38; Pliny, *Historia naturalis* 8.77.206, 11.68.179; Isidore, *Etymologiae* 12.5.16; Fergus Kelly, *Early Irish Farming*, 208–9.

60. E.g., Baker, "The Vertebrate Remains," 439; Finbar McCormick and Murray, *Excavations at Knowth 3*, 68; O'Connor, "Animals in Medieval Urban Lives," 118; Benseddik and Potter, *Fouilles du Forum de Cherchel*, 1:167 (faunal analysis by Gill Clark); Kierdorf and Kierdorf, "The Histiopathy of Fluorotic Dental Enamel in Wild Boar and Domestic Pigs"; Dobney and Ervynck, "Interpreting Developmental Stress in Archaeological Pigs"; Marcellus, *De medicamentis liber* 23.49.

61. Pliny, *Historia naturalis* 8.41.98; Palladius, *Opus agriculturae* 14.38.3. Ancient moralists drew different conclusions about what animals' self-medicating ought to teach humans: see Holmes, "The Generous Text," esp. 238–42; and Spittler, *Animals in the Apocryphal Acts of the Apostles*, esp. 33.

62. "Animalium hoc maxime brutum": Pliny, *Historia naturalis* 8.77.207.

63. Various kinds of animal enclosures: Hitchner, "Image and Reality," 35–39; Seaver, *Meithal*, 28–30, 37–39; Arge, Church, and Brewington, "Pigs in the Faroe Islands," 23–28; Hamerow, *Rural Settlements and Society in Anglo-Saxon England*, 88–90; *Lex Salica* 2.3 (*sutis [qui] clauem habuerit*), 16.4 (*sutis cum porcis*); *Lex Alamannorum* 67 [74].1, 77.1 [83.3] (*porcaritia domus*), 94 [97].1 (*burica porcorum*); *Polyptychon von Saint-Germain-des-Prés*, no. 25.1 (a stone wall for piglets); and on the difficulty of identifying certain structures as animal pens see Catteddu, *Archéologie médiévale*, 32–33. Jumping: Varro, *Res rusticae* 2.4.14–15; Columella, *De re rustica* 7.9.9–13; Morelle et al., "Towards Understanding Wild Boar *Sus scrofa* Movement," 18. Swimming: Masseti, "The Economic Role of *Sus* in Early Human Fishing Communities," 159–61. Piglet leader: *Ancient Laws of Ireland*, 4:108–11 (= *Corpus iuris Hibernici* 1.72.18); see the discussion in Fergus Kelly, *Early Irish Farming*, 81, 137. The text assumes that the culprit here was a pet piglet, which may account for the frequency of its trespassing. Tethering: Crabtree, *West Stow*, 28.

64. Kittawornrat and Zimmerman, "Toward a Better Understanding of Pig Behavior," 27 (quotation). On the complex motor functioning of pigs' snouts: Goursot et al., "Behavioural Lateralization in Domestic Pigs."

65. Fergus Kelly, *Early Irish Farming*, 142–43; *Edictus Rothari* 350 (on ditchdigging). On the agrarian character of urban space, see Chapter 3, and more generally Goodson, *Urban Gardening*. In the high and late Middle Ages, pigs became a more pressing problem in cities: see the Epilogue.

66. *Edictus Rothari* 326 (biting); *Lex Alamannorum* 96.4 [99.20] (killing a man); *Lex Baiwariorum* 19.7 (corpses; see also Chapter 4); *Pactus Legis Alamannorum* 27 (male pig killing another male pig); Fergus Kelly, *Early Irish Farming*, 154, 180 (on women, children, and the calf story). The wild pigs in the U.S. South also kill and eat calves: Frazier, "Hogs Wild," 73.

67. Fergus Kelly, *Early Irish Farming*, 81, 137.

68. Vigil-Escalera Guirado et al., "Productive Strategies and Consumption Patterns."

69. "Iste sues locus enutrit custodit & [corr: ad]ultas": Plan of Saint Gall. On the Plan of Saint Gall as a "meditation machine" see especially Carruthers, *The Craft of*

Thought, 228–31. Viewable with interactive features at www.stgallplan.org. For more on the work of swineherding, see Chapter 4.

70. E.g., *Lex Salica* 9.8–9, 34; *Liber constitutionum* 27.1; *Lex Ribuaria* 73.2; *Edictus Rothari* 358; *Liber iudiciorum* 8.4.28; Laws of Ine 42.1, in *Gesetze der Angelsachsen*, 106–8; *Lex Baiwariorum* 14.1.

71. VI Æthelstan 8.7, in *Gesetze der Angelsachsen* ("forðam we wenað, þæt mænige gimeléase menn ne reccean, hú heora yrfe fare, for þam ofertruan on þam friðe"). This is one of the few early medieval records we have for livestock causing problems in urban environments specifically. Towns were often fairly open and agrarian in these centuries, in contrast to the more densely settled spaces of the high and late Middle Ages, when pigs became a more pressing urban problem. See the Epilogue.

72. *Lex Salica* 9.5, 9.8; *Liber constitutionum* 27.6; *Lex Ribuaria* 85; *Edictus Rothari* 343–48; *Liber iudiciorum* 8.3–4, 8.3.13–14; *Lex Baiwariorum* 14.17; *Lex Alamannorum* 67.2 [74.2]; *Cartulaire de l'abbaye de Gorze*, no. 11 (765 CE, in which Chrodegang of Metz describes best practices on the estate of Flamersheim); Charlemagne, *Capitula apud Ansegisum servata* 6 (= *Capitularia regum Francorum* 70.6); *Lex Frisionum* 4.2 (owner determines replacement value); *Lex Saxonum* 57; *Lex Thuringorum* 52.

73. *Liber constitutionum* 23.4–5, 89.2; *Edictus Rothari* 349–50; Laws of Ine 42.1, in *Gesetze der Angelsachsen*.

74. Fergus Kelly, *Early Irish Farming*, 134–38, 141–42, 154–55; *Edictus Rothari* 323–24.

75. Berkowitz, *Animals and Animality in the Babylonian Talmud*, 37–62.

76. *Lex Salica* 9.1–4, 9.6–7; *Liber constitutionum* 23, 64, 89; *Lex Ribuaria* 85; *Liber iudiciorum* 8.3.13 (*iracundia inmoderationis*), 8.3.17, 8.4.8; *Edictus Rothari* 352–53, 357; *Lex Alamannorum* 67.3 [74.3]; *Lex Baiwariorum* 14.3, 14.4–16 (14.7: "Ut nemo praesumat alienum animal occidere neque porcum, quamvis in damnum eum inveniret"). *Non moleste sed modeste*: Chrodegang of Metz discusses the obligations of the tenants of Flamersheim: *Cartulaire de l'abbaye de Gorze*, no. 11 (765 CE). This policy applied specifically to the breeding males that tenants owed the estate every year, so the trespasses of these particular animals would have been especially infuriating.

77. In five out of six *securitas* formulas in the Formulary of Angers (nos. 5–6, 39, 42, 44, in *Formulae Merowingici et Karolini aevi*, pp. 6–7, 17, 19), *securitas* serves to confirm rights to something when those rights had been in dispute, and three out of six of them involve accusations of theft or seizure. Nos. 42 and 44 also state that appropriate compensation has been paid. See also the discussion in Rio, *The Formularies of Angers and Marculf*, 52–54, 80–81, 84–86.

78. The slate is edited in *Pizarras visigodas*, no. 92.

79. *Tombo de Celanova*, vol. 1, nos. 189–90. On the probable status of the defendants see Davies, *Windows on Justice in Northern Iberia*, 179.

80. *Edictus Rothari* 353, repeated in a ninth-century compilation of Lombard laws, *Liber legis Langobardorum concordia dictus* 10.5; *Edictus Rothari* 326 ("ipse conponat

homicidium aut damnum, cuius animales fuerit, cessante in hoc capitulo faida, quod est inimicitia; quia muta res fecit, nam non hominis studium").

2. From the Mud to the Cosmos

1. Upper air: Augustine, *De Genesi ad litteram* 3.3; *Liber de ordine creaturarum* 6; Bede, *Libri quatuor in principium Genesis* 1.2, 1.21. Stars: Augustine, *De Genesi ad litteram* 2.14; Isidore, *De natura rerum* 22; Bede, *Libri quatuor in principium Genesis* 1.14. Saturn: Augustine, *De Genesi ad litteram* 2.5; Eriugena, *Periphyseon* 3, lines 3257–58 (= PL 122:697C). Cf. [Wigbod], *Explanatio sex dierum*, which posited an icy barrier between the hot stars and earth, cols. 210D–211A. (Wigbod was an abbot of Lorsch and archbishop of Trier who became Charlemagne's official commentator on Genesis: Gorman, "Wigbod and Biblical Studies under Charlemagne"; and Gorman, "Wigbod, Charlemagne's Commentator," with attribution of the *Explanatio* at p. 23.) Vision: Basil *Hexaemeron* 6.9; Ambrose, *Exameron* 4.6. Suspension of the earth: Basil, *Hexaemeron* 1.9–10; Ambrose, *Exameron* 1.6, 2.3; Isidore, *De natura rerum* 45; Bede, *Libri quatuor in principium Genesis* 1.6. Sea creatures: Basil, *Hexaemeron* 7.6; Bede, *Libri quatuor in principium Genesis* 2.19–20. Insect breathing: Basil, *Hexaemeron* 8.7; Ambrose, *Exameron* 5.22. Decomposition: Augustine, *De Genesi ad litteram* 3.14; *Intexuimus*, lines 257–63; [Wigbod], *Explanatio sex dierum*, cols. 215A–B; Remigius of Auxerre, *Expositio super Genesim* 1.25.

2. Remigius of Auxerre, *Expositio super Genesim*, introduction, lines 14–15 ("Constat autem hunc Geneseos librum multiplicibus etiam ad litteram profunditatibus involutum").

3. Prescriptions for how to work like a "scientist" originally developed from evolutionary, psychological, and philosophical theories about how nature and the mind already worked: see Cowles, *The Scientific Method*. For the argument that natural history in the ancient world was not science, see French, *Ancient Natural History*. On early modern criticisms of ancient and medieval writers for their dependence on observation rather than experimentation: Merchant, "The Violence of Impediments"; but for ancient examples of "empirical methodologies" (namely of Ptolemy and Galen) see Lehoux, *What Did the Romans Know?*, esp. 106–32. On the evolving parameters of what researchers since the eighteenth century thought the impediments to knowledge were, and what they did to surmount them: Daston and Galison, *Objectivity*.

4. As Lehoux argues, premodern science may not seem to predict or explain things accurately from our perspective, but Roman science was nevertheless sufficiently predictive and coherent within the Romans' conceptual schema, and researchers operated on the conviction that they were describing a world that was real and knowable: *What Did the Romans Know?*, 200–242. "Exegetical cultures": Fowden, *Before and After Muḥammad*, 56–68, 127–97.

5. Robbins, "The Hexaemeral Literature," 42–72; for more on the reception of these authors see the second and third sections of this chapter.

6. Van Dam, *Kingdom of Snow*, 26–36; Van Dam, *Becoming Christian*, 105–31. On hexameral exegesis prior to Basil see Bouteneff, *Beginnings*, esp. 170–73.

7. Basil, *Hexaemeron* 2.2, 2.4, 3.9, 9.1 (against figural interpretation), 1.2, 1.3–4, 3.8, 6.1 (against "worldly wisdom"). On Basil's pedagogical motives for speaking this way: Lim, "The Politics of Interpretation."

8. Basil, *Hexaemeron* 5.9 (plants), 6.11 (sun and moon), 9.1 (shape of earth, eclipses). Influences on Basil's *Hexaemeron:* Robbins, "The Hexaemeral Literature," 1–52; Giet's comments to his edition of Basil's *Hexaemeron*, 47–96; French, *Ancient Natural History*, 287–89. For the broader context to Christians' attitudes about Aristotle in particular, see Fowden, *Before and After Muḥammad*, 136–46.

9. Basil, *Hexaemeron* 2.1 (approaching the sacred), 2.7 (light), 5.2 (plants and fruit), 5.5 (grain), 5.6 (trees), 5.9 (mountains), 7.1 (waters); Rousseau, *Basil of Caesarea*, 319–49 (on the *Hexaemeron* as Basil's vision of "a biological and spiritual community,"346). Cappadocian industries: Van Dam, *Kingdom of Snow*, 20–24, 41; Van Dam, *Becoming Christian*, 113, 116.

10. Basil, *Hexaemeron* 1.7 (ditchdiggers; likewise Bede, *Libri quatuor in principium Genesis* 1.9), 3.10 (goodness), 4.6–7 (hydrology), 5.7 (tree structure), 7.2 (shellfish/ *ostrakoderma*).

11. Ball metaphor: Basil, *Hexaemeron* 9.2. Animal soul: ibid., 7.1, 8.1, 9.3–4. See also Chapter 1.

12. Basil, *Hexaemeron* 8.2 (animal souls' mortality), 9.3–4 (exemplars for human souls).

13. See e.g. Robbins, *Hexaemeral Literature*, 58–59; Nicolaidis et al., "Science and Orthodox Christianity," 547–49.

14. Ambrose, *Exameron* 3.17 (view from a villa), 6.1 (tour guide), 3.7, 5.1, 6.1–2 (reevaluating priorities); Basil, *Hexaemeron* 6.1 (a tour through the "city" of the universe). Basil had spoken briefly of nature as a treasure (*Hexaemeron* 5.4), but Ambrose amplified that metaphor to make it a centerpiece of his sermon cycle. On the congregation of Milan: McLynn, *Ambrose of Milan;* Peter Brown, *Through the Eye of a Needle*, 120–47.

15. Ambrose, *Exameron* 3.1 (poor attendance), 6.2 ("non possumus plenius nos cognoscere, nisi prius quae sit omnium natura animantium cognoverimus").

16. Ambrose, *Exameron* 5.12 (audience interest in birds), 5.14 (diversity of birds), elaborating a theme in Basil, *Hexaemeron* 8.3. Cf. Isidore, *Etymologiae* 12.7.1 and Hrabanus Maurus, *De rerum naturis* 8.6: "Unum nomen avium, sed genus diversum. . . . Neque enim omnia Indiae et Aethiopiae aut Scythiae deserta quis penetrare poterit, qui earum genus vel differentias nosset" (Birds have one name, but there are diverse kinds. . . . No one could possibly personally visit the deserts of India, Ethiopia, or Scythia and become acquainted with all the species and their differences).

17. Ambrose, *Exameron* 3.2.9 (hydraulic engineers/*artifices*), 3.13.55 (arborists/*cultores lucorum*), 5.2.6 (fishermen/*piscatores;* see Basil, *Hexaemeron* 7.2), 5.12.39 (peasants/*rusticani*).

18. Sarah Iles Johnson, *Ancient Greek Divination,* 7–9, 128–30; Bouché-Leclercq, *Histoire de la divination,* 1:127–45. By the late Republic, the use of birds had shifted: by Cicero's day augurs would perform ritualistic feedings of birds, usually chickens (Foti, "Funzioni e caratteri del 'pullarius'"). But the knowledge of birds that diviners had developed exercised a powerful influence on natural history. See, for example, the source material that Pliny cited for his book on birds: *Historia naturalis* 1, pp. 80–81, citing *auctores* for book 10. Isidore knew that diviners had developed a rich knowledge of birds, but he rejected their ability to base predictions on them: *Etymologiae* 12.8.75–79.

19. Swartz, *The Signifying Creator,* 65, 68–69, 75, 89–90.

20. Ambrose, *Exameron* 3.13 (cedar), 5.21 (honey), 3.14 (grape leaves), 5.24 (bats; likewise Basil, *Hexaemeron* 8.7), 3.7 (grasses; see Isaiah 40:6 and Basil, *Hexaemeron* 5.2), 1.7 (creation in stages). God as craftsman: Ambrose, *Exameron* 1.5; Basil, *Hexaemeron* 1.7, 3.10, 4.1.

21. Ambrose, *Exameron* 5.15 (*politia quaedam et militia naturalis,* cranes), 5.16 (storks), 5.17 (swallows), 5.18 (crows).

22. Basil, *Hexaemeron* 8.5.

23. Ambrose, *Exameron* 5.10 (the implication that fish cannot conceive of breaking the law), 5.21 ("ipsae [apes] sibi regem ordinant, ipsae populos creant et licet positae sub rege sunt tamen liberae"); Basil, *Hexaemeron* 7.4, 8.3.

24. "Quod utique ex specie instructionis humanae quadam videntur ratione colligere": Ambrose, *Exameron* 5.23. Cf. Basil, who said more simply that this behavior was "not far from human reason": *Hexaemeron* 8.7.

25. "Censes eum sentiendi sagacitate vim sibi rationis asciscere": Ambrose, *Exameron* 6.4.

26. "'Aut in hanc partem' inquit 'deflexit aut in illam, aut certe in hunc se anfractum contulit, sed nec in istam nec in illam ingressus est uiam. Superest igitur, ut in istam se partem sine dubitatione contulerit.'" Ambrose, *Exameron* 6.4, a close match to Basil, *Hexaemeron* 9.4.

27. French, *Ancient Natural History,* 183–84, 288.

28. The translation of *ad litteram* as "word for word," rather than "in its literal meaning" as it is more typically rendered, is James Halporn's: Cassiodorus, *Institutiones,* trans. Halporn, 112.

29. Augustine, *De Genesi ad litteram* 1.1 (*in principio*), 8.1 (*gesta*). Augustine had written his figural commentary on Genesis, *De Genesi contra Manichaeos,* in 388–89.

30. Augustine, *De Genesi ad litteram* 4.29 (*rationes*), 4.33 ("quas [sc. rationes] tamquam seminaliter sparsit deus in ictu condendi"), 5.20 ("explicat . . . plicita indiderat"), 5.23 (*vi potentiaque causali*), 6.8 (*causae*), 6.10 (*causae*), 6.14–15 (*causales rationes*), 9.17–18 (*ratio*), 10.2 (*ratio causalis*).

31. See esp. Augustine, *De Genesi ad litteram* 1.2–5, 3.20, 4.22, 4.32, 5.18. Pigs specifically: 3.11. The Vetus Latina (Augustine's version of the Bible) renders Gen. 1.24 as "Et dixit deus: educat terra animam uiuam secundum genus: quadrupedia et reptilia et bestias terrae secundum genus et pecora secundum genus." Cf. the Vulgate: "Dixit quoque Deus: producat terra animam viventem in genere suo: iumenta et reptilia et bestias terrae secundum species suas."

32. Augustine, *De Genesi ad litteram* 2.1 (firmament), 2.11 (land and sea), 3.1–2 (birds and aquatic animals), 3.11 (pigs).

33. Augustine, *De Genesi ad litteram* 3.2.

34. Augustine, *De Genesi ad litteram* 3.3–5. On Augustine's probable sources here see the notes by Agaësse and Solignac in their edition, 1:615–19.

35. Augustine, *De Genesi ad litteram* 3.6–7, 3.9–10.

36. Augustine, *De Genesi ad litteram* 1.19–21 (Augustine's audiences), 7.18 (medical model of the brain), 12.2 (a peasant's dream). See further Agaësse and Solignac's comments on Augustine's medical knowledge in their edition, 1:710–14.

37. Augustine, *De Genesi ad litteram* 2.18 (life force of the celestial bodies), 3.14 (insects), 10.1–10 (the creation of souls), 1.20 (*multipliciter*). On inter-Christian debates see for example Alan Scott, *Origen and the Life of the Stars*, esp. 113–64 (my thanks to Peter Brown for this reference).

38. Augustine, *De Genesi ad litteram* 2.15 (moon), 4.30 (day and night), 1.15–18, 4.32 (simultaneity and narrative).

39. Augustine, *De Genesi ad litteram* 3.8. For Basil's position that fish were an "imperfect" form of life that could barely sense things, let alone remember or reflect upon them, see his *Hexaemeron* 8.1.

40. Augustine, *De Genesi ad litteram* 3.20, 4.4, 4.7, 7.21, 8.23–24, 9.12–14, 11.2, 11.12, 11.28, 12.11, 12.28, 12.31.

41. Augustine, *De Genesi ad litteram* 3.20, 9.14.

42. Jeremy Cohen, *Be Fertile and Increase*, esp. 67–76, 184–87, 224–29, which definitively refutes Lynn White, "The Historical Roots of Our Ecologic Crisis."

43. "Inest enim omnibus quoddam naturae sui generis decus": *De Genesi ad litteram* 3.14.

44. Some rough diagnostics: in the sixth century, Cassiodorus started off his recommended-reading list for monks with the Genesis commentaries of Basil, Ambrose, and Augustine: *Institutiones* 1.1–4. Among the surviving manuscripts produced in Europe before 800, there are at least five copies of Ambrose's *Exameron* (CLA 2.124, 533, 622, 807, and 1464), one of Basil's *Hexaemeron* (CLA 621), and four of Augustine's *De Genesi ad litteram* (CLA 418, 547, 855, 1745). The library catalogues that survive from early medieval monasteries mention copies of Ambrose's *Exameron* at Reichenau, Saint Gall, Würzburg, and Lorsch; and Augustine's *De Genesi ad litteram* at Reichenau, Fontanelle, Würzburg, Saint Gall, Lorsch, and Bobbio (*Catalogi bibliothecarum antiqui*,

nos. 6.45, 6.308, 7.2, 15.118–20, 9.52, 22.169, 22.180, 32.68, 37.290, 37.567). On the use of these authors in subsequent commentaries, see the following discussion.

45. Claudius to Dructeramnus (a preface to his *Expositio libri Genesis*), *Ep.* 1, pp. 590, 592; cf. Is. 11:9. The commentary itself is printed as the *Commentariorum in Genesim*, ed. Brassicanus (but misattributed to Eucherius of Lyons), with an inferior edition in PL 50. The essential guide here is Gorman, "The Commentary of Genesis of Claudius of Turin." Other comments on the depth of the Genesis/creation literature: Bede to Acca of Hexham, *Libri quatuor in principium Genesis*, pp. 1–2; Hrabanus Maurus, preface to *De rerum naturis*, cols. 11–12.

46. Wigbod, *Quaestiones in Octateuchum*, col. 1104c ("Et quae nota tibi vel quae percepta legendo / Ad virtutis opus studio converte regali"). For an introduction to early medieval exegetical practices see Contreni, "Carolingian Biblical Culture"; Stansbury, "Early-Medieval Biblical Commentaries"; Keskiaho, "The Annotation of Patristic Texts." This is not to say all Carolingian scholarship on the natural world focused exclusively on compilation. For example, the field of *computus*—the science of building calendars—was a rapidly developing field in these centuries, which in turn advanced the study of astronomy and of "spiritual mathematics." See Borst, *Die karolingische Kalendarreform;* Wallis, "'Number Mystique'"; Borst, *Schriften zur Komputistik;* Eastwood, *Ordering the Heavens;* Ramírez-Weaver, *A Saving Science.*

47. Jeffrey Jerome Cohen, *Stone.*

48. "Neque enim earum rerum naturam noscere superstitiosae scientiae est, si tantum sana sobriaque doctrina considerentur." Isidore, preface to *De natura rerum,* 167–69. For an overview of royal patronage of learned culture (including what today we would call the arts and sciences, as well as theology and law) in the early Middle Ages, see Hen, *Roman Barbarians.*

49. Isidore, *De natura rerum* 3 (planets), 37 (winds), 38 (dolphins).

50. Sisebut, *Epistula,* line 15 ("His tamen incuruus, per pondera terrea nitens"). See also Fontaine's introduction to the poem, pp. 151–61. Cf. Isidore, *De natura rerum* 21 (lunar eclipses).

51. Sisebut, *Epistula,* lines 12–14.

52. "Haec cum nascitur, aut regni mutationem fertur ostendere, aut bella et pestilentias surgere." Isidore, *De natura rerum* 26. Historical writing and environmental events: Kreiner, *Social Life of Hagiography,* 149; Squatriti, "Barbarizing the *Bel Paese*," 399; Newfield, "Early Medieval Epizootics and Landscapes of Disease," 99–100; and Belser, *Power, Ethics, and Ecology in Jewish Late Antiquity,* 59–83, and 84–114 on the Talmud's cautionary notes about interpreting divine communications through creation. Fontaine suggests that Isidore and Sisebut wanted to refute interpretations of natural phenomena that tended toward the apocalyptic—especially because there had been a string of solar and lunar eclipses in the previous two years: Isidore, *De natura rerum,* pp. 5–6; see further discussion in Kendall and Wallis's translation, 18–26.

53. Doody, *Pliny's Encyclopedia*, 14–23; Borst, *Das Buch der Naturgeschichte*. Medieval scribes produced around three hundred copies of the *Historia naturalis,* and another two hundred late antique and medieval authors had read at least parts of it (Borst, *Das Buch der Naturgeschichte,* 35–36). For an overview of Isidore's influences in the *De natura rerum* see Fontaine's remarks to his edition, pp. 11–15.

54. Doody, *Pliny's Encyclopedia*, 23.

55. Pliny, *Historia naturalis* 8.83.227 (frogs), 9.17.62–63 (*scarus,* the *novus incola*), 10.29.76 (on organisms' vulnerability to new places in general), 10.15.37 (bird extinction).

56. Basil, *Hexaemeron* 1.6, 3.5–7, 6.10. Giet notes in his edition (pp. 228–30n) that the battle of the elements and the eventual vanquishing by fire was originally a Stoic idea, though in *Hexaemeron* 3.8 Basil rejected the Stoic theory that the universe is continually being extinguished and reborn: for him this cosmic history happens only once.

57. "Inexplicabile est singularum rerum exquirere proprietates et vel diversitates earum manifesta testificatione distinguere vel latentes occultasque causas indeficientibus aperire documentis. [U]na nempe atque eadem aqua et diversas plerumque se mutat in species." Ambrose, *Exameron* 3.15.

58. Ambrose, *Exameron* 5.10; Pliny, *Historia naturalis* 9.54–56. According to Borst (*Das Buch der Naturgeschichte,* 61–62), only a few passages in Ambrose's *Exameron* draw upon either the *Historia naturalis* or an intermediary text that transmitted parts of Pliny's work. He does not discuss this particular passage. For the economic activity and sensibility that Pliny is describing here, see the discussion in Shaw, "A Hidden History of the Equites?" Sea monsters: Basil, *Hexaemeron* 7.3–4.

59. *Liber de ordine creaturarum,* nos. 5 (moon and sun, mourning), 10 (deterioration of environments), 11 (seasons, immutability after salvation). The author of the *Liber* thought that God might even create an entirely new cosmos to constitute this changeless realm after the Resurrection (11), in stark contrast to Augustine, for example, who argued that God made everything that would ever be made in the first six days of creation: *De Genesi ad litteram* 4.12, 5.12, 5.20. Consequences of the Fall: Basil, *Hexaemeron* 5.5–6; Augustine, *De Genesi ad litteram* 8.8, 11.32, 11.37–38. Augustine thought it was at least possible that thorns had predated original sin: *De Genesi ad litteram* 3.18. His later readers asserted this point much more confidently: *Intexuimus,* lines 177–90; Claudius, *Expositio libri Genesis* 1.4.

60. Isidore, *De natura rerum* 39. Isidore's discussion of pestilential "seeds" was greatly influenced by Lucretius, *De rerum natura* 6.769–830; see Kendall and Wallis's commentary to their translation of Isidore, 14–15, 167, 243–46. For prelapsarian physics in Augustine: *De Genesi ad litteram* 5.20, 5.22.

61. Isidore, *De natura rerum* 9. On the diagrams more generally see Fontaine, in his edition of *De natura rerum,* 15–18; and the translation of Kendall and Wallis, 27–50,

esp. 28–30. The micro/macrocosmic concept was an ancient one, and although Isidore and his modern readers call it a "mystical" reading, it is also a good example of the scientific interest in finding similar patterns in different parts of the physical world— an investigative principle that Lehoux dubs "symmetry": *What Did the Romans Know?* 176–99; also Obrist, *La cosmologie médiévale* 1:298–304. The idea still had play into the nineteenth century: Coen, *Climate in Motion*, 31–37.

62. In medieval cognitive practice, readers or listeners would have carefully "filled in" or supplemented visual images with concepts from the accompanying text (or better yet, with associations and analysis that they made as they read or listened): Carruthers, *The Book of Memory*, 274–337; Carruthers, *Craft of Thought*, 116–70.

63. Bede names his literary influences: *Libri quatuor in principium Genesis*, letter to Acca of Hexham, pp. 1–2. Calculating the Flood: Kendall, introduction to his translation the text, 6–8; Bede, *Libri quatuor in principium Genesis* 2.7.10–2.8.18a. The metrics of life: ibid., 1.14, 1.17–18.

64. Augustinus Hibernicus, *De mirabilibus* 1.7 (waters of the flood), 1.8 (sun and moon). Cf. 2.4 (on how the sun and moon *both* stood still at Joshua's orders—because if just one and not the other had frozen, time would have been warped).

65. Augustinus Hibernicus, *De mirabilibus* 1.11 (*medici*), 1.7 (boars and water), 2.1 (Cyrus), 2.23 (*ars pincernaria*). On the Cyrus episodes cf. Herodotus, *The Persian Wars* 1.189–91; Bruce, "The Dark Age of Herodotus," 56–62. As it happens, we still do not how wild boars reached Ireland, since they were not present on the island until the Early Holocene. See Finbar McCormick and Murray, *Excavations at Knowth 3*, 17–18.

66. "Etiam omnes res, quas possidemus, ex parte vix novimus": Augustinus Hibernicus, *De mirabilibus* 1.7.

67. Augustinus Hibernicus, *De mirabilibus* 3.10.

68. Dal Santo, *Debating the Saints' Cult*, 129–236; Dal Santo, "The God-Protected Empire?"; Kreiner, "A Generic Mediterranean," 206–8, 213.

69. Eriugena, *Periphyseon* 3, lines 2082–85 (= PL 122:670A). "Nam et saepe contra consuetum naturae cursum multa solent fieri; ut nobis ostendatur quod diuina prouidentia non uno sed multiplici modo atque infinito potest omnia administrare." Ethics in rhetoric: Carruthers, *The Book of Memory*, 195–233.

70. Eriugena, *Periphyseon* 3, lines 417–74, 3367–69 (= PL 122: 628C–630A, 700B).

71. For Eriugena's affinity with literary traditions around the Irish Sea, which like Eriugena focused on the potential of specific vantage points to transport a person to new and enlarged vistas, see Siewers, *Strange Beauty*, esp. 1–33, 67–95. Unlike Siewers, however, I am also inclined to see Eriugena's work as both Augustinian and "Western" (though not exclusively) in light of the Latin traditions that appear in this chapter.

72. Pliny had applied the term *physicus* strictly to Greek students of the natural world (astronomers, zoologists, doctors), but in the fourth century we see Ammianus Marcellinus and Jerome designating Pliny by the same label: Borst, *Das Buch der*

Naturgeschichte, 51–52, 62–64. See also Isidore, *Etymologiae* 8.6.4; Hrabanus Maurus, *De rerum naturis* 15.1.

73. Basil, *Hexaemeron* 9.4; Bede, *De temporum ratione* 7, lines 51–59, Remigius of Auxerre, *Expositio super Genesim* 1.5. For a different take cf. Isidore, *Etymologiae* 5.31.1 and [Wigbod], *Explanatio sex dierum*, col. 212D; Eriugena, *Periphyseon* 3, lines 4336–50, 4945–5068 (= PL 122:723B–C, 736C–739B).

74. Holmes, "The Generous Text," 231–51; Holmes, "The Poetic Logic of Negative Exceptionalism."

75. Walahfrid Strabo, *Vita sancti Galli* 2.18.

76. Basil, *Hexaemeron* 2.6. The "Syrian" was probably Eusebius, Ephraem Syrus, or Theophilus of Antioch (Lim, "The Politics of Interpretation," 354, citing E. Schweizer, "Diodor von Tarsus als Exeget," *Zeitschrift für die neutestamentliche Wissenschaft* 40 [1941–2]: 69). Iterations of Basil's remark: Ambrose, *Exameron* 1.8.29; Augustine, *De Genesi ad litteram* 1.18; *Intexuimus*, lines 56–61; Claudius, *Expositio libri Genesis* 1.

77. Isidore, *De natura rerum* 1, 3, 4, 6; see also Bede, *De temporum ratione* 2; Hrabanus Maurus, *De rerum naturis* 10.1.

78. Dorofeeva, "Miscellanies"; Orchard, *Pride and Prodigies*; Zuwiyya, *A Companion to Alexander Literature*.

79. See Michael Herren's introduction to his edition of *Cosmographia*, lxiii–lxiv; for the tenth-century catalogue, which was probably copied from a late ninth-century exemplar, *Catalogi bibliothecarum antiqui*, no. 32.

80. Jeffrey Jerome Cohen, "Monster Culture," 6–7 ("disturbing hybrids"). The *monstrare* etymology is, of course, Isidore's: *Etymologiae* 11.3.3; reiterated by Hrabanus Maurus in *De rerum naturis* 7.7, with his own emphasis about the naturalness of all creatures at cols. 199A–B.

81. Van Duzer, "*Hic sunt dracones*"; Daston and Park, *Wonders and the Order of Nature*, esp. 173–214; Bruce, "Hagiography as Monstrous Ethnography"; see also Wood, "Where the Wild Things Are."

82. On the flat-earth theory of Cosmas Indicopleustes: *Cosmographia*, l–li; Wolska, *La topographie chrétienne de Cosmas Indicopleustès*, 147–51, 246–48. Alexander's submarine: *Cosmographia* 36b–c. Pseudo-Jerome's sources and references to modern events (which may be allusions to the real author's personal history): *Cosmographia*, xxxiii–lv, lxxiii–lxxviii. See further Shanzer, "The *Cosmographia*," 82–86 (on the text as a "parody . . . of learning itself.")

83. As Augustinus Hibernicus pointed out: *De mirabilibus* 1.2; echoed by Alcuin, *Quaestiones in Genesim* 3. For an overview of Alcuin's text: Fox, "Alcuin the Exegete."

84. [Wigbod], *Explanatio sex dierum*, col. 210A ("quaedam luculenta rationis affectio"). On the primacy of angels: *Intexuimus*, lines 86–91 ("Oportebat enim ut creatura inconcusse deo adhaerens, etsi non suo creatori aequalis, omni saltem creaturae prior esset et melior").

85. Hrabanus Maurus, following Gennadius of Marseille (whose work was often misidentified as Augustine's), suggested that everything except God is "bodied" (*corporeus*), but by this he meant that everything had a finite nature—in angels' case, an "intellectual nature"—rather than that everything took physical, fleshy form: *De rerum naturis* 4.10, col. 98; cf. Gennadius, *De ecclesiasticis dogmatibus* 11–13.

86. Augustine, *De Genesi ad litteram* 1.5; Eriugena, *Periphyseon* 3, lines 4336–50 (= PL 122:723B–C).

87. Augustine, *De Genesi ad litteram* 11.16–19; Augustinus Hibernicus, *De mirabilibus* 1.2; *Liber de ordine creaturarum* 8; [Wigbod], *Explanatio sex dierum*, cols. 214A–B.

88. On the "psychological similarity" of angels and humans in late antique Christianity, see Muehlberger, "Angel."

89. "Quia ipse dies, hoc est natura angelorum, quando creatura ipsa, quam deus faciebat, contemplabatur, quodam modo vesperescebat. Verumtamen quia non permanebat in eius creaturae contuitu, sed laudem eius ad deum referens, eam melius in divina ratione conspiciebat, tunc continuo quasi mane fiebat. Nam si permaneret neglecto creatore in aspectu creaturae, iam non uespera sed nox utique fieret." *Intexuimus*, lines 118–26; nearly identical is Isidore, *Sententiae* 1.8.13, p. 23, and he was himself drawing on the theories of Augustine, *De Genesi ad litteram* 4.22. See also Claudius, *Expositio libri Genesis* 1.2. For the reception of *Intexuimus* see Gorman's introduction to the text.

90. Moses: Basil, *Hexaemeron* 1.1; Hrabanus Maurus, *De rerum naturis*, prologue to book 9, cols. 257D–259A; Eriugena, *Periphyseon* 3, lines 2918–20 (= PL 122:689C). The Lombard case: *Leges Liutprandi*, a. 733, no. 136: "quia non fuit animal sed sensum rationalem habuit, sicut homo debit habere, sicut homo debit habere, prospicere debuit in qualem locum se ponere ad standum, aut qualem pondus super se habebat."

91. Eriugena, *Periphyseon* 1, lines 1–10 (= PL 122:441A): *physis/natura* was "the general term for everything that is and is not (omnium quae sunt et quae non sunt)."

92. Cf. Hoffmann, *Environmental History of Medieval Europe*, 85–112; Pluskowski, "The Zooarchaeology of Medieval 'Christendom.'" More subtle if still schematic is Herlihy, "Attitudes Toward the Environment in Medieval Society."

3. Salvaged Lands

1. Vos, "The Rural Landscape of Thugga," 169 (Aïn Wassel); Aramburu-Zabala Higuera, *El abrigo del Puig de s'Escolà;* Arthur et al., "Masseria Quattro Macine"; Prummel, *Early Medieval Dorestad*, esp. 18–20; Gilchrist, "A Reappraisal of Dinas Powys," 56–58. Because they do not have sweat glands, pigs cool themselves by drinking and wallowing in water, and they drink about three times the volume of what they eat: Redding, "The Pig and the Chicken," 340–41.

2. Fifty kg pork: MacKinnon, *Production and Consumption of Animals in Roman Italy*, 191–92. Sixty-four kg pork (estimating meat weight at 80 percent of 80 kg live weight):

Seaver, *Meithal*, 107 (faunal analysis by Emily Murray). Seventy kg pork: Miró i Miró, "La fauna," 412. Live pig weights of 100 kg: Grassi, *L'insediamento medievale*, 143–44 (faunal analysis by Frank Salvadori); Valenti, *Miranduolo*, 368 (faunal analysis by Frank Salvadori); *Flixborough 3* with a slightly lower live weight of 85 kg (p. 123). Ratios of meat to carcass: Miró i Miró, "La fauna," citing Lucien Jourdan, *La faune du site gallo-romain et paléo-chrétien de la Bourse (Marseille)* (Paris: Centre National de Recherche Scientifique, 1976); Redding, "The Pig and the Chicken," 346–47. Buglione, De Venuto, and Volpe, "Agricoltura e allevamento nella Puglia settentrionale," section 13, reports that a pig can grow to 200 kg in only six months, but this figure is unreliable and is double the weight of modern pigs fed grain and supplements (for which see Redding, "The Pig and the Chicken," 344–48).

3. Hence Pliny, *Historia naturalis* 8.77.207: "Animalium hoc maxime brutum, animamque ei pro sale datam, non inlepide existimabatur." Likewise Varro, *Res rusticae* 2.4.10; and further Holmes, "The Generous Text," 239; French, *Ancient Natural History*, 165. Cf. Clutton-Brock, *The Walking Larder*.

4. Claudius, *Expositio libri Genesis* 1.4: "quae noxia sunt usibus hominum innoxium praebent feris et avibus pabulum."

5. Tsing, *The Mushroom at the End of the World*, 63–66.

6. Igo, *The Averaged American*; Bouk, *How Our Days Became Numbered*; and on the diversity of peasant experiences in Late Antiquity: Grey, *Constructing Communities*, esp. 15–19, 25–57.

7. Jonas, *Vita Columbani*, preface (comparing the exotics to writers he admired and the European products to his own work), 1.16 (beer).

8. One can count the number of total bone fragments on site (which in Anglophone publications goes by the acronym NISP, or number of individual specimens), the minimum number of individuals that must have been present (MNI), or less commonly, bone weight, estimated weight in meat, or the minimum number of anatomical elements on a site (MNE/NME). Typically a careful bone study will discuss the pros and cons of these measures with respect to the conditions of a particular site, but see generally O'Connor, *Archaeology of Animal Bones*, 54–67; Albarella et al., *Oxford Handbook of Zooarchaeology*, s.vv. "MNE," "MNI," "NISP," "Quantification," and "Weight method"; and the methodological arguments in Ikeguchi, "Beef in Roman Italy," esp. 9–24.

9. Finbar McCormick and Murray, "The Zooarchaeology of Medieval Ireland"; Smiarowski et al., "Zooarchaeology of the Scandinavian Settlements"; Enghoff, *Hunting, Fishing and Animal Husbandry*, 79 (on the virtual absence of pig in Greenland); Arge, Church, and Brewington, "Pigs in the Faroe Islands," 23–24; O'Connor, "Livestock and Animal Husbandry"; O'Connor, "Livestock and Deadstock"; Benecke, *Archäozoologische Studien*, 150–55, 195–202, 370–71 (table 41), 382–83 (table 53); Clavel and Yvinec, "L'archéozoologie du Moyen Âge"; Forest, "Alimentation carnée"; Iwaszczuk, "Animal Husbandry on the Polish Territory"; Salvadori, "L'allevamento nell'Italia me-

dievale"; Salvadori, *Uomini e animali nel Medioevo*, 87–122; Grau-Sologestoa, *Zooarchaeology of Medieval Álava*, 122–42; Dolores Carmen Morales Muñiz, "Pig Husbandry in Visigoth Iberia"; Moreno García, "Gestión y aprovechamiento de cabañas ganaderas"; Arturo Morales Muñiz et al., "¿El origen de una disyunción alimentaria?"; García García, "Explotación y consumo de los animales," esp. 632–44; King, "Diet in the Roman World," esp. 187–89 (Egypt and North Africa); Mattingly and Hitchner, "Roman Africa," 197; Veen, Grant, and Barker, "Romano-Libyan Agriculture"; Kroll, "Animals in the Byzantine Empire."

10. Schroeder, *Lehrbuch der Pflanzengeographie*, 201, 237–39, 268–70, 310–11; Devèze, "Forêts françaises et forêts allemandes," 348–53; Hoffmann, *Environmental History of Medieval Europe*, 21–50; Kallala and Sanmartí, *Althiburos* 1, 2:491–515; Barker, "A Tale of Two Deserts"; Mattingly, *Archaeology of Fazzān*, 1:47–48. For the historical and geographical delineation of the Maghreb: Shaw, "A Peculiar Island."

11. Porte, *Larina*, 1:463–80 (faunal analysis by Philippe Columeau). Measured as proportions of total animal remains or NISP, Larina's bones are roughly 5 percent cow, 27 percent pig, 60 percent ovicaprid, and 8 percent wild animal. For Marseille, see Columeau, *Alimentation carnée en Gaule du sud*, "Moyen Âge," §9–12.

12. Kerr, "Livestock Farming," 85–89; more generally Finbar McCormick and Murray, *Excavations at Knowth 3*, 103–16; Clavel and Yvinec, "L'archéozoologie du Moyen Âge," esp. fig. 5; Jiménez-Camino et al., "¿Continuidad o cambio en la dieta?" Algeciras was under Byzantine control from the 550s into the seventh century: its ceramic and coin finds suggest trade with other cities under the empire's control, and some of the city was rebuilt to house troops (Reynolds, "Material Culture and the Economy," 187–90; Vizcaíno Sánchez, *La presencia bizantina en Hispania*, 148–51).

13. See, generally, Horden and Purcell, *Corrupting Sea*, esp. 53–88.

14. Azuar, "Arqueologías ambientales," 149–52.

15. Cantini, *Il castello di Montarrenti*, 186–91, 213–15.

16. Valenti, *Miranduolo*, 323–70; Dall'Olio and Putti, "Bioarcheologia in un sito di potere altomedievale." On chestnuts as a cultivated species in the early Middle Ages see Squatriti, *Landscape and Change*.

17. Putelat, "L'homme, l'animal et L'Ajoie," 103–6 (the village near Courtedoux); Saint Jores and Hincker, "Les habitats mérovingien et carolingien de la 'Delle sur le Marais,'" 10–11 (faunal analysis by Jean-Hervé Yvinec); Humphrey, *Excavations at Carthage*, 6:191–258 (faunal analysis by David S. Reese, George E. Watson, and Alwyne Wheeler); *Flixborough 3*, 36–58, 196–207; Arge, Church, and Brewington, "Pigs in the Faroe Islands," 20–23; Smiarowski et al., "Zooarchaeology of the Scandinavian Settlements," 150; Lucas, *Hofstaðir*, 222–26 (faunal analysis by Thomas H. McGovern).

18. *Liber iudiciorum* 8.4.31; *Capitulare saxonicum* 11 (= *Capitularia regum Francorum* 27). Compare the agricultural landscape of Frisia, just west of northern Saxon territory: Hoffmann, *Environmental History of Medieval Europe*, 71–75.

19. For pigs' love of acorns and beechnuts, see Chapter 1. Humans' disdain for acorns: Mason, "Acornutopia?"; Squatriti, *Landscape and Change*, 6–10; Braudel, *La Méditerranée*, 8. Humans' love of acorn-fed pigs: Varro, *Res rusticae* 2.4.6. The Old Irish adage is from Fergus Kelly, *Early Irish Farming*, 83.

20. Woodbridge, Roberts, and Fyfe, "Vegetation and Land-Use Change in Northern Europe"; López-Sáez et al., "A Late Antique Vegetation History"; Kouli et al., "Regional Vegetation Histories"; Squatriti, *Landscape and Change*, esp. 1–26; Vanpoucke et al., "Pig Husbandry and Environmental Conditions." For the pig:cow ratios see Cantini, *Il castello di Montarrenti*, 181 (1 cow:5 pigs, faunal analysis by Gill Clark); *Flixborough 3*, 123 (1 cow:3.12 pigs). In the early Middle Ages many factors affected these changes in vegetation, depending on the region: lower population levels, the disappearance of Roman agricultural taxes and extractive initiatives, the reduction in volume of long-distance trade, increasing emphasis on animal husbandry, and the "climatic anomaly" of colder (and correspondingly wetter or more arid) conditions between the fifth and eighth centuries or longer.

21. García-Blanco and Vila, "Restos animales y vegetales"; Alarcón Hernández, "Estudio arqueofaunístico"; Vigil-Escalera Guirado et al., "Productive Strategies and Consumption Patterns"; Malalana Ureña, Barroso Cabrera, and Morín de Pablos, *La Quebrada II*, 465–522. This mountain range underwent substantial deforestation in the early Middle Ages, though as always there was pronounced local variation: Blanco-González et al., "Medieval Landscapes in the Spanish Central System," esp. 6–8. In any case, the pigs of Gózquez were definitely free-range: García-Collado, "Food Consumption Patterns and Social Inequality," 68–70 (for the pigs' diet) and 70–73 (for the humans').

22. Woods without pigs: Casivico (with woods to feed 200 pigs), Cublas (100), Mantivado (100), Capursa (60), Sextuna (60), Albinago (20), Macharegia (15), and a property at the edge of Parma ("in finibus Parmensis," with woods for 3 pigs). Pigs without woods: Cardulina (1 pig), Rivariolas (2), Temulina (3), Isula Rosberga (3), Barbada (4), Mantevado (6), Audalvico (8), Casale Ermanfridi (8), Cardena (10), Trevoncio (10), Glociano (11), a property "in vico Porzano" (12), Cinctura (12), Canellas (13), two properties in Plasentia (13 and 20), Temulina (the *curtis*, 16), Cervinica (18), Flosola (19), Clusune (20), Kebaharti (21), Cabriana (23), Alfiano (23), Valcamoniga (29), Gummolfi (50). From the Polyptych of S. Giulia di Brescia, *Inventari altomedievali* V, ed. Gianfranco Pasquali.

23. Kallala and Sanmartí, *Althiburos II*, 421–48 (faunal analysis by Silvia Valenzuela-Lamas), 449–90 (carpological analysis by Dani López and Francisco José Cantero), 491–515 (anthracological analysis by Francisco José Cantero and Raquel Piqué). An even higher rate of pork consumption (48.9 percent NISP) appears in fifth-century Sétif, also in the Tell, but paleobotanical evidence is lacking for this spot: Mohamedi et al., *Fouilles de Sétif*, 247–59 (faunal analysis by Anthony King). See more generally Vos,

"The Rural Landscape of Thugga"; Hitchner, "Image and Reality" (but whose comments on the *annona* have been superseded by the Thugga project).

24. Quirós Castillo, *Arqueología del campesinado medieval;* Grau-Sologestoa, *Zooarchaeology of Medieval Álava,* 41–55.

25. Porte, *Larina,* 25–30, 463–80 (faunal analysis by Philippe Columeau). These figures derive from MNI ratios—that is, the proportions between the minimum number of individual animals of each species that would have been present at Larina.

26. Arthur, *Naples,* 116–17; Salvadori, "L'allevamento nell'Italia medievale," 137–42; Salvadori, "Animals in Italian Medieval Towns," 133–34; Salvadori, *Uomini e animali nel Medioevo,* 249–51.

27. Devroey, *Puissants et misérables,* 551–59, "center of centers," 552; Lebecq, "The Role of Monasteries"; Crabtree, "Agricultural Innovation," 129–33. Bobbio: ChLA2 57.19, line 111; ChLA2 57.21, line 91. Saint-Germain: Elmshäuser and Hedwig, *Studien zum Polyptychon von Saint-Germain-des-Prés,* 130–34, 194–95, 365–99, 490 (= map 2); *Polyptychon von Saint-Germain-des-Prés,* nos. 11–13 (the western properties). Elmshäuser and Hedwig suggest that the 120 monks at Saint-Germain probably only drank about 15 percent of all this wine; the rest would have been sold in the Paris markets or farther afield. This still left the monks with more than two bottles of wine per person per day, but other texts from the Carolingian period suggest that this was exactly what monks expected (Marios Costambeys, "The Production and Consumption of Wine in Carolingian Europe: Monasteries and Markets," paper delivered at the Medieval Academy of America, March 2018).

28. See e.g., Martín Viso, "Un mundo en transformación," esp. 50–54; Quirós Castillo, "Los comportamientos alimentarios del campesinado medieval," 26–27, 28–29; Vigil-Escalera Guirado and Quirós Castillo, "Early Medieval Rural Societies in North-Western Spain," 47–49; Valenti, *L'insediamento altomedievale nelle campagne Toscane,* esp. 11–15, 65–77; Smiarowski et al., "Zooarchaeology of the Scandinavian Settlements," 151; Finbar McCormick, O'Sullivan, and Kerr, "The Farming Landscape of Early Medieval Ireland"; Barbiera and Dalla-Zuanna, "Population Dynamics in Italy," 369–65; Hoffmann, *Environmental History of Medieval Europe,* 57–67; Horden and Purcell, *Corrupting Sea,* 175–230; and, precociously, Montanari, *L'alimenzatione contadina,* 19–70. Pollen samples can be a good proxy for the changing balances among field cultivation, pasture, and woodland: see, e.g., López-Sáez et al., "A Late Antique Vegetation History"; Izdebski et al., "The Environmental, Archaeological and Historical Evidence for Regional Climatic Changes," 192 (on the eastern Mediterranean). Individual diets varied considerably within this general pattern: see, e.g., Reitsema, Vercellotti, and Boano, "Subadult Dietary Variation"; and further discussion in Chapter 4.

29. Moreno García, "Gestión y aprovechamiento de cabañas ganaderas," esp. 87.

30. Guélat et al., *Develier-Courtételle.* This volume is one of five (Cahiers d'Archéologie Jurassienne 13–17), amounting to a truly extraordinary analysis of an early medieval

settlement. All five volumes are open-access, available at https://www.jura.ch/fr/ Autorites/Archeologie-2017/Publications/Les-cahiers-d-archeologie-jurassienne-CAJ .html.

31. Rackham, "Savanna in Europe."

32. Mattingly, *Archaeology of Fazzān*, 1:37–106, 350–61, 4:473–536.

33. Volpe and Turchiano, *Faragola 1*.

34. Pig figures for this period: Buglione, De Venuto, and Volpe, "Agricoltura e allevamento nella Puglia settentrionale," §9. On transhumance in medieval Apulia, before the rise of the vast *mesta* system that Aragon introduced to the Kingdom of Naples see §5–12; De Venuto, "Carne, lane e pellame"; cf. Marino, *Pastoral Economics in the Kingdom of Naples;* Pascua, *Señores del paisaje;* Klein, *The Mesta.*

35. Volpe and Turchiano, *Faragola I,* 205–12 (faunal analysis by Antonietta Buglione), 213–22 (botanical analysis by Valentina Caracuta and Girolamo Fiorentino).

36. Redding, "The Pig and the Chicken," 340–48, with further bibliography.

37. Columella, *De re rustica* 7.9.4; Palladius, *Opus agriculturae* 2.26.2. Walter of Henley, *Hosbondrye* 94; Walter of Henley, *The Husbandry* 17, 22; and Walter of Henley, "The Gloucester Husbandry" (Gloucester Cathedral, Library of the Dean and Chapter, MS 33, fol. 54r); all in *Walter of Henley,* 33–34, 424–27, 472. Fertility rates and litter sizes among wild boar are lower, and litter sizes of free-range domesticated pigs today are higher: see, for example, Gamelon et al., "The Relationship Between Phenotypic Variation Among Offspring and Mother Body Mass in Wild Boar"; Graves, "Behavior and Ecology of Wild and Feral Swine," 484; Albarella, Manconi, and Trentacoste, "A Week on the Plateau," 152–53; Halstead and Isaakidou, "A Pig Fed by Hand," 164–66.

38. Varro, *Res rusticae* 2.4.13–14, 22; Columella, *De re rustica* 7.9.2–3, 13; Palladius, *Opus agriculturae* 3.26.4–5. For the early manuscript tradition of Palladius, see Rodgers, *An Introduction to Palladius,* 18–26. In the sixth century Cassiodorus included Columella and Palladius on his reading list for readers who were serious about their education: *Institutiones* 1.28.6.

39. Stone, "Medieval Farm Management and Technological Mentalities," 631–32.

40. Peytremann, *En marge du village,* 97, 268–69 (osteoarchaeological analysis by Gaëtan Jouanin and Jean-Hervé Yvinec); the detail about the skinning comes from Jean-Hervé Yvinec, personal communication (14 April 2015). Cf. Varro, *Res rusticae* 2.4.6–8; Columella, *De re rustica* 7.9.2–3; Palladius, *Opus agriculturae* 3.26.

41. Special diet: Varro, *Res rusticae* 2.4.21; Columella, *De re rustica* 7.9.13; and for the high Middle Ages see, for example, Biddick, *The Other Economy,* 122–23. Sties: Varro, *Res rusticae* 2.4.14–15; Columella, *De re rustica* 7.6.9–10; Palladius, *Opus agriculturae* 3.26.4; MacKinnon, "High on the Hog," 665–66. For the lack of clear evidence in early medieval contexts, see for example Catteddu, Clavel, and Ruas, "L'habitat rural mérovingien de Genlis," 57–64; Catteddu, *Archéologie médiévale,* 32–33; Buglione, De Venuto, and Volpe, "Agricoltura e allevamento nella Puglia settentrionale," section 13.

42. Herd sizes: *Lex Salica* 2.20 (fifty pigs); *Lex Alamannorum* 72 [79] (forty); *Lex Baiwariorum* 4.26 (seventy). Marking and branding: *Lex Salica* 9.2; *Liber iudiciorum* 8.5.8; and the elaborate and probably unrealistic example of Columella, *De re rustica* 7.9.12–13. Single herd with different owners: *Liber iudiciorum* 5.5.6.

43. *Edictus Rothari* 249–52, 371; see also *Codex Euricanus* 278–79; *Lex Salica* 9.3; *Liber constitutionum* 49.1–2; *Liber iudiciorum* 5.4.1–2, 5.4.4, 5.4.6; *Lex Ribuaria* 75.6–8; *Lex Baiwariorum* 13.4–5, 15.1; *Pactus legis Alamannorum* 22, 27; *Lex Alamannorum* 83.1 [86.1], 94.4 [98.1]; Lothar, *Concessio generalis* 2 (= *Capitularia regum Francorum* 159.2); *Pactum Hlotharii* 21 (= *Capitularia regum Francorum* 233.21), echoed in *Pactum Karoli III* 21 (= *Capitularia regum Francorum* 236.21) and *Pactum Berengarii I* 21 (= *Capitularia regum Francorum* 238.21); and the Old Irish legal commentary from Trinity College Dublin, MS H 3.18, ed. and trans. Fergus Kelly, "Livestock Not to Be Distrained," in *Early Irish Farming*, Appendix A, Text 2, pp. 521–32. For the countless damaged pigs (*porcos sine numero*): *Colección documental del Monasterio de Santa María de Otero de las Dueñas*, no. 40 (995 CE).

44. Ireland: Fergus Kelly, *Early Irish Farming*, 176. Lucca: ChLA 73.5 (807 CE); ChLA 75.9 (822).

45. *Lex Ribuaria* 11.1, 19.1. On the code's context, see Esders, "Eliten und Raum." The same unit of six sows plus a boar also appears in the Carolingian *Lex Thuringorum* 37.

46. *Liber pontificalis* 97.54 (on the *domusculta* of Capracorum); *Colección documental del archivo de la Catedral de León*, vol. 3, no. 555 (993 CE); *Polyptyque . . . de Saint-Remi de Reims*, p. 76 (late ninth/early tenth century); *Polyptyque . . . de l'abbaye Saint-Pierre de Lobbes*; Polyptych of S. Giulia di Brescia, *Inventari altomedievali* V. Unfortunately Bobbio did not record how many pigs it was keeping on its *porcaritia*, or pig farm, near Piacenza (in modern Porcile!): Bobbio inventory of 862, ChLA2 57.19, lines 26–28.

47. *Charters of Christ Church Canterbury*, vol. 1, nos. 96 (= Sawyer 1508, 871 x 889 CE) and 97 (= Stockholm, Royal Library, A. 135, fol. 11r: "Ic Aelfred aldormon 7 Weburg min gefera begetan ðas bec æt hæðnum herge mid uncre claene feo ðæt ðonne wæas mid clæne golde"). On the Weald see Witney, *The Jutish Forest*; and further discussion in the next chapter.

48. Agrarian-urban spaces: Jones, Straker, and Davis, "Early Medieval Plant Use and Ecology"; Prummel, *Dorestad*, 8, 11; Arthur, *Naples*, 109–18; Mohamedi et al., *Fouilles de Sétif*, 93–96; Alba, "Diacronía de la vivienda señorial de *Emerita*," 177; García García, "Some Remarks on the Provision of Animal Products"; Goodson, "Garden Cities in Early Medieval Italy." Patterns of local, regional, and long-distance trade: Horden and Purcell, *Corrupting Sea*, 89–122; Michael McCormick, *Origins of the European Economy*, 573–613; Wickham, *Framing the Early Middle Ages*, 693–824; Loseby, "Post-Roman Economies"; Loveluck, *Northwest Europe*, 178–212; Reynolds, "Material Culture and the Economy."

49. Arthur and Bruno, *Apigliano*; Arthur, Imperiale, and Tinelli, *Apigliano*. On Glazed White Ware II: Vroom, "Ceramics," 178–80.

50. The best overview of the pork annona is Sirks, *Food for Rome*, esp. 368–74. On the Ostrogoths' adaptation of the annona system in Italy, see Cracco Ruggini, *Economia e società nell' "Italia Annonaria,"* esp. 312–21 (on pork). On the Merovingians' possible adaptation of it, see the next section of this chapter.

51. Jagt et al., "An Insight into Animal Exchange in Early Medieval Oegstgeest" (my thanks to Frans Theuws and Lisette Kootker for bringing my attention to this work); *Prümer Urbar*, no. 114 (at Rhein-Gönheim).

52. Newfield, "Early Medieval Epizootics," esp. 108–11.

53. Galinié, *Tours antique et médiéval*, 73 (analysis of pit deposits by Cécile Bébien). On oyster values as variable, see Hitchner, "More Italy Than Province?" Export of pig carcasses, minus their heads: Crabtree, "Production and Consumption in an Early Complex Society," 68–70 (Wicken Bonhunt).

54. Francovich and Valenti, *Poggio Imperiale*, 107–24 (faunal analysis by Frank Salvadori).

55. Tuscany: Valenti, *L'insediamento altomedievale nelle campagne Toscane*, 110, 114; on the tax see Andreolli, "I prodotti alimentari nei contratti agrari toscani dell'alto medioevo," in Andreolli, *Contadini su terre di signori*, 201–9, at 206–7, originally published in *Archeologia Medievale* 8 (1981): 117–26. Earlier payments in cured pork: see, e.g., the obligations of the massarii of Migliarina, an estate in the possession of S. Giulia di Brescia: ChLA2 92.41, line 47 (*porco salario de soldo*); an inventory of the same estate at some point in the ninth century showed 50 pork flitches/*baffas de lardo* in its stores (ChLA2 91.24); a pork shoulder/*armo de porco* paid to the bishopric of Lucca in the second half of the ninth century (*Inventari altomedievali* XI.1, ed. Michele Luzzati, p. 220 line 4); and shoulders/*spallas* paid in the ninth century to S. Lorenzo di Tortona (*Inventari altomedievali* VII, ed. Andrea Castagnetti). English towns: O'Connor, "Livestock and Animal Husbandry," who raises the possibly of both trade and tribute/rent.

56. These are my calculations based on the Bobbio inventories from 862 and 883 (ChLA 57.19, 57.21, also in *Inventari altomedievali* VIII.1–2, ed. Andrea Castagnetti), the Polyptych of S. Giulia di Brescia dating between 879 and 906 (*Inventari altomedievali* V); and the inventory from Wissembourg, specifically its core layer dating between 860 and 870 (*Liber possessionum Wizenburgensis*). Wissembourg's totals exclude the *silva communis* at Hoveheim (no. 26); for more on *silva communis* see the next section of this chapter. Pannage rates in Britain: Laws of Ine 49.3, in *Gesetze der Angelsachsen*. The payment of one-third to one-fifth of one's pigs, depending on how fat they had gotten, might represent punitive rates for unauthorized grazing—i.e., what a swineherd owed if he got caught.

57. Inventories of Bobbio from 862 and 883, ChLA 57.19, 57.21; Polyptych of S. Giulia di Brescia, *Inventari altomedievali* V; see also Andreolli and Montanari, *L'azienda curtense*, 152–53.

58. Rose, Greenberg, and Fearer, "Acorn Production Prediction Models"; Paul Johnson, Shifley, and Rogers, *The Ecology and Silviculture of Oaks*, 68–73. For European

oaks, which offer less specific figures, see Espelta et al., "Masting Mediated by Summer Drought" (*Quercus ilex* and *Q. humilis*); Pons and Pausas, "The Coexistence of Acorns with Different Maturation Patterns" (*Q. suber*); Biano and Schirone, "On *Quercus coccifera*." Beech: Packham et al., "Biological Flora of the British Isles: *Fagus sylvatica*."

59. ChLA 91.26 (804 CE). By this point a libellarius was a tenant who agreed that both he and his descendants would farm a given property in addition to paying an annual rent (in cash, kind, or labor). See further Andreolli, "Il contratto di livello," in Andreolli, *Contadini su terre di signori*, 39–67, esp. 48–57; orig. publ. as "Per una semantica storica dello ius libellarium nell'alto e nel pieno Medioevo," *Bullettino dell'Istituto Storico Italiano per il Medio Evo e Archivio Muratoriano* 89 (1980–81): 151–91. This kind of contract (sometimes called *emphyteusis* in the sources) may have taken on a coercive character in the ninth century: Andreolli argues that it forced small-time landowners into dependent relationships. But in earlier centuries, the setup was attractive to members of elite families, who used arrangements like these to expand their access to (state and ecclesiastical) property and build alliances in the process: Santos Salazar, "Las transformaciones de la fiscalidad," 137–43.

60. *Polyptyque . . . de Lobbes*, p. 10; *Liber possessionum Wizenburgensis*, nos. 3, 17–18, 65, 68, 74, 229 (all provisional on pannage), and 5, 11, 15, 20, 46, 73, 241 (pig feeding regardless of pannage).

61. "Quando ipso loco glande non est dunat ipsis solidos in argento": here *solidos* is a metonym for *porco de soldo* (that is, a pig worth one solidus or gold coin), and *argento* means cash. Inventory of Migliarina, ChLA2 91.24. When Santa Giulia di Brescia included Migliarina's assets in its overarching inventory, it halved the number of pigs it expected the estate's woods to feed (Polyptych of S. Giulia di Brescia, *Inventari altomedievali* V, p. 85). It is possible that one of these records was in error, but it is also possible that in the time between the two inventories, half of the woodland at Migliarina was assarted and converted into arable, since the accounts point to a concomitant reduction in the number of sheep, goats, and chickens on-site and an increase in draft animals (twelve oxen and donkeys, up from five).

62. Andreolli, "I prodotti alimentari nei contratti agrari toscani dell'alto medioevo," in Andreolli, *Contadini su terre*, 201–9.

63. Swine-renders as a unit of calculation in southeast England: *Flixborough* 3, 190. Various forms of pastio payment: *Polyptychon von Saint-Germain-des-Prés*, nos. 2–8, 14–17; *Polyptychon . . . von Saint-Maur-des-Fossés*, nos. 14, 16; *Polyptichon von Montierender*, nos. 28, 34–35. The caveat here is that *pastio* may not actually refer to pannage in these cases, since some tenants were paying for pastio even when there was no private woodland nearby to tax. We may be seeing the results of a tax in transition: possibly pastio was originally a pannage or generic pasture tax, which gradually came to be collected in different commodities that were available or that a monastery wanted, and over time the name of the tax (and its original function) was changed to reflect that. Some wine payments made to Saint-Germain, for example, lack the commoner

pastio designation and were simply registered as wine taxes: Elsmhäuser and Hedwig, *Studien zum Polyptychon von Saint-Germain-des-Prés*, 394, referring to *Polyptychon von Saint-Germain-des-Prés*, nos. 19–23.

64. *Polyptyque . . . de Reims*, p. 59; *Liber possessionum Wizenburgensis*, no. 45; *Polyptyque . . . de Lobbes*, pp. 18, 23; *Prümer Urbar*, pp. 219, 222, 225, 226, 236. For more on silva communis see the following section.

65. Polyptych of S. Giulia di Brescia, *Inventari altomedievali* V.

66. *Pannage* in English can refer to both the nut crop and the payment for it, but the terminology was split in early medieval Latin. The tax specifically was called *decima porcorum* (sixth century on), *cellarinsis* (seventh century), *glandaticum* (eighth century on), *pastionaticum* (ninth century), *pasnagium/pagsnaticum* (eleventh century on), or the more generic terms of *scaticum* and *datio*. The crop is called *glans/glando, saginatio, sagina, pastio*, or *pastus* (though the last two terms can also refer to animal fodder more generally).

67. Gregory of Tours, *Libri historiarum X* 4.48–51, 5; Fredegar, *Chronicae* 3.55–4.42; *Liber historiae Francorum* 30–40; Halsall, "The Preface to Book V of Gregory of Tours' Histories"; Peter Brown, *Ransom of the Soul*, 149–58; Wood, *The Merovingian Kingdoms*, 88–101.

68. "Quicumque vero haec deliberationem, quem cum pontificibus vel tam magnis viris optematibus aut fidelibus nostris in synodale concilio instruemus, temerare praesumpserit, in ipso capitale sententia iudicetur, qualiter alii non debeant similia perpetrare." *Chlotharii II. edictum* 24. For the context: Wood, *Merovingian Kingdoms*, 140–58; Yaniv Fox, *Power and Religion in Merovingian Gaul*, esp. 27–49; Reimitz, *History, Frankish Identity and the Framing of Western Ethnicity*, 166–281; Kreiner, *The Social Life of Hagiography*, 140–229.

69. "Porcarii fescalis in silvas ecclesiarum aut privatorum absque voluntate possessoris in silvas eorum ingredere non praesumant. . . . Et quandoquidem passio [sc. pastio] non fuerit, unde porci debeant saginare, cellarinsis in publico non exegatur." *Chlotharii II. edictum* 21, 23.

70. "Agraria, pascuaria, vel decimas porcorum aeclesiae pro fidei nostrae divucione concedemus ita, ut actor aut decimatur in rebus ecclesiae nullus accedat. Aeclesiae vel clerecis nullam requirant agentes publice functione, qui avi vel genetoris aut germani nostri immunitatem meruerunt": *Praeceptio Chlotharii*, in Esders, *Römische Rechtstradition und merowingisches Königtum*, 82–83. An older edition is also available in *Capitularia regum Francorum*, 1:19. Although the identity of the "Clothar" who issued the precept has been debated (was it Clothar II, or Clothar I, who ruled about a century earlier?), Esders's study convincingly situates the precept in the political culture of the late sixth and seventh centuries.

71. Alexander Callander Murray, "Immunity"; Esders, *Römische Rechtstradition und merowingisches Königtum*, 237–38; Rosenwein, *Negotiating Space*, esp. 42–96. See, for

example, *Urkunden der Merowinger,* vol. 1, no. 173: Chilperic II (r. 715/16–721) specifically forbade tax officials from collecting revenue in a forest that he granted to Saint-Denis.

72. Allen, "Vegetation and Ecosystem Dynamics"; Peterken, *Natural Woodland;* Devèze, "Forêts françaises et forêts allemandes"; Fabre, "Écologie des forêts et exploitation des bois."

73. Peterken, *Natural Woodland,* 86–116; Rackham, "Savanna in Europe"; Chabal, *Forêts et sociétés en Languedoc,* esp. 77–85.

74. The contrast between rights and territorial sovereignty appears in Costambeys, Innes, and MacLean, *The Carolingian World,* 63; see further Rio, *Slavery After Rome;* Innes, "Rituals, Rights and Relationships," esp. 36–39 (and thanks to Marios Costambeys for this last reference). Woodland rights in general: Wickham, "European Forests in the Early Middle Ages."

75. Silva communis: the most relevant law here is *Lex Ribuaria* 79; see also *Liber constitutionum* 13; Montanari, "La foresta come spazio economico e culturale." For *materia* as timber, see Ulrich, *Roman Woodworking,* 271. For timber as the main building material in Gaul, see Catteddu, *Archéologie médiévale,* 31–32. For centralized timber management in Achaemenid, Hellenistic, and then Roman regimes, see John Pairman Brown, "Paradise and the Forest of Lebanon."

76. For example, a judgment from 747 in the cartulary of Farfa (in Lazio) mentions a *gualdo publico* that also has private parcels or *casales* within it (Gregory of Catino, *Registrum Farfense* 2:35); a grant by Æthelwulf of Kent in the 830s mentions *silvam ad perfruendum in communi pastura* and *communionem in silvis* (*Charters of Christ Church Canterbury,* vol. 1, no. 67 = Sawyer 323); and a dispute between Santa Maria del Puerto (in Cantabria) and one Revelio ends with Revelio recognizing that the woodlands concerned were common pasture (*ut quicquid silva est sit pastus communis*): *Cartulario de Santa Maria del Puerto,* no. 1 (863 CE). For Ireland see Fergus Kelly, *Early Irish Farming,* 379–90, 407.

77. *Liber constitutionum* 28; *Lex Salica* 27.23–26; *Lex Ribuaria* 79.

78. Private woodland: *Edictus Rothari* 236–37, 300–302, 319 (where King Rothari refers to the public rights to trees in private woodlands as "natural law," *ius naturalis*); similarly *Liber constitutionum* 28.1 (regarding the collection of firewood in private woodland in Burgundian Gaul). Lombard law seems to have excluded royal woodland (*gahagius regis*) from this entitlement: *Edictus Rothari* 319–20. Oxcarts of wood: *Liber iudiciorum* 8.3.8; and see the contrasting policies of King Liutprand and (later on) Aregis, the duke and *princeps* of Benevento: *Leges Liutprandi* 82 [XIII], *Aregis principis capitula* 11.

79. Woodland resources in general: Squatriti, *Landscape and Change;* Montanari, "La foresta come spazio economico e culturale"; Horden and Purcell, *Corrupting Sea,* 182–86. Bees: *Lex Salica* 33. Domesticated deer: *Lex Salica* 33.2–3; *Lex Ribuaria* 46.2. Birds: *Lex Alamannorum* 95 [99].14–16, 96.1 [99.17]; *Lex Baiwariorum* 12.8. Fish: *Urkunden der Merowinger,* vol. 1, no. 80 (643–647/8 CE). Songbirds: *Lex Baiwariorum*

21.6. Wildcat, chamois, ibex: Putelat, "L'homme, l'animal et l'Ajoie," 106; Guélat et al., *Develier-Courtételle,* 167–68 (faunal analysis by Claude Olive). Pet foxes: Dierkens, Le Bec, and Périn, "Sacrifice animal et offrandes alimentaires," 285. Thrushes and fly-catcher pair: MacKinnon, *The Excavations of San Giovanni di Ruoti 3,* 183–8 (analysis of avian remains by A. Eastham).

80. *Lex Salica* 33.4–5; *Pactus legis Alamannorum* 23–26 (note the domesticated pigs included among these concerns at 25.3); *Edictus Rothari* 311–21; *Liber iudiciorum* 8.3.3.

81. Pannage payments in royal woodlands are most visible when rulers gifted the forests along with their revenues: e.g., *Urkunden der Merowinger,* vol. 1, no. 46 (a grant to Speyer forged in the Carolingian period, posing as a Merovingian charter); *Salzburger Urkundenbuch,* vol. 2, no. 48a (Otto I, 959 CE). Various pannage stipulations in rental agreements: ChLA2 72.38 (Lucca, 806); ChLA2 62.14 (Lucca, 830); *Breviarium ecclesiae Ravennatis,* no. 111. Acorn collection: ChLA2 74.37 (Lucca, 818); ChLA2 76.18 (Lucca, 829), ChLA2 79.46 (Lucca, 849); ChLA2 80.1 (Lucca, 850), ChLA2 80.8 (Lucca, 850); ChLA2 54.22 (Ravenna, 896); *Liber possessionum Wizenburgensis* 68; *Prümer Urbar* 10–14, 18, 20, 23–27. Acorns and children: Palladius, *Opus agriculturae* 12.14.

82. ChLA2 88.32; Wickham, "Space and Society," 564–65; Montanari, *L'alimentazione contadina,* 91–93. On the general location: Bonacini, *Terre d'Emilia,* 213–33. On the range of possible norms and forms of legal recourse that were available to litigants and judges in Italy: Costambeys, "Disputes and Courts."

83. Esders, *Römische Rechtstradition und merowingisches Königtum,* 220–41; Barnish, "Pigs, Plebeians and *Potentes*"; A. H. M. Jones, *The Later Roman Empire,* 396–97, 1158 n. 63; Vera, "Dalla liturgia al contratto," 59; Cracco Ruggini, *Economia e società nell' "Italia Annonaria,"* 19–152, 207–96; Sato, "*L'agrarium*"; and on the tension between local agrarian regimes and the Roman tax system see Grey, *Constructing Communities,* 189–91. For a late-Roman criticism of the cellaria, see Severus, *Chronica* 2.41.

84. *Liber iudiciorum* 8.5.1–4; *Marculfi formularum libri duo,* nos. 1.1–2 (*nova carmina*).

85. Esders, *Römische Rechtstradition und merowingisches Königtum,* 222–23; Alexander Callander Murray, "Immunity," 31–32.

86. Montanari, "La foresta come spazio economico e culturale," 339–40; Baruzzi and Montanari, *Porci e porcari,* 31. For example: *Vita Genovefae* 18; *Vita Aviti* 7; Gregory of Tours, *Liber vitae patrum* 12.2. The conspicuous ancient example is Virgil, *Aeneid* 8.42–48, 81–85.

87. *Urkunden der Merowinger,* vol. 1, nos. 81 (Sigibert III) and 108 (Childeric II); Wickham, "European Forests in the Early Middle Ages," 513–14. For the demarcation of the "little woodland" (*silvula*): ChLA 23.738 (Sovana, 760 CE).

88. *Liber iudiciorum* 8.5.1–3.

89. *Aliud eius meriti: Liber iudiciorum,* 5.4.1, 8.3.3, 8.4.13; see also *Codex Euricanus* 278–79, issued in Iberia in 475 and using identical language.

90. *Pace* Andreolli, who suggested that the difference in prices reflected a change in the value of pigs over time ("I prodotti alimentari," in his *Contadini su terre*). See, for

example, a pig worth 3 denarii (*Inventari altomedievale* VII, S. Lorenzo di Tortona, ninth century, p. 116 line 16), pigs worth a tremissis [= 4d] (ChLA 33.974, Lucca, 762 CE; ChLA 22.723, Lucca, 777); an "average-sized pig" worth 6d (ChLA2 72.32, Lucca, 804); pigs worth 1 solidus [= 12d or 3 tremisses] (*porco soldale*: inventory of Tivoli, 945, *Inventari altomedievali* XII, ed. Augusto Vasina, p. 268, line 6); pigs worth 4 tremisses (ChLA 39.1146, Lucca, 795); pigs worth 20d [= 4 tremisses] (*Inventari altomedievali* III, ed. Andrea Castagnetti = curtis Lemunta, in Como, before 24 January 835); *Prümer Urbar*, e.g., no. 54; *Liber possessionum Wizenburgensis*, passim. Pigs are measured in ages rather than coin: ChLA 35.1011 (Lucca, 770, *porco annotino bono*), ChLA 35.1055 (Lucca, 776, *porco annotino*); ChLA2 76.5 (Lucca, 827, *porcus annotinus*). Occasionally animals and money were treated interchangeably, e.g., a payment of either a pig worth 12d or 12d in cash (ChLA2 74.25, Lucca, 815; ChLA2 78.6, Lucca, 843); *Polyptychon . . . von Saint-Maur-des-Fossés* 9; and Prüm's commutation of pig payments to cash in the first half of the tenth century: see Morimoto, "Le polyptyque de Prüm n'a-t-il pas été interpolé? À propos de sa nouvelle édition," in Morimoto, Études sur l'économie rurale, 253–60, at 258; orig. publ. in *Le Moyen Âge* 92 (1986): 265–76. Irish lords also specified that their free clients pay them in pigs of specific value: Fergus Kelly, *Early Irish Farming*, 83. *Porci crassi*: *Polyptychon von Saint-Germain-des-Prés* 9.2, 9.158; *Liber possessionum Wizenburgensis* 8, 10, 12, 19, 21, 68, all but no. 68 reflecting an earlier polyptych drawn up before 818/19.

91. *Lex Salica* 2, but these values were not market prices: see the "Soldiers and States" section of Chapter 4.

92. But not *much* better: only a 4 percent profit. The joke driving this math problem is that sellers should know better than try to fatten pigs quickly just after pannage season had ended! *Propositiones ad acuendos iuvenes*, no. 6, pp. 47–8.

93. This was a problem that the *Lex Baiwariorum* (16.9) anticipated with livestock sales.

94. A. H. M. Jones, *Later Roman Empire*, 702–3, 1290 n. 36; Einhard, Ep. 9 ("nec aliud aliquid nisi triginta porcos et illos ipsos non bonos, sed mediocres"), in Einhard, *Epistolae*.

95. For example, *Urkunden der Merowinger*, vol. 1, no. 168 (716 CE).

96. For herding difficulties, see *Lex Baiwariorum* 4.26; Redding, "The Pig and the Chicken," 342–43 (with further literature); Pliny, *Historia naturalis* 30.53.147. For Roman losses, see Barnish, "Pigs, Plebeians and *Potentes*," 162–63; A. H. M. Jones, *Later Roman Empire*, 703. The miracle: Walahfrid Strabo, *Vita sancti Galli* 2.18 (*mirabili ordine*). Taxes in kind to cash: Kreiner, "Pigs in the Flesh and Fisc," 37–39.

97. Barnish, "Pigs, Plebeians and *Potentes*," esp. 165–68, 173–75; Banaji, *Agrarian Change in Late Antiquity*, 53–60.

98. Wickham, *Framing the Early Middle Ages*, 102–15; Esders, "Nordwestgallien um 500."

99. Santos Salazar, "Las transformaciones de la fiscalidad," 132–35, 138–40. On the variable reconfigurations of the imperial tax system in the early medieval West, see

more generally Díaz and Martín Viso, *Between Taxation and Rent;* Martín Viso, "Circuits of Power"; Fernández, "Statehood, Taxation, and State Infrastructural Power"; Costambeys, "Settlement, Taxation, and the Condition of the Peasantry," 108–14; Wickham, *Framing the Early Middle Ages,* 56–150; Bjornlie, "Law, Ethnicity and Taxes."

100. Cronon, *Nature's Metropolis,* 207–59.

101. For some useful reference points, see Keßler and Ott, "*Nec provident futuro tempori*"; Warde, *The Invention of Sustainability.*

102. See, for example, Peter Brown, *Ransom of the Soul;* Freu, *Les figures du pauvre;* Devroey, *Puissants et misérables,* esp. 317–50; Kreiner, *Social Life of Hagiography.*

4. Partnerships

1. Crane, *Animal Encounters,* esp. 137–68; Crane, "Medieval Animal Studies"; Haraway, *When Species Meet,* 3–4; Buell, "The Microbes and Pneuma," e.g., p. 79 ("Some early Christian texts also exhort the ingestion of 'probiotic' agents, especially figured as the body and blood of Christ").

2. Among recent syntheses: James C. Scott, *Against the Grain,* 68–92; Trautmann, Feeley-Harnik, and Mitani, "Deep Kinship."

3. Severus, *Dialogi* 2.10.3–4, p. 192. My thanks to Peter Brown for sneaking away on a coffee break to hunt for this reference in the library. The New Testament figures of the Prodigal Son and the Gadarene swineherds contributed to the negative portraiture of swineherds in Christian exegesis: e.g., Chromatius, *Tractatus in Matthaeum* 43.6; Augustine, *Quaestiones evangeliorum* 2.13; Bede, *In Lucae evangelium* 3, lines 793–97.

4. *Tombo de Celanova,* vol. 1, no. 158 (Aulfus and Petro Aquilion: 942–977 CE); ChLA 33.965 (Barulo and Aurulus: Lucca, 761 CE); Gregory of Catino, *Registrum Farfense* 2:35 (Adoald and Maurulo: 747 CE), 2:158 (Gratiolus: 786 CE); *Cartulario della Berardenga,* no. 53 (Amulo: 867 CE); Remigius of Reims, *Testamentum* (ca. 533), p. 337 (Melloricus and Pascasiola); ChLA 14.592 (Agnechild and Baccio, Gundilanis: will of Ermintrude, Gaul, late seventh century); Heidrich, "Das Breve der Bischofskirche von Mâcon," 22 (Idoldo); *Polyptychon von Saint-Germain-des-Prés,* 9.285 (Eusebius, Beroild, Bernard), 11.9 (Bertlinus, Lantsida), 13.90 (Frotgius, Ragambolda, Ontbold), 24.39 (Gisleuold, Adalind, Gisloin, Dominica); *Will of Æthelgifu,* lines 25 (Eadstan/Eatstan), 26 (Byrnstan), and 31 (Brihtelm); Fergus Kelly, *Early Irish Farming,* 443 (Dub, Dorm, Dorchae). Sometimes charters mention the transfer of swineherds without naming them, e.g., *Traditiones Wizenburgenses,* no. 54 (774 CE).

5. ChLA 33.965 (Lucca, 761 CE): their brother is Prandulo, and their father is Roppulo.

6. *Bethu Brigte* 9. The episode doesn't appear in the two earliest hagiographies about Brigit, Cogitosus's *Vita sanctae Brigidae* and the anonymous *Vita prima sanctae Brigidae.*

7. See now Rio, *Slavery After Rome.*

8. *Will of Æthelgifu,* lines 10, 25–26.

9. "Porcarius quidam vir nobilissimus, eiusdem agri dominus": *Martyrium Prisci et sociorum* 2, col. 366F. The name may have been the hagiographer's idea of a joke, since this Porcarius does not comport himself as would befit an aristocrat living in Gaul (according to this author, anyway): see Kreiner, *Social Life of Hagiography,* 193–94. But whether fictional or not, he was not the only high-ranking person to have the name: e.g., introduction to *Martyrium Porcarii,* 734–35 (two abbots of the prestigious monastery of Lérins). Christian Iberian elites sometimes named their children Suarius, which (perhaps only coincidentally) had been the late Roman term for state officials who procured and herded pigs for the annona of the city of Rome: e.g., *Documentación del Tumbo A de la Catedral de Santiago de Compostela,* nos. 23 (912 CE, witness to a charter of Ordoño II of Galicia), 33 (927 CE, same king and probably same witness), 59 (1002 CE, witness to a judgement of Alfonso V), 62 (1020 CE, a bishop witnessing a charter of Alfonso V), 63 (1022 CE, same as 62).

10. Gregory of Tours, *Libri de virtutibus sancti Martini* 4.5.

11. Rio, *Slavery After Rome,* 19–174; Rio, "Freedom and Unfreedom." Enslavement as punishment: *Liber iudiciorum* 3.3.1, 6.2.1, 6.3.1; *Lex Baiwariorum* 1.10, 2.1. Different swineherd arrangements: *Polyptychon von Saint-Germain-des-Prés,* nos. 9.285 (described as *lidus* and *lida*), 11.9 (*lidus, colona*), 13.90 (*ancilla* married to a man of unspecified status), 24.39 (two *servi* married to two *ancillae*)

12. Rio, *Slavery After Rome,* esp. 80–82, 175–211, 236–42.

13. Rio, *Legal Practice and the Written Word,* 198–237; Rio, "Freedom and Unfreedom." These two contractual arrangements that Rio discusses appear in *Marculfi formularum libri duo* 2.27 (loan repayment plan), 2.29 (*servus* and free woman).

14. *Liber iudiciorum* 8.5.1; *Edictus Rothari* 136, p. 31 ("De illos vero pastoris [sic] dicimus, qui ad liberos homines serviunt, et de sala propria exeunt"); *Rectitudines singularum personarum,* nos. 4.2, 6, 7. On this last source see Harvey, "Rectitudines Singularum Personarum." Part-time herders: *Prümer Urbar,* pp. 166 (Rommersheim), 175 (Ettelsdorf), 193 (Weinsheim), 218 (Iversheim), 255 (Alisheim); *Liber possessionum Wizenburgensis,* nos. 3, 5, 11, 15, 17–18, 20, 46, 65, 73–74, 229, 241; *Codex Laureshamensis,* no. 3672 (all tenants at Nierstein care for five pigs each in the winter, amounting to nearly seven hundred pigs).

15. *Rectitudines singularum personarum* 4.2; Polyptych of Saint-Victor (also known as the Polyptych of Wadaldus): *Descriptio mancipiorum ecclesie Massiliensis,* at p. 640 (= G.10, in Castellane, Alpes de Haute Provence). Deidona's son may have been working as a transhumant pastoralist on the slopes with the family's sheep and goats for the summer: see Devroey, *Puissants et misérables,* 291. This polyptych was concerned more with the unit of the "work group" than the household: see Faith, "Farms and Families in Ninth-Century Provence," 191. But in this case, the work group on the property *was* the nuclear family.

16. *Edictus Rothari* 352–53; *Liber legis Langobardorum concordia dictus* 10.4–5. On the date of the concordance see Pertz's introduction to this volume, p. xv.

17. *Lex Salica, A* version 35.9, *C* and *K* versions, 10.6 (cf. 10.1 for *servi/ancillae* of lower value); *Lex Salica [Karolina], D* and *E* versions, no. 11.2, cf. 11.1 (*A* represents the original version, the *C* version was issued by Chilperic I in the later sixth century, the *D* version by Pippin in the 760s, the *E* version was endorsed or possibly even commissioned by Charlemagne in the late 780s or early 790s, and the *K* version was coordinated by Charlemagne around 802: Ubl, *Sinnstiftungen eines Rechtsbuchs,* 120–27, 137–81); *Liber constitutionum* 10; *Edictus Rothari,* 133–36. For a hint of the difference between ancient and early medieval attitudes toward specialized workers, see Long, *Openness, Secrecy, Authorship,* 77–78.

18. Gregory of Catino, *Registrum Farfense* 2:35. Another swineherd in this case (Maurulo) is also documented as having owned and sold property.

19. Ascough et al., "Stable Isotopic (δ^{13}C and δ^{15}N) Characterization," 37–38; Lucas, *Hofstaðir,* 26–54 (environmental analysis by Ian T. Lawson), esp. 34–38 (woodland) and 38–50 (on soil improvement through manuring, attesting to the practice in this region), 169–252 (faunal analysis by Thomas H. McGovern), esp. 216–20 (pigs). On Hrísheimar see Evardsson and McGovern, "Hrísheimar 2006: Interim Report." For unpublished reports on Sveigakot, see FSÍ Archaeological Reports, NABO: North Atlantic Biocultural Organisation, at http://www.nabohome.org/cgi-bin/fsi_reports.pl— but the zooarchaeological data are discussed at greater length in the other publications cited here.

20. Discipuli: *Edictus Rothari* 135. Iunior: *Lex Alamannorum* 72 [79.1]. Varro calls them companions or helpers (*comites*): *Res rusticae* 2.4.22. Dogs specifically tasked with herding pigs: *Lex Alamannorum* 72 [79.1] (*canis doctus*), 78.4 [82.4] (*bonus canis porcaritius*); *Lex Salica, K* version, no. 6.2 (*veltris porcarius*).

21. *Rectitudines singularum personarum* 6.2, 7. Possibly the swineherds were in charge of slaughter and butchery, although these passages do not offer enough information to be sure. Basic veterinary care: MacKinnon, *The Excavations of San Giovanni di Ruoti 3,* 69; more generally Grau-Sologestoa, *Zooarchaeology of Medieval Álava,* 158. For an example of healed periostitis (an inflammation of the connective tissue around bone) in a pig's foot, which may or may not have involved a swineherd's caretaking: Hardy, Charles, and Williams, *Death and Taxes,* 148 (faunal analysis by Emma-Jayne Evans and Lena Strid).

22. Varro, *Res rusticae* 2.10.10; Charlemagne, Capitulary of Aachen 19 (= *Capitularia regum Francorum* 77.19); on the documentary explosion on English estates in the high Middle Ages see the overview in Mark Bailey, *The English Manor.*

23. Varro, *Res rusticae* 2.4.6–8, 2.4.15–16, 2.4.19–20; Columella, *De re rustica* 7.6.9–13, 7.10.6–7; Palladius, *Opus agriculturae* 3.26. Some farms had separate terminology for castrated pigs, as at the monastery of Saint-Remi in the later ninth or early tenth

century, which counted its boars (*verres*), female pigs (*scrofae*), castrated males (here *maiales*, though this is not always what the term meant), and younger pigs or piglets (*genales*): *Polyptyque de Saint-Remi de Reims*, 76. Horns in the early medieval codes (*bucina, cornus*): *Lex Baiwariorum* 4.26; *Lex Alamannorum* 72 [79.1]. Bell (*tintinnum de porcina*): *Lex Salica* 27.1.

24. "Nam quamvis praedictum animal in pabulatione spurce versetur, mundissimum tamen cubile desiderat": Columella, *De re rustica* 7.9.14. Compare free- and semi-free-range pigs in western Iberia today: "The local veterinarian and the breeders stressed that Iberian pigs are clever animals that know how to find suitable spots to feed and rest. At nights they usually sleep outdoors in groups and tend to use the same spot as a *cama* (bed), which over time ends up devoid of stones and vegetation and develops into a comfortable layer of softened fine soil": Hadjikoumis, "Traditional Pig Herding Practices," 358.

25. Horowitz, *Being a Dog*, esp. 220–31. Pigs require less motivation from their trainers for truffle hunting because the fungus releases the same pheromone (androstenone) that male boars do in mating season: Lavelle et al., "Attractants for Wild Pigs." On wild pigs' navigation with reference to the geomagnetic field: Čverný et al., "Magnetic Alignment."

26. *Lex Salica* 122 (= *Capitulare V*); *Lex Baiwariorum* 4.26; *Pactus legis Alamannorum* 22.2 (= *Lex Alamannorum* 94.5 [98.2]).

27. The *Liber iudiciorum* assumed that swineherds would leave the woods only after pannage was paid (or slightly earlier than the seasonal deadline, if they were trying to evade the payment): *Liber iudiciorum* 8.5.3. The laws of the Alamans (drawn up in a duchy of the Merovingian kingdom) mention pigsties located in woodland (*burica in silva*): *Pactus legis Alamannorum* 21; *Lex Alamannorum* 94.1 [97.1]. For place-name evidence of woodland shelters in Kent: Witney, *The Jutish Forest*, 69–77.

28. Witney, *The Jutish Forest*, 60–66, quotation 73.

29. Witney, *The Jutish Forest*, 29–30, 129–30.

30. Arge, Church, and Brewington, "Pigs in the Faroe Islands," 24–28.

31. Witney, *The Jutish Forest*, 31–55, 60–66, 85–90. For one of many examples of a jaggedly plotted den, shaped sort of like a squashed can, see *Charters of Christ Church Canterbury*, vol. 1, no. 118 (948 CE = Sawyer 535). With the help of the editors' identifications this can be mapped using the route-mapping tool on the online Ordnance Survey: https://osmaps.ordnancesurvey.co.uk/.

32. City predation: Gregory of Tours, *Libri de virtutibus sancti Martini* 4.5. Tree felling: *Edictus Rothari* 138; *Liber iudiciorum* 8.3.3. Hunting traps: *Liber constitutionum* 46 (traps on farms), 72 (traps *in desertis*); *Liber iudiciorum* 8.4.22 (quotation—"quadrupedis sibi ea cauere non potuit"—and types of traps); *Edictus Rothari* 309 (hunter, dogs, and prey), 310 (trapped animal causing harm); *Lex Saxonum* 58; *Lex Thuringorum* 61 (traps in the woods).

33. Augustine, *De Genesi ad litteram* 4.10–19; *Intexuimus*, lines 352–69; Bede, *Libri quatuor in principium Genesis* 2.2; Alcuin, *Quaestiones in Genesim* 1; Wigbod, verses on the seven days of creation, preface to *Quaestiones in Octateuchum*, PL 96: 1105A; Remigius of Auxerre, *Expositio super Genesim* 2.2. For the exegesis of the unit of a "day" as a dialectical process between Creator and creation (or between God and the angels), see Chapter 2.

34. Lisa Kaaren Bailey, *Religious Worlds of the Laity*, 131.

35. Bishops' admonitions: *Episcoporum ad Hludovicum relatio* 45 (= *Capitularia regum Francorum* 196.45); *Concilium Meldense-Parisiense* 80 (= *Capitularia regum Francorum* 293.80). Charlemagne: *Admonitio generalis* 81 (= *Capitularia regum Francorum* 22.81). Other royal endorsements: Laws of Wihtred 9 and Laws of Ine 3, both in *Gesetze der Angelsachsen*; *Grágás*, vol. 1, K8, Add. 14, and vol. 2, K204. See further Jong, *In Samuel's Image*, 11–12.

36. Distinctions between slave's and owner's guilt: *Edictus Rothari* 238–39 and 241 (altering boundary markers); see also *Edictus Rothari* 249 (seizing a herd of animals as surety), 259 (theft); *Lex Alamannorum, B* version, 5.3 (theft of church property); *Lex Saxonum* 18 (murder). Slave and owner share guilt: *Edictus Rothari* 142 (poisoning); *Liber iudiciorum* 6.1.3, 7.6.1 (both mentioning counterfeiting); *Lex Baiwariorum* 1.6 (church arson), 2.5 (unauthorized despoliation). Unlawful grazing: *Leges Liutprandi* 151. Avoiding pannage collection: *Liber iudiciorum* 8.5.3.

37. Bringing a slave to court: *Lex Salica* 40; *Lex Salica* 82 (= *Pactus pro tenore pacis*, an agreement between Childebert I and Clothar I); *Liber iudiciorum* 6.1.1; similarly *Leges Ahistulfi* 9 (750 CE). Implicating an owner in the course of torture: *Liber iudiciorum* 2.4.4, 7.6.1, and 6.1.4 (the death or debilitation of a tortured slave). Owner's responsibility for slave's crimes: *Lex Ribuaria* 20–31. Lord or slave owner who will not take an oath: *Leges Liutprandi* 151; see also *Lex Ribuaria* 32.

38. Mikhail, *Nature and Empire in Ottoman Egypt*, 38–81, quotation 21.

39. Bede, *Historia ecclesiastica* 4.24; Wallis, "Cædmon's Created World." *Ruminare* had the same double meaning in Latin that it has in English: Carruthers, *The Book of Memory*, 206–10.

40. These differences broke down in the third and fourth centuries, when the emperors restructured the military's organization and recruitment strategies. For an overview see Mark Hassall, "The Army," in *Cambridge Ancient History*, 11:320–43; Brian Campbell, "The Army," ibid., 12:110–30; A. D. Lee, "The Army," ibid., 13:211–37.

41. *Genesis Rabbah* 65.1; Lange, "Jewish Attitudes to the Roman Empire," esp. 274–75 (my thanks to Brent Shaw for this reference). On the Gadarene swine episode in Mark and Luke as a subversion of Roman imperial authority, see Burdon, "To the Other Side"; Garroway, "The Invasion of a Mustard Seed"; Carter, "Cross-Gendered Romans"; Elizabeth Arnold and McConnell, "Hijacked Humanity." See Chapter 5 for further discussion of the rabbinic texts that linked Rome and pigs.

42. Legio X Fretensis: Deines, "How Long?," 207–12; Har-Peled, "The Dialogical Beast," 117–31. Coins: Carradice and Buttrey, *The Roman Imperial Coinage*, 129–30, nos. 982–84, 986; cf. Virgil, *Aeneid* 8.42–48, 81–85. Vespasian and Titus were not the only politicians to use this iconography. See also a silver denarius struck by C. Sulpicius C. F. Galba in 106 BCE, and a medallion issued in 140–43 CE by Antoninus Pius, leading up to the nine hundredth anniversary of Rome in 148: Crawford, *Roman Republican Coinage*, 1:315 (no. 312/1); Hill, *The Dating and Arrangement of the Undated Coins of Rome*, 89–101.

43. Pliny, *Historia naturalis* 8.77.209 (Anthony Bourdain, whose interests ranged as much as Pliny's did, would say in 1999, "Pork tastes different depending on what you do with it, but chicken always tastes like chicken": Bourdain, "Don't Eat Before Reading This," 60); Apicius, *De re coquinaria*, esp. books 7 and 8; Petronius, *Satyricon* 45.4.1, Ruden's translation, italics mine.

44. Ikeguchi, "Beef in Roman Italy"; MacKinnon, *Production and Consumption of Animals in Roman Italy*, 77–100, 139–69.

45. See the contributions in Valenzuela-Lamas and Albarella, eds., "Animal Husbandry in the Western Roman Empire"; King, "Diet in the Roman World"; MacKinnon, "'Romanizing' Ancient Carthage"; Kallala and Sanmartí, *Althiburos II*, 421–48 (faunal analysis by Silvia Valenzuela-Lamas); Benseddik and Potter, *Fouilles du Forum de Cherchel*, 1:159–95 (faunal analysis by Gill Clark), esp. table 3 on p. 187 (where estimated beef weight also outranks pork consistently); Kroll, "Animals in the Byzantine Empire."

46. Pronounced pork consumption at military sites: Stallibrass and Thomas, *Feeding the Roman Army*, esp. 4–5, 69–98; Deschler-Erb, "Animal Husbandry in Roman Switzerland," 419; Groot, "Developments in Animal Husbandry," 454–57, 462–63. An early exploration is King, "Animals and the Roman Army." Will of a Piglet: *Testamentum porcelli*; Champlin, "The Testament of the Piglet"; Graham Anderson, "The Cognomen of M. Grunnius Corocotta." Shinomori, "*Testamentum porcelli*," persuasively suggests the testator here is represented as a fugitive slave. But this text is so densely layered that the pig is never a single figure: he is speaking like a soldier, a slave, and an animal all at once.

47. Thomas, "Supply-Chain Networks," 36–37; Cavallo, Koosistra, and Dütting, "Food Supply to the Roman Army," 72–74; Groot, "Developments in Animal Husbandry," 459 and fig. 7. The same point for the early post-imperial period: Crabtree, *West Stow*, 11–13, 16, 18–19, 106; Benecke, *Archäozoologische Studien*, 201–2.

48. Sirks, *Food for Rome*, esp. 368–74.

49. Parker, *Ancient Shipwrecks*, no. 282, pp. 133–34; Bagnall, *Egypt in Late Antiquity*, 29 (papyri attesting to the collection of cured pork for the annona, including sausage and pork pickled in wine); Kolias, "Essgewohnheiten und Verpflegung im byzantinischen Heer," 199–200 (a discussion of Procopius, *Persian War* 1.8.14–17, in which soldiers rinse the salt off their pork rations in a stream); Columella, *De re rustica* 12.55

(on the methods of smoking and packing in salt); Apicius, *De re coquinaria* 1.7.1 (preserving pork in honey).

50. Local livestock suppliers: Thomas, "Supply-Chain Networks"; Groot, "Developments in Animal Husbandry"; Pigière, "The Evolution of Cattle Husbandry Practices"; Rizzetto, Crabtree, and Albarella, "Livestock Changes"; Toplyn, "Livestock and *Limitanei*," 475–82, 502–6. Imported garum and plants: Thomas and Stallibrass, "For Starters," 5–8. Ceramics: Wickham, *Framing the Early Middle Ages*, 77–78, and Map 2 (p. xvii); Reynolds, "From Vandal *Africa* to Arab *Ifrīqiya*," 133; Vokaer, "Pottery Production and Exchange," 590–98; Jeremy Evans, "Balancing the Scales." Wine could also be shipped in skins and barrels; because leather and wood are much less likely to survive than pottery, it is harder to be certain when wine imports end. Garum production: Zerbini, "The Late Antique Economy," 66–67.

51. Bökönyi, "Animal Breeding on the Danube," quotation at 175; Deschler-Erb, "Animal Husbandry in Roman Switzerland," 424–25 (speaking of Raetia and Belgica/Germania Superior/Maxima Sequanorum).

52. Fernández, "Statehood, Taxation, and State Infrastructural Power"; Díaz and Martín Viso, "Una contabilidad esquiva"; Vera, "Dalla liturgia al contratto." On reduced rates in Rome's pork annona: Cracco Ruggini, *Economia e società nell' "Italia Annonaria,"* 312–21.

53. Lucania and the imperial pork annona: Sirks, *Food for Rome*, 380–81, referring in particular to edicts of Valentinian (Nov. Val. 36, 452 CE) and Majorian (Nov. Mai. 2.1, 458 CE); *Expositio totius mundi et gentium* 53. On lucanicae sausages see *Edictum Diocletiani* 4.15; Apicius, *De re coquinaria* 2.4, 4.2.13, 5.3.2, 5.3.8, 5.4.2, 5.4.6; Isidore, *Etymologiae* 20.2.28. One "Lucanicus" is also a testamentary witness to the satirical *Will of a Piglet* (*Testamentum porcelli* 4).

54. Small and Buck, *The Excavations of San Giovanni di Ruoti 1*; MacKinnon, *The Excavations of San Giovanni di Ruoti 3*, esp. 50–69, 111–23. Pigs are 73 percent NISP and 70 percent MNI in the villa's last major phase.

55. Small and Buck, *The Excavations of San Giovanni di Ruoti 1*, esp. pp. 92–97, 117 (on room 61, the dining room); Simpson, *The Excavations of San Giovanni di Ruoti 2*, nos. 59–60 (bird brooches), 70 (ring), 109 (buckle tongue), and cf. 375 (arrowhead). On the unfixed nature of personal adornment: Rummel, *Habitus barbarus*; Rummel, "L'aquila gotica"; Halsall, *Barbarian Migrations*, 332–38.

56. The archaeologists who excavated the site were the first to raise the possibility that it was an annona supplier (MacKinnon, *The Excavations of San Giovanni di Ruoti 3*); and Barnish, "Pigs, Plebeians and *Potentes*," who consulted the excavation reports before their publication. For an unconvincing rejection of this hypothesis, based on the supposition that annona pigs were always herded on foot, see Francovich and Hodges, *Villa to Village*, 48–49. On the collecting of Lucania's annona payments in cash: Cassiodorus, *Variae* 11.39. On the granting of estates to veterans: Halsall, "The

Ostrogothic Military," 176–83. On the decline of tax obligations in the Ostrogothic countryside: Bjornlie, "Law, Ethnicity and Taxes," esp. 153–58.

57. Ubl, *Sinnstiftungen eines Rechtsbuchs*, esp. 67–98 (on the code's creation). The essential resource for the manuscript traditions is Karl Ubl with Dominik Trump and Daniela Schulz, eds., *Bibliotheca legum: Eine Handschriftendatenbank zum weltlichen Recht im Frankenreich*, at http://www.leges.uni-koeln.de/.

58. Childeric and Clovis: Becher, "Chlodwig"; Jussen, "Chlodwig der Gallier," esp. 35–38; Halsall, *Barbarian Migrations*, 269–70, 303–8; Wood, *The Merovingian Kingdoms*, 32–54; Rummel, *Habitus barbarus*, 368–75. Rex: Hoffmann-Salz, "Roms 'arabische' Grenze"; Dick, "Childerich und Chlodwig"; Wiemer, "Odovakar und Theoderich." On Clovis's tax and legal negotiations: Esders, "Nordwestgallien um 500." On the kingdom's connections to the Mediterranean: Esders et al., *East and West in the Early Middle Ages*.

59. Ubl, *Sinnstiftungen eines Rechtsbuchs*, 69–77.

60. *Lex Salica* 2.7–8, 14, 18–19. Strictly speaking, a title concerning miscellaneous thefts (*Lex Salica* 27) was slightly longer than the pig list, and one manuscript witness to the oldest version (A) had more variants for the murder of free persons (*Lex Salica* 41, manuscript A3/Munich, Clm 4115)—but overall it is the pig thefts that are most carefully differentiated in the original version of the code.

61. Varro, *Res rusticae* 2.4.10–12; Stern, "Les calendriers romains illustrés," esp. 445–53; Anthimus, *De obseruatione ciborum* 14.

62. On northern Gaul as a key supply source for the lower Rhine: Wickham, *Framing the Early Middle Ages*, 78. Iberia may have been an annona supplier to the same area, but historians are increasingly suggesting that its exports to the Rhine were less important than had previously been assumed. See Fernández-Ochoa and Morillo, "Walls in the Urban Landscape," 334–35; refuted by Bowes, "Villas, Taxes and Trade," 206–13; and qualified by Fernández, *Aristocrats and Statehood*, 90–119.

63. Ubl, "Im Bann der Traditionen," esp. 439–44; Ubl, *Sinnstiftungen eines Rechtsbuchs*, 79–81. See also Siems, "La vie économique des Francs," 613–16. For the bell see *Lex Salica* 27.1.

64. *Edictum Theoderici* 56–57, drawing on *Pauli Sententiae* 5.18.1; *Digesta* 47.14.3. On the *Edictum Theoderici* see Lafferty, *Law and Society in the Age of Theoderic the Great*. On rustling's close relationship to banditry as far as the Roman state was concerned: Shaw, "Bandits in the Roman Empire," esp. 20, 31–32. Thanks to Brent Shaw for asking why *Lex Salica* 2 is titled *De furtis porcorum*.

65. *Lex Salica* 2.9, 10, 18–20.

66. Ubl, *Sinnstiftungen eines Rechtsbuchs*, esp. 133–92, "mystisches Fundament für neue Gesetzgebung" at p. 254.

67. Ubl, *Sinnstiftungen eines Rechtsbuchs*, 101–7, 120–27, 133–35.

68. *Lex Salica* 2.1–3, 6, 10–11 (the italicized text, and the bracketed text in no. 10, represent the C version).

69. *Lex Salica [Karolina]*, *D* version, 2.8; on Pippin and this version see Ubl, *Sinnstiftungen eines Rechtsbuchs*, 137–64.

70. *Lex Salica*, *K* version, 2.4. On this version of the code, see Ubl, *Sinnstiftungen eines Rechtsbuchs*, 174–81.

71. Ubl, *Sinnstiftungen eines Rechtsbuchs*, 78–79, 171–72, 180; Fruscione, "Malbergische Glossen." By the Carolingian period some copyists could not even recognize the language: one scribe writing around 800 guessed that it was Greek! See the manuscript of *Lex Salica* known as A3, Munich, Bayerische Staatsbibliothek, Clm 4115, fol. 44r: "abstulimus hinc verba grecorum (we've taken the Greek words out of here)."

72. Höfinghoff, "Haustier und Herde," 63–108, at 63–66, 81–83, 87–92, 101–2. *Narechalti/focichalti*: *Lex Salica* 2.5. *Sundeba/leodeba*: *Lex Salica* 16.4. *Maialis sacrivus* and its variants: *Lex Salica* 2.17. Charlemagne's *K* version went for the middle ground and spoke of "a *sacrivus* a.k.a. *votivus* pig (maialem sacrivum qui dicitur votivus)"!

73. Ubl, *Sinnstiftungen eines Rechtsbuchs*, esp. 188–91, 195–205.

74. Fulton, "Taste and see that the Lord is sweet"; Harvey, *Scenting Salvation*, 99–155; Buell, "The Microbes and Pneuma," 78–80. Late antique preachers still expected that the physical senses would be guided and corrected by "interior senses" (their informed judgment): Frank, "'Taste and See,'" esp. 627–30.

75. Carrion: *Canones Adomnani* 6–7; *Paenitentiale Oxoniense II* 55, in *Paenitentialia minora*; *Paenitentiale Halitgarii*, col. 704B; cf. *Paenitentiale Merseburgense A*, appendix 150, in *Paenitentialia minora*; *Paenitentiale Pseudo-Theodori* 25.19, 25.20; Meens, "Pollution," 9–10; and for the context to these sources more generally see Meens, *Penance in Medieval Europe*. Figs and "figged" liver (called *skyôtos* or *ficatum*): Galen, *De alimentorum facultatibus* 3.11; Pliny, *Historia naturalis* 8.77.209; Apicius, *De re coquinaria* 7.3.1–2; Anthimus, *De obseruatione ciborum* 21. Roots: Pliny, *Historia naturalis* 28.37.136.

76. Michelle Alexander et al., "Diet, Society, and Economy in Late Medieval Spain."

77. Piglets: Apicius, *De re coquinaria* 5.4.6, 8.7 (seventeen recipes); Vindarius, *Excerpta* 20–26; Anthimus, *De obseruatione ciborum* 10. Lips: Apicius, *De re coquinaria* 7.1.4. Shoulder: ibid., 4.3.4, 4.3.6–7, 5.4.2, 7.10. Belly: ibid., 5.3.2. Udders: ibid., 4.2.14–15; Anthimus, *De obseruatione ciborum* 19. Haunches: Apicius, *De re coquinaria* 7.9.1–2. Loins (*lumbus*): ibid., 7.8; Anthimus, *De obseruatione ciborum* 9. Feet: Apicius, *De re coquinaria* 7.1.4. Tail: ibid., 7.1.4. Entrails: ibid., 7.4, 7.7.1–2; Anthimus, *De obseruatione ciborum* 16, 21. Sweetbreads: Apicius, *De re coquinaria* 4.3.3. Skin: Ibid., 1.7.2; see also 7.1.4. Intestines: *Testamentum porcelli* 3; Apicius, *De re coquinaria* 2.4. Lard on bread: Fergus Kelly, *Early Irish Farming*, 86. Bacon fat on vegetables: Anthimus, *De obseruatione ciborum* 14. Brains: Apicius, *De re coquinaria* 4.2.13. Greasy bones: Chapman, *West Cotton*, 526 (faunal analysis by Umberto Albarella and Simon Davis). Uterus (most commonly *vulva*, but also *uterus, sterilis, eiecticia, porcaria*, and *abdomen*): Pliny, *Historia naturalis* 11.64.209–11; Ambrose, *De Tobia* 14.50; Apicius, *De re coquinaria* 2.3.1, 7.1.1–3, 7.1.5; Anthimus, *De obseruatione ciborum* 18.

78. Scarcity of pigskin in codices: Szirmai, *Archaeology of Medieval Bookbinding*, 112, 117, 127–29, 162, 225–27; Gameson, "The Material Fabric of Early British Books," 14–15; Reed, *Ancient Skins*, 37–38, 212–13. Shoemaking: *Testamentum porcelli* 3; Isidore, *Etymologiae* 19.34.1; Hrabanus Maurus, *De rerum naturis* 21.26. Lard as grease: Pliny, *Historia naturalis* 28.37.136 (*adeps suillus* = *axungia*); *Vita sancti Cuthberti* 3.5. Lard (*adeps porcorum*) as lighting: *Appendix ad Hrabanum* 2, MGH Epp. 5, p. 517 (my thanks to Paul Fouracre for this reference and for sharing from his current book project on lighting). Bladder as toy: *Testamentum porcelli* 3. "Buzz bones": Chapman, *West Cotton*, 352, 355 (analysis by Graeme Lawson). Brains and blood: Pliny, *Historia naturalis* 28.42.152, 28.60.213. Blood without brains: Marcellus, *De medicamentis* 34.59. Brains without blood: Serenus, *Liber medicinalis* 58 (the teething baby case, which is a variation of Pliny, *Historia naturalis* 28.78.258–59); *Medicina Plinii* 2.20.4, 3.8.4; *Physica Plinii* 61.2; Marcellus, *De medicamentis* 33.37. Bacon: *Medicina Plinii* 3.25.2; Anthimus, *De obseruatione ciborum* 14; other possibilities in *Medicina Plinii* 2.1.4, where in place of the expected pig fat or *adeps/axungia/pinguis/sevum* for a tuberculosis cure, the compiler has replaced it with bacon (*laridum*) from a female pig, which is repeated with some emendations in *Curationes* 2.60, in Stoll, *Lorscher Arzneibuch*; *Medicina Plinii* 2.10.7; Marcellus, *De medicamentis* 9.68, 27.76, 34.47. Spleen: *Physica Plinii* 83.15. Marrow: Pliny, *Historia naturalis* 28.47.172, 28.80.261. Lungs: ibid., 28.80.262. Liver: Marcellus, *De medicamentis* 26.128, 27.96. Feet: Pliny, *Historia naturalis*, 28.43.179, 28.60.215, 28.62.222; Serenus, *Liber medicinalis* 14; *Medicina Plinii* 2.19.2; Marcellus, *De medicamentis* 12.32, 13.10 ("dentes candidissimos praestant"), 20.9; *Curationes* 2.9, 2.106, in Stoll, *Lorscher Arzneibuch*. Testicles: Pliny, *Historia naturalis* 28.63.224; *Medicina Plinii* 3.21.1. Genitals: Marcellus, *De medicamentis* 36.102. Semen: Pliny, *Historia naturalis*, 28.48.175; Marcellus, *De medicamentis* 9.100; cf. 29.51. Milk: Pliny, *Historia naturalis*, 28.74.250. Feces: ibid., 28.56.198, 28.58.204, 28.62.222, 28.67.233, 28.70.234, 28.71.235, 28.74.241, 28.77.249; Serenus, *Liber medicinalis* 6, 42 (both including the advice *nec pudeat*); *Medicina Plinii* 2.22.3, 2.26.4, 3.30.7; Marcellus, *De medicamentis* 4.22, 16.11, 19.48, 24.9, 28.68, 32.23, 34.52; *Curationes* 2.6, in Stoll, *Lorscher Arzneibuch*. Urine: Marcellus, *De medicamentis* 9.9, 9.71, 9.101, 9.130. Gall: Pliny, *Historia naturalis* 28.48.173–74, 28.51.190, 28.57.200, 28.61.218, 28.62.221, 28.62.223, 28.74.241, 28.80.261; *Medicina Plinii* 2.13.7, 2.23.1; *Physica Plinii* 11.8; Marcellus, *De medicamentis*, 4.36, 9.5, 9.99, 36.69; *Curationes* 2.162, in Stoll, *Lorscher Arzneibuch*. Pig fat (*adeps, axungia*): see the lengthy discussion in Pliny, *Historia naturalis* 28.37; also Serenus, *Liber medicinalis* 18, 59 (describing it as an "amazing remedy" or *mira . . . forma medelae*); *Medicina Plinii* 3.6.9, 3.9.5, 3.13.2, 3.24.7; *Physica Plinii* 48.19, 57.25, 82.69–70; Marcellus, *De medicamentis* 4.32, 8.157, 16.71, 16.100, 19.40, 20.148, 21.14, 26.46, 31.1, 32.10, 35.9, 35.12; *Curationes* 1.8, 4.84, 5.20, in Stoll, *Lorscher Arzneibuch*. There are many other references to *axungia* in which the animal providing this product is not specified (e.g., *Alphabetum Galieni* 288), but I am certain that they all mean lard, not only because of

Pliny's comment in *Historia naturalis* 28.37.176, but also because *axungia* is never associated with any other animal besides the pig. I have omitted these examples—there are a *lot* of them—but they are easily found in the excellent indexes of any of the medical texts cited here. For the firmer kind of pig fat, *sevum*, that sits between the skin and the softer layer of fat: Serenus, *Liber medicinalis* 18; Marcellus, *De medicamentis* 36.69. And for the fat between the belly and skin, *pinguis:* Marcellus, *De medicamentis* 15.46.

79. On the uptick in medical writing and compilations in the Carolingian period, see Leja, "The Sacred Art."

80. Nasrallah, *Annals of the Caliphs' Kitchens,* esp. 15–22.

81. Fentress, Goodson, and Maiuro, *Villa Magna,* 229–64; Colonese et al., "The Identification of Poultry Processing," 187–89 (Flixborough); Hammon, "Understanding the Romano-British-Early Medieval Transition," 294, 297–98 (Wroxeter).

82. Montanari, *Cheese, Pears, and History,* 31–35.

83. MacKinnon, *The Excavations of San Giovanni di Ruoti 3,* 114; MacKinnon, *Production and Consumption of Animals in Roman Italy,* 225–26; Parker, *Ancient Shipwrecks,* no. 316, pp. 316–17 (sunk off the island of Panier in France, 60–40 BCE).

84. Elite Romanness: Hen, "Food and Drink in Merovingian Gaul." Liver patties: Apicius, *De re coquinaria* 2.1.4. Uterus dumplings: ibid., 2.3.1. Mushrooms: ibid., 7.15.6. Snails: ibid., 7.18.4. Chopped meat: Vindarius, *Excerpta* 5.

85. Guélat et al., *Develier-Courtételle,* 119–20 (botanical analysis by Christoph Brombacher with Marlies Klee). The mustard greens might have been wild plants, but their seeds were nevertheless found in the occupied areas of the village. Cf. Apicius, *De re coquinaria* 5.3.1, 5.6.1, 5.6.3.

86. Less meat: Quirós Castillo, "Los comportamientos alimentarios del campesinado medieval," 24–6. Preserved meat: Cirelli, "La dieta dei monaci," 231 (speaking of lay diets here). On pork preservation see also Putelat, "L'homme, l'animal et L'Ajoie," 103; Guélat et al., *Develier-Courtételle,* 174 (faunal analysis by Claude Olive).

87. Fresh meat: Clavel and Yvinec, "L'archéozoologie du Moyen Âge," 80–82. Elite consumers in the "ecclesiastical complex" zone of Carthage from the late fifth to seventh centuries were roasting some of their pork: Humphrey, *Excavations at Carthage,* 6:204–19 (faunal analysis of the cisterns by David S. Reese, George E. Watson, and Alwyne Wheeler). Barbecue in the United States: Cobb, "From 'Cracklins' to 'Gourmet Bacon Puffs,'" 168.

88. *Scéla Mucce Meic Dathó* 6. Roman villas: Valenzuela-Lamas and Albarella, "Animal Husbandry Across the Roman Empire," 404–5. Early medieval elites and pork: Grau-Sologestoa, "Faunal Remains and Social Inequality," 53–54; Loveluck, *Northwest Europe,* 124–50; Audoin-Rouzeau, "Compter et mesurer les os animaux," 292–94.

89. Hammon, "Understanding the Romano-British-Early Medieval Transition,"; Doll, "'Im Essen jedoch konnte er nicht so enthaltsam sein . . . ,'" 445–46; Ettel, *Karlburg—Rosstal—Oberammerthal,* 305–16 (faunal analysis by Katrin Vagedes);

François Gentili and Valais, "Composantes aristocratiques," 101–7; François Gentili, "L'organisation spatiale des habitats ruraux du haut Moyen Âge," 19 (fig. 8, chart by Jean-Hervé Yvinec).

90. Bougard, Goetz, and Le Jan, *Théorie et pratiques des élites au haut Moyen Âge;* Loveluck, *Northwest Europe,* laying out the argument on pp. 9–29; and see the first section of this chapter.

91. Saint Jores and Hincker, "Les habitats mérovingien et carolingien de la 'Delle sur le Marais,'" 10–11 (faunal analysis by Jean-Hervé Yvinec). For a similar proportion of suckling piglets at an Icelandic feasting hall see Lucas, *Hofstaðir,* 216–20, 252.

92. *Prümer Urbar,* no. 114 (Rhein-Gönheim), and piglets paid *in adventu regis* at nos. 7, 9, 15.

93. Dall'Olio and Putti, "Bioarcheologia in un sito di potere altomedievale."

94. Fernández, *Aristocrats and Statehood,* esp. 147, 196–224; Vigil-Escalera Guirado and Quirós Castillo, "Early Medieval Rural Societies in North-Western Spain"; Fenwick, "From Africa to Ifrīqiya," esp. 18–19, 20–30; Mattingly and Hitchner, "Roman Africa," 185; Francovich and Hodges, *Villa to Village;* Martín Viso, "Un mundo en transformación," 37–45; Catteddu, *Archéologie médiévale,* 136–57; Valenti, *L'insediamento altomedievale nelle campagne Toscane,* esp. 92–115; Hamerow, *Rural Settlements and Society in Anglo-Saxon England,* 67–119; Finbar McCormick and Murray, "The Zooarchaeology of Medieval Ireland," esp. 197–200; Pedersen and Widgren, "Agriculture in Sweden," 67–68; Loveluck, *Northwest Europe,* 77–79, 92–95, 105–13; Loveluck, "Problems of the Definition and Conceptualisation of Early Medieval Elites," 45–51; Buko, *Archaeology of Early Medieval Poland,* 223–349; Grau-Sologestoa, "Faunal Remains and Social Inequality," 53–54, with some qualifications. On elite expenses see also Wickham, *Framing the Early Middle Ages,* 153–257, 303–36; Wood, "Entrusting Western Europe to the Church"; Peter Brown, *Ransom of the Soul.*

95. Sykes, *The Norman Conquest,* 42; Janssen and Janssen, *Die frühmittelalterliche Niederungsburg bei Haus Meer,* 191–92 (cherries, analyzed by Karl-Heinz Knörzer), 225–49 (faunal analysis by Hans Reichstein); Sancho i Planas, *Mur,* esp. 147–69 (faunal analysis by Sílvia Valenzuela Lamas and Lídia Colominas Barberà); Colardelle and Verdel, *Les habitats du lac de Paladru,* esp. 98–115 (faunal analysis by Claude Olive); Grassi, *L'insediamento medievale,* esp. 141–60 (faunal analysis by Frank Salvadori).

96. Smiarowski et al., "Zooarchaeology of the Scandinavian Settlements," 152; Loveluck, *Northwest Europe,* 124–50, quotation at 107; MacKinnon, *The Excavations of San Giovanni di Ruoti 3,* xxiv n. 8, 189–93; Rossiter, Reynolds, and MacKinnon, "A Roman Bath-House." On the house in Tours see Galinié, *Tours antique et médiéval,* 73 (summary of pit deposits by Cécile Bébien et al.) and discussion in the previous chapter.

97. Kuchenbuch, "Porcus donativus," esp. 207, 215–17.

98. See also the general remarks of Grau-Sologestoa, "Faunal Remains and Social Inequality."

99. Loveluck, *Northwest Europe*, 178–212, 302–27; Loveluck, "Dynamics of Portable Wealth"; Loveluck and Tys, "Coastal Societies."

100. Putelat, "Des littoraux nordiques à la Bourgogne?" Cf. the six-horned sheep found at the town of Birka, in eastern Sweden: this town had trading connections with the Indian Ocean, Russia, Central Asia, the Middle East, and Europe. Wigh, *Animal Husbandry in the Viking Age Town of Birka*, 19, 92.

101. For the "uncanny" quality of exotics among late antique courts as a contrast to the everyday: Peter Brown, "'Charismatic' Goods," quotation 103.

102. *Liber iudiciorum* 12.2.17.

103. "De suillis vero carnibus id observare promittimus, ut si eas pro consuetudine minime percipere potuerimus, ea tamen, que cum ipsis decocta sunt, absque fastidio et orrore sumamus": *Liber iudiciorum* 12.2.17. On the tannaitic tradition of treating certain foods both as metonyms for identity ("sole" foods) and as identity-transforming substances ("soul" foods) see Rosenblum, *Food and Identity in Early Rabbinic Judaism*, 11, 49–53.

104. *Liber iudiciorum* 12.2.17.

5. The Christianization of the Pig

1. On the Christian significance of the cosmos, see Chapter 2. On the concept of commonplaces in medieval mnemonics, see Carruthers, *The Book of Memory*, 224–26.

2. Pastoureau, *Le roi tué par un cochon*, and further context in Jordan, "The Historical Afterlife," 114–25. Not everyone agreed with the "porcus diabolicus" assessment: to many of the Capetians' contemporaries, this "diabolical" pig seemed altogether typical, and many liturgies and histories simply noted this as the day when Philip was killed by a plain old pig—*Philippus rex a porco interfectus*.

3. Shachar, *The "Judensau"*; Fabre-Vassas, *The Singular Beast*, esp. 97–128.

4. Fabre-Vassas, *The Singular Beast*, esp. 233–57.

5. Kallala and Sanmartí, *Althiburos II*, 421–48 (faunal analysis by Silvia Valenzuela-Lamas); Kallala and Sanmartí, *Althiburos I*, 31–43; MacKinnon, "'Romanizing' Ancient Carthage."

6. Har-Peled, "The Dialogical Beast"; Rosenblum, "Why Do You Refuse to Eat Pork?"

7. Deines, "How Long?"; Har-Peled, "The Dialogical Beast," 95–115.

8. *Midrash Psalms* 80.6; *Sifre Deuteronomy* 317.

9. Esau/sow: *Genesis Rabbah* 63.8 (לְחֲזִירַתְכוֹן); less obviously *Leviticus Rabbah* 13.5 (חֲזִיר); Har-Peled, "The Dialogical Beast," 67–69, 100, 149–52. Interlingual punning: Har-Peled, "The Dialogical Beast," 153–54; Hasan-Roken, "An Almost Invisible Presence."

10. *Midrash Psalms* 80.6, also 120.6 ("Esau hates peace . . . and the boar is none other than the wicked Esau"); *Genesis Rabbah* 65.1.

11. *Genesis Rabbah* 65.1; similarly *Midrash Psalms* 80.6.

12. Har-Peled, "The Dialogical Beast," 40–54, 73, 161–65; discussing in particular Leviticus 18:1–5, 20:22–26, *Leviticus Rabbah* 13, and *Sifra, Qeodoshim* 9.13. Maimonides: Har-Peled, "The Dialogical Beast," 24, citing Maimonides, *The Guide for the Perplexed*, trans. M. Friedländer (London: Routledge, 1919), 370–71.

13. The splitting of Christian and Roman triumphalism: Meier, "Nachdenken über 'Herrschaft'"; Peter Brown, *Through the Eye of a Needle*, 430–32; Fowden, *Before and After Muḥammad*, 68–82. Post-imperial experiments: see, e.g., Pohl, Gantner, et al., *Transformations of Romanness*; Pohl and Heydemann, *Post-Roman Transitions*; Bolgia, McKitterick, and Osborne, *Rome Across Time and Space*.

14. Eucherius, *Formulae spiritalis intelligentiae*, line 480; Eucherius, *Instructionum libri duo* 1.791–95; Cassiodorus, *Expositio psalmorum* 79.14. Augustine had obliquely commented that the *aper* of the psalm stands for a king (*rex*) who overthrew Judea, but as noted in Chapter 4 the title *rex* was never applied to Roman emperors, only to non-Roman rulers. In any case, Augustine is not at all sympathetic to this figural boar, which he sees as an instance of ferocity and pride. See Augustine, *Enarrationes in Psalmos*, vol. 2, 79.11. For an analogous case of Christian identification with Jewish oppression—rather than with pigs—in the early Middle Ages see Blennemann, "Altestamentarische Modelle" (on Maccabees 1 and 2).

15. Jerome, *Commentariorum in Danielem* 2.7a. Thanks to Gerda Heydemann for discussing this passage of Cassiodorus with me. For the evidence Jewish communities in Constantinople and the post-imperial West: Toch, *The Economic History of European Jews*, 12–15, 38–46, 66–74, 104–19, 153–68.

16. *Pace* Har-Peled, who suggests that Cassiodorus and other Christians saw the boar/emperors as "executers of punishment of the Jews for their rejection of Christ": "The Dialogical Beast," 199–203, at 202. Eucherius and Cassiodorus on the *vinea* as *ecclesia*: Eucherius, *Formulae spiritalis intelligentiae*, lines 286–87; Cassiodorus, *Expositio psalmorum* 79.9. The verb *vastare* also echoes the language of the Old Latin version of the psalm, which describes the boar's action with *devastavit*, rather than *exterminavit*, as the Vulgate (Jerome's translation) had it. Eusebius and Cassiodorus were using the Vulgate, but they would have noticed that Augustine had used the Vetus Latina: see, e.g., Augustine, *Enarrationes in Psalmos*, vol. 2, 79.11.

17. Cook, *Studies in Muslim Apocalyptic*, 175–76, and 178 on the specificity of Jesus-as-Mahdī to the Umayyad apocalyptic traditions.

18. Bashear, "Apocalyptic and Other Materials" (thanks to Peter Brown for this reference); Cook, *Studies in Muslim Apocalyptic*, 49–80, and 143–44 on Muslim apocalyptic as frequently cyclical rather than terminating in the end of time.

19. Anthony, *Crucifixion and Death as Spectacle*, esp. 4, 42; *Theophilus of Edessa's Chronicle*, 189 (= Theophilus of Edessa, Agapius of Manbij, Michael the Syrian, and the *Chronicle of 1234*).

20. Anthony, *Crucifixion and Death as Spectacle*, esp. 1–39; Cook, *Studies in Muslim Apocalyptic*, 51.

21. On the endurance of the Roman Empire: Haldon, *The Empire That Would Not Die*. "Echo chamber": Peter Brown, *The Rise of Western Christendom*, xix, xx, 2, 286; for further discussion of this point of view see Fowden, *Before and After Muḥammad*; and Kreiner and Reimitz, introduction to *Motions of Late Antiquity*.

22. Toch, *Dunkle Jahrhunderte*; Michael Toch, "The Jews in Europe, 500–1000," in *New Cambridge Medieval History*, 1:545–70.

23. E.g., Redding, "The Pig and the Chicken," which is a more sophisticated version of the theory found in Harris, *Good to Eat*, 67–87. Cf. Jerome, who was talking about nomadic "barbarians" who lived in the desert: *Adversus Iovinianum* 2.7.

24. Faust, "Pigs in Space (and Time)"; Sapir-Hen, "Food, Pork Consumption, and Identity in Ancient Israel." (Thanks to Baruch Halpern for both references.) Faust and Sapir-Hen disagree on the reasons why pork consumption varied from site to site: Faust argues that Israelites reduced their pork intake as a gesture of ethnic self-definition against the Philistines, whereas Sapir-Hen argues that it had more to do with differences between rural and urban settlements and changing patterns of provisioning. For more extensive discussion about the interplay between ecology and religious culture, see Sapir-Hen et al., "Pig Husbandry in Iron Age Israel and Judah."

25. al-Jāḥiẓ, *Kitāb al-al-ḥayawān* 1.234, 4.51–52, trans. Souami, pp. 333–35; Brethren of Purity, *The Case of the Animals versus Man*, pp. 119–21 (pp. 59–60 for the Arabic). Christian legends about Muhammad in central and high Middle Ages: Rubenstein, *Armies of Heaven*, 124; Har-Peled, "Configurations porcines," 145–52. On the dissemination of the letters of the Brethren of Purity to Spain see Borst, *Das Buch der Naturgeschichte*, 203; and for further context see Foltz, *Animals in Islamic Tradition*, 49–53; Fowden, *Before and After Muḥammad*, 205–7. Ancient explanations were equally varied: Schäfer, *Judeophobia*, 72–77.

26. Iberia: García García, "Explotación y consumo de los animales," esp. 183–243 (Tolmo de Minateda, on the southeast edge of the meseta), 297–354 (Šaqunda), 355–454 (Cercadilla), 482–86, 632–44. See also Grau-Sologestoa, "Socio-Economic Status and Religious Identity," 196–97; Arturo Morales Muñiz et al., "711 ad.," 305–6, 308–9, 310–11; Moreno García, "Gestión y aprovechamiento de cabañas ganaderas," esp. 82; and Chapter 3 for more examples of Visigothic-era rates of pig husbandry. North Africa: Mattingly, *The Archaeology of Fazzān*, 4:495–501; Clark, "ULVS XIV"; Siracusano, "The Fauna of Leptis Magna." The changes in Africa Proconsularis, where pork had been eaten in greater proportion, were more pronounced between the Roman and Muslim periods: Rossiter, Reynolds, and MacKinnon, "A Roman Bath-House"; Vitelli, *Islamic Carthage*, 33–35; Humphrey, *Excavations at Carthage*, 3:131–64 (see phase IV, late seventh century, probably after the conquest); Benseddik and Potter, *Fouilles du Forum de Cherchel*; Mohamedi et al., *Fouilles de Sétif*, 247–59 (faunal analysis by Anthony King).

On conversion to Islam as a highly variable process in the early Middle Ages: Tannous, *The Making of the Medieval Middle East*, 353–99. On variable arrangements between Muslim officials and their non-Muslim subjects in the eastern Mediterranean: Levy-Rubin, *Non-Muslims in the Early Islamic Empire*, 58–87, esp. 83 (on pigs in public places).

27. García García, "Some Remarks on the Provision of Animal Products," esp. 91–93; García García, "Explotación y consumo de los animales," 355–454.

28. Lorrio, Almagro-Gorbea, and Sánchez de Prado, *El Molón*, 44–56. Hunting prohibitions and Jahangir: Foltz, *Animals in Islamic Tradition*, 20, 33, 37–39. Wild fauna in Muslim settlements: Arturo Morales Muñiz et al., "711 ad.," 310–11. Egypt: Alkhateeb Shehada, *Mamluks and Animals*, 38, 75–76, 305 (pork as dog food).

29. Safran, *Defining Boundaries in al-Andalus*, 27 (pig dowry), 73–77 (Abu al-Khayr), 139–40 (sex, kissing), 140–41 (wet nurses), 149 n. 60 (poll tax); Arcas Campoy, "El criterio de los juristas malikíes sobre los alimentos y las bebidas de los dimmíes," 89 (debtors, citing Ibn Abī Zamanīn, Ibn Ḥabīb, and Abū al-Muṭarrif).

30. *Colección canónica hispana*, 6:258 (Elvira, fourth century, no. 50); *Concilia Galliae*, 1:154 (Vannes 461–491 CE, no. 12), 210 (Agde 506, no. 210), 2:27–28 (Epaone, 517, no. 15), 102 (Orléans 533, no. 20), 191–92 (Tours 567, no. 23), 226 (Mâcon 581–83, no. 15).

31. Agobard of Lyon, *De iudaicis superstitionibus et erroribus* 3–5, and Michel Rubellin's discussion ibid., pp. 211–50; Rebillard, *Christians and Their Many Identities*; Lisa Kaaren Bailey, *The Religious Worlds of the Laity*. On interfaith commensality see Hosang, "Will You Join Us for a Meal?"; Halfond, "A Hermeneutical Feast."

32. Alcuin, *Quaestiones in Genesim* 132; Hrabanus Maurus, *Commentariorum in Genesim* 2.9, at 524B; Remigius of Auxerre, *Expositio super Genesim* 9.3. The aversion to meat that was imputed to so-called Priscillianists was probably a rhetorical fabrication: Ferreiro, "*De prohibitione carnis*."

33. Peter Brown, *The Body and Society*, 237; Grumett and Muers, *Theology on the Menu*, 1–16.

34. Lisa Kaaren Bailey, *The Religious Worlds of the Laity*, 21–52.

35. Constantius, *Vita Germani* 3; cf. Evagrius of Antioch's translation of Anthansius of Alexandria, *Vita Antonii* 6: "Sumebat vero panem et sal, potumque aquae perparvum. De carnibus vero et vino tacere melius puto quam quidquam dicere, quando nec apud plurimos quidem monachorum istiusmodi aliquid reperiatur"; Fortunatus, *Vita Radegundis* 4, 15, 17, 21–22, quotation chap. 6, p. 367. These extreme forms of self-denial would go out of fashion in the seventh and eighth centuries, even in hagiographical portraiture: Diefenbach, "'Bischofsherrschaft,'" esp. 114–23; Kreiner, *Social Life of Hagiography*, 176.

36. *Regula Magistri* 26.13; *Regula Benedicti* 39.10, 40.5; [Jonas of Bobbio], *Regula cuiusdam ad virgines* 10.11. Anthimus used some of the same terms to suggest eating sparingly (*parcius*) rather than to excess (*nimietas*), particularly when it came to raw

foods, "because as the ancients said, too much of anything causes harm" (*De obserua-tione ciborum*, pp. 2–3).

37. See in particular the work of Albrecht Diem, e.g., "Rewriting Benedict"; and for the many monastic rules composed in the early Middle Ages see Vogüé, *Les règles monastiques anciennes*. Examples of diversity in the monastic diets of a given zone: Murray, McCormick, and Plunkett, "The Food Economies of Atlantic Island Monasteries"; Andrade Cernadas, "En el refectório."

38. *Regula Benedicti* 40.1 (1 Cor. 7:7); Augustine of Hippo, *Praeceptum* 3.3–4; Cassian, *Institutiones* 5.23; *Regula magistri* 23.2 ("ut a caelo videatur operariis Dei annona descendere"). In addition to Vogüé's editions of the *Regula Benedicti* and the *Regula Magistri*, see Diem, *Das monastische Experiment*, 235–39, on the ways the *Regula Benedicti* draws on and departs from the *Regula Magistri*.

39. Galen, *De alimentorum facultatibus* 3.1; Anthimus, *De obseruatione ciborum* 9 (*levior* = *apta ad digestionem*); *Problemata Aristotilis philosophi* 35, in Stoll, *Lorscher Arzneibuch*, p. 72 ("Quare carnis porcina leviores sunt a pane? Quia mixturata sunt acriora sunt tenues autem evanat tota vana sunt"). The latter text is based on a Latin translation of a third-century Greek text, but this particular example is not attested in the Greek tradition and may well be the addition of an early medieval compiler. The *Alphabetum Galieni* was especially clear about its theories of astringency: see Everett's commentary, pp. 40–45. On Galen in early medieval traditions, see the remarks and bibliography in Leja, "Dissecting the Inner Life," 33–40.

40. *Regula Magistri* 26.11–12 (sweets), 53.26–33 ("ne abstinentium uideatur munditia inquinari, ut comedentes agnoscant quanta sit inter utrosque distantia, qui aut suis serviunt desideriis aut qui imperant ventri"). This arrangement was more about hierarchy than purity: the concern about *munditia* is that the fasters should not "seem" to be contaminated by the meat eaters.

41. *Regula Benedicti* 39.1; see further Vogüé's commentary in his edition, 6:1125–42; [Jonas of Bobbio], *Regula cuiusdam ad virgines* 10.4 ("duo fercula, exceptis pomorum donis, de leguminibus uel de holeribus conferta, seu farina qualibet consparsione"); Bazell, "Strife Among the Table-Fellows," 80–85. On Jonas's authorship of the *Regula cuiusdam ad virgines*: O'Hara and Wood, *Jonas of Bobbio*, 36–37, 287–97 (appendix by Albrecht Diem).

42. Variety of Benedictine diets: Cirelli, "La dieta dei monaci," 229–30. For a longer view of Christians' disagreements about meat eating, see Grumett and Muers, *Theology on the Menu*, esp. 94–100. Similarity between lay and ecclesiastical estates: see Christopher Loveluck's cautious remarks in *Flixborough 4*, 151–54. For animal consumption in this phase see *Flixborough 3*, 36–58.

43. Hunting prohibition: Kreiner, "About the Bishop," 348. Women as cooks: *Concilia Galliae*, 2:179 (Tours 567, no. 10). Saint-Julien: Loveluck, *Northwest Europe*, 166–67. San Pietro in Canosa: Volpe, "Città apule fra destrutturazione e trasformazione"; Buglione, "People and Animals in Northern Apulia," 198–206.

44. "Quia valde videtur equitati contrarium, ut quod manifesta operum Christi nobilitat fides, pro sola reiectione unius cibi teneantur notabiles": *Liber iudiciorum* 12.3.7 (King Erwig, 681 CE). Royal and ecclesiastical legislation against viewing some foods as unclean or unacceptable to eat: *Liber iudiciorum* 12.2.8; *Colección canónica hispana,* 4:344 (Toledo I, 400 CE, no. 17), 5:482–85 (Toledo VIII, 653, no. 17), 6:176 (Toledo XII, 681, no. 9).

45. Genesis 7:2; Alcuin, *Quaestiones in Genesim* 111–12, 129; Hrabanus Maurus, *Commentariorum in Genesim* 2.6; Angelomus of Luxeuil, *Commentarius in Genesin* 6.19, 8.11; Remigius of Auxerre, *Expositio super Genesim* 7.2.

46. Goldberg, "'The Hunt Belongs to Man.'"

47. For an introduction to Hrabanus and his massive output, see Depreux, "Raban, l'abbé, l'archevêque"; Padberg and Klein, "Hrabanus Maurus." For an introduction to early medieval monastic culture: Mayke De Jong, "Carolingian Monasticism: The Power of Prayer," in *New Cambridge Medieval History,* 2:622–53; Davies, "Monastic Landscapes and Society."

48. Hrabanus Maurus, *De rerum naturis,* introductory prologues, cols. 9–13.

49. "Tardiores pascantur per historiam, et velociores ingenio per allegoriam": Hrabanus Maurus, *De rerum naturis,* prologue to book 9, col. 257D, more generally cols. 257–61. On *scientia . . . sine moralis vitae fidelis institutio*: Hrabanus Maurus, *De rerum naturis* 15.1, col. 416B.

50. Hrabanus Maurus, *De rerum naturis,* introductory prologues, cols. 9–13.

51. Hrabanus Maurus, *De rerum naturis* 22.1, cols. 591–92; Heyse, *Hrabanus Maurus' Enzyklopädie,* 151; more generally Schipper, "Rabanus Maurus and His Sources."

52. Isidore, *Etymologiae* 8.6.15, trans. Barney et al. (with my slight modifications); Hrabanus Maurus, *De rerum naturis* 15.1, col. 415A.

53. Warren, *Epicurus and Democritean Ethics,* 129–42; Konstan, "Epicurean Happiness." Bronze pig in the free-ranging form: MacKinnon, "High on the Hog," 661.

54. Severus, *Dialogi* 2.10.4 ("fornicationis imaginem foedam"); *Concilia Galliae* 2: 247 ("in merda . . . ut sues teterrimi conuoluuntur," no. 18)—a more clinical word for animal dung would have been *ficus,* or even *stercus;* see further Ubl, *Inzestverbot und Gesetzgebung,* 166–67; Isidore, *Etymologiae* 12.1.25.

55. Drake, Fraser, and Weary, "Parent-Offspring Resource Allocation in Domestic Pigs," 310; Gamelon et al., "The Relationship Between Phenotypic Variation Among Offspring and Mother Body Mass in Wild Boar," 942–43.

56. *Propositiones ad acuendos iuvenes,* no. 41.

57. Apuleius, *Metamorphoses* 2.7; Camille, "At the Sign of the 'Spinning Sow'"; for the sign/sculpture (now at Wellesley's Jewett Art Center) see Gillerman, *Gothic Sculpture in America,* vol. 1, no. 195 (where the curled tail and razorback of the pig makes clear it is not a dog, contrary to the artifact's heading). Thanks to William Diebold for sharing Camille's article with me. For the legacy of women as pigs as women in more recent Mediterranean history, see Fabre-Vassas, *The Singular Beast,* e.g., 29–32. Not all

links between pigs, women, and sex were negative: in antiquity, "pig" (*porcus, choiros*) was the word that women taught girls to use for their vulvas *before* they were sexually active (Adams, *Latin Sexual Vocabulary*, 82).

58. Jonas, *Vita Columbani* 2.22.

59. Matthew 8:28–34, Mark 5:1–20, Luke 8:26–39.

60. Bede, *In Lucae evangelium* 3, lines 773–79; see also Bede, *In Marci evangelium* 2, lines 186–92, which was written about two decades later and is nearly identical in its treatment of the story, though with fewer accounts about exorcisms in Bede's own time, plus an interpretation of "legion" to mean many varieties of idolatry (lines 160–62).

61. "Homo ipse sibi est auctor aerumnae. Nam nisi quis porci more uixisset, numquam accepisset in eum diabolus potestatem": Ambrose, *Expositio evangelii secundum Lucam* 6.48. See also Hilary, *In Matthaeum*, vol. 1, 8.3–4; Chromatius, *Tractatus in Matthaeum* 43; Augustine, *Quaestiones evangeliorum* 2.13.

62. "Si de eadem substantia et ex eodem auctore hominum bestiarumque sunt animae, quomodo ob unius hominis salutem duo milia porcorum suffocantur?" Jerome, *Commentariorum in Matheum* 1, lines 1209–15; repeated by Bede, *In Lucae evangelium* 3, lines 766–73. Wigbod, *Quaestiunculae super evangelium* 73 [86 in Gorman's synopsis in "Wigbod, Charlemagne's Commentator"] also opts for the *occasio salutis* interpretation above all others. His text is not available in a printed edition, but see Karlsruhe, Badische Landesbibliothek, Aug. perg. 191, fol. 35r (ninth century, digitized); Munich, Bayerische Staatsbibliothek, Clm 14426, fols. 41v–42r (ninth century, also digitized); and Gorman, "Wigbod, Charlemagne's Commentator."

63. BeDuhn, *The Manichaean Body*, 163–87, esp. 171–72, with a discussion of the Elects' foods and ritual meals at 126–62, esp. 130–31, 149–50. For more on the profound porousness of life in Manichaean culture (which could be both positive and negative), see Townsend, "The Manichaean Body and Society," esp. 65–67.

64. On the emergence of this spiritual economy, see Magnani, "Almsgiving"; Kreiner, *Social Life of Hagiography*, 175–88, 201–29; Peter Brown, *Ransom of the Soul*; Peter Brown, *Treasure in Heaven*; Goodson, "Garden Cities in Early Medieval Italy," 350–54. On tithes see Eldevik, *Episcopal Power and Ecclesiastical Reform*. Miracle for the travelers: Patrick, *Confessio* 19.

65. ChLA 30.898 (Petruald, Lucca, 720 CE); *Traditiones Wizenburgenses*, no. 273 (Gebolt, 838 CE); ChLA2 81.50 (Rosselmus, Lucca, 865 CE); *Tombo de Celanova*, vol. 1, no. 247 (Adosinda, 927 CE); will of Æthelflæd, in Whitelock, *Anglo-Saxon Wills*, no. 14 (962–991 CE).

66. *Charters of St Augustine's Abbey Canterbury*, no. 24 (= Sawyer 1198, ca. 850 CE); "*for mine saule 7 minra frionda 7 mega ðe me to gode gefultumedan*": *Charters of Christ Church Canterbury*, vol. 2, no. 84 (= Sawyer 1197, 843 x 863). There are some examples of this sort of gift on the Continent: see, e.g., *Recueil des chartes de l'abbaye de Saint-Germain-des-Prés*, no. 29 (829): Louis the Pious and Lothar grant the monastery an annual food stipend, including twenty *modii* of lard (*pinguedine*) or fifty pigs.

67. ChLA 1.54 (mid-eighth century), 60 (763 CE), 71 (770), 72 (771), 73 (771), 83 (777), 85 (776), 86 (778), 89 (778), 90 (781), 95 (779), 96 (782), 97 (782), 100 (786?), 102 (791), 104 (783); ChLA 2.122 (789), 132 (793), 136 (796), 138 (797), 140 (797), 163 (754), 164 (762), 165 (761); ChLA2 100.1 (801), 7 (802), 35 (809), 46 (813/14); ChLA2 101.9 (812–816?), 34 (818); ChLA2 103.17 (829), 23 (830), 44 (833/34), 37 (845); ChLA2 105.23 (848/54); ChLA2 106.13 (838), 20 (839), 55 (865). See also *Traditionen des Hochstifts Regensburg*, no. 136 (889); *Codex Laureshamensis*, vol. 2, no. 252 (mid-tenth century).

68. Herefrid: *Recueil des chartes de l'abbaye de Stavelot-Malmedy*, no. 49 (905 CE). The Met: Keefe, "The Family That Built an Empire of Pain," 34. Liturgical economy: Diem, *Das monastische Experiment;* Diem, "Disimpassioned Monks and Flying Nuns"; Peter Brown, *Through the Eye of a Needle*, esp. 83–88. "Usque minima gallina": see, e.g., *Cartulario de San Millán de la Cogolla*, no. 12 (872 CE?); *Colección documental del archivo de la Catedral de León*, vol. 1, no. 121 (937); *Cartulario de Valpuesta*, no. 43 (973); *Colección documental del Monasterio de Santa María de Otero de las Dueñas*, no. 20 (976).

69. "Euangelicum, inquit, mandatum ista conpleuit: duas habuit tunicas, unam earum largita est non habenti: ita ergo et uos facere debetis." Severus, *Dialogi* 2.10.1–2; for the cutting of the wool *chlamys* see Sulpicius Severus's earlier composition, *Vita Martini* 3.

70. Kay, *Animal Skins and the Reading Self;* Kay, "Legible Skins"; Clanchy, *From Memory to Written Record*, 263–64; Holsinger, "Of Pigs and Parchment." On figures for early medieval book production, see, e.g., McKitterick, *Carolingians and the Written Word*, 138–41.

71. For the contexts of figs. 5.1–5.3: Deichmann, *Ravenna*, 1:181–82, 2.1:172–73; Deliyannis, *Ravenna in Late Antiquity*, 153–58; Gaborit-Chopin, "Les trois fragments d'ivoire"; Volbach, *Elfenbeinarbeiten der Spätantike und des frühen Mittelalters*, no. 221, pp. 95–96.

72. Irmscher, "Otto III. und Byzanz"; Effenberger, "Byzantinische Kunstwerke."

73. For the Gadarene swine examples discussed in this paragraph see *Bernward von Hildesheim*, vol. 2, no. II-14e (the Magdeburg ivories); Martin, *Die ottonischen Wandbilder der St. Georgskirche*, esp. 23–24, 102; Mütherich, "Der neutestamentliche Zyklus"; Deichmann, *Ravenna*, 2.1:172–73; Budny, "The *Biblia Gregoriana*," esp. 267–68. My thanks to Beatrice Kitzinger, William Diebold, Cecily Hillsdale, and Mildred Budny for their pointers here. Additional Latin manuscripts of the late tenth and eleventh centuries that included this scene but are not discussed here: Codex Egberti (Reichenau, 980–993), Trier Cod. 24, fol. 26v; Liuthar Gospels (another Gospel book of Otto III made at Reichenau, 990–1002), Aachen Domschatzkammer, fol. 88v; Hitda of Meschede's Gospel Book (Ottonian, 1000–1020), Darmstadt, Landesbibliothek 1640, fol. 76r; Codex Aureus of Echternach (1030–50), Nuremberg, Germanisches Nationalmuseum, Ms. 156142, fol. 35r. For a completely different iconography, cf. Greek Gospel books from the eleventh and twelfth centuries that take advantage of their margins to show demons plunging on pig-back, down the length of the page, into the water below:

e.g., Florence, Biblioteca Medicea Laurenziana Plut. 6.23 fol. 70v; London, British Library, Add.19352, fol. 85r; Biblioteca Apostolica Vaticana, Barb. gr. 372, fol. 112r; and Paris, Bibliothèque nationale de France, Ms. suppl. gr. 27, fol. 68r.

74. Hilary, *In Matthaeum*, vol. 1, 8.3–4; Chromatius, *Tractatus in Matthaeum* 43.4, 7; Ambrose, *Expositio evangelii secundum Lucam* 6.50–53; Augustine, *Quaestiones evangeliorum* 2.13; Bede, *In Lucae evangelium* 3, lines 788–817; Bede, *In Marci evangelium* 2, lines 206–37.

75. For this context see Fricke, "Jesus Wept!"

76. Mundó, *Les bíblies de Ripoll*, esp. 79–81, 139–42. Mundó identifies the three figures in the upper left part of the frame as additional demons (pp. 258–59, no. 12), but I would identify them as the inhabitants of Gerasa: they are clothed, unlike the demons; they are standing above the sea in a place that is normally occupied by Gerasa in the Ottonian examples; and the gestures they are making with their hands are also very similar to what the Gerasenes are doing in the Bernulfus Codex at the Museum Catherijneconvent, ABM Ms. 3, fol. 33v (Reichenau, 1027–1054 CE), and in Gospel book of Henry III, also known as the Codex Aureus of Speyer, El Escorial, Monasterio de San Lorenzo de El Escorial, Real Biblioteca, Vit. 17, fol. 31r (Echternach, 1045–46).

77. Bynum, *Christian Materiality*; Ritchey, *Holy Matter*.

78. Bolzoni, *Web of Images*, 177; the *lardarium* appears in the *Tabula exemplorum secundum ordinem alphabeti: Recueil d'exempla compilé en France à la fin du XIIIe siècle*, ed. J.-Th. Welter (Paris: Guitard, 1927), no. 219, p. 49, cited by Fabre-Vassas, *The Singular Beast*, 255.

79. Galen: Von Staden, "Anatomy as Rhetoric"; Mattern, *The Prince of Medicine*, 149–55; Kreiner, "A Generic Mediterranean," 213 (evidence for this anatomical legacy in the early Middle Ages); on the *Anatomia porci* see Vico, "Gli scritti anatomici."

80. *Anatomia porci*, p. 144. On terms for the pig uterus see the previous chapter, note 77.

81. Meditation as butchery: Carruthers, *The Experience of Beauty*, 3–5; for cognition as digestion see further Carruthers, *The Book of Memory*, 205–11. Amiens: Stephen Murray, *A Gothic Sermon*, 119.

82. Zchomelisdse, *Santa Maria Immacolata in Ceri*, esp. 35–68, 109–30, 161–74.

83. Zchomelidse, *Santa Maria Immacolata in Ceri*, 137–40, quotation at 167. My thanks to Nino Zchomelidse and Giovanni Freni for their assistance in locating digital images of this fresco.

84. Zchomelidse, *Santa Maria Immacolata in Ceri*, 141–47.

85. Zchomelidse, *Santa Maria Immacolata in Ceri*, 90–93, 137–40.

86. Kessler, *Seeing Medieval Art*, 126, 134; Carruthers, *The Experience of Beauty*, 5 n. 5. One medieval midrashic tradition associated Joseph's refusal to sleep with Potiphar's wife with a refusal to eat pork: Har-Peled, "The Dialogical Beast," 70–71, citing Midrash Tannaim, Vayshev 8.

87. Carruthers, *The Experience of Beauty*, 8.

88. Shachar, *The "Judensau"*; Duque, "Staging Martyrdom"; for the modern Mediterranean legacy see Fabre-Vassas, *The Singular Beast*, esp. 233–57.

Epilogue

1. Iceland: Arge, Church, and Brewington, "Pigs in the Faroe Islands," 23–24. Land clearance: Hoffmann, *Environmental History of Medieval Europe*, 113–54, 181–88. Venice and its increasingly careful management of woodland resources: Appuhn, *A Forest on the Sea*. Later pannage regulations: Regnath, *Schwein im Wald*; Clemente Ramos, "Ganadería porcina," 222–26; Vassberg, "Concerning Pigs," 52–54; Grant, *Royal Forests of England*, 35–36, 65, 125–26, 129 (on the agistment system in England).

2. Slavin, "Flogging a Dead Cow," 128–32.

3. Biddick, "Pig Husbandry"; Ervynck et al., "An Investigation"; Sykes, *The Norman Conquest*, 14–16, 34; Thomas, *Animals, Economy and Status*, 51; Sam White, "From Globalized Pig Breeds to Capitalist Pigs," 102–9. Efforts to preserve woodland resources in the West Midlands: Birrell, "Common Rights in the Medieval Forest," 31, 41; J. D. Hurst, "Fuel Supply," 113, 115–18, 122–24; Dyer, "Salt-Making at Droitwich"; Rackham, *Ancient Woodland*, 1, 5, 135–37; Hilton, *A Medieval Society*, 119–20. Iberia: Vassberg, "Concerning Pigs"; Parsons, "The Acorn-Hog Economy"; Hadjikoumis, "Traditional Pig Herding Practices."

4. Elite consumption: Quirós Castillo, "Los comportamientos alimentarios del campesinado medieval," 24–26, 28–30; Grau-Sologestoa, "Socio-Economic Status and Religious Identity," 194, 195–97; Grau-Sologestoa, *Zooarchaeology of Medieval Álava*, 125–26, and fig. 13.1; Sykes, *The Norman Conquest*, 28–34, 42; Clavel and Yvinec, "L'archéozoologie du Moyen Âge," 81–82; Clavel, "L'animal dans l'alimentation," 83–84, 98–99; García García, "Some Remarks on the Provision of Animal Products," especially on Madīnat Ilbīrah. A noticeable exception to this trend is Languedoc-Roussillon, in southwest France: Forest and Rodet-Belarbi, "Viandes animales dans le Languedoc-Roussillon," 93–100. Cash payments: Britnell, *The Commercialization of English Society*, 31–47, 70–71, 111–12, 191–94; Duby, *L'économie rurale*, 436–46, 462–500; Sée, *Les classes rurales*, 405–8; García de Cortázar, *La sociedad rural*, 95–121; and see pannage literature in note 1 to this chapter. Livestock markets and fairs: Stephan R. Epstein, "Regional Fairs," esp. 463–64. *Tak* (or *thac, tac, take, tack, takk*) sometimes resembled a pannage fee, but more often it was the fee owed for selling a pig: *Cartulary of Worcester Cathedral Priory*, 25a, 66a, 69a, 72a, 73a–b, 79a, 102a, 104a; *Red Book of Worcester*, 19, 20, 79; *Inquisitiones Post Mortem for the County of Worcester*, part 2, pp. 84, 102.

5. Burgundy: Santiard, "Un aspect du commerce des porcs." On large-scale sheep transhumance in Italy and Iberia in the later Middle Ages and early modern period, see Chapter 3. For comments about the decline of pig husbandry in favor of sheep

husbandry see Salvadori, "L'allevamento nell'Italia medievale," 137–42; Audoin-Rouzeau, "Compter et mesurer les os animaux," 288–91, 294; Pascua Echegaray, "From Forest to Farm and Town," 92–95.

6. Arthur, Imperiale, and Tinelli, *Apigliano*, 3–33 (faunal analysis by Jacopo De Grossi Mazzorin and Giovanni De Venuto, analysis of textile production by Marco Leo Imperiale and Domenico Sancio); Bianchi, *Campiglia*, esp. 485–92 (faunal analysis by Frank Salvadori), 512–17 (anthracological analysis by Gaetano Di Pasquale).

7. For an introduction to the new manorial accounting practices in England, see Mark Bailey, *The English Manor;* Slavin, "The Sources for Manorial and Rural History." A few of these manorial accounts have been published, e.g., *Medieval Oxfordshire Village: Cuxham,* which contains the account for that particular side of pork (210, 227).

8. Beullens, "Like a Book Written by God's Finger," esp. 127–30, 135–42; Leemans and Klemm, "Animals and Anthropology in Medieval Philosophy"; Crane, *Animal Encounters;* Crane, "Medieval Animal Studies"; Norton, "Going to the Birds," 54–58.

9. Beullens, "Like a Book Written by God's Finger," esp. 147–50.

10. On the connections between scholastics and their urban environments: Kaye, *Economy and Nature in the Fourteenth Century.* York: Hammond and O'Connor, "Pig Diet in Medieval York." Pigs fed within the confines of English towns: Sykes, *The Norman Conquest,* 38–42. There was a commercial pig operation in the thirteenth-century town of Podium Bonizi (Poggibonsi), but we know nothing about the logistical details beyond the fact that the residents were eating juvenile animals almost exclusively: Francovich and Valenti, *Poggio Imperiale,* 197 (faunal analysis by Frank Salvadori).

11. Antiquity: Plautus, *Captivi* 4.1.807–10; Bagnall, *Egypt in Late Antiquity,* 49–50; Bryen, "Law in Many Pieces," 355–56. High and late Middle Ages: Ruhland, "Schweinehaltung in und vor der Stadt"; Jørgensen, "Running Amuck?"; Geltner, "Finding Matter out of Place"; Jordan, "The Historical Afterlife," 123. Theories of sight pollution: Geltner, "Healthscaping a Medieval City," 404–5.

12. Camphuijsen and Coomans, "De middeleeuwse stad en zijn varkens"; Cantwell, "Anthropozoological Relationships in Late Medieval Dublin," 76–77; Ruhland, "Schweinehaltung in und vor der Stadt"; Geltner, *Roads to Health,* 44–46, 54, 89, 121–26; Maltby, "From Bovid to Beaver," 237.

13. I have found the most illuminating analysis of late medieval–early modern animal trials to be Pastoureau, "Une justice exemplaire"; see also Dinzelbacher, "Animal Trials." The painting of a sow's execution was done for the church of Sainte-Trinité in Falaise in the late fourteenth century; the original is lost but a nineteenth-century interpretive engraving survives: Pastoureau, "Une justice exemplaire," 180–81.

14. Pastoureau, "Une justice exemplaire," esp. 175–78, 194–98; Esther Cohen, "Law, Folklore and Animal Lore," with discussion of early criticisms on pp. 20–24 and putative Germanic origins on p. 27. As Cohen points out, a separate sort of animal trial started in the fifteenth century that involved ecclesiastical courts prosecuting whole

swarms of pests (usually insects or rodents) and pronouncing them anathema: these should be treated as a different juridical class.

15. See also the remarks about the trials' rough sense of human-animal equivalency in Holsinger, "Of Pigs and Parchment," 618–19; Enders, "Homicidal Pigs."

16. Crosby, *Ecological Imperialism*, 173–76, quotations at 173 and 175; Crosby, *The Columbian Exchange*, 75–76, 77–78; and for a similar description of pigs as "weed creatures" see Cronon, *Changes in the Land*, 135. The population of pigs on Hispaniola did not descend entirely from these eight pigs: settlers occasionally seeded the stock with imports from Europe: Río Moreno, "El cerdo," 15, 17.

17. Río Moreno, "El cerdo"; Clynes, "Twenty Americans Die Each Day Waiting for Organs."

18. Pigs and early colonizers: Río Moreno, "El cerdo," 15; Cronon, *Changes in the Land*, 129, with caveats about the problems pigs entailed, pp. 135–37. Pig husbandry in Extremadura: Clemente Ramos, "Ganadería porcina"; Vassberg, "Concerning Pigs."

19. The pioneering work here is Virginia DeJohn Anderson, *Creatures of Empire*, and for what follows in this paragraph, including the phrase "wild gangs of the Chesapeake," see esp. 107–40, 184–90. On the "ungulate irruption" in the Valle del Mezquital of central Mexico in the sixteenth century, see Melville, *A Plague of Sheep*—but this focuses on the effects of pastoralism rather than pigs. Alfred Crosby noted (*Ecological Imperialism*, 173–76) that pigs could greatly transform a landscape, but he left it to others to investigate the possibility.

20. Calls for more pig history: Mancall, "Pigs for Historians"; Derby, "Bringing the Animals Back In," esp. 605–7. Cities and public health: Río Moreno, "El cerdo," 27–29; McCrea, "Pest to Vector"; Hartog, "Pigs and Positivism," 904, 908–12, 923–24, quotation 924.

21. Virginia DeJohn Anderson, *Creatures of Empire*, 211–18. Difference in local environments: Alexander and Hernández Álvarez, "Agropastoralism and Household Ecology in Yucatán."

22. Norton, "The Chicken or the *Iegue*," esp. 28–29 and 53–54. For further context on the contrast between Amerindian and European concepts of animals see Norton, "Going to the Birds."

23. García Garagarza, "The Year the People Turned into Cattle."

BIBLIOGRAPHY

Ancient and Medieval Texts

Agobard of Lyon. *De iudaicis superstitionibus et erroribus.* Edited by L. Van Acker, in *Agobard de Lyon: Oeuvres,* vol. 1, under the direction of Michel Rubellin. SC 583. Paris: Cerf, 2016.

Alcuin. *Quaestiones in Genesim.* PL 100, cols. 515–70 [= *Interrogationes et responsiones in Genesin*]. Paris: Migne, 1851.

Alphabetum Galieni. Edited and translated by Nicholas Everett, *The Alphabet of Galen: Pharmacy from Antiquity to the Middle Ages.* Toronto: University of Toronto Press, 2012.

Ambrose of Milan. *Exameron.* Edited by Karl Schenkl. CSEL 32.1. Vienna: Tempsky, 1896.

———. *Expositio evangelii secundum Lucam.* Edited by M. Adriaen. CCSL 14. Turnhout: Brepols, 1956.

———. *De Tobia.* Edited by Karl Schenkl. CSEL 32.2. Vienna: Tempsky, 1897.

Anatomia porci. Edited by Karl Sudhoff, in "Die erste Tieranatomie von Salerno und ein neuer salernitanischer Anatomietext." *Archiv für Geschichte der Mathematik, der Naturwissenschaft und der Technik* 10 (1927): 136–54, at 141–45.

Ancient Laws of Ireland. Vol. 4: *Din Techtugad and Certain Other Selected Brehon Law Tracts.* Dublin: A. Thom; London: Longmans, 1879.

Angelomus of Luxeuil. *Commentarius in Genesin.* PL 115, cols. 107–244. Paris: Migne, 1852.

Anthansius of Alexandria. *Vita Antonii.* Translated by Evagrius of Antioch. PL 73, cols. 125–69. Paris: Migne, 1849.

Anthimus. *De obseruatione ciborum ad Theodoricum regem Francorum epistula.* Edited by Eduard Liechtenhan. Corpus Medicorum Latinorum 8.1. Berlin: Akademie, 1963.

Apicius. *De re coquinaria.* Edited by Jacques André, *L'art culinaire.* Paris: Belles Lettres, 1974.

Appendix ad Hrabanum: Epistolarum Fuldensium fragmenta ex octava, nona, et decima centuriis ecclesiasticae historiae. Edited by E. Dümmler. MGH Epp. 5. Berlin: Weidmann, 1899.

Apuleius. *Metamorphoses/Asinus aureus.*

   Edited by D. S. Robertson, *Les métamorphoses.* 3 vols. Paris: Belles Lettres, 1940–1946.

   Translated by Sarah Ruden, *The Golden Ass.* New Haven: Yale University Press, 2011.

Aregis principis capitula. Edited by Friedrich Bluhme, in *Leges Langobardorum.* MGH LL 4. Hannover: Hahn, 1868.

Augustine of Hippo. *De civitate Dei.* Edited by Bernard Dombart and Alfonse Kalb. CCSL 47–48. Turnhout: Brepols, 1955.

———. *Confessiones.* Edited by James O'Donnell. Oxford: Clarendon, 1992.

———. *Enarrationes in Psalmos.* Edited by D. Eligius Dekkers and Jean Fraipont. CCSL 38–40. Turnhout: Brepols, 1956.

———. *De Genesi ad litteram libri duodecim.*

   Edited by Joseph Zycha, CSEL 28A. Vienna: Tempsky, 1894.

   Edited and translated by P. Agaësse and A. Solignac, *La Genèse au sens littéral en douze livres.* Bibliothèque Augustinienne 48–49. Paris: Desclée de Brouwer, 1972.

———. *De Genesi contra Manichaeos.* Edited by Dorothea Weber. CSEL 91. Vienna: Österreichischen Akademie der Wissenschaften, 1998.

———. *Praeceptum.* Edited and translated by George Lawless, *Augustine of Hippo and His Monastic Rule.* Oxford: Oxford University Press, 1987.

———. *Quaestiones evangeliorum.* Edited by Almut Mutzenbecher. CCSL 44B. Turnhout: Brepols, 1980.

Augustinus Hibernicus. *De mirabilibus sacrae scripturae libri tres.* PL 35, cols. 2149–200. Paris: Migne, 1841.

Basil of Caesarea. *Hexaemeron.*

   Edited by Emmanuel Amand de Mendieta and Stig Y. Rudberg, *Homilien zum Hexaemeron.* Berlin: Akademie, 1997.

   Edited and translated by Stanislas Giet, *Homélies sur l'Hexaéméron.* SC 26. 2nd ed. Paris: Cerf, 1968.

   Translated into Latin by Eustatius, PL 53, cols. 867–966. Paris: Migne, 1847.

Bede. *Historia ecclesiastica gentis Anglorum.* Edited and translated by Bertram Colgrave and R. A. B. Mynors. Oxford: Clarendon, 1969.

———. *Libri quatuor in principium Genesis.*

   Edited by C. W. Jones. CCSL 118A. Turnhout: Brepols, 1967.

   Translated by Calvin B. Kendall, *Bede: On Genesis.* Liverpool: Liverpool University Press, 2008.

———. *In Lucae evangelium expositio.* Edited by D. Hurst. CCSL 120. Turnhout: Brepols, 1960.

———. *In Marci evangelium expositio.* Edited by D. Hurst. CCSL 120. Turnhout: Brepols, 1960.

———. *De temporum ratione*. Edited by C. W. Jones. CCSL 123B. Turnhout: Brepols, 1977.

Bethu Brigte. Edited and translated by Donnchadh Ó hAodha. Dublin: Dublin Institute for Advanced Studies, 1978.

Boethius. *In Isagogen Porphyrii commenta*. Edited by Samuel Brandt. CSEL 48. Vienna: Tempsky, 1906.

Brethren of Purity. *The Case of the Animals Versus Man Before the King of the Jinn: An Arabic Critical Edition and English Translation of Epistle 22*. Edited and translated by Lenn E. Goodman and Richard McGregor. Oxford: Oxford University Press and the Institute of Ismaili Studies, 2009.

Breviarium ecclesiae Ravennatis (Codice Bavaro) secoli VII–X. Edited by Giuseppe Rabotti. Rome: Istituto Storico Italiano per il Medio Evo, 1985.

Canones Adomnani. Edited by Ludwig Bieler, *The Irish Penitentials*. Dublin: Dublin Institute for Advanced Studies, 1963.

Capitularia regum Francorum. Edited by Alfred Boretius and Victor Krause. 2 vols. MGH LL 2.1–2. Hannover: Hahn, 1883–1897.

Cartulaire de l'abbaye de Gorze: Ms. 826 de la Bibliothèque de Metz. Edited by A. D'Herbomez. Paris: Klincksieck, 1898.

Cartulario de Alaón (Huesca). Edited by José Luis Corral Lafuente. Zaragoza: Anubar, 1984.

Cartulario della Berardenga, Il. Edited by Eugenio Casanova. Siena: L. Lazzeri, 1914.

Cartulario de San Millán de la Cogolla (759–1076). Edited by Antonio Ubieto Arteta. Valencia: Instituto de Estudios Riojanos, Monasterio de San Millán de la Cogolla, and Anubar, 1976.

Cartulario de Santa María del Puerto. Edited by Juan Abad Barrasus, *El monasterio de Santa María de Puerto (Santoña), 863–1210*, appendix 2. Santander: Institución Cultural de Cantabria, 1985.

Cartulario de "Sant Cugat" del Vallés. Edited by José Rius. Vol. 1. Barcelona: Consejo Superior de Investigaciones Científicas, 1945.

Cartulario de Valpuesta. Edited by M. Desamparados Pérez Soler. Valencia: Anubar, 1970.

Cartulary of Worcester Cathedral Priory, The. Edited by R. R. Darlington. London: J. W. Ruddock and Sons, 1968.

Cassian, John. *Institutiones*. Edited and translated by Jean-Claude Guy, *Institutions cénobitiques*. SC 109. Paris: Cerf, 1965.

Cassiodorus. *Expositio psalmorum*. Edited by M. Adriaen. 2 vols. CCSL 98. Turnhout: Brepols, 1958.

———. *Institutiones divinarum et saecularium litterarum*.

Edited by R. A. B. Mynors. Oxford: Clarendon, 1937.

Translated by James W. Halporn, *"Institutions of Divine and Secular Learning" and "On the Soul."* Liverpool: Liverpool University Press, 2004.

————. *Variae.* Edited by Theodor Mommsen. MGH Auct. ant. 12. Hannover: Hahn, 1894.

Catalogi bibliothecarum antiqui. Vol. 1: *Catalogi saeculo XIII vetustiores.* Edited by Gustav Heinrich Becker. Bonn: Cohen, 1885.

Chartae Latinae Antiquiores: Facsimile Edition of the Latin Charters Prior to the Ninth Century. Edited by Albert Bruckner and Robert Marichal et al. 49 volumes. Zurich: Urs Graf, 1954–1997.

Chartae Latinae Antiquiores: Facsimile Edition of the Latin Charters, Second Series, Ninth Century. Edited by Guglielmo and Giovanna Nicolaj et al. 69 volumes. Zurich: Urs Graf, 1997–2019.

Charters of Christ Church Canterbury. Edited by N. P. Brooks and S. E. Kelly. 2 vols. Oxford: Oxford University Press, 2013.

Charters of St Augustine's Abbey Canterbury and Minster-in-Thanet. Edited by S. E. Kelly. Oxford: Oxford University Press, 1995.

Chartes de l'abbaye de Saint-Étienne de Dijon. Vol. 1: *VIIIe, IXe, X^e et XIe siècles.* Edited by J. Courtois. Paris: Librairie Picard; Dijon: Nourry, 1908.

Chlotharii II. edictum. In *Capitularia regum Francorum,* 1:20–23.

Chromatius of Aquileia. *Tractatus in Matthaeum.* Edited by R. Étaix and J. Lemarié. CCSL 9A. Turnhout: Brepols, 1974.

Claudius of Turin. *Epistolae.* Edited by Ernst Dümmler. MGH Epp. 4. Berlin: Weidmann, 1895.

————. *Expositio libri Genesis.* Edited by Iohannes Alexander Brassicanus, *Commentariorum in Genesim,* in *Diui Eucherii Lugdunensis episcopi doctissimi lucubrationes.* Basel: Froben, 1591.

Codex Euricanus. Edited by Alvaro D'Ors, *El Código de Eurico.* Estúdios visigóticos 2. Cuadernos del Instituto Jurídico Español 12. Rome: Consejo Superior de Investigaciones Científicas, 1960.

Codex Laureshamensis. Edited by Karl Glöckner. 3 vols. Darmstadt: Verlag des Historischen Vereins für Hessen, 1929–1936.

Cogitosus. *Vita sanctae Brigidae.* Edited by Karina Hochegger, "Untersuchungen zu den ältesten *Vitae sanctae Brigidae.*" M.Phil. Thesis, Universität Wien, 2009.

Colección canónica hispana, La. Edited by Gonzalo Martínez Diez and Félix Rodríguez. Madrid: Consejo Superior de Investigaciones Científicas.

Vol. 4, *Concilios galos, concilios hispanos: primera parte.* 1984.

Vol. 5, *Concilios hispanos: segunda parte.* 1992.

Vol. 6, *Concilios hispánicos: tercera parte.* 2002.

Colección documental del archivo de la Catedral de León (775–1230). León: Caja de Ahorros y Monte de Piedad de León and Archivo Histórico Diocesano de León.

Vol. 1, *775–952,* edited by Emilio Sáez. 1987.

Vol. 2, *953–985,* edited by Emilio Sáez and Carlos Sáez. 1990.

Vol. 3, *986–1031*, edited by José Manuel Ruíz Ascencio, 1987.

Colección documental del Monasterio de Santa María de Otero de las Dueñas. Vol. 1, *854–1108*, edited by José Antonio Fernández Flórez and Marta Herrero de la Fuente. León: Caja España de Inversiones and Archivo Histórico Diocesano de León, 1999.

Columella. *De re rustica.* In *L. Iuni Moderati Columellae opera quae exstant*, vols. 2–8, edited by V. Lundström, Å. Josephson, and S. Hedberg. Uppsala: Lundquist, 1917–1958.

Concilia Galliae. Edited by Charles de Clerq. 2 vols. CCSL 148, 148A. Turnhout: Brepols, 1963.

Constantius of Lyon. *Vita Germani episcopi Autissiodorensis.* Edited by Bruno Krusch and Wilhelm Levison. MGH SS rer. Merov. 7. Hannover: Hahn, 1920.

Cosmographia. Edited and translated by Michael W. Herren, *The "Cosmography of Aethicus Ister": Edition, Translation, and Commentary.* Turnhout: Brepols, 2011.

Cyprianus of Toulon, Firminus of Uzès, Viventius, Messianus, and Stephanus. *Vita Caesarii episcopi Arelatensis libri duo.* Edited by Bruno Krusch. MGH SS rer. Merov. 3. Hannover: Hahn, 1896.

Descriptio mancipiorum ecclesie Massiliensis. Edited by M. Guérard, in *Cartulaire de l'abbaye de Saint-Victor de Marseilles.* Vol. 2, 634–54. Collection des Cartulaires de France 9. Paris: Lahure, 1857.

Dhuoda. *Liber manualis.* Edited by Pierre Riché, *Manuel pour mon fils.* SC 225. Paris: Cerf, 1975.

Digesta. Edited by Theodore Mommsen. Vol. 1 of *Corpus Iuris Civilis.* 16th ed. Berlin: Weidmann, 1954.

Documentación del Tumbo A de la Catedral de Santiago de Compostela, La. Edited by Manuel Lucas Álvarez. León: Caja España de Inversiones, Caja de Ahorros y Monte de Piedad, and Archivo Histórico Diocesano de León, 1997.

Edictum Diocletiani et Collegarum de pretiis rerum venalium. Edited by Marta Giacchero. 2 vols. Genoa: Istituto di Storia Antica e Scienze Asuiliare, 1974.

Edictum Theoderici regis. Edited by Pierre Pithou and Friedrich Bluhme. MGH LL 5. Hannover: Hahn, 1875–1889.

Edictus Rothari. Edited by Friedrich Bluhme, in *Leges Langobardorum.* MGH LL 4. Hannover: Hahn, 1868.

Einhard. *Epistolae.* Edited by Karl Hampe. MGH Epp. 5. Hannover: Hahn, 1899.

Eriugena, John Scottus. *Periphyseon.* Edited by Edward Jeauneau. 5 vols. CCCM 161–65. Turnhout: Brepols, 1996–2003.

Eucherius of Lyon. *Formulae spiritalis intelligentiae.* Edited by C. Mandolfo. CCSL 66. Turnhout: Brepols, 2004.

———. *Instructionum libri duo.* Edited by C. Mandolfo. CCSL 66. Turnhout: Brepols, 2004.

Expositio totius mundi et gentium. Edited by Jean Rougé. Paris: Cerf, 1966.

Formulae Merowingici et Karolini aevi. Edited by Karl Zeumer. Hannover: Hahn, 1886.

Fortunatus, Venantius. *Vita Radegundis*. Edited by Bruno Krusch. MGH SS rer. Merov. 2. Hannover: Hahn, 1888.

Fredegar. *Chronicae*. Edited by Bruno Krusch. MGH SS rer. Merov. 2. Hannover: Hahn, 1888.

Galen. *De alimentorum facultatibus*. Translated by Owen Powell, *On the Properties of Foodstuffs*. Cambridge: Cambridge University Press, 2003.

Genesis Rabbah. Translated by H. Freedman, *Midrash Rabbah: Genesis 2*. 3rd ed. London: Soncino, 1983.

Gennadius of Marseille. *De ecclesiasticis dogmatibus*. PL 42, cols. 1211–22. Paris: Migne, 1845.

Gesetze der Angelsachsen, Die. Edited by F. Liebermann. Vol. 1: *Text und Übersetzung*. Halle: Niemeyer, 1903.

Grágás. Translated by Andrew Dennis, Peter Foote, and Richard Perkins, *Laws of Early Iceland: Grágás; The Codex Regius of Grágás with Material from Other Manuscripts*. 2 vols. Winnipeg: University of Manitoba Press, 1980–2000.

Gregory of Catino. *Registrum Farfense*. Edited by I. Giorgi and U. Balzani. 5 vols. Rome: Società romana di storia patria, 1879–1914.

Gregory of Tours. *Liber vitae patrum*. Edited by Bruno Krusch. 2nd ed. MGH SS rer. Merov. 1.2. Hannover: Hahn, 1969.

———. *Libri de virtutibus sancti Martini episcopi*. Edited by Bruno Krusch. 2nd ed. MGH SS rer. Merov. 1.2. Hanover: Hahn, 1969.

———. *Libri historiarum X* [= *Historiae*]. Edited by Bruno Krusch and Wilhelm Levison. 2nd ed. MGH SS rer. Merov. 1.1. Hannover: Hahn, 1951.

Gregory the Great. *Dialogi*. Edited by Adalbert de Vogüé, *Dialogues*. SC 251, 260, 265. Paris: Cerf, 1978–1980.

Heidrich, Ingrid. "Das Breve der Bischofskirche von Mâcon aus der Zeit König Pippins (751–768) mit Textedition." *Francia* 24 (1997): 17–37.

Herodotus. *The Persian Wars*. Edited and translated by A. D. Godley. Vol. 1: *Books I–II*. Rev. ed. Loeb Classical Library. Cambridge: Harvard University Press, 1926.

Hilary of Poitiers. *In Matthaeum*. Edited by Jean Doignon, *Sur Matthieu*. SC 254, 258. Paris: Cerf, 1979.

Hrabanus Maurus. *Commentariorum in Genesim libri quatuor*. PL 107, cols. 439–670. Paris: Migne, 1864.

———. *De rerum naturis/De universo*. PL 111, cols. 9–614. Paris: Migne, 1852.

Inquisitiones Post Mortem for the County of Worcester, The. Edited by J. W. Willis-Bund. Oxford: Parker, 1909.

Intexuimus. Edited by Michael Gorman, "The Visigothic Commentary on Genesis in Autun 27 (S. 29)." *Recherches Augustiniennes et Patristiques* 30 (1997): 167–277, at 241–66.

Inventari altomedievali di terre, coloni, et redditi. Rome: Storico Italiano per il Medio Evo, 1979.

Isidore of Seville. *Etymologiarum sive originum libri XX* [*Etymologiae*].

    Edited by W. M. Lindsay. Oxford: Clarendon, 1911, repr., 1966.

    Translated by Stephen A. Barney, W. J. Lewis, J. A. Beach, and Oliver Berghof, with the collaboration of Muriel Hall, *The "Etymologies" of Isidore of Seville.* Cambridge: Cambridge University Press, 2006.

―――. *De natura rerum.*

    Edited by Jacques Fontaine, *Isidore de Séville: Traité de la nature suivi de l'épître en vers du roi Sisebut à Isidore.* Bordeaux: Féret et Fils, 1960.

    Translated by Calvin B. Kendall and Faith Wallis, *Isidore of Seville: On the Nature of Things.* Liverpool: Liverpool University Press, 2016.

―――. *Sententiae.* Edited by Pierre Cazier. CCSL 111. Turnhout: Brepols, 1998.

al-Jāḥiẓ, Abū 'Uthman 'Amr ibn Baḥr al-Kinānī al-Baṣrī. *Kitāb al-ḥayawān.*

    Edited by 'Abd al-Salām Muḥammad Hārūn. 8 vols. Cairo: Mustafā al-Bābī al-Halabī, 1357–1364/1938–1945.

    Partially translated by Lakhdar Souami, in *Le cadi et la mouche: Anthologie du "Livre des Animaux."* Paris: Sindbad, 1988.

Jerome. *Adversus Iovinianum.* PL 23, cols. 205–338. Paris: Migne, 1863.

―――. *Commentariorum in Danielem libri III <IV>.* Edited by Francis Glorie. CCSL 75A. Turnhout: Brepols, 1964.

―――. *Commentariorum in Matheum libri IV.* Edited by D. Hurst and M. Adriaen. CCSL 77. Turnhout: Brepols, 1969.

Jonas of Bobbio. *Vita Columbani abbatis discipulorumque eius.* Edited by Bruno Krusch. MGH SS rer. Germ. 37. Hannover: Hahn, 1905.

[Jonas of Bobbio.] *Regula cuiusdam ad virgines.* Edited by Albrecht Diem, in *The Pursuit of Salvation: Discipline, Space, and Community in Early Medieval Monasticism,* forthcoming. Otherwise see PL 88, cols. 1053–70. Paris: Migne, 1850.

Leges Ahistulfi regis. Edited by Friedrich Bluhme, in *Leges Langobardorum.* MGH LL 4. Hannover: Hahn, 1868.

Leges Liutprandi regis. Edited by Friedrich Bluhme, in *Leges Langobardorum.* MGH LL 4. Hannover: Hahn, 1868.

Leviticus Rabbah. Translated by J. Israelstam and Judah J. Slotki, *Midrash Rabbah: Leviticus.* London: Socino, 1983.

Lex Alamannorum. Edited by Karl August Eckhardt. MGH LL nat. Germ. 5.1. 2nd ed. Hannover: Hahn, 1966.

Lex Baiwariorum. Edited by Ernst von Schwind. MGH LL nat. Germ. 5.2. Hannover: Hahn, 1926.

Lex Frisionum. Edited by Karl August Eckhardt and Albrecht Eckhardt. MGH Fontes iuris Germanici antiqui in usum scholarum separatim editi 12. Hannover: Hahn, 1982.

Lex Ribuaria. Edited by Franz Beyerle and Rudolf Buchner. MGH LL nat. Germ. 3.2. Hannover: Hahn, 1954.

Lex Salica. Edited by Karl August Eckhardt, *Pactus legis Salicae.* MGH LL nat. Germ. 4.1. Hannover: Hahn, 1962.

Lex Salica [Karolina] = *Lex Salica* versions D and E. Edited by Karl August Eckhardt. MGH LL nat. Germ. 4.2. Hannover: Hahn, 1969.

Lex Saxonum. Edited by Karl Freiherr von Richthofen and Karl Friedrich von Richthofen. MGH LL 5. Hannover: Hahn, 1875–1889.

Lex Thuringorum. Edited by Karl Friedrich von Richthofen. MGH LL V. Hannover: Hahn, 1875–1889.

Liber constitutionum. Edited by Louis Rodolphe de Salis, in *Leges Burgundionum.* MGH LL nat. Germ. 2.1. Hannover: Hahn, 1892.

Liber de ordine creaturarum: Un anónimo irlandés del siglo VII. Edited by Manuel Díaz y Díaz. Santiago de Compostela: University of Santiago de Compostela, 1972.

Liber historiae Francorum. Edited by Bruno Krusch. MGH SS rer. Merov. 2. Hannover: Hahn, 1888.

Liber iudiciorum [= *Lex Visigothorum*]. Edited by Karl Zeumer, in *Leges Visigothorum.* MGH LL nat. Germ. 1.1. Hannover: Hahn, 1902.

Liber legis Langobardorum concordia dictus. Edited by Friedrich Bluhme, in *Leges Langobardorum,* edited by Georg Heinrich Pertz. MGH LL 4. Hannover: Hahn, 1868.

Liber pontificalis. Edited by L. Duchesne. 3 vols. Paris: De Boccard, 1955–1957.

Liber possessionum Wizenburgensis. Edited by Christoph Dette. Mainz: Gesellschaft für mittelrheinische Kirchengeschichte, 1987.

Lucretius. *De rerum natura libri sex.* Edited by Joseph Martin. Leipzig: Teubner, 1953.

Luxorius. *Liber epigrammaton.* In *Anthologia Latina sive Poesis Latinae supplementum.* 2nd ed. Vol. 1: *Libri Salmasiani aliorumque carmina,* edited by Alexander Riese. Leipzig: Teubner, 1894.

Marcellus. *De medicamentis liber.* 2nd ed. Edited by Max Niedermann. Corpus Medicorum Latinorum 5. Berlin: Akademie, 1968.

Marculfi formularum libri duo. Edited by Alf Uddholm. Uppsala: Eranos, 1962.

Martin of Braga. *Opera omnia.* Edited by Claude W. Barlow. New Haven: Yale University Press, 1950.

Martyrium Porcarii. AASS, August II. Antwerp: Société des Bollandistes, 1735.

Martyrium Prisci et sociorum. AASS, May VI. Antwerp: Société des Bollandistes, 1688.

Medicina Plinii. Edited by Alf Önnerfors, *Plinii Secundii Iunioris qui feruntur de medicina libri tres.* Corpus Medicorum Latinorum 3. Berlin: Akademie-Verlag, 1964.

Medieval Oxfordshire Village, A: Cuxham, 1240 to 1400. Edited by P. D. A. Harvey. London: Oxford University Press, 1965.

Midrash Psalms. Translated by William J. Braude. 2 vols. New Haven: Yale University Press, 1959.

Paenitentiale Halitgarii Cameracensis. PL 105, cols. 693–710. Paris: Migne, 1851.

Paenitentiale Pseudo-Theodori. Edited by Carine van Rhijn. CCSL 156B. Turnhout: Brepols, 2009.

Paenitentialia minora Franciae et Italiae saeculi VIII–IX. Edited by Raymund Kottje. CCSL 156. Turnhout: Brepols, 1994.

Pactus legis Alamannorum. Edited by Karl August Eckhardt. MGH LL nat. Germ. 5.1. 2nd ed. Hannover: Hahn, 1966.

Palladius. *Opus agriculturae*. Edited by Charles Guiraud and René Martin, *Traité d'agriculture*. 2 vols. Paris: Belles Lettres, 1976–2010.

Patrick. *Confessio*. Edited by Ludwig Bieler, in *Libri epistolarum sancti Patricii episcopi*. Dublin: Royal Irish Academy, 1993; orig. published 1950.

Paul the Deacon. Epitome of Sextus Pompeius Festus, *De verborum significatu*. Edited by Wallace M. Lindsay. Leipzig: Teubner, 1913.

Petronius. *Satyricon*.
Edited by Konrad Müller and Wilhelm Ehlers, *Satyrica*. Munich: Heimeran, 1965.
Translated by Sarah Ruden, *Satyricon*. Indianapolis: Hackett, 2000.

Physica Plinii Bambergensis (Cod. Bamb. med. 2, fol. 93v–232r). Edited by Alf Önnerfors. Hildesheim: Georg Olms 1975.

Pizarras visigodas, Las (Entre el latín y su disgregación: La lengua hablada en Hispania, siglos VI–VIII). Edited by Isabel Velázquez Soriano. Burgos: Fundación Instituto Castellano Leonés de la Lengua, 2004.

Plan of Saint Gall. St. Gallen, Stiftsbibliothek, Cod. Sang. 1092. Digitized at https://www.e-codices.unifr.ch/de/csg/1092/recto.

Plautus. *Captivi*. Edited by Friedrich Leo, in *Plauti Comoediae*, vol. 1. Berlin: Weidmann, 1895.

Pliny the Elder. *Historia naturalis*. 37 vols. Edited and translated by A. Ernout et al. Paris: Belles Lettres, 1947–2015.

Polyptichon von Montierender, Das: Kritische Edition und Analyse. Edited by Claus-Dieter Droste. Trier: Trierer Historische Forschungen, 1988.

Polyptychon und die Notitia de Areis von Saint-Maur-des-Fossés, Das. Edited by Dieter Hägermann and Andreas Hedwig. Sigmaringen: Thorbecke, 1990.

Polyptychon von Saint-Germain-des-Prés, Das: Studienausgabe. Edited by Dieter Hägermann, with Konrad Elmshäuser and Anreas Hedwig. Cologne: Böhlau, 1993.

Polyptyque et les listes de biens de l'abbaye Saint-Pierre de Lobbes, Le (IXᵉ–XIᵉ siècles). Edited by Jean-Pierre Devroey. Brussels: Commission Royale d'Histoire, 1986.

Polyptyque et les listes de cens de l'abbaye de Saint-Remi de Reims, Le (IXᵉ–XIᵉ siècles). Edited by Jean-Pierre Devroey. Reims: Académie Nationale, 1984.

Portugaliae Monumenta Historica. Vol. 1: *Diplomata et chartae*. Nendeln, Liechtenstein: Kraus 1967; reprint of 1867 edition.

Propositiones ad acuendos iuvenes. Edited by Menso Fölkerts, *Die älteste mathematische Aufgabensammlung in lateinische Sprache: Die Alkuin zugeschriebenen Propositiones ad acuendos iuvenes. Überlieferung, Inhalt, Kristische Edition*. Vienna: Springer, 1978.

Prümer Urbar, Das. Edited by Ingo Schwab. Düsseldorf: Droste, 1983.

Rectitudines singularum personarum. In *Gesetze der Angelsachsen*, 444–53.

Recueil des chartes de l'abbaye de Saint-Germain-des-Prés. Edited by René Poupardin. Vol. 1: *558–1182.* Paris: Champion, 1909.

Recueil des chartes de l'abbaye de Stavelot-Malmedy. Edited by J. Halkin and C.-G. Roland. Vol. 1. Brussels: Académies Royales de Belgiques, 1909.

Red Book of Worcester, The. Edited by Marjory Hollings. London: Worcestershire Historical Society, 1934.

Regula Benedicti. Edited by Adalbert de Vogüé and Jean Neufville, *La Régle de Saint Benoît.* 7 vols. SC 181–86. Paris: Cerf, 1971–1977.

Regula Magistri. Edited by Adalbert de Vogüé, *La Régle du Maître.* 3 vols. SC 105–7. Paris: Cerf, 1964–65.

Remigius of Auxerre. *Expositio super Genesim.* Edited by Burton Van Name Edwards. CCSM 136. Turnhout: Brepols, 1999.

Remigius of Reims. *Testamentum.* In Hincmar of Reims, *Vita Remigii episcopi Remensis.* MGH SS rer. Merov. 3, edited by Bruno Krusch. Hannover: Hahn, 1896.

Salzburger Urkundenbuch. Edited by Willibald Hauthaler and Franz Martin. 3 vols. Salzburg: Gesellschaft für Salzburger Landeskunde, 1910–1918.

Scéla mucce Meic Dathó. Edited by Rudolf Thurneysen. Dublin: Dublin Institute for Advanced Studies, 1969.

Serenus, Quintus. *Liber medicinalis.* Edited by Friedrich Vollmer. Corpus Medicorum Latinorum 2.3. Leipzig: Teubner, 1916.

Severus, Sulpicius. *Chronica.* Edited by C. Halm. CSEL 1. Vienna: Gerold, 1866.

———. *Dialogi.* Edited by C. Halm. CSEL 1. Vienna: Gerold, 1866.

———. *Vita Martini.* Edited by Jacques Fontaine, *Vie de Saint Martin.* 3 vols. SC 133–35. Paris: Cerf, 1967–1969.

Sifra, Qeodoshim. Translated by Jacob Neusner, *Sifra: An Analytical Translation.* 3 vols. Atlanta: Scholars, 1988.

Sifre Deuteronomy. Translated by Reuven Hammer, *Sifre: A Tannaitic Commentary on the Book of Deuteronomy.* New Haven: Yale University Press, 1986.

Sisebut. *Epistula.* Edited by Jacques Fontaine, *Isidore de Séville: Traité de la nature suivi de l'épître en vers du roi Sisebut à Isidore.* Bordeaux: Féret et Fils, 1960.

Statutes of the Realm (1225–1713), The, Printed by Command of His Majesty King George the Third. Vol. 1. London, Eyre and Strahan, 1810.

Stoll, Ulrich, ed. *Das Lorscher Arzneibuch: Ein medizinisches Kompendium des 8. Jahrhunderts (Codex Bambergensis Medicinalis 1). Text, Übersetzung und Fachglossar.* Stuttgart: Steiner, 1992.

Stubbs, William. *Select Charters and Other Illustrations of English Constitutional History from the Earliest Times to the Reign of Edward the First.* 9th ed., revised by H. W. C. Davis. Oxford: Clarendon, 1960.

Testamentum porcelli. Edited by Alvaro d'Ors, "Testamentum Porcelli: Introduccion, Texto, Traduccion y Notas." *Supplementos de "Estudios Classicos": Serie de Textos 3* (1953): 74–83.

Theophilus of Edessa's Chronicle and the Circulation of Historical Knowledge in Late Antiquity and Early Islam. Translated by Robert G. Hoyland. Liverpool: Liverpool University Press, 2011.

Tombo de Celanova, O: Estudio introductorio, edición e índices (ss. IX–XII). Edited by José Miguel Andrade Cernadas. 2 vols. Santiago de Compostela: Consello da Cultura Galega, 1995.

Traditionen des Hochstifts Regensburg und des Klosters S. Emmeram, Die. Edited by Josef Widemann. Munich: Scientia Verlag Aalen, 1969.

Traditiones Wizenburgenses: Die Urkunden des Klosters Weissenburg, 661–864. Edited by Anton Doll. Darmstadt: Hessichen Historischen Kommission, 1979.

Triads of Ireland, The. Edited by Kuno Meyer. Royal Irish Academy Todd Lecture Series 13. Dublin: Hodges, Figgis; London: Williams and Norgate, 1906.

Tumbos del Monasterio de Sobrado de los Monjes. Edited by Pilar Loscertales de G. de Valdeavellano. Vol. 1. Madrid: Archivo Histórico Nacional, 1976.

Urkunden der Merowinger, Die. Edited by Theo Kölzer. 2 vols. Hannover: Hahn, 2001.

Varro. *Res rusticae*. Edited by Georg Goetz. 2nd ed. Leipzig: Teubner, 1929.

Vindarius. *Excerpta*. Edited by Jacques André, *L'art culinaire*. Paris: Belles Lettres, 1974.

Virgil. *Aeneid*. Edited by R. A. B. Mynors, *P. Vergili Maronis opera*. Oxford: Clarendon, 1969.

Vita Aviti confessoris Aurelianensis. Edited by Bruno Krusch. MGH SS rer. Merov. 3. Hannover: Hahn, 1896.

Vita Genovefae virginis Parisiensis. Edited by Bruno Krusch. MGH SS rer. Merov. 3. Hannover: Hahn, 1896.

Vita prima sanctae Brigidae. Edited by Karina Hochegger, "Untersuchungen zu den ältesten *Vitae sanctae Brigidae*." M.Phil. Thesis, Universität Wien, 2009.

Vita sancti Cuthberti auctore anonymo. Edited by Bertram Colgrave, *Two Lives of Saint Cuthbert*. Cambridge: Cambridge University Press, 1940.

Walahfrid Strabo. *Vita sancti Galli confessoris*. Edited by Bruno Krusch. MGH SS rer. Merov. 4. Hannover: Hahn, 1902.

Walter of Henley and Other Treatises on Estate Management and Accounting. Edited by Dorothea Oschinsky. Oxford: Clarendon, 1971.

Whitelock, Dorothy, ed. *Anglo-Saxon Wills*. Cambridge: Cambridge University Press, 1930.

Wigbod. *Quaestiones in Octateuchum*. PL 96, cols. 1103–68. Paris: Migne, 1851.

———. *Quaestiunculae super evangelium*. Munich, Bayerische Staatsbibliothek 14426, fols. 6v–140r; Karlsruhe, Badische Landesbibliothek Aug. perg. 191, fols. 2r–116r; Brussels, Bibliothèque Royale, Ms. 8654–72, fols. 1r–98v.

[Wigbod]. *Explanatio sex dierum*. PL 93, cols. 207–34 [= *De sex dierum creatione liber sententiarum ex patribus collectarum*]. Paris: Migne, 1850.

Will of Æthelgifu, The: A Tenth Century Anglo-Saxon Manuscript. Edited by Dorothy Whitelock. Oxford: Oxford University Press, 1968.

Modern Research

Adams, J. N. *The Latin Sexual Vocabulary.* Baltimore: Johns Hopkins University Press, 1982.

Alarcón Hernández, Alejandra. "Estudio arqueofaunístico del yacimiento arqueológico 'La Huelga.'" In *La investigación arqueológica de la época visigoda en comunidad de Madrid,* 974–81. Zona Arqueológica 8.3. Alcalá de Henares: Museo Arqueológico Regional, 2006.

Alba, Miguel. "Diacronía de la vivienda señorial de *Emerita (Lusitania, Hispania)*: desde las *domus* alto imperiales y tardoantiguas a las residencia palaciales omeyas (siglos I–IX)." In *Archeologia e societá tra tardo antico e alto medioevo,* edited by Gian Pietro Brogiolo and Alexandra Chavarría Arnau, 163–92. Padua: SAP, 2007.

Albarella, Umberto, Keith Dobney, Anton Ervynck, and Peter Rowley-Conwy. *Pigs and Humans: 10,000 Years of Interaction.* Oxford: Oxford University Press, 2007.

Albarella, Umberto, Keith Dobney, and Peter Rowley-Conwy. "The Domestication of the Pig (*Sus scrofa*): New Challenges and Approaches." In *Documenting Domestication: New Genetic and Archaeological Paradigms,* edited by Melinda A. Zeder et al., 209–27. Berkeley: University of California Press, 2006.

Albarella, Umberto, Filippo Manconi, and Angela Trentacoste. "A Week on the Plateau: Pig Husbandry, Mobility, and Resource Exploitation in Central Sardinia." In *Ethnozooarchaeology: The Present and Past of Human-Animal Relationships,* edited by Umberto Albarella and Angela Trentacoste, 143–59. Oxford: Oxbow, 2011.

Albarella, Umberto, Filippo Manconi, Jean-Denis Vigne, and Peter Rowley-Conwy. "Ethnoarchaeology of Pig Husbandry in Sardinia and Corsica." In Albarella, Dobney, et al., *Pigs and Humans,* 285–307.

Albarella, Umberto, Mauro Rizzetto, Hannah Russ, Kim Vickers, and Sarah Viner-Daniels, eds. *The Oxford Handbook of Zooarchaeology.* Oxford: Oxford University Press, 2017.

Alexander, Michelle, Christopher M. Gerrard, Alejandra Gutiérrez, and Andrew R. Millard. "Diet, Society, and Economy in Late Medieval Spain: Stable Isotope Evidence from Muslims and Christians from Gandía, Valencia." *American Journal of Physical Anthropology* 156 (2015): 263–73.

Alexander, Rani T., and Héctor Hernández Álvarez. "Agropastoralism and Household Ecology in Yucatán after the Spanish Invasion." *Environmental Archaeology* 23 (2018): 69–79.

Alkhateeb Shehada, Housni. *Mamluks and Animals: Veterinary Medicine in Medieval Islam.* Leiden: Brill, 2013.

Allen, Harriet. "Vegetation and Ecosystem Dynamics." In *The Physical Geography of the Mediterranean,* edited by Jamie C. Woodward, 203–27. Oxford: Oxford University Press, 2009.

Allsen, Thomas T. *The Royal Hunt in Eurasian History*. Philadelphia: University of Pennsylvania Press, 2006.

Anderson, Graham. "The Cognomen of M. Grunnius Corocotta: A Dissertatiuncula on Roast Pig." *American Journal of Philology* 101, no. 1 (1980): 57–58.

Anderson, Virginia DeJohn. *Creatures of Empire: How Domestic Animals Transformed Early America*. Oxford: Oxford University Press, 2004.

Andersson, Leif. "The Molecular Basis for Phenotypic Changes During Pig Domestication." In Albarella, Dobney, et al., *Pigs and Humans*, 42–54.

Andrade Cernadas, José Miguel. "En el refectório: la alimentación en el mundo monástico de la Galicia medieval." *Sémata: Ciencias Sociais e Humanidades* 21 (2009): 45–64.

Andreae, Bernard. *Die römischen Jagdsarkophäge*. Vol. 2 of *Die Sarkophage mit Darstellungen aus dem Menschleben*. Berlin: Mann, 1980.

Andreolli, Bruno. *Contadini su terre di signori: Studi sulla contrattualistica agraria dell'Italia medievale*. Bologna: CLUEB, 1999.

———. "Misurare la terra: metrologie altomedievali." In *Uomo e spazio nell'alto medioevo*, 151–87. Settimane di studio 50. Spoleto: Centro Italiano di Studi sull'Alto Medioevo, 2003.

Andreolli, Bruno, and Massimo Montanari, *L'azienda curtense: Proprietà della terra e lavoro contadino nei secoli VIII–XI*. Bologna: Cooperativa Libraria Universitaria, 1983.

Anthony, Sean W. *Crucifixion and Death as Spectacle: Umayyad Crucifixion in Its Late Antique Context*. New Haven, Conn.: American Oriental Society, 2014.

Appuhn, Karl. *A Forest on the Sea: Environmental Expertise in Renaissance Venice*. Baltimore: Johns Hopkins University Press, 2009.

Aramburu-Zabala Higuera, Javier. *El abrigo del Puig de s'Escolà (Llucmajor, Mallorca)*. N.p., unpublished, 2011. Downloaded 1 November 2017 from www.academia.edu/20195298/El_abrigo_del_puig_de_sEscol%C3%A0_Llucmajor_Mallorca.

Arcas Campoy, María. "El criterio de los juristas malikíes sobre los alimentos y las bebidas de los ḏimmíes: Entre la teoría y la práctica." In *Law and Religious Minorities in Medieval Societies: Between Theory and Praxis*, edited by Ana Echevarria, Juan Pedro Monferrer-Sala, and John Tolan, 85–100. Turnhout: Brepols, 2016.

Arge, Símun V., Mike J. Church, and Seth D. Brewington. "Pigs in the Faroe Islands: An Ancient Facet of the Islands' Paleoeconomy." *Journal of the North Atlantic* 2 (2009): 19–32.

Arnold, Elizabeth, and James McConnell. "Hijacked Humanity: A Postcolonial Reading of Luke 8:26–39." *Review & Expositor* 112 (2015): 591–606.

Arnold, Ellen F. *Negotiating the Landscape: Environment and Monastic Identity in the Medieval Ardennes*. Philadelphia: University of Pennsylvania Press, 2012.

Arthur, Paul. *Naples: From Roman Town to City-State*. London: British School at Rome, 2002.

Arthur, Paul, Umberto Albarella, Brunella Bruno, and Sarah King. "'Masseria Quattro Macine'—A Deserted Medieval Village and Its Territory in Southern Apulia: An Interim Report on Field Survey, Excavation and Document Analysis." *Papers of the British School at Rome* 64 (1996): 181–237.

Arthur, Paul, and Brunella Bruno. *Apigliano: Un villagio bizantino e medioevale in Terra d'Otranto. L'ambiente, il villaggio, la popolazione.* Galatina: Arti Grafiche Panico, [2009].

Arthur, Paul, M. Leo Imperiale, and M. Tinelli. *Apigliano: Un villaggio bizantino e medievale in Terra d'Otranto. I reperti.* Lecce: In-Cul.Tu.Re. and Università del Salento, 2015.

Ascough, Philippa L., Mike J. Church, Gordon T. Cook, Árni Einarsson, Thomas H. McGovern, Andrew J. Dugmore, and Kevin J. Edwards. "Stable Isotopic (δ^{13}C and δ^{15}N) Characterization of Key Faunal Resources from Norse Period Settlements in North Iceland." *Journal of the North Atlantic* 7 (2014): 25–42.

Audoin-Rouzeau, Frédérique. "Compter et mesurer les os animaux: Pour un histoire de l'élevage et de l'alimentation en Antiquité aux Temps Modernes." *Histoire & Mesure* 10 (1995): 277–312.

Azuar, Rafael. "Arqueologías ambientales para el conocimiento del paleo-paisaje y del aprovechamiento de sus recursos en el *Sharq Al-Andalus* (Siglos VIII–X d.C.)." *MARQ: Arqueología y Museos* 6 (2015): 147–58.

Bagnall, Roger. *Egypt in Late Antiquity.* Princeton: Princeton University Press, 1996.

Bailey, Lisa Kaaren. *The Religious Worlds of the Laity in Late Antique Gaul.* London: Bloomsbury, 2016.

Bailey, Mark. *The English Manor, c. 1200–c. 1500.* Manchester, UK: Manchester University Press, 2002.

Baker, Polydora. "The Vertebrate Remains from the Longobard and 9th–10th C. Occupation at S. Giulia, Brescia." In Gian Pietro Brogiolo, *S. Giulia di Brescia: Gli scavi dal 1980 al 1992, reperti preromani, romani e alto medievali,* 425–49. Florence: All'Insegna del Giglio, 1999.

Ballari, Sebastián A., and M. Noelia Barrios-García. "A Review of Wild Boar *Sus scrofa* Diet and Factors Affecting Food Selection in Native and Introduced Ranges." *Mammal Review* 44 (2014): 124–34.

Balmelle, Catherine. *Les demeures aristocratiques d'Aquitaine: Société et culture de l'Antiquité tardive dans le Sud-Ouest de la Gaule.* Bordeaux: Ausonius, 2001.

Banaji, Jairus. *Agrarian Change in Late Antiquity: Gold, Labour, and Aristocratic Dominance.* Oxford: Oxford University Press, 2001.

Barbiera, Irene, and Gianpiero Dall-Zuanna. "Population Dynamics in Italy in the Middle Ages: New Insights from Archaeological Findings." *Population and Development Review* 35 (2009): 367–89.

Barker, Graeme. "A Tale of Two Deserts: Contrasting Desertification Histories on Rome's Desert Frontiers." *World Archaeology* 33 (2002): 488–507.

Barnish, S. J. B. "Pigs, Plebeians and *Potentes:* Rome's Economic Hinterland, *c.* 350–600 A.D." *Papers of the British School at Rome* 55 (1987): 157–85.

Baruzzi, Marina, and Massimo Montanari. *Porci e porcari nel medioevo: Paesaggio, economia, alimentazione.* Bologna: Cooperativa Libraria Universitaria Editrice Bologna, 1981.

Bashear, Suliman. "Apocalyptic and Other Materials on Early Muslim-Byzantine Wars: A Review of Arabic Sources." *Journal of the Royal Asiatic Society,* 3rd ser., 1 (1991): 173–207.

Bazell, Dianne M. "Strife Among the Table-Fellows: Conflicting Attitudes of Early and Medieval Christians Toward the Eating of Meat." *Journal of the American Academy of Religion* 65 (1997): 73–99.

Becher, Matthias. "Chlodwig: Zwischen Biographie und Quellenkritik." In Meier and Patzold, *Chlodwigs Welt,* 45–66.

Beck, Heinrich. *Das Ebersignum im Germanischen: Ein Beitrag zur germanischen Tier-Symbolik.* Berlin: de Gruyter, 1965.

BeDuhn, Jason David. *The Manichaean Body in Discipline and Ritual.* Baltimore: Johns Hopkins University Press, 2000.

Belser, Julia Watts. *Power, Ethics, and Ecology in Jewish Late Antiquity: Rabbinic Responses to Drought and Disaster.* Cambridge: Cambridge University Press, 2015.

Benecke, Norbert. *Archäozoologische Studien zur Entwicklung der Haustierhaltung im Mitteleuropa und Südskandinavien von der Anfängen biz zum ausgehenden Mittelalter.* Berlin: Akademie, 1994.

Benseddik, N., and T. W. Potter. *Fouilles du Forum de Cherchel, 1977–1981.* 2 vols. Algiers: Agence Nationale d'Archéologie et de Protection des Sites et Monuments Historiques, 1993.

Berkowitz, Beth A. *Animals and Animality in the Babylonian Talmud.* Cambridge: Cambridge University Press, 2018.

Bernward von Hildesheim und das Zeitalter der Ottonen: Katalog der Austellung, Hildesheim 1993. 2 vols. Hildesheim: Bernward Verlag; Mainz am Rhein: Philipp von Zabem, 1993.

Beullens, Pieter. "Like a Book Written by God's Finger: Animals Showing the Path Toward God." In Resl, *A Cultural History of Animals,* 127–51.

Bianchi, Giovanna. *Campiglia: un castello e il suo territorio.* 2 vols. Siena: All'Insegna del Giglio, 2005.

Biano, P., and B. Schirone. "On *Quercus coccifera* L. s.l.: Variation in Reproductive Phenology." *Taxon* 34 (1985): 436–39.

Biddick, Kathleen. *The Other Economy: Pastoral Husbandry on a Medieval Estate.* Berkeley: University of California Press, 1989.

———. "Pig Husbandry on the Peterborough Abbey Estate from the Twelfth to the Fourteenth Century A.D." *Animals and Archaeology* 4 (1984): 161–77.

Birrell, Jean. "Common Rights in the Medieval Forest: Disputes and Conflicts in the Thirteenth Century." *Past and Present* 117 (1987): 22–49.

Bjornlie, Shane. "Law, Ethnicity and Taxes in Ostrogothic Italy: A Case for Continuity, Adaptation and Departure." *Early Medieval Europe* 22 (2014): 138–70.

Blanco-González, Antonio, José Antonio López Sáez, Francisca Alba, Daniel Abel, and Sebastián Pérez. "Medieval Landscapes in the Spanish Central System: A Palaeoenvironmental and Historical Perspective." *Journal of Medieval Iberian Studies* 7 (2015): 1–17.

Blázquez, José María. *Mosaicos romanos de España.* Madrid: Ediciones Cátedra, 1993.

——. "Nombres de aurigas, de possessores, de cazadores y perros en mosaicos de Hispania y Africa." In *L'Africa romana: Atti del IX convegno di studio,* edited by Attilio Mastino, 954–63. Sassari: Edizioni Gallizzi, 1992.

Blennemann, Gordon. "Altestamentarische Modelle für den 'Populus Christianus': Hrabanus Maurus' Kommentar zu den Makkabäerbüchern 1 und 2." In *Vom Blutzeugen zum Glaubenszeugen? Formen und Vorstellungen des christlichen Martyriums im Wandel,* edited by Gordon Blennemann and Klaus Herbers, 101–22. Stuttgart: Steiner, 2014.

Bökönyi, S. "Animal Breeding on the Danube." In *Pastoral Economies in Classical Antiquity,* edited by C. R. Whittaker, 171–76. Cambridge: Cambridge Philological Society, 1988.

Bolgia, Claudia, Rosamond McKitterick, and John Osborne, eds.. *Rome Across Time and Space: Cultural Transmission and the Exchange of Ideas,* c. 500–1400. Cambridge: Cambridge University Press, 2011.

Bolzoni, Lina. *The Web of Images: Vernacular Preaching from Its Origins to St Bernardino da Siena.* Translated by Carole Preston and Lisa Chien. Aldershot: Ashgate, 2004.

Bonacini, Pierpaolo. *Terre d'Emilia: Distretti pubblici, comunità locali e poteri signorili nell'esperienza di una regione italiana (secoli VIII–XII).* Bologna: CLUEB, 2001.

Borst, Arno. *Das Buch der Naturgeschichte: Plinius und seine Leser im Zeitalter des Pergaments.* Heidelberg: Universitätsverlag C. Winter, 1994.

——. *Die karolingische Kalendarreform.* Hannover: Hahnsche Buchhandlung, 1998.

——. *Schriften zur Komputistik im Frankenreich von 721 bis 818.* 3 vols. Hannover: Hahnsche Buchhandlung, 2006.

Bouché-Leclercq, A. *Histoire de la divination dans l'antiquité.* 4 vols. Paris: Leroux, 1879–1882.

Bougard, François, Hans-Werner Goetz, and Régine Le Jan, eds. *Théorie et pratiques des élites au haut Moyen Âge: Conception, perception et réalisation sociale.* Turnhout: Brepols, 2011.

Bouk, Dan. *How Our Days Became Numbered: Risk and the Rise of the Statistical Individual.* Chicago: University of Chicago Press, 2015.

Bourdain, Anthony. "Don't Eat Before Reading This." *New Yorker,* 19 April 1999.

Bouteneff, Peter C. *Beginnings: Ancient Christian Readings of the Biblical Creation Narratives.* Grand Rapids: Baker Academic, 2008.

Bowersock, G. W. *Mosaics as History: The Near East from Late Antiquity to Islam*. Cambridge, Mass.: Belknap, 2006.

Bowes, Kim. "Villas, Taxes and Trade in Fourth Century Hispania." *Late Antique Archaeology* 10 (2013): 191–226.

Braudel, Fernand. *La Méditerranée et le Monde méditerranéen à l'époque de Phillippe II*. Paris: Librairie Armand Colin, 1949.

Britnell, R. H. *The Commercialisation of English Society, 1000–1500*. Cambridge: Cambridge University Press, 1993.

Brogan, Olwen, and D. J. Smith. *Ghirza: A Libyan Settlement in the Roman Period*. Tripoli: Department of Antiquities, 1984.

Brown, John Pairman. "Paradise and the Forest of Lebanon." In John Pairman Brown, *Israel and Hellas*, 3 vols., 3:119–51. Berlin: De Gruyter, 2001.

Brown, Peter. *The Body and Society: Men, Women, and Sexual Renunciation in Early Christianity*. New York: Columbia University Press, 1988.

———. "'Charismatic' Goods: Commerce, Diplomacy, and Cultural Contacts Along the Silk Road in Late Antiquity." In *Empires and Exchanges in Eurasian Late Antiquity: Rome, China, Iran, and the Steppe, ca. 250–750*, edited by Nicola di Cosmo and Michael Maas, 96–107. Cambridge: Cambridge University Press, 2018.

———. *The Ransom of the Soul: Afterlife and Wealth in Early Western Christianity*. Cambridge: Harvard University Press, 2015.

———. *The Rise of Western Christendom: Triumph and Diversity, AD 200–1000*, 2nd ed. Malden, Mass.: Wiley-Blackwell, 2003; 10th anniversary edition, 2013.

———. *Through the Eye of a Needle: Wealth, the Fall of Rome, and the Making of Christianity in the West, 350–550 AD*. Princeton: Princeton University Press, 2012.

———. *Treasure in Heaven: The Holy Poor in Early Christianity*. Charlottesville: University of Virginia Press, 2016.

Bruce, Scott. "The Dark Age of Herodotus: Shards of a Fugitive History in Early Medieval Europe." *Speculum* 94 (2019): 47–67.

———. "Hagiography as Monstrous Ethnography: A Note on Ratramnus of Corbie's Letter Concerning the Conversion of the Cynocephali." In *Insignis sophiae arcator: Essays in Honour of Michael W. Herren on His 65th Birthday*, edited by Gernot R. Wieland, Carin Ruff, and Ross G. Arthur, 45–56. Turnhout: Brepols, 2006.

Bryen, Ari Z. "Law in Many Pieces." *Classical Philology* 109 (2014): 346–65.

Budny, Mildred. "The *Biblia Gregoriana*." In *St Augustine and the Conversion of England*, edited by Richard Gameson, 237–84. Stroud: Sutton, 1999.

Buell, Denise Kimber. "The Microbes and Pneuma That Therefore I Am." In *Divinanimality: Animal Theory, Creaturely Theology*, edited by Stephen D. Moore, 63–87. New York: Fordham University Press, 2014.

Buglione, Antonietta. "People and Animals in Northern Apulia from Late Antiquity to the Early Middle Ages: Some Considerations." In *Breaking and Shaping Beastly*

Bodies: Animals as Material Culture in the Middle Ages, edited by Aleksander Pluskowski, 189–215. Oxford: Oxbow, 2007.

Buglione, Antonietta, Giovanni De Venuto, and Giuliano Volpe. "Agricoltura e allevamento nella Puglia settentrionale tra età romana e Medioevo: il contributo delle bioarcheologie." *Mélanges de l'École française de Rome* 128, no. 2 (2016), https://mefra.revues.org/3475.

Buko, Andrzej. *The Archaeology of Early Medieval Poland: Discoveries—Hypotheses—Interpretations.* Leiden: Brill, 2008.

Burdon, Christopher. "'To the Other Side': Construction of Evil and Fear of Liberation in Mark 5.1–20." *Journal for the Study of the New Testament* 27 (2004): 149–67.

Bynum, Caroline Walker. *Christian Materiality: An Essay on Religion in Late Medieval Europe.* Cambridge: MIT Press, 2011.

Cambridge Ancient History. 2nd ed. Cambridge: Cambridge University Press.

    Vol. 11, *High Empire, A.D. 70–192,* edited by Alan K. Bowman, Peter Garnsey, and Dominic Rathbone. 2000.

    Vol. 12, *The Crisis of Empire, A.D. 193–337,* edited by Alan K. Bowman, Averil Cameron, and Peter Garnsey. 2005.

    Vol. 13, *The Late Empire, A.D. 337–425,* edited by Averil Cameron and Peter Garnsey. 1998.

Cambridge History of Science. Vol. 2, *Medieval Science,* edited by David C. Lindberg and Michael H. Shank. Cambridge: Cambridge University Press, 2003.

Cameron, Alan. *The Last Pagans of Rome.* Oxford: Oxford University Press, 2011.

Camille, Michael. "At the Sign of the 'Spinning Sow': The 'Other' Chartres and Images of Everyday Life of the Medieval Street." In *History and Images: Towards a New Iconology,* edited by Axel Bolvig and Phillip Lindley, 249–76. Turnhout: Brepols, 2003.

Camphuijsen, Frans, and Janna Coomans. "De middeleeuwse stad en zijn varkens." *Madoc: Tijdschrift over de Middeleeuwen* 28 (2015): 140–48.

Cantini, Federico. *Il castello di Montarrenti: lo scavo archeologico (1982–1987). Per la storia della formazione del villagio medievale in Toscana (secc. VII–XV).* Siena: All'Insegna del Giglio, 2003.

Cantwell, Ian. "Anthropozoological Relationships in Late Medieval Dublin." *Dublin Historical Record* 54 (2001): 73–80.

Carradice, I. A., and T. V. Buttrey. *The Roman Imperial Coinage.* 2nd ed. Vol. 2, part 1, *From AD 69–96: Vespasian to Domitian.* London: Spink, 2007.

Carruthers, Mary. *The Book of Memory: A Study of Memory in Medieval Culture.* 2nd ed. Cambridge: Cambridge University Press, 2008.

———. *The Craft of Thought: Meditation, Rhetoric and the Making of Images, 400–1200.* Cambridge: Cambridge University Press, 1998.

———. *The Experience of Beauty in the Middle Ages.* Oxford: Oxford University Press, 2013.

Carter, Warren. "Cross-Gendered Romans and Mark's Jesus: Legion Enters the Pigs (Mark 1:5–20)." *Journal of Biblical Literature* 134 (2015): 139–55.

Cate, C. L. ten. *"Wan god mast gift . . .": Bilder aus der Geschichte der Schweinezucht im Walde.* Wageninger, Netherlands: Centre for Agricultural Publishing and Documentation, 1972.

Catteddu, Isabelle. *Archéologie médiévale en France: le premier Moyen Âge, Ve–XIe siècle.* Paris: La Découverte, 2009.

Catteddu, Isabelle, Benoît Clavel, and Marie-Pierre Ruas. "L'habitat rural mérovingien de Genlis (Côte-d'Or)." *Revue archéologique de l'est et du centre-est* 43 (1992): 38–98.

Cavallo, Chiara, Laura I. Koositra, and Monica K. Dütting. "Food Supply to the Roman Army in the Rhine Delta in the First Century A.D." In Stallibrass and Thomas, *Feeding the Roman Army,* 69–82.

Chabal, Lucie. *Forêts et sociétés en Languedoc (Néolithique final, Antiquité tardive): L'anthracologie, méthode et paléoécologie.* Paris: Maison des Sciences de l'Homme, 1997.

Champlin, Edward. "The Testament of the Piglet." *Phoenix* 41 (1987): 174–83.

Chapman, Andy. *West Cotton, Raunds: A Study of Medieval Settlement Dynamics, AD 450–1450; Excavation of a Deserted Medieval Hamlet in Northamptonshire, 1985–89.* Oxford: Oxbow, 2010.

Choyke, Alice M., and Gerhard Jaritz, eds. *Animaltown: Beasts in Medieval Urban Space.* Oxford: BAR, 2017.

Cirelli, Enrico. "La dieta dei monaci: Cultura materiale e alimentazione nei monasteri benedettini tra IX e XI secolo." *Hortus Artium Medievalium* 19 (2013): 227–40.

Clanchy, M. T. *From Memory to Written Record: England, 1066–1307.* 3rd ed. Malden, Mass.: Wiley-Blackwell, 2013.

Clark, Gillian. "ULVS XIV: Archaeological Evidence for Stock-Raising and Stock-Management in the Pre-Desert." *Libyan Studies* 17 (1986): 49–64.

Clavel, Benoît. "L'animal dans l'alimentation médiévale et moderne en France du Nord (XIIIᵉ–XVIIᵉ siècles)." *Revue archéologique de Picardie,* numéro spécial 19 (2001): 9–204.

Clavel, Benoît, and Jean-Hervé Yvinec. "L'archéozoologie du Moyen Âge au début de la période moderne dans la moitié nord de la France." In *Trente ans d'archéologie médiévale en France: Un bilan pour un avenir,* edited by Jean Chapelot, 71–87. Caen: Publications du CRAHM, 2010.

Clemente Ramos, Julián. "Ganadería porcina y campesinado en Extremadura (1450–1550)." *Debates de Arqueología Medieval* 3 (2013): 221–40.

Clutton-Brock, J., ed. *The Walking Larder: Patterns of Domestication, Pastoralism, and Predation.* London: Unwin Hyman, 1989.

Clynes, Tom. "20 Americans Die Each Day Waiting for Organs: Can Pigs Save Them?" *New York Times Magazine,* 14 November 2018. Accessed same day. https://www.nytimes.com/interactive/2018/11/14/magazine/tech-design-xenotransplantation.html.

Cobb, James C. "From 'Cracklins' to 'Gourmet Bacon Puffs': The Complex Origins and Shifting Shape of Southern Foodways." In *Citizen-Scholar: Essays in Honor of Walter Edgar,* edited by Robert H. Brinkmeyer, Jr., 165–78. Columbia: University of South Carolina Press, 2016.

Coen, Deborah R. *Climate in Motion: Science, Empire, and the Problem of Scale.* Chicago: University of Chicago Press, 2018.

Cohen, Esther. "Law, Folklore and Animal Lore." *Past & Present* 110 (1986): 6–37.

Cohen, Jeffrey Jerome. "Monster Culture (Seven Theses)." In *Monster Theory: Reading Culture,* edited by Jeffrey Jerome Cohen, 3–25. Minneapolis: University of Minnesota Press, 1996.

———. *Stone: An Ecology of the Inhuman.* Minneapolis: University of Minnesota Press, 2015.

Cohen, Jeremy. *"Be Fertile and Increase, Fill the Earth and Master It": The Ancient and Medieval Career of a Biblical Text.* Ithaca: Cornell University Press, 1989.

Colardelle, Michel, and Eric Verdel. *Les habitats du lac de Paladru (Isère) dans leur environnement: La formation d'un terroir au XIe siècle.* Paris: Éditions de la Maison des Sciences de l'Homme, 1993.

Colominas, Lídia, Carlos Fernández Rodríguez, and Maria Pilar Iborra Eres. "Animal Husbandry and Hunting Practices in Hispania Tarraconensis: An Overview." *European Journal of Archaeology* 20, no. 3 (2017): 510–34.

Colonese, A. C., et al. "The Identification of Poultry Processing in Archaeological Ceramic Vessels Using *In-situ* Isotope References for Organic Residue Analysis." *Journal of Archaeological Science* 78 (2017): 179–92.

Columeau, Philippe. *Alimentation carnée en Gaule du sud (VIIe s. av. J.-C.–XIVe s.).* Travaux de Centre Camille Jullian 29. Aix-en-Provence: Presses universitaires de Provence, 2002; online edition 2013, http://books.openedition.org/pup/609.

Conant, Jonathan. *Staying Roman: Conquest and Identity in North Africa and the Mediterranean, 439–700.* Cambridge: Cambridge University Press, 2012.

Contreni, John J. "Carolingian Biblical Culture." In *Iohannes Scottus Eriugena: The Bible and Hermeneutics,* edited by Gerd Van Riel, Carlos Steel, and James McEvoy, 1–23. Leuven: Leuven University Press, 1996.

Cook, David. *Studies in Muslim Apocalyptic.* Princeton, N.J.: Darwin Press, 2002.

Costambeys, Marios. "Disputes and Courts in Lombard and Carolingian Central Italy." *Early Medieval Europe* 15 (2007): 265–89.

———. "Settlement, Taxation, and the Condition of the Peasantry in Post-Roman Central Italy." *Journal of Agrarian Change* 9 (2009): 92–119.

Costambeys, Marios, Matthew Innes, and Simon MacLean. *The Carolingian World.* Cambridge: Cambridge University Press, 2011.

Cowles, Henry. *The Scientific Method: An Evolution of Thinking from Darwin to Dewey.* Cambridge: Harvard University Press, 2020.

Crabtree, Pam J. "Agricultural Innovation and Socio-Economic Change in Early Medieval Europe: Evidence from Britain and France." *World Archaeology* 42 (2010): 122–36.

———. "Production and Consumption in an Early Complex Society: Animal Use in Middle Saxon East Anglia." *World Archaeology* 28 (1996): 58–75.

———. *West Stow, Suffolk: Early Anglo-Saxon Animal Husbandry.* East Anglian Archaeology Report 47. Ipswich, UK: Suffolk County Planning Department, 1987.

Cracco Ruggini, Lellia. *Economia e società nell' "Italia Annonaria": rapporti fra agricoltura e commercio dal IV al VI secolo d.C.* Rev. ed. Bari: Edipuglia, 1995; orig. publ. 1961.

Crane, Susan. *Animal Encounters: Contacts and Concepts in Medieval Britain.* Philadelphia: University of Pennsylvania Press, 2013.

———. "Medieval Animal Studies: Dogs at Work." *Oxford Handbooks Online.* May 2015. DOI: 10.1093/oxfordhb/9780199935338.013.103.

Crary, Alice. *Inside Ethics: On the Demands of Moral Thought.* Cambridge: Harvard University Press, 2016.

Crawford, Michael H. *Roman Republican Coinage.* 2 vols. Cambridge: Cambridge University Press, 1974.

Cronon, William. *Changes in the Land: Indians, Colonists, and the Ecology of New England.* New York: Hill and Wang, 1983.

———. *Nature's Metropolis: Chicago and the Great West.* New York: Norton, 1990.

Crosby, Alfred W. *The Columbian Exchange: Biological and Cultural Consequences of 1492.* Westport, Conn.: Greenwood, 1972.

———. *Ecological Imperialism: The Biological Expansion of Europe, 900–1900.* Cambridge: Cambridge University Press, 1986.

Čverný, Jaroslav, Hynek Burda, Miloš Ježek, Tomáš Kušta, Václav Husinec, Petra Nováková, Vlastimil Hart, Veronika Harvtová, Sabine Begall, and E. Pascal Malkemper. "Magnetic Alignment in Warthogs *Phacochoerus africanus* and Wild Boars *Sus scrofa.*" *Mammal Review* 47 (2017): 1–5.

Dall'Olio, Lisa, and Manuele Putti. "Bioarcheologia in un sito di potere altomedievale (VII–X secolo): il caso di Miranduolo." In *VII Congresso Nazionale di Archeologia Medievale,* edited by Paul Arthur and Marco Leo Imperiale, 1:401–5. Florence: All'Insegna del Giglio, 2015.

Dal Santo, Matthew. *Debating the Saints' Cult in the Age of Gregory the Great.* Oxford: Oxford University Press, 2012.

———. "The God-Protected Empire? Skepticism Towards the Cult of the Saints in Early Byzantium." In *An Age of Saints? Power, Conflict and Dissent in Early Medieval Christianity,* edited by Peter Sarris, Matthew Dal Santo, and Phil Booth, 129–49. Leiden: Brill, 2011.

Daston, Lorraine, and Peter Galison. *Objectivity.* Cambridge: MIT Press, 2007.

Daston, Lorraine, and Katherine Park. *Wonders and the Order of Nature, 1150–1750.* New York: Zone, 1998.

Davies, Wendy. "Monastic Landscapes and Society." In *The Oxford Handbook of Medieval Christianity,* edited by John Arnold, 132–47. Oxford: Oxford University Press, 2014.

———. *Windows on Justice in Northern Iberia, 800–1000.* London: Routledge, 2016.

Deichmann, Friedrich Wilhelm. *Ravenna: Hauptstadt des spätantiken Abendlandes.* 3 vols. Wiesbaden: Franz Steiner, 1969–1989.

Deines, Roland. "How Long? God's Revealed Schedule for Salvation and the Outbreak of the Bar Kokhba Revolt." In *Judaism and Crisis: Crisis as a Catalyst in Jewish Cultural History,* edited by Armin Lange, K. F. Diethard Römheld, and Matthias Weigold, 201–34. Göttingen: Vandenhoeck & Ruprecht, 2011.

Deliyannis, Deborah Mauskopf. *Ravenna in Late Antiquity.* Cambridge: Cambridge University Press, 2010.

Depreux, Philippe. "Raban, l'abbé, l'archevêque: Le champ d'action d'un grand ecclésiastique dans la société carolingienne." In *Raban Maur et son temps,* edited by Philippe Depreux, Stéphane Lebecq, Michel J.-L. Perrin, and Olivier Szerwiniack, 49–61. Turnhout: Brepols, 2010.

Depreux, Philippe, François Bougard, and Régine Le Jan, eds. *Les élites et leurs espaces: Mobilité, rayonnement, domination, du VIᵉ au XIᵉ siècle.* Turnhout: Brepols, 2007.

Derby, Lauren. "Bringing the Animals Back In: Writing the History of Quadrupeds into the Environmental History of Latin America and the Caribbean." *History Compass* 9, no. 8 (2011): 602–21.

Deschler-Erb, Sabine. "Animal Husbandry in Roman Switzerland: State of Research and New Perspectives." *European Journal of Archaeology* 20, no. 3 (2017): 416–30.

De Venuto, Giovanni. "Carne, lane e pellame nell'Italia del medio e basso versante adriatico, tra X e XV secolo." *European Journal of Postclassical Archaeologies* 3 (2013): 199–219.

Devèze, Michel. "Forêts françaises et forêts allemandes: Étude historique comparée (1ʳᵉ partie)." *Revue Historique* 235 (1966): 347–80.

Devroey, Jean-Pierre. *Puissants et misérables: Système social et monde paysan dans l'Europe des Francs (VIᵉ–IXᵉ siècles).* Louvain-la-Neuve: Académie Royale de Belgique, 2006.

Díaz, Pablo C., and Iñaki Martín Viso. "Una contabilidad esquiva: las pizarras numerales visigodas y el caso de El Cortinal de San Juan (Salvatierra de Tormes, España)." In Díaz and Martín Viso, *Between Taxation and Rent,* 221–50.

Díaz, Pablo C., and Iñaki Martín Viso, eds. *Between Taxation and Rent: Fiscal Problems from Late Antiquity to Early Middle Ages / Entre el impuesto y la renta: Problemas de la fiscalidad tardoantigua y altomedieval.* Bari: Edipuglia, 2011.

Dick, Stephanie. "Childerich und Chlodwig: Fränkische Herrschafts-und Gesellschaftsorganisation um 500." In Meier and Patzold, *Chlodwigs Welt,* 365–81.

Diefenbach, Steffen. "'Bischofsherrschaft': Zur Transformation der politischen Kultur im spätantiken und frühmittelalterlichen Gallien." In *Gallien in Spätantike und Frühmittelalter: Kulturgeschichte einer Region*, edited by Steffan Diefenbach and Gernot Michael Müller, 91–149. Berlin: De Gruyter, 2013.

Diem, Albrecht. "Disimpassioned Monks and Flying Nuns: Emotion Management in Early Medieval Rules." In *Funktionsräume, Wahrnehmungsräume, Gefühlsräume: Mittelalterliche Lebensformen zwischen Kloster und Hof*, edited by Christina Lutter, 17–39. Munich: Oldenbourg, 2011.

———. *Das monastische Experiment: Die Rolle der Keuschheit bei der Entstehung des westliche Klosterwesens*. Münster: LIT, 2005.

———. "Rewriting Benedict: The *Regula cuiusdam ad virgines* and Intertextuality as Tool to Construct a Monastic Identity." *Journal of Medieval Latin* 17 (2007): 313–28.

Dierkens, Alain, Claire Le Bec, and Patrick Périn. "Sacrifice animal et offrandes alimentaires en Gaule mérovingienne." In *Archéologie du sacrifice animal en Gaule romaine: Rituels et pratiques alimentaires*, edited by Sébastien Lepetz and William van Andriga, 279–99. Montagnac: Mergoil, 2008.

Dinzelbacher, Peter. "Animal Trials: An Interdisciplinary Approach." *Journal of Interdisciplinary History* 32 (2002): 405–21.

Dobney, Keith, and Anton Ervynck. "Interpreting Developmental Stress in Archaeological Pigs: The Chronology of Linear Enamel Hypoplasia." *Journal of Archaeological Science* 27 (2000): 597–607.

Dobney, Keith, Deborah Jaques, James Barrett, and Cluny Johnstone. *Farmers, Monks, and Aristocrats: The Environmental Archaeology of Anglo-Saxon Flixborough*. Oxford: Oxbow, 2007.

Doll, Monika. "'Im Essen jedoch konnte er nicht so enthaltsam sein . . . ': Fleischverzehr in der Karolingerzeit." In *799: Kunst und Kultur der Karolingerzeit: Karl der Große und Papst Leo III. in Paderborn. Beiträge zum Katalog der Ausstellung, Paderborn 1999*, edited by Christoph Stiegemann and Matthias Wemhoff, 445–49. Mainz: Philipp von Zabern, 1999.

Doody, Aude. *Pliny's Encyclopedia: The Reception of the "Natural History."* Cambridge: Cambridge University Press, 2010.

Dorofeeva, Anna. "Miscellanies, Christian Reform and Early Medieval Encyclopaedism: A Reconsideration of the Pre-Bestiary Latin *Physiologus* Manuscripts." *Historical Research* 90 (2017): 665–82.

Drake, Anna, David Fraser, and Daniel M. Weary. "Parent-Offspring Resource Allocation in Domestic Pigs." *Behavioral Ecology and Sociobiology* 62, no. 3 (2008): 309–19.

Duby, Georges. *L'économie rurale et la vie des campagnes dans l'occident médiéval (France, Angleterre, Empire, IXᵉ–XVᵉ siècles: Essai de synthèse et perspectives de recherches*. Paris: Aubier, 1962.

DuCange, Charles du Fresne, et al. *Glossarium mediæ et infimæ latinitatis.* Niort: L. Favre, 1883–1887.

Duque, Adriano. "Staging Martyrdom in the Trial of El Niño de La Guardia." *Journal of Medieval Iberian Studies* 10 (2018): 88–105.

Dyer, Joseph. "Salt-Making at Droitwich, Worcestershire, in the Fourteenth Century." *Transactions of the Worcestershire Archaeological Society,* 3rd ser., 19 (2004): 133–39.

Eastwood, Bruce. *Ordering the Heavens: Roman Astronomy and Cosmology in the Carolingian Renaissance.* Leiden: Brill, 2007.

Effenberger, Arne. "Byzantinische Kunstwerke im Besitz deutscher Kaiser, Bischöfe und Klöster im Zeitalter der Ottonen." In *Bernward von Hildesheim,* 1:145–59.

Effros, Bonnie. *Uncovering the Germanic Past: Merovingian Archaeology in France, 1830–1914.* Oxford: Oxford University Press, 2012.

Eldevik, John. *Episcopal Power and Ecclesiastical Reform in the German Empire: Tithes, Lordship, and Community, 950–1150.* Cambridge: Cambridge University Press, 2012.

Electronic Sawyer, The: Online Catalogue of Anglo-Saxon Charters. https://esawyer.lib .cam.ac.uk. Last updated 1 October 2010. Revised and expanded version of Peter Sawyer, *Anglo-Saxon Charters: An Annotated List and Bibliography.* London: Royal Historical Society, 1968.

Elmshäuser, Konrad, and Andreas Hedwig. *Studien zum Polyptychon von Saint-Germain-des-Prés.* Cologne: Böhlau, 1993.

Elsner, Jás. "Sacrifice in Late Roman Art." In *Greek and Roman Animal Sacrifice: Ancient Victims, Modern Observers,* edited by Christopher A. Faraone and F. S. Naiden, 120–63. Cambridge: Cambridge University Press, 2012.

Enders, Jody. "Homicidal Pigs and the Antisemitic Imagination." *Exemplaria* 14 (2002): 201–38.

Enghoff, Inge Bødker. *Hunting, Fishing and Animal Husbandry at the Farm Beneath the Sand, Western Greenland: An Archaeozoological Analysis of a Norse Farm in the Western Settlement.* Copenhagen: Danish Polar Center, 2003.

Ennaïfer, M. "La Maison des deuz chasses à Kélibia." In *La mosaïque gréco-romaine VII, Tunis 3–7 octobre 1994,* 233–48. Tunis: Institut National du Patrimoine, 1999.

Epstein, Stephan R. "Regional Fairs, Institutional Innovation, and Economic Growth in Late Medieval Europe." *Economic History Review,* n.s. 47 (1994): 459–82.

Epstein, Steven A. *The Medieval Discovery of Nature.* Cambridge: Cambridge University Press, 2012.

Ervynck, Anton, An Lentacker, Gundula Müldner, Mike Richards, and Keith Dobney. "An Investigation into the Transition from Forest Dwelling Pigs to Farm Animals in Medieval Flanders, Belgium." In Albarella, Dobney, et al., *Pigs and Humans,* 171–93.

Escalona, Julio, and Andrew Reynolds. eds. *Scale and Scale Change in the Early Middle Ages: Exploring Landscape, Local Society, and the World Beyond.* Turnhout: Brepols, 2011.

Esders, Stefan. "Eliten und Raum nach frühmittelalterlichen Rechtstexten: Überlegungen zu einem Spannungsverhältnis." In Depreux, Bougard, and Le Jan, *Les élites et leurs espaces*, 11–29.

————. "Nordwestgallien um 500: Von der militarisierten spätrömischen Provinzgesellschaft zur erweiterten Militäradministration des merowingischen Königtums." In Meier and Patzold, *Chlodwigs Welt*, 339–61.

————. *Römische Rechtstradition und merowingisches Königtum: Zum Rechtscharakter politischer Herrschaft in Burgund im 6. und 7. Jahrhundert.* Göttingen: Vandenhoeck & Ruprecht, 1997.

Esders, Stefan, Yitzhak Hen, Laury Sarti, and Yaniv Fox, eds. *East and West in the Early Middle Ages: The Merovingian Kingdoms in Mediterranean Perspective.* Cambridge: Cambridge University Press, 2019.

Espelta, Josep Maria, Pilar Cortés, Roberto Molowny-Horas, Belén Sánchez-Humanes, and Javier Retana. "Masting Mediated by Summer Drought Reduces Acorn Predation in Mediterranean Oak Forests." *Ecology* 89 (2008): 805–17.

Essig, Mark. *Lesser Beasts: A Snout-to-Tail History of the Humble Pig.* New York: Basic, 2015.

Ettel, Peter. *Karlburg—Rosstal—Oberammerthal: Studien zum frühmittelalterlichen Burgenbau in Nordbayern.* 2 vols. Rahden: Leidorf, 2001.

Evans, D. H., and Christopher Loveluck. *Life and Economy at Early Medieval Flixborough, c. AD 600–1000: The Artefact Evidence.* Oxford: Oxbow, 2009.

Evans, Jeremy. "Balancing the Scales: Romano-British Pottery in Early Late Antiquity." *Late Antique Archaeology* 10 (2013): 425–50.

Evardsson, Ragnar, and Thomas H. McGovern. "Hrísheimar 2006: Interim Report." Unpublished field report, 31 May 2007. http://www.nabohome.org/publications/fieldreports/Hrisheimar2006InterimReportMcGeditMay07.pdf. Accessed 7 March 2018.

Fabre, Laurent. "Écologie des forêts et exploitation des bois: L'apport de l'anthracologie." In *Habitats, nécropoles et paysages dans la moyenne et la basse vallée du Rhône (VIIᵉ–XVᵉ s.): Contribution des travaux du TGV-Méditerranée à l'étude des sociétés rurales médiévales*, edited by Odile Maufras, 209–16. Paris: Éditions de la Maison des sciences de l'homme, 2006.

Fabre-Vassas, Claudine. *The Singular Beast: Jews, Christians, and the Pig.* Translated by Carol Volk. New York: Columbia University Press, 1997.

Faith, Rosamond. "Farms and Families in Ninth-Century Provence." *Early Medieval Europe* 18 (2010): 175–201.

Farnum, Jerome H. *The Positioning of the Roman Imperial Legions.* Oxford: Archaeopress, 2005.

Faust, Avraham. "Pigs in Space (and Time): Pork Consumption and Identity Negotiations in the Late Bronze and Iron Ages of Ancient Israel." *Near Eastern Archaeology* 84, no. 1 (2018): 276–99.

Fentress, E., A. Drine, and R. Holod, eds. *An Island Through Time: Jerba Studies.* Vol. 1, *The Punic and Roman Periods.* Portsmouth, R.I.: Journal of Roman Archaeology, 2009.

Fentress, Elizabeth, Caroline Goodson, and Marco Maiuro, eds. *Villa Magna: An Imperial Estate and Its Legacies; Excavations 2006–10.* London: British School at Rome, 2016.

Fenwick, Corisande. "From Africa to Ifrīqiya: Settlement and Society in Early Medieval North Africa (650–800)." *Al-Masāq* 25 (2013): 9–33.

Fernández, Damián. *Aristocrats and Statehood in Western Iberia, 300–600 C.E.* Philadelphia: University of Pennsylvania Press, 2017.

———. "Statehood, Taxation, and State Infrastructural Power in Visigothic Iberia." In *Ancient States and Infrastructural Power: Europe, Asia, and America,* edited by Clifford Ando and Seth Richardson, 243–71. Philadelphia: University of Pennsylvania Press, 2017.

Fernández-Galiano, Dimas. "La villa de Materno." In *Mosaicos romanos: Actas de la I Mesa Redonda Hispano-Francesa sobre Mosaicos Romanos habida en Madrid en 1985,* 255–69. Madrid: Asociación Española del Mosaico, 1989.

Fernández-Ochoa, Carmen, and Ángel Morillo. "Walls in the Urban Landscape of Late Roman Spain: Defense and Imperial Strategy." In *Hispania in Late Antiquity,* edited by Kim Bowes and Michael Kulikowski, 299–340. Leiden: Brill, 2005.

Ferreiro, Alberto. "*De prohibitione carnis:* Meat Abstention and the Priscillianists." *Zeitschrift für antikes Christentum* 11 (2008): 464–78.

Few, Martha, and Zeb Tortorici, eds. *Centering Animals in Latin American History.* Durham, N.C.: Duke University Press, 2013.

Focardi, S., F. Morimando, S. Capriotti, A. Ahmed, and P. Genov. "Cooperation Improves the Access of Wild Boars (*Sus scrofa*) to Food Sources." *Behavioural Processes* 121 (2015): 80–86.

Foltz, Richard C. *Animals in Islamic Tradition and Muslim Cultures.* Oxford: Oneworld, 2006.

Fonrobert, Charlotte Elisheva, and Martin S. Jaffee, eds. *The Cambridge Companion to the Talmud and Rabbinic Literature.* Cambridge: Cambridge University Press, 2007.

Forest, V. "Alimentation carnée dans le Languedoc médiéval: Les témoignages archéozoologiques des vertébrés supérieurs." *Archéologie du Midi Médiéval* 15-16 (1997–1998): 141–60.

Forest, Vianney, and Isabelle Rodet-Belarbi. "Viandes animales dans le Languedoc-Roussillon rural médiéval: Bilan 2010." In *Processing, Storage, Distribution of Food: Food in the Medieval Rural Environment,* edited by Jan Klápště and Petr Sommer, 91–112. Turnhout: Brepols, 2011.

Förstemann, Ernst. *Altdeutsches Namenbuch.* Vol. 1: *Personennamen.* Bonn: Hanstein, 1901; repr., Munich: Fink, 1966.

Foti, Giuseppina. "Funzioni e caratteri del 'pullarius' in età repubblicana e imperiale." *ACME: Annali della Facoltà di Lettere e Filosofia dell'Università degli Studi di Milano* 64 (2011): 89–121.

Fowden, Garth. *Before and After Muḥammad: The First Millennium Refocused*. Princeton: Princeton University Press, 2014.

Fox, Michael. "Alcuin the Exegete: The Evidence of the *Quaestiones in Genesim*." In *The Study of the Bible in the Carolingian Era*, edited by Celia Chazelle and Burton Van Name Edwards, 39–60. Turnhout: Brepols, 2003.

Fox, Yaniv. *Power and Religion in Merovingian Gaul: Columbanian Monasticism and the Frankish Elites*. Cambridge: Cambridge University Press, 2014.

Francovich, Riccardo, and Richard Hodges. *Villa to Village: The Transformation of the Roman Countryside in Italy, c. 400–1000*. Duckworth Debates in Archaeology. London: Duckworth, 2003.

Francovich, Riccardo, and Marco Valenti. *Poggio Imperiale a Poggibonsi: Il territoria, lo scavo, il parco*. Milan: Silvana Editoriale, 2007.

Frank, Georgia. "'Taste and See': The Eucharist and the Eyes of Faith in the Fourth Century." *Church History* 70 (2001): 619–43.

Frazier, Ian. "Hogs Wild." *New Yorker*, 12 December 2005.

Frémondeau, Delphine, Pauline Nuviala, and Colin Duval. "Pigs and Cattle in Gaul: The Role of Gallic Societies in the Evolution of Husbandry Practices." *European Journal of Archaeology* 20, no. 3 (2017): 494–509.

French, Roger. *Ancient Natural History: Histories of Nature*. London: Routledge, 1994.

Freu, Christel. *Les figures du pauvre dans les sources italiennes de l'antiquité tardive*. Paris: De Boccard, 2007.

Fricke, Beate. "Jesus Wept! On the History of Anthropophagy in Christianity: A New Reading of a Miniature from the Gospel Book of Otto III as *Kippfigur*." *RES: Anthropology and Aesthetics* 59–60 (2011): 192–205.

Fruscione, Daniela. "Malbergische Glossen." In *Handwörterbuch zur deutschen Rechtsgeschichte*, 3:1210–15. 2nd ed. Berlin: Erich Schmidt, 2016.

Fulton, Rachel. "'Taste and See That the Lord Is Sweet' (Ps. 33:9): The Flavor of God in the Monastic West." *Journal of Religion* 86 (2006): 169–204.

Gaborit-Chopin, Danielle. "Les trois fragments d'ivoire de Berlin, Paris et Nevers." In *Byzantine East, Latin West: Art-Historical Studies in Honor of Kurt Weitzmann*, edited by Doula Mouriki, Christopher Moss, and Katherine Kiefer, 49–63. Princeton: Princeton University Department of Art and Archaeology, 1995.

Galinié, Henri, ed. *Tours antique et médiéval: Lieux de vie, temps de la ville*. Revue archéologique du Centre de la France, Supplement 30. Tours: FERACF, 2007.

Gamelon, Marlène, Jean-Michel Gaillard, Eric Baubet, Sébastien Devillard, Ludovic Say, Serge Brandt, and Olivier Gimienz. "The Relationship Between Phenotypic Variation Among Offspring and Mother Body Mass in Wild Boar: Evidence of Coin-Flipping?" *Journal of Animal Ecology* 82 (2013): 937–45.

Gameson, Richard. "The Material Fabric of Early British Books." In *The Cambridge History of the Book in Britain*. Vol. 1, *c. 400–1100*, edited by Richard Gameson, 13–93. Cambridge: Cambridge University Press, 2012.

Garcia, Maxime, Bruno Gingras, Daniel L. Bowling, Christian T. Herbst, Markus Boeckle, Yann Locatelli, and W. Tecumseh Fitch. "Structural Classification of Wild Boar (*Sus scrofa*) Vocalizations." *Ethology* 122, no. 4 (2016): 329–42.

García-Blanco, Víctor, and Sara Vila. "Restos animales y vegetales del yacimiento visigodo de Prado de los Galápagos, interpretación ambiental." In *La investigación arqueológica de la época visigoda en comunidad de Madrid*, 962–72. Zona Arqueológica 8.3. Alcalá de Henares: Museo Arqueológico Regional, 2006.

García-Collado, Maite Iris. "Food Consumption Patterns and Social Inequality in an Early Medieval Rural Community in the Centre of the Iberian Peninsula." In *Social Complexity in Early Medieval Rural Communities: The North-western Iberia Archaeological Record*, edited by Juan António Quirós Castillo, 59–78. Oxford: Archaeopress, 2016.

García de Cortázar, José Angel. *La sociedad rural en la España medieval*. Madres: Siglo Veintiuno Editores, 1989.

García Garagarza, León. "The Year the People Turned into Cattle: The End of the World in New Spain, 1558." In Few and Tortorici, *Centering Animals in Latin American History*, 31–61.

García García, Marcos. "Explotación y consumo de los animales en el sudeste de la península ibérica durante la alta edad media (siglos VII–XII): Perspectivas históricas y arqueozoológicas." Ph.D. Diss., University of Granada, 2019.

———. "Some Remarks on the Provision of Animal Products to Urban Centres in Medieval Islamic Iberia: The Cases of Madinat Ilbirah (Granada) and Cercadilla (Cordova)." *Quaternary International* 460 (2017): 86–96.

Garroway, Joshua. "The Invasion of a Mustard Seed: A Reading of Mark 5:1–20." *Journal for the Study of the New Testament* 32 (2009): 57–75.

Geltner, Guy. "Finding Matter out of Place: Bologna's *Fango* ('Dirt') Notary in the History of Premodern Public Health." In *The Far-Sighted Gaze of Capital Cities: Essays in Honor of Francesca Bocchi*, edited by Rosa Smurra, Hubert Houben, and Manuela Ghizzoni, 307–21. Rome: Viella, 2014.

———. "Healthscaping a Medieval City: Lucca's *Curia viarum* and the Future of Public Health History." *Urban History* 40 (2013): 395–415.

———. *Roads to Health: Infrastructure and Urban Wellbeing in Later Medieval Italy*. Philadelphia: University of Pennsylvania Press, 2019.

Gentili, François. "L'organisation spatiale des habitats ruraux du haut Moyen Âge: L'apport des grandes fouilles préventives. Deux exemples franciliens: Serris 'Les Ruelles' (Seine-et-Marne) et Villers-le-Sex (Val-d'Oise)." In *Trente ans d'archéologie médiévale en France: Un bilan pour un avenir*, edited by Jean Chapelot, 119–31. Caen: Publications du CRAHM, 2010.

Gentili, François, and Alain Valais. "Composantes aristocratiques et organisation de l'espace au sein de grands habitats ruraux du haut Moyen Âge." In Depreux, Bougard, and Le Jan, *Les élites et leurs espaces*, 99–134.

Gentili, Gino Vinicio. *La Villa Romana di Piazza Armerina, Palazzo Erculio*. 3 vols. Osimo: Fondazione Don Carlo, 1999.

Gilchrist, Roberta. "A Reappraisal of Dinas Powys: Local Exchange and Specialized Livestock Production in 5th- to 7th-Century Wales." *Medieval Archaeology* 32 (1988): 50–62.

Gillerman, Dorothy. *Gothic Sculpture in America*. Vol. 1, *The New England Museums*. New York: Garland, 1989.

Gitner, Adam. "Porcus Does Not Just Mean Piglet Either: The TLL Pigs Up the Gauntlet in Our Pugna Porcorum." *In Medias Res*, 25 February 2019. https://medium.com/in-medias-res/schweinerei-at-the-tll-e74430f5146d.

Godfrey-Smith, Peter. *Other Minds: The Octopus, the Sea, and the Deep Origins of Consciousness*. New York: Farrar, Straus and Giroux, 2016.

Goffart, Walter A. *Barbarian Tides: The Migration Age and the Later Roman Empire*. Philadelphia: University of Pennsylvania Press, 2006.

Goldberg, Eric J. "'The Hunt Belongs to Man': Some Neglected Treatises Related to Hunting and Falconry from the Court of Louis the German." In *Discovery and Distinction in the Early Middle Ages: Studies in Honor of John J. Contreni*, edited by Cullen J. Chandler and Steven A. Stofferahn, 31–56. Kalamazoo, Mich.: Medieval Institute Publications, 2013.

———. "Louis the Pious and the Hunt." *Speculum* 88 (2013): 613–43.

Goodson, Caroline. "Garden Cities in Early Medieval Italy." In *Italy and Early Medieval Europe: Papers for Chris Wickham*, edited by Ross Balzaretti, Julia Barrow, and Patricia Skinner, 339–55. Oxford: Oxford University Press, 2018.

———. *Urban Gardening in Early Medieval Italy*. Cambridge: Cambridge University Press, 2020.

Gorman, Michael. "The Commentary of Genesis of Claudius of Turin and Biblical Studies Under Louis the Pious." *Speculum* 72 (1997): 279–329.

———. "Wigbod, Charlemagne's Commentator: The *Quaestiunculae super evangelium*." *Revue Bénédictine* 114 (2004): 5–74.

———. "Wigbod and Biblical Studies Under Charlemagne." *Revue Bénédictine* 107 (1997): 40–76.

Goursot, Charlotte, Sandra Düpjan, Armin Tuchscherer, Birger Puppe, and Lisette M. C. Leliveld. "Behavioural Lateralization in Domestic Pigs (*Sus scrofa*)—Variations Between Motor Functions and Individuals." *Laterality: Asymmetries of Body, Brain and Cognition* 23, no. 5 (2018): 576–98.

Grant, Raymond. *The Royal Forests of England*. Wolfeboro Falls, N.H.: Alan Sutton, 1991.

Grassi, Francesca. *L'insediamento medievale nelle Colline Metallifere (Toscana, Italia): Il sito minerario di Rochette Pannocchieschi dall'VIII al XIV secolo*. Oxford: BAR, 2013.

Grau-Sologestoa, Idoia. "Faunal Remains and Social Inequality in the Basque Country During the Early Middle Ages." In *Social Complexity in Early Medieval Rural Communities: The North-western Iberia Archaeological Record*, edited by Juan António Quirós Castillo, 47–58. Oxford: Archaeopress, 2016.

———. "Socio-Economic Status and Religious Identity in Medieval Iberia: The Zooarchaeological Evidence." *Environmental Archaeology* 22 (2017): 189–99.

———. *The Zooarchaeology of Medieval Álava in Its Iberian Context.* Oxford: BAR, 2015.

Grau-Sologestoa, Idoia, and Juan António Quirós Castillo. "Peasant Economy in Late Roman Álava: Zooarcheology of Zornoztegi." *Archaeofauna* 26 (2017): 87–102.

Gravel, Martin. "Of Palaces, Hunts, and Pork Roast: Deciphering the Last Chapters of the Capitulary of Quierzy (*a.* 877)." *Florilegium* 29 (2012): 89–115.

Graves, H. B. "Behavior and Ecology of Wild and Feral Swine (*Sus scrofa*)." *Journal of Animal Science* 58 (1984): 482–92.

Greenfield, Haskel J. "Bone Consumption by Pigs in a Contemporary Serbian Village: Implications for the Interpretation of Prehistoric Faunal Assemblages." *Journal of Field Archaeology* 15 (1988): 473–79.

Grey, Cam. *Constructing Communities in the Late Roman Countryside.* Cambridge: Cambridge University Press, 2011.

Groot, Maaike. "Developments in Animal Husbandry and Food Supply in Roman Germania Inferior." *European Journal of Archaeology* 20, no. 3 (2017): 451–71.

———. "Surplus Production of Animal Products for the Roman Army in a Rural Settlement in the Dutch River Area." In Stallibrass and Thomas, *Feeding the Roman Army,* 83–98.

Grumett, David, and Rachel Muers. *Theology on the Menu: Asceticism, Meat and Christian Diet.* London: Routledge, 2010.

Guardia Pons, Milagros. *Los mosaicos de la antigüedad tardía en Hispania: Estudios de iconografía.* Barcelona: PPU, 1992.

Guélat, Michel, Christoph Brombacher, Claude Olive, and Lucia Wick. *Develier-Courtételle: Un habitat rural mérovingien.* Vol. 4, *Environnement et exploitation du terroir.* Cahier d'Archéologie Jurassienne 16. Porrentruy: Société jurassienne d'Émulation, 2008.

Hadjikoumis, Angelos. "Traditional Pig Herding Practices in Southwest Iberia: Questions of Scale and Zooarchaeological Implications." *Journal of Anthropological Archaeology* 31 (2012): 353–64.

Haldon, John. *The Empire That Would Not Die: The Paradox of Eastern Roman Survival, 640–740.* Cambridge: Harvard University Press, 2016.

Halfond, Gregory I. "A Hermeneutical Feast: Interreligious Dining in Early Medieval Conciliar Legislation." *Haskins Society Journal* 26 (2014): 31–45

Halsall, Guy. *Barbarian Migrations and the Roman West, 376–568.* Cambridge: Cambridge University Press, 2007.

————. *Cemeteries and Society in Merovingian Gaul: Selected Studies in History and Archaeology, 1992–2009.* Leiden: Brill, 2010.

————. "The Ostrogothic Military." In *A Companion to Ostrogothic Italy,* edited by Jonathan J. Arnold, M. Shane Bjornlie, and Kristina Sessa, 173–99. Leiden: Brill, 2016.

————. "The Preface to Book V of Gregory of Tours' *Histories:* Its Form, Context, and Significance." *English Historical Review* 122 (2007): 297–317.

Halstead, Paul, and Valasia Isaakidou. "A Pig Fed by Hand Is Worth Two in the Bush: Ethnoarchaeology of Pig Husbandry in Greece and Its Archaeological Implications." In *Ethnozooarchaeology: The Present and Past of Human-Animal Relationships,* edited by Umberto Albarella and Angela Trentacoste, 160–74. Oxford: Oxbow, 2011.

Hamerow, Helena. *Rural Settlements and Society in Anglo-Saxon England.* Oxford: Oxford University Press, 2012.

Hammon, Andy. "Understanding the Romano-British-Early Medieval Transition: A Zooarchaeological Perspective from Wroxeter (*Viroconium Cornoviorum*)." *Britannia* 42 (2011): 275–305.

Hammond, Clare, and Terry O'Connor. "Pig Diet in Medieval York: Carbon and Nitrogen Stable Isotopes." *Archaeological and Anthropological Sciences* 5, no. 2 (2013): 123–27.

Haraway, Donna. *When Species Meet.* Minneapolis: University of Minnesota Press, 2008.

Hardy, Alan, Bethan Mair Charles, and Robert J. Williams. *Death and Taxes: The Archaeology of a Middle Saxon Estate Centre at Higham Ferrers, Northamptonshire.* Oxford: Oxford Archaeology, 2007.

Har-Peled, Misgav. "Configurations porcines: Étiologies et jeux identitaires entre juifs, chrétiens et musulmans autour du cochon au Moyen Âge." In *Byzance et l'Europe: L'héritage historiographique d'Évelyne Patlagean,* edited by Claudine Delacroix-Besnier, 143–68. Paris: Centre d'études byzantines, néo-helléniques et sud-est européennes, 2016.

————. "The Dialogical Beast: The Identification of Rome with the Pig in Early Rabbinic Literature." Ph.D. Diss., Johns Hopkins University, 2013.

Harris, Marvin. *Good to Eat: Riddles of Food and Culture.* New York: Simon and Schuster, 1985.

Hartog, Hendrik. "Pigs and Positivism." *Wisconsin Law Review* 899 (1985): 899–935.

Harvey, P. D. A. "Rectitudines Singularum Personarum and Gerefa." *English Historical Review* 108 (1993): 1–22.

Harvey, Susan Ashbrook. *Scenting Salvation: Ancient Christianity and the Olfactory Imagination.* Berkeley: University of California Press, 2006.

Hasan-Roken, Galit. "An Almost Invisible Presence: Multilingual Puns in Rabbinic Literature." In Fonrobert and Jaffee, *The Cambridge Companion to the Talmud and Rabbinic Literature,* 222–39.

Hen, Yitzhak. "Food and Drink in Merovingian Gaul." In *Tätigkeitsfelder und Erfah-rungshorizonte des ländlichen Menschen in der frühmittelalterlichen Grundherrschaft (bis ca. 1000): Festschrift für Dieter Hägermann zum 65. Geburtstag*, edited by Brigitte Kasten, 99–110. Stuttgart: Franz Steiner, 2006.

———. *Roman Barbarians: The Royal Court and Culture in the Early Medieval West.* Basingstoke, UK: Palgrave Macmillan, 2007.

Herlihy, David J. "Attitudes Toward the Environment in Medieval Society." In *Historical Ecology: Essays on Environment and Social Change*, edited by Lester J. Bilsky, 100–116. Port Washington, N.Y.: Kennikat, 1980.

Heyse, Elisabeth. *Hrabanus Maurus' Enzyklopädie "De rerum naturis": Untersuchungen zu den Quellen und zur Methode der Kompilation.* Munich: Arbeo-Gesellschaft, 1969.

Hill, Philip V. *The Dating and Arrangement of the Undated Coins of Rome, A.D. 98–148.* London: Spink, 1970.

Hilton, R. H. *A Medieval Society: The West Midlands at the End of the Thirteenth Century.* London: Weidenfeld and Nicolson, 1966.

Hitchner, R. Bruce. "Image and Reality: The Changing Face of Pastoralism in the Tu-nisian High Steppe." In *Landuse in the Roman Empire*, edited by Jesper Carlsen, Peter Ørsted, and Jens Erik Skydsgaard, 27–43. Rome: "L'Erma" di Bretschneider, 1994.

———. "More Italy Than Province? Archaeology, Texts, and Culture Change in Roman Provence." *Transactions of the American Philological Association* 129 (1999): 375–79.

Hoffmann, Richard C. *An Environmental History of Medieval Europe.* Cambridge: Cam-bridge University Press, 2014.

Hoffmann-Salz, Julia. "Roms 'arabische' Grenze: Herrschaftsorganisation an der Ost-grenze des Reiches." In Meier and Patzold, *Chlodwigs Welt*, 269–92.

Höfinghoff, Hans. "Haustier und Herde: Die volkssprachigen Tierbezeichnungen in den frühmittelalterlichen Leges." Inaugural-Dissertation, Westfälischen Wilhelms-Universität, 1987.

Holmes, Brooke. "The Generous Text: Animal Intuition, Human Knowledge and Writ-ten Transmission in Pliny's Books on Medicine." In *Knowledge, Text and Practice in Ancient Medical Writing*, edited by Marco Formisano and Philip van der Eijk, 231–51. Cambridge: Cambridge University Press, 2017.

———. "The Poetic Logic of Negative Exceptionalism in Lucretius, Book Five." In *Lu-cretius: Poetry, Philosophy, Science*, edited by Daryn Lehoux, A. D. Morrison, and Aly-son Sharrock, 153–91. Oxford: Oxford University Press, 2013.

Holsinger, Bruce. "Of Pigs and Parchment: Medieval Studies and the Coming of the Animal." *PMLA* 124 (2009): 616–23.

Horden, Peregrine, and Nicholas Purcell. *The Corrupting Sea: A Study of Mediterranean History.* Oxford: Blackwell, 2000.

Horowitz, Alexandra. *Being a Dog: Following the Dog into a World of Smell.* New York: Scribner, 2016.

Horst, Koert van der. "The Utrecht Psalter: Picturing the Psalms of David." In *The Utrecht Psalter in Medieval Art: Picturing the Psalms of David*, edited by Koert van der Horst, William Noel, and Wilhelmina C. M. Wüstefeld, 22–84. 't Goy, Netherlands: HES, 1996.

Hosang, Elizabeth Boddens. "Will You Join Us for a Meal? Jewish and Christian Interaction in Early Council Texts." In *Sanctifying Texts, Transforming Rituals: Encounters in Liturgical Studies*, edited by Paul van Geest, Marcel Poorthuis, and Else Rose, 331–48. Leiden: Brill, 2017.

Humphrey, J. H., ed. *Excavations at Carthage . . . Conducted by the University of Michigan*. 7 vols. Ann Arbor: University of Michigan, 1975–1981.

Hurst, H. R. *Excavations at Carthage: The British Mission*. Vol. 2.1, *The Circular Harbor, North Side: The Site and Finds Other Than Pottery*. Oxford: Oxford University Press, 1994.

Hurst, H. R., and S. P. Rostams. *Excavations at Carthage: The British Mission*. Vol. 1.1, *The Avenue du Président Habib Bourguiba, Salammbo: The Site and Finds Other Than Pottery*. Sheffield: British Academy, 1984.

Hurst, J. D. "Fuel Supply and the Medieval Salt Industry in Droitwich." *Transactions of the Worcestershire Archaeological Society*, 3rd ser., 19 (2004): 111–32.

Igo, Sarah E. *The Averaged American: Surveys, Citizens, and the Making of a Mass Public*. Cambridge: Harvard University Press, 2007.

Ikeguchi, Mamoru. "Beef in Roman Italy." *Journal of Roman Archaeology* 30 (2017): 7–37.

Innes, Matthew. "Rituals, Rights and Relationships: Some Gifts and Their Interpretation in the Fulda Cartulary, c. 827." *Studia Historica: Historia Medieval* 31 (2013): 25–50.

Irmscher, Johannes. "Otto III. und Byzanz." In *Byzanz und das Abendland im 10. und 11. Jahrhundert*, edited by Evangelos Konstantinou, 207–29. Cologne: Böhlau, 1997.

Iwaszczuk, Urszula. "Animal Husbandry on the Polish Territory in the Early Middle Ages." *Quaternary International* 346 (2014): 69–101.

Izdebski, Adam, Jordan Pickett, Neil Roberts, and Tomasz Waliszewski. "The Environmental, Archaeological and Historical Evidence for Regional Climatic Changes and Their Societal Impacts in the Eastern Mediterranean in Late Antiquity." *Quaternary Science Reviews* 136 (2016): 189–208.

Jagt, Inge M. M. van der, Lisette M. Kootker, Thijs van Kolfschoten, Henk Kars, and Gareth R. Davies. "An Insight into Animal Exchange in Early Medieval Oegstgeest: A Combined Archaeozoological and Isotopic Approach." In *A Bouquet of Archaeozoological Studies: Essays in Honour of Wietske Prummel*, ed. D. C. M. Raemaekers, E. Esser, R. C. G. M. Lauwerier, and J. T. Zeiler, 139–49. Eelde: Barkhuis, 2012.

Janssen, Walter. "Das Tier im Spiegel der archäologischen Zeugnisse." In *L'uomo di fronte al mondo animale nell'alto medioevo*, 2:1231–1309. Settimane di Studio 31. Spoleto: Centro Italiano di Studi sull'Alto Medioevo, 1985.

Janssen, Walter, and Brigitte Janssen. *Die frühmittelalterliche Niederungsburg bei Haus Meer, Kreis Neuss: Archäologische und naturwissenschaftliche Untersuchungen.* Cologne: Rheinland-Verlag, 1999.

Jarnut, Jörg. "Die frühmittelalterliche Jagd unter rechts- und sozialgeschichtlichen Aspekten." In *L'uomo di fronte al mondo animale nell'alto medioevo,* 1:765–98. Settimane di Studio 31. Spoleto: Centro Italiano di Studi sull'Alto Medioevo, 1985.

Jiménez-Camino, Rafael, Darío Bernal Casasola, José Antonio Riquelme Cantal, Mila Soriguer, José Antonio Hernando, and Cristina Zabala Jiménez. "¿Continuidad o cambio en la dieta entre la población bizantina y paleoandalusí? Aproximación a partir del registro faunístico de dos intervenciones arqueológicas en Algeciras." In *Espacios urbanos en el occidente mediterráneo (s. VI–VIII),* edited by Alfonso García, 153–64. Toledo: Toletum Visigodo, 2010.

Johnson, Paul S., Stephen R. Shifley, and Robert Rogers. *The Ecology and Silviculture of Oaks.* 2nd ed. Wallingford, UK: CABI, 2009.

Johnson, Sarah Iles. *Ancient Greek Divination.* Malden, Mass.: Wiley-Blackwell, 2008.

Jones, A. H. M. *The Later Roman Empire, 284–602: A Social, Economic and Administrative Survey.* Baltimore: Johns Hopkins University Press, 1986; reprint of 1964 ed.

Jones, Glynis, Vanessa Straker, and Anne Davis. "Early Medieval Plant Use and Ecology." In *Aspects of Saxo-Norman London II: Finds and Environmental Evidence,* edited by Alan Vince, 347–85. London: London and Middlesex Archaeological Society, 1991.

Jones, Jennifer R., and Jacqui A. Mulville. "Norse Animal Husbandry in Liminal Environments: Stable Isotope Evidence from the Scottish North Atlantic Islands." *Environmental Archaeology* 23 (2018): 338–51.

Jones, Richard. "Understanding Medieval Manure." In *Manure Matters: Historical, Archaeological and Ethnographic Perspectives,* edited by Richard Jones, 145–58. Farnham: Ashgate, 2012.

Jong, Mayke de. *In Samuel's Image: Child Oblation in the Early Medieval West.* Leiden: Brill, 1996.

Jordan, William Chester. "Count Robert's 'Pet' Wolf." *Proceedings of the American Philosophical Society* 155 (2011): 404–17.

———. "The Historical Afterlife of Two Capetian Co-Kings Who Predeceased Their Fathers." In *Louis VII and His World,* edited by Michael L. Bardot and Laurence W. Mavin, 114–25. Leiden: Brill, 2018.

Jørgensen, Dolly. "Running Amuck? Urban Swine Management in Late Medieval England." *Agricultural History* 87 (2013): 429–51.

Jussen, Bernhard. "Chlodwig der Gallier. Zur Strukturgeschichte einer historischen Figur." In Meier and Patzold, *Chlodwigs Welt,* 27–43.

Kallala, Nabil, and Joan Sanmartí. *Althiburos I: La fouille dans l'aire du capitale et dans la nécropole méridionale.* Tarragona: Institut Català d'Arqueologia Clàssica, 2011.

———. *Althiburos II: L'aire du capitole et la nécropole méridionale: études.* Edited by Maria Carme Belarte. Tarragona: Institut Català d'Arqueologia Clàssica, 2016.

Kay, Sarah. *Animal Skins and the Reading Self in Medieval Latin and French Bestiaries.* Chicago: University of Chicago Press, 2017.

———. "Legible Skins: Animals and the Ethics of Medieval Reading." *postmedieval: a journal of medieval cultural studies* 2 (2011): 13–32.

Kaye, Joel. *Economy and Nature in the Fourteenth Century: Money, Market Exchange, and the Emergence of Scientific Thought.* Cambridge: Cambridge University Press, 1998.

Kearney, Milo. *The Role of Swine Symbolism in Medieval Culture.* Lewiston, N.Y.: Edwin Mellen, 1991.

Keefe, Patrick Radden. "The Family That Built an Empire of Pain." *New Yorker,* 30 October 2017.

Keller, Otto. *Die Antike Tierwelt.* 2 vols. Leipzig: Wilhelm Engelmann, 1909–1913.

Kelly, Fergus. *Early Irish Farming: A Study Based Mainly on the Law-Texts of the 7th and 8th Centuries AD.* Rev. ed. Dublin: Dublin Institute for Advanced Studies, 2000.

Kelly, Thomas Forest, ed. *Oral and Written Transmission in Chant.* Farnham: Ashgate, 2009.

Kerr, Thomas R. "Livestock Farming." In *Early Medieval Agriculture: Livestock and Cereal Production in Ireland, AD 400–1100,* edited by Finbar McCormick, 61–100. Oxford: Archaeopress, 2014.

Keskiaho, Jesse. "The Annotation of Patristic Texts as Curatorial Activity? The Case of Marginalia to Augustine's *De Genesi ad litteram* in Late Antiquity and the Middle Ages." In *The Annotated Book in the Early Middle Ages: Practices of Reading and Writing,* edited by Mariken Teeuwen and Irene van Renswoude, 673–704. Turnhout: Brepols, 2017.

Kessler, Herbert. *Seeing Medieval Art.* Peterborough, Ont.: Broadview, 2004.

Keßler, Lars, and Konrad Ott. "*Nec provident futuro tempori, sed quasi plane in diem vivant*—Sustainable Business in Columella's *De Re Rustica?*" In Schliephake, *Ecocriticism, Ecology, and the Cultures of Antiquity,* 197–216.

Kierdorf, Horst, and Uwe Kierdorf. "The Histiopathy of Fluorotic Dental Enamel in Wild Boar and Domestic Pigs." In Albarella, Dobney, et al., *Pigs and Humans,* 255–68.

King, Anthony. "Animals and the Roman Army: The Evidence of Animal Bones." In *The Roman Army as a Community,* edited by Adrian Goldsworthy and Ian Haynes, 139–49. Portsmouth, R.I.: Journal of Roman Archaeology, 1999.

———. "Diet in the Roman World: A Regional Inter-Site Comparison of the Mammal Bones." *Journal of Roman Archaeology* 12 (1999): 168–202.

Kittawornrat, Apisit, and Jeffrey J. Zimmerman. "Toward a Better Understanding of Pig Behavior and Pig Welfare." *Animal Health Research Reviews* 12 (2011): 25–32.

Klein, Julius. *The Mesta: A Study in Spanish Economic History, 1273–1836.* Cambridge: Harvard University Press, 1920.

Klingshirn, William. "Charity and Power: Caesarius of Arles and the Ransoming of Captives in Sub-Roman Gaul." *Journal of Roman Studies* 35 (1985): 183–203.

Kolias, Taxiarchis. "Essgewohnheiten und Verpflegung im byzantinischen Heer." In *Byzantios: Festschrift für Herbert Hunger zum 70. Geburtstag*, edited by Wolfram Hörandner, Johannes Koder, Otto Kresten, and Erich Trapp. 193–202. Vienna: Trapp, 1984.

Konstan, David. "Epicurean Happiness: A Pig's Life?" *Journal of Ancient Philosophy* 6, no. 1 (2012): 1–24.

Kornum, Birgitte R., and Gitte M. Knudsen. "Cognitive Testing of Pigs (*Sus scrofa*) in Translational Biobehavioral Research." *Neuroscience & Biobehavioral Reviews* 35 (2011): 437–51.

Kouli, Katerina, Alessia Masi, Anna Maria Mercuri, Assunta Florenzano, and Laura Sadori. "Regional Vegetation Histories: An Overview of the Pollen Evidence from the Central Mediterranean." *Late Antique Archaeology* 11 (2018): 69–82.

Krebs, Christopher. *A Most Dangerous Book: Tacitus's "Germania" from the Roman Empire to the Third Reich*. New York: Norton, 2011.

Kreiner, Jamie. "About the Bishop: The Episcopal Entourage and the Economy of Government in Post-Roman Gaul." *Speculum* 86 (2011): 321–60.

———. "A Generic Mediterranean: Hagiography in the Early Middle Ages." In Esders et al., *East and West in the Early Middle Ages*, 202–17.

———. "Pigs in the Flesh and Fisc: An Early Medieval Ecology." *Past & Present* 236 (2017): 3–42.

———. *The Social Life of Hagiography in the Merovingian Kingdom*. Cambridge: Cambridge University Press, 2014.

Kreiner, Jamie, and Helmut Reimitz, eds. *Motions of Late Antiquity: Essays on Religion, Politics, and Society in Honour of Peter Brown*. Turnhout: Brepols, 2016.

Kroll, Henriette. "Animals in the Byzantine Empire: An Overview of the Archaeozoological Evidence." *Archeologia Medievale* 39 (2012): 93–121.

Kuchenbuch, Ludolf. "Porcus donativus: Language Use and Gifting in Seigniorial Records Between the Eighth and the Twelfth Centuries." In *Negotiating the Gift: Pre-Modern Figurations of Exchange*, edited by Gadi Algazi, Valentin Groebner, and Bernhard Jussen, 193–246. Göttingen: Vandenhoeck & Ruprecht, 2003.

Kuhner, John Byron. "A Definitive Guide to Pig Latin: Final Thoughts on the Meaning of Porcus." *In Medias Res*, 25 March 2019. https://medium.com/in-medias-res/a-definitive-guide-to-pig-latin-7bfbd490a96d.

———. "Porcus Does Not Mean Pig: Reading Varro and Columella Can Be Surprising." *In Medias Res*, 4 February 2019. https://medium.com/in-medias-res/porcus-does-not-mean-pig-d413592572fb.

Lafferty, Sean D. W. *Law and Society in the Age of Theoderic the Great: A Study of the "Edictum Theoderici."* Cambridge: Cambridge University Press, 2013.

Lange, Nicholas de. "Jewish Attitudes to the Roman Empire." In *Imperialism in the Ancient World*, edited by P. D. A. Garnsey and C. R. Whittaker, 255–81. Cambridge: Cambridge University Press, 1978.

Larson, Greger, Umberto Albarella, Keith Dobney, and Peter Rowley-Conwy. "Current Views on *Sus* Phylogeography and Pig Domestication as Seen Through Modern mtDNA Studies." In Albarella, Dobney, et al., *Pigs and Humans*, 30–41.

Lavelle, Michael J., Nathan P. Snow, Justin W. Fischer, Joe M. Halseth, Eric H. Van-Natta, and Kurt C. VerCauteren. "Attractants for Wild Pigs: Current Use, Availability, Needs, and Future Potential." *European Journal of Wildlife Research* (2017) 63:86. https://doi.org/10.1007/s10344-017-1144-z.

Lebecq, Stéphane. "The Role of Monasteries in the Systems of Production and Exchange of the Frankish World Between the Seventh and the Beginning of the Ninth Centuries." In *The Long Eighth Century: Production, Distribution and Demand*, edited by Inge Lyse Hansen and Chris Wickham, 121–48. Leiden: Brill, 2000.

Leemans Pieter de, and Matthew Klemm. "Animals and Anthropology in Medieval Philosophy." In Resl, *A Cultural History of Animals*, 153–77.

Lehoux, Daryn. *What Did the Romans Know? An Inquiry into Science and Worldmaking*. Chicago: University of Chicago Press, 2012.

Leja, Meg. "Dissecting the Inner Life: Body and Soul, Medicine and Metaphor in the Carolingian Era." Ph.D. Diss., Princeton University, 2015.

———. "The Sacred Art: Medicine in the Carolingian Renaissance." *Viator* 27 (2016): 1–34.

Levy-Rubin, Milka. *Non-Muslims in the Early Islamic Empire: From Surrender to Coexistence*. Cambridge: Cambridge University Press, 2011.

Lim, Richard. "The Politics of Interpretation in Basil of Caesarea's *Hexaemeron*." *Vigiliae Christianae* 44 (1990): 351–70.

Lindberg, David C. *The Beginnings of Western Science: The European Scientific Tradition in Philosophical, Religious, and Institutional Context, 600 B.C. to A.D. 1450*. 2nd ed. Chicago: University of Chicago Press, 2007; 1st ed. 1992.

Long, Pamela O. *Openness, Secrecy, Authorship: Technical Arts and the Culture of Knowledge from Antiquity to the Renaissance*. Baltimore: Johns Hopkins University Press, 2001.

López-Sáez, José Antonio, Sebastián Pérez-Díaz, Didier Galop, Francisca Alba-Sánchez, and Daniel Abel-Schaad. "A Late Antique Vegetation History of the Western Mediterranean in Context." *Late Antique Archaeology* 11 (2018): 83–104.

Lorrio, Alberto J., Martín Almagro-Gorbea, and M. Dolores Sánchez de Prado. *El Molón (Camporrobles, Valencia): "Oppidum" prerromano y "ḥiṣn" islámico*. Camporrobles: Ayuntamiento de Camporrobles, 2009.

Lorzen, Sönke. "Der Königsforst (*forestis*) in den Quellen der Merowinger- und Karolingerzeit: Prolegomena zu einer Geschichte mittelalterlicher Nutzwälder." In *Mönchtum, Kirche, Herrschaft, 750–1000*, edited by Dieter R. Bauer, 261–85. Sigmaringen: Thorbecke, 1998.

Loseby, Simon T. "Post-Roman Economies." In *The Cambridge Companion to the Roman Economy*, edited by Walter Scheidel, 334–60. Cambridge: Cambridge University Press, 2012.

Loveluck, Christopher. "The Dynamics of Portable Wealth: Social Status and Competition in the Ports, Coastal Zones, and River Corridors of Northwest Europe, c. AD 650–1100." In *Acquérir, prélever, contrôler: Les ressources en compétition (400–1100)*, edited by Vito Loré, Geneviève Bührer-Thierry, and Régine Le Jan, 299–322. Turnhout: Brepols, 2017.

———. *Northwest Europe in the Early Middle Ages, c. AD 600–1150: A Comparative Archaeology.* Cambridge: Cambridge University Press, 2013.

———. "Problems of the Definition and Conceptualisation of Early Medieval Elites, AD 450–900: The Dynamics of the Archaeological Evidence." In Bougard, Goetz, and Le Jan, *Théorie et pratiques des élites*, 21–67.

———. *Rural Settlement, Lifestyles, and Social Change in the Later First Millennium AD: Anglo-Saxon Flixborough and Its Wider Context.* Oxford: Oxbow, 2007.

Loveluck, Christopher, and David Atkinson. *The Early Medieval Settlement Remains from Flixborough, Lincolnshire: The Occupation Sequence, c. AD 600–1000.* Oxford: Oxbow, 2007.

Loveluck, Christopher, and Dries Tys. "Coastal Societies, Exchange and Identity Along the Channel and Southern North Sea Shores of Europe, AD 600–1000." *Journal of Maritime Archaeology* 1 (2006): 140–69.

Lowe, E. A., ed. *Codices Latini Antiquiores: A Paleographical Guide to Latin Manuscripts Prior to the Ninth Century.* 11 vols. Oxford: Clarendon, 1934–1966.

Lucas, Gavin. *Hofstaðir: Excavations of a Viking Age Feasting Hall in North-Eastern Iceland.* Reykjavík: Institute of Archaeology, 2009.

MacKinnon, Michael. *The Excavations of San Giovanni di Ruoti 3: The Faunal and Plant Remains.* Toronto: University of Toronto Press, 2002.

———. "High on the Hog: Linking Zooarchaeological, Literary, and Artistic Data for Pig Breeds in Roman Italy." *American Journal of Archaeology* 105 (2001): 649–73.

———. *Production and Consumption of Animals in Roman Italy: Integrating the Zooarchaeological and Textual Evidence.* Portsmouth, R.I.: Journal of Roman Archaeology, 2004.

———. "'Romanizing' Ancient Carthage: Evidence from Zooarchaeological Remains." In *Anthropological Approaches to Zooarchaeology: Colonialism, Complexity, and Animal Transformations*, edited by D. Campana, P. Crabtree, S. D. deFrance, J. Lev-Tov, and A. M. Choyke, 168–77. Oxford: Oxbow, 2010.

Magnani, Eliana. "Almsgiving, Donatio *pro anima* and Eucharistic Offering in the Early Middle Ages of Western Europe (4th–9th Century)." In *Charity and Giving in Monotheistic Religions*, edited by Miriam Frenkel and Yaacov Lev, 111–24. Berlin: De Gruyter, 2009.

Malalana Ureña, Antonio, Rafael Barroso Cabrera, and Jorge Morín de Pablos. *La Quebrada II: un hábitat de la tardoantigüedad al siglo XI. La problemática de los "silos" en la Alta Edad Media hispana.* Alcázar de San Juan: MArq Audema, 2012.

Malone, Stephen James. *Legio XX Valeria Victrix: Prosopography, Archaeology and History*. Oxford: Archaeopress, 2006.

Maltby, Mark. "From Bovid to Beaver: Mammal Exploitation in Medieval Northwest Russia." In Albarella et al., *Oxford Handbook of Zooarchaeology*, 230–44.

Mancall, Peter C. "Pigs for Historians: *Changes in the Land* and Beyond." *William and Mary Quarterly*, 3rd ser., 67, no. 2 (2010): 347–75.

Marino, John A. *Pastoral Economics in the Kingdom of Naples*. Baltimore: Johns Hopkins University Press, 1988.

Martin, Kurt. *Die ottonischen Wandbilder der St. Georgskirche Reichenau-Oberzell*. Sigmaringen: Thorbecke, 1975.

Martín Viso, Iñaki. "Circuits of Power in a Fragmented Space: Gold Coinage in the Meseta del Duero (Sixth–Seventh Centuries)." In Escalona and Reynolds, *Scale and Scale Change in the Early Middle Ages*, 215–52.

———. "Un mundo en transformación: Los espacios rurales en la Hispania postromana (siglos V–VII)." In *Visigodos y Omeyas: El territorio*, edited by Luis Caballero Zoreda, Pedro Mateos Cruz, and Tomás Cordero Ruiz, 31–63. Mérida: Instituto de Arqueología, 2012.

Marzluff, John M. *Welcome to Subirdia: Sharing Our Neighborhoods with Wrens, Robins, Woodpeckers, and Other Wildlife*. New Haven: Yale University Press, 2014.

Marzluff, John M., and Tony Angell. *Gifts of the Crow: How Perception, Emotion, and Thought Allow Smart Birds to Behave Like Humans*. New York: Atria, 2012.

Mason, Sarah. "Acornutopia? Determining the Role of Acorns in Past Human Subsistence." In *Food in Antiquity*, edited by John Wilkins, David Harvey, and Mike Dobson, 12–24. Exeter: University of Exeter Press, 1995.

Masseti, Marco. "The Economic Role of *Sus* in Early Human Fishing Communities," in Albarella, Dobney et al., *Pigs and Humans*, 156–70.

Mattern, Susan. *The Prince of Medicine: Galen in the Roman Empire*. Oxford: Oxford University Press, 2013.

Mattingly, David J., ed. *The Archaeology of Fazzān*. 4 vols. Tripoli: Department of Antiquities; London: Society for Libyan Studies, 2003–2013.

Mattingly, David J., and R. Bruce Hitchner. "Roman Africa: An Archaeological Review." *Journal of Roman Studies* 85 (1995): 165–213.

McCormick, Finbar, and Emily Murray. *Excavations at Knowth 3: Knowth and the Zooarchaeology of Early Christian Ireland*. Dublin: Royal Irish Academy, 2007.

———. "The Zooarchaeology of Medieval Ireland." In Albarella et al., *Oxford Handbook of Zooarchaeology*, 195–213.

McCormick, Finbar, Aidan O'Sullivan, and Thomas R. Kerr. "The Farming Landscape of Early Medieval Ireland." In *Early Medieval Agriculture: Livestock and Cereal Production in Ireland, AD 400–1100*, edited by Finbar McCormick, 1–38. Oxford: Archaeopress, 2014.

McCormick, Michael. *Origins of the European Economy: Communications and Commerce, AD. 300–900.* Cambridge: Cambridge University Press, 2001.

McCrea, Heather. "Pest to Vector: Disease, Public Health, and the Challenges of State-Building in Yucatán, Mexico, 1833–1922." In Few and Tortorici, *Centering Animals in Latin American History,* 149–79.

McKitterick, Rosamond. *The Carolingians and the Written Word.* Cambridge: Cambridge University Press, 1989.

McLynn, Neil. *Ambrose of Milan: Church and Court in a Christian Capital.* Berkeley: University of California Press, 1994.

Meens, Rob. *Penance in Medieval Europe, 600–1200.* Cambridge: Cambridge University Press, 2014.

———. "Pollution in the Early Middle Ages: The Case of the Food Regulation in Penitentials." *Early Medieval Europe* 4 (1995): 3–19.

Meier, Mischa. "Nachdenken über 'Herrschaft': Die Bedeutung des Jahres 476." In Meier and Patzold, *Chlodwigs Welt,* 143–215.

Meier, Mischa, and Steffen Patzold, eds. *Chlodwigs Welt: Organisation von Herrscahft um 500.* Stuttgart: Franz Steiner, 2014.

Melville, Elinor G. K. *A Plague of Sheep: Environmental Consequences of the Conquest of Mexico.* Cambridge: Cambridge University, 1994.

Merchant, Carolyn. "The Violence of Impediments: Francis Bacon and the Origins of Experimentation." *Isis* 99 (2008): 731–60.

Mikhail, Alan. *Nature and Empire in Ottoman Egypt: An Environmental History.* New York: Cambridge University Press, 2011.

Miró i Miró, Josep M. "La fauna." In *Un abocador del segle V d.C. en el fórum provincial de Tàrraco,* 403–15. Tarragona: Taller Escola d'Arqueologia, 1989.

Mohamedi, A., A. Benmansour, A. A. Amamra, and E. Fentress. *Fouilles de Sétif (1977–1984).* Algiers: Agence Nationale d'Archéologie et de Protection des Sites et Monuments Historiques, 1991.

Montanari, Massimo. *L'alimentazione contadina nell'alto medioevo.* Naples: Liguori Editore, 1979.

———. *Cheese, Pears, and History in a Proverb.* Translated by Beth Archer Brombert. New York: Columbia University Press, 2010.

———. "La foresta come spazio economico e culturale." In *Uomo e spazio nell'alto medioevo,* 301–40. Settimane di studio 50. Spoleto: Centro Italiano di Studi sull'Alto Medioevo, 2003.

Morales Muñiz, Arturo, Marta Moreno García, Eufrasia Roselló Izquierdo, Laura Llorente Rodríguez, and Dolores Carmen Morales Muñiz. "711 ad. ¿El origen de una disyunción alimentaria?" In *711: arqueología e historia entre dos mundos,* 303–19. Zona Arqueológica 15.2. Alcalá de Henares: Museo Arqueológico Regional, 2011.

Morales Muñiz, Dolores Carmen. "Pig Husbandry in Visigoth Iberia: Fact and Theory." *Archaeofauna* 1 (1992): 147–55.

Morelle, Kevin, Tomasz Podgórski, Céline Prévot, Oliver Keuling, François Lehaire, and Philippe Lejeune. "Towards Understanding Wild Boar *Sus scrofa* Movement: A Synthetic Movement Ecology Approach." *Mammal Review* 45 (2015): 15–29.

Moreno García, Marta. "Gestión y aprovechamiento de cabañas ganaderas en al-Andalus: aportaciones desde la arqueozoología." *Debates de Arqueología Medieval* 3 (2013): 75–98.

Morimoto, Yoshiki. *Études sur l'économie rurale du haut Moyen Âge: Historiographie, régime domaniale, polyptyques carolingiens.* Brussels: De Boeck, 2008.

Muehlberger, Ellen. "Angel." In *Late Ancient Knowing: Explorations in Intellectual History,* edited by Catherine M. Chin and Moulie Vidas, 117–33. Berkeley: University of California Press, 2015.

Mundó, Anscari M. *Les bíblies de Ripoll: Estudi dels mss. Vaticà, Lat. 5729 i Paris, BNF, Lat. 6.* Vatican City: Biblioteca Apostlica Vaticana, 2002.

Murphy, Eimar, Rebecca E. Nordquist, and Franz Josef van der Staay. "A Review of Behavioural Methods to Study Emotion and Mood in Pigs, *Sus scrofa.*" *Applied Animal Behaviour Science* 159 (2014): 9–28.

Murray, Alexander Callander. "Immunity, Nobility, and the Edict of Paris." *Speculum* 69 (1994): 18–39.

Murray, Emily, Finbar McCormick, and Gill Plunkett. "The Food Economies of Atlantic Island Monasteries: The Documentary and Archaeo-Environmental Evidence." *Environmental Archaeology* 9 (2004): 179–88.

Murray, Stephen. *A Gothic Sermon: Making a Contract with the Mother of God, Saint Mary of Amiens.* Berkeley: University of California Press, 2004.

Mütherich, Florentine. "Der neutestamentliche Zyklus." In *Das Evangeliar Ottos III: Clm 4453 der Bayerischen Staatsbibliothek München,* edited by Florentine Mütherich and Karl Dachs, 46–71. Munich: Prestel, 2001.

Nasrallah, Nawal. *Annals of the Caliphs' Kitchens: Ibn Sayyār al-Warrāq's Tenth-Century Baghdadi Cookbook.* Leiden: Brill, 2007.

New Cambridge History of Islam. Vol. 1, *The Formation of the Islamic World, Sixth to Eleventh Centuries.* Edited by Chase F. Robinson. Cambridge: Cambridge University Press, 2010.

New Cambridge Medieval History. Cambridge: Cambridge University Press.

Vol. 1, *c. 500–c. 700.* Edited by Paul Fouracre. 2005.

Vol. 2, *c. 700–c. 900.* Edited by Rosamond McKitterick. 1995.

Vol. 3, *c. 900–c. 1024.* Edited by Timothy Reuter. 2000.

Newfield, Timothy P. "Early Medieval Epizootics and Landscapes of Disease: The Origins and Triggers of European Livestock Pestilences, 400–1000 CE." In *Landscapes and Societies in Medieval Europe East of the Elbe: Interactions Between Environmental Settings and Cultural Transformations,* edited by Sunhild Kleingärtner, Timothy Newfield, Sébastien Rossignol, and Donat Wehner, 73–113. Toronto: Pontifical Institute of Medieval Studies, 2013.

————. "Livestock Plagues in Late Antiquity, with a Disassembling of the Bovine Panzootic of A.D. 376–386." *Journal of Roman Archaeology* 30 (2017): 490–508.

Nicolaidis, Efthymios, Eudoxie Delli, Nikolaos Livanos, Kostas Tampakis, and George Vlahakis. "Science and Orthodox Christianity: An Overview." *Isis* 107 (2016): 542–66.

North, Richard. "You Sexy Beast: The Pig in a Villa in Vandalic North Africa, and Boar-Cults in Old Germanic Heathendom." In *Representing Beasts in Early Medieval England and Scandinavia*, edited by Michael D. J. Bintley and Thomas J. T. Williams, 151–75. Woodbridge, UK: Boydell and Brewer, 2015.

Norton, Marcy. "The Chicken or the *Iegue*: Human-Animal Relationships and the Columbian Exchange." *American Historical Review* 120 (2015): 28–60.

————. "Going to the Birds: Animals as Things and Beings in Early Modernity." In *Early Modern Things: Objects and Their Histories, 1500–1800*, edited by Paula Findlen. 53–83. London: Routledge, 2013.

Nyhart, Lynn K. *Modern Nature: The Rise of the Biological Perspective in Germany*. Chicago: University of Chicago Press, 2009.

Obrist, Barbara. *La cosmologie médiévale: Textes et images*. Vol. 1, *Les fondements antiques*. Florence: SISMEL and Edizioni del Galluzzo, 2004.

O'Connor, Terry. "Animals in Medieval Urban Lives: York as a Case Study." In Choyke and Jaritz, *Animaltown*, 115–28.

————. *The Archaeology of Animal Bones*. Stroud: Sutton, 2000.

————. "Livestock and Animal Husbandry in Early Medieval England." *Quaternary International* 346 (2014): 109–18.

————. "Livestock and Deadstock in Early Medieval Europe from the North Sea to the Baltic." *Environmental Archaeology* 15, no. 1 (2010): 1–15.

O'Hara, Alexander, and Ian Wood. *Jonas of Bobbio: Life of Columbanus, Life of John of Réomé, and Life of Vedast*. Liverpool: Liverpool University Press, 2017.

Oostindjer, Marije, Bas Kemp, Henry van den Brand, and J. Elizabeth Bolhuis. "Facilitating 'Learning from Mom How to Eat Like a Pig' to Improve Welfare of Piglets Around Weaning." *Applied Animal Behaviour Science* 160 (2014): 19–30.

Orchard, Andy. *Pride and Prodigies: Studies in the Monsters of the "Beowulf"-Manuscript*. Woodbridge, UK: Brewer, 1995.

Pacioni, G. "Truffle Hunting in Italy." *Bulletin of the British Mycological Society* 20 (1986): 80–81.

Packham, Jack R., Peter A. Thomas, Mark D. Atkinson, and Thomas Degen. "Biological Flora of the British Isles: *Fagus sylvatica*." *Journal of Ecology* 100 (2012): 1557–1608.

Padberg, L. E. von, and T. A.-P. Klein. "Hrabanus Maurus." In *Reallexikon der germanischen Altertumskunde*, vol. 15, edited by Heinrich Beck, Dieter Geuenich, and Heiko Steuer, 139–46. Berlin: De Gruyter, 2000.

Parker, A. J. *Ancient Shipwrecks of the Mediterranean and the Roman Provinces*. Oxford: BAR, 1992.

Parkes, M. B. *Pause and Effect: An Introduction to the History of Punctuation in the West.* Aldershot: Scolar, 1992.

Parsons, James J. "The Acorn-Hog Economy of the Oak Woodlands of Southwestern Spain." *Geographical Review* 52, no. 2 (1962): 211–35.

Pascua Echegaray, Esther. "From Forest to Farm and Town: Domestic Animals from ca. 1000 to ca. 1450." In Resl, *A Cultural History of Animals,* 81–102.

———. *Señores del paisaje: ganadería y recursos naturales en Aragón, siglos XIII–XVII.* Valencia: Universidad de Valencia, 2012.

Pastoureau, Michel. "La chasse au sanglier: Histoire d'une dévalorisation (IVe–XIVe siècle)." In *La chasse au Moyen Âge: Société, traités, symboles,* edited by Agostino Paravicini Bagliani and Baudouin Van den Abeele, 7–23. Turnhout: SISMEL / Edizioni del Galluzzo, 2000.

———. *Le cochon: histoire d'un cousin mal aimé.* Paris: Gallimard, 2009.

———. "Une justice exemplaire: Les procès faits aux animaux (XIIIe–XVIe siècle)." In *Les rites de la justice: Gestes et rituels judiciaires au Moyen Âge,* edited by Claude Gauvard and Robert Jacob, 173–200. Paris: Le Léopard d'Or, 1999.

———. *Le roi tué par un cochon: Une mort infâme aux origines des emblèmes de la France?* Paris: Seuil, 2015.

Pedersen, Ellen Anne, and Mats Widgren. "Agriculture in Sweden, 800 BC–AD 1000." In *The Agrarian History of Sweden, 4000 BC to AD 2000,* edited by Janken Myrdal and Mats Morell, 46–71. Lund: Nordic Academic Press, 2011.

Pensabene, Patrizio. *Piazza Armerina: Villa del Casale e la Sicilia tra tardoantico e medioevo.* Rome: "L'Erma" Brentschneider, 2010.

Peterken, George F. *Natural Woodland: Ecology and Conservation in Northern Temperate Regions.* Cambridge: Cambridge University Press, 1996.

Peytremann, Édith. *En marge du village: La zone d'activités spécifiques et les groups funéraires de Sermersheim (Bas-Rhin) du VIe au XIIe siècle.* Dijon: Revue Archéologique de l'Est, 2018.

Phillips, Sarah. "The Pig in Medieval Iconography." In Albarella, Dobney, et al., *Pigs and Humans,* 373–87.

Pigière, Fabienne. "The Evolution of Cattle Husbandry Practices in the Roman Period in Gallia Belgica and Western Germania Inferior." *European Journal of Archaeology* 20, no. 3 (2017): 472–93.

Pluskowski, Aleksander. "The Zooarchaeology of Medieval 'Christendom': Ideology, the Treatment of Animals, and the Making of Medieval Europe." *World Archaeology* 42 (2010): 201–14.

Podgórski, Thomasz, Grzegorz Baś, Bogumiła Jędrzejewska, Leif Sönnichsen, Stanisław Śnieżko, Włodzimierz Jędrzejewski, and Henryk Okarma. "Spatiotemporal Behavioral Plasticity of Wild Boar (*Sus scrofa*) Under Contrasting Conditions of Human Pressure: Primeval Forest and Metropolitan Area." *Journal of Mammalogy* 94 (2013): 109–19.

Pohl, Walter. *Die Germanen*. Munich: Oldenbourg, 2000.

———. "Der Germanenbegriff." In *Zur Geschichte der Gleichung "germanisch-deutsch,"* edited by Heinrich Bech, Dieter Geuenich, Heiko Steuer, and Dietrich Hakelberg, 163–83. Reallexikon der Germanischen Altertumskunde, Ergänzungsband 34. Berlin: De Gruyter, 2004.

Pohl, Walter, Clemens Gantner, Cinzia Grifoni, and Marianne Pollheimer-Mohaupt, eds. *Transformations of Romanness: Early Medieval Regions and Identities*. Berlin: De Gruyter, 2018.

Pohl, Walter, Clemens Gantner, and Richard Payne, eds. *Visions of Community in the Post-Roman World: The West, Byzantium and the Islamic World, 300–1100*. Burlington, Vt: Ashgate, 2012.

Pohl, Walter, and Gerda Heydemann, eds. *Post-Roman Transitions: Christian and Barbarian Identities in the Early Medieval West*. Turnhout: Brepols, 2013.

———. *Strategies of Identification: Ethnicity and Religion in Early Medieval Europe*. Turnhout: Brepols, 2013.

Pohl, Walter, and Helmut Reimitz, eds. *Strategies of Distinction: The Construction of Ethnic Communities, 300–800*. Leiden: Brill, 1998.

Pons, Josep, and Juli G. Pausas. "The Coexistence of Acorns with Different Maturation Patterns Explains Acorn Production Variability in Cork Oak." *Oecologia* 169 (2012): 723–31.

Porte, Patrick. *Larina de l'Antiquité au Moyen Âge*. 2 vols. Biarritz: Atlantica, 2011.

Prummel, Wietske. *Early Medieval Dorestad: An Archaeozoological Study*. Excavations at Dorestad 2. Amersfoort: ROB, 1983.

Putelat, Olivier. "L'homme, l'animal et L'Ajoie au premier Moyen Âge: Le bestiaire ostéologique de Courtedoux, Creugenat (Jura, Suisse)." In *L'Austrasie: Sociétés, économies, territoires, christianisation. Actes des XXVIᵉˢ Journées internationales d'archéologie mérovingienne, Nancy 22–25 septembre 2005*, edited by Jacques Guillaume and Édith Peytremann, 99–108. Nancy: Presses universitaires de Nancy, 2008.

———. "Des littoraux nordiques à la Bourgogne? Le périple d'un mouton à quatre cornes (Malay-le-Grand, VIᵉ–VIIᵉ s.)." In *Villes et campagnes en Neustrie: Sociétés—Économies—Territoires—Christianisation*, edited by Laurent Verslype, 261–71. Montagnac: Éditions Monique Mergoil, 2007.

Quirós Castillo, Juan Antonio. *Arqueología del campesinado medieval: la aldea de Zaballa*. Bilbao: Universidad del País Vasco, 2012.

———. "Los comportamientos alimentarios del campesinado medieval en el País Vasco y su entorno (siglos VIII–XIV)." *Historia Agraria* 59 (2013): 13–41.

Rackham, Oliver. *Ancient Woodland: Its History, Vegetation and Uses in England*. London: Edward Arnold, 1980.

———. "Savanna in Europe." In *The Ecological History of European Forests*, edited by Keith J. Kirby and Charles Watkins, 1–24. Wallingford, UK: CAB International, 1998.

Ramírez-Weaver, Eric M. *A Saving Science: Capturing the Heavens in Carolingian Manuscripts.* University Park: Pennsylvania State University Press, 2017.

Rebillard, Éric. *Christians and Their Many Identities in Late Antiquity: North Africa, 200–450 CE.* Ithaca: Cornell University Press, 2012.

Redding, Richard W. "The Pig and the Chicken in the Middle East: Modeling Human Subsistence Behavior in the Archaeological Record Using Historical and Animal Husbandry Data." *Journal of Archaeological Research* 23 (2015): 325–68.

Reed, R. *Ancient Skins, Parchments, and Leathers.* London: Seminar, 1972.

Regnath, R. Johanna. *Das Schwein im Wald: Vormoderne Schweinehaltung zwischen Herrschaftstrukturen, ständischer Ordnung und Subsistenzökonomie.* Ostfildern: Thorbecke, 2008.

Reimitz, Helmut. *History, Frankish Identity and the Framing of Western Ethnicity, 550–850.* Cambridge: Cambridge University Press, 2015.

Reitsema, Laurie J., Giuseppe Vercellotti, and Rosa Boano. "Subadult Dietary Variation at Trino Vercellese, Italy, and Its Relationship to Adult Diet and Mortality." *American Journal of Physical Anthropology* 160 (2016): 653–64.

Resl, Brigitte, ed. *A Cultural History of Animals.* Vol. 2, *In the Medieval Age.* New York: Berg, 2007.

Reynolds, Paul. "From Vandal *Africa* to Arab *Ifrīqiya:* Tracing Ceramic and Economic Trends Through the Fifth to the Eleventh Centuries." In *North Africa Under Byzantium and Early Islam,* edited by Susan T. Stevens and Jonathan P. Conant, 129–71. Washington, D.C.: Dumbarton Oaks, 2016.

———. "Material Culture and the Economy in the Age of Saint Isidore of Seville (6th and 7th Centuries)." *Antiquité Tardive* 23 (2015): 163–210.

Riera Rullan, Mateu, Miguel Ángel Cau Ontiveros, and Magdalena Salas Burguera, eds. *Cent anys de Son Peretó: descobrint el passat cristià.* Palma: Consell de Mallorca, 2012.

Rio, Alice. *The Formularies of Angers and Marculf: Two Merovingian Legal Handbooks.* Liverpool: Liverpool University Press, 2008.

———. "Freedom and Unfreedom in Early Medieval Francia: The Evidence of the Formulae." *Past & Present* 193 (2006): 7–40.

———. *Legal Practice and the Written Word in the Early Middle Ages: Frankish Formulae, c. 500–1000.* Cambridge: Cambridge University Press, 2009.

———. *Slavery After Rome, 500–1100.* Oxford: Oxford University Press, 2017.

Río Moreno, Justo L. del. "El cerdo: Historia de un elemento esencial de la cultura castellana en la conquista y colonización de América (siglo XVI)." *Anuario de estudios americanos* 53 (1996): 13–35.

Ritchey, Sara. *Holy Matter: Changing Perceptions of the Material World in Late Medieval Christianity.* Ithaca: Cornell University Press, 2014.

Rizzetto, Mauro, Pam J. Crabtree, and Umberto Albarella. "Livestock Changes at the Beginning and End of the Roman Period in Britain: Issues of Acculturation, Adaptation, and 'Improvement.'" *European Journal of Archaeology* 20, no. 3 (2017): 535–56.

Robbins, Frank Egleston. "The Hexaemeral Literature: A Study of the Greek and Latin Commentaries on Genesis." Ph.D. Diss., University of Chicago, 1912.

Rodgers, R. H. *An Introduction to Palladius*. London: Institute of Classical Studies, 1975.

Rose, Anita K., Cathryn H. Greenberg, and Todd M. Fearer. "Acorn Production Prediction Models for Five Common Oak Species of the Eastern United States." *Journal of Wildlife Management* 76 (2012): 750–58.

Rosenblum, Jordan D. *Food and Identity in Early Rabbinic Judaism*. Cambridge: Cambridge University Press, 2010.

———. "'Why Do You Refuse to Eat Pork?' Jews, Food, and Identity in Roman Palestine." *Jewish Quarterly Review* 100 (2010): 95–110.

Rosenwein, Barbara H. *Negotiating Space: Power, Restraint, and the Privileges of Immunity in Early Medieval Europe*. Ithaca: Cornell University Press, 1999.

Rossiter, Jeremy, Paul Reynolds, and Michael MacKinnon. "A Roman Bath-House and a Group of Early Islamic Middens at Bir Ftouha, Carthage." *Archeologia Medievale* 39 (2012): 245–82.

Rousseau, Philip. *Basil of Caesarea*. Berkeley: University of California Press, 1994.

Rubenstein, Jay. *Armies of Heaven: The First Crusade and the Quest for Apocalypse*. New York: Basic, 2011.

Ruhland, Florian. "Schweinehaltung in und vor der Stadt." In *Nürnberg: Archäologie und Kulturgeschichte*, edited by Birgit Friedel and Claudia Frieser, 319–25. Büchenbach: Dr. Faustus, 1999.

Rummel, Philipp von. "L'aquila gotica: Sull'interpretazione di un simbolo." In *La trasformazione del mondo romano e le grandi migrazioni: Nuovi popoli dall'Europa settentrionale e centro-orientale alle coste del Mediterraneo*, ed. Carlo Ebanista and Marcello Rotili, 51–66. Naples: Tavolario Edizione, 2012.

———. *Habitus barbarus: Kleidung und Repräsentation spätantiker Eliten im 4. und 5. Jahrhundert*. Berlin: De Gruyter, 2007.

Safran, Janina M. *Defining Boundaries in al-Andalus: Muslims, Christians, and Jews in Islamic Iberia*. Ithaca: Cornell University Press, 2013.

Saint Jores, Jean-Xavier de, and Vincent Hincker. "Les habitats mérovingien et carolingien de la 'Delle sur le Marais' à Giberville (Calvados)." *Archéologie médiévale* 30–31 (2001): 1–38.

Salvadori, Frank. "L'allevamento nell'Italia medievale (secc. X–XIV): i dati archeozoologici." *Debates de Arqueología Medieval* 3 (2013): 117–48.

———. "Animals in Italian Medieval Towns: From Late Antiquity to the Late Middle Ages." In Choyke and Jaritz, *Animaltown*, 129–45.

———. *Uomini e animali nel Medioevo: Ricerche archeozoologische in Italia, tra analisi di laboratorio e censimento dell'edito*. Saarbrücken: Edizioni Accademiche Italiane, 2015.

Sancho i Planas, Marta. *Mur: La història d'un castell feudal a la llum de la recerca històrico-arqueològica*. Tremp: Garsineu, 2009.

Sandom, Christopher J., Joelene Huges, and David W. Macdonald. "Rooting for Rewilding: Quantifying Wild Boar's *Sus scrofa* Rooting Rate in the Scottish Highlands." *Restoration Ecology* 3 (2013): 329–35.

Santiard, M.-Th. "Un aspect du commerce des porcs en Bourgogne au XIVe siècle." *Annales de Bourgogne* 48 (1976): 100–106.

Santos Salazar, Igor. "Las transformaciones de la fiscalidad en el territorio de Rávena entre los siglo V y VIII." In Díaz and Martín Viso, *Between Taxation and Rent*, 107–46.

Sapir-Hen, Lidar. "Food, Pork Consumption, and Identity in Ancient Israel." *Near Eastern Archaeology* 82, no. 1 (2019): 52–59.

Sapir-Hen, Lidar, Guy Bar-Oz, Yuval Gadot, and Israel Finkelstein. "Pig Husbandry in Iron Age Israel and Judah: New Insights Regarding the Origin of the 'Taboo.'" *Zeitschrift des Deutschen Palästina-Vereins* 129 (2013): 1–20.

Sato, Shoichi. "L'*agrarium*: La charge paysanne avant le régime domanial, VIe–VIIIe siècles." *Journal of Medieval History* 24 (1998): 103–25.

Scandura, Massimo, Laura Iacolina, and Marco Apollonio. "Genetic Diversity in the European Wild Boar *Sus scrofa*: Phylogeography, Population Structure, and Wild x Domestic Hybridization." *Mammal Review* 41, no. 2 (2011): 125–37.

Schäfer, Peter. *Judeophobia: Attitudes Toward the Jews in the Ancient World*. Cambridge: Harvard University Press, 1997.

Schipper, William. "Rabanus Maurus and His Sources." In *Schooling and Society: The Ordering and Reordering of Knowledge in the Western Middle Ages*, edited by Alasdair A. MacDonald and Michael W. Twomey, 1–21. Leuven: Peeters, 2004.

Schliephake, Christopher, ed. *Ecocriticism, Ecology, and the Cultures of Antiquity*. London: Lexington, 2017.

Schroeder, F.-G. *Lehrbuch der Pflanzengeographie*. Wiesbaden: Quelle & Meyer, 1998.

Scott, Alan. *Origen and the Life of the Stars: A History of an Idea*. Oxford: Clarendon, 1991.

Scott, James C. *Against the Grain: A Deep History of the Earliest States*. New Haven: Yale University Press, 2017.

Seaver, Matthew. *Meithal: The Archaeology of Lives, Labours and Beliefs at Raystown, Co. Meath*. Dublin: Transport Infrastructure Ireland, 2016.

Sée, Henri. *Les classes rurales et le régime domanial en France au Moyen Âge*. Paris: Giard & Brière, 1901.

Sessa, Kristina. "The New Environmental Fall of Rome: A Methodological Consideration." *Journal of Late Antiquity* 12 (2019): 211–55.

Shachar, Isaiah. *The "Judensau": A Medieval Anti-Jewish Motif and Its History*. London: Warburg Institute, 1974.

Shanzer, Danuta. "The *Cosmographia* Attributed to Aethicus Ister as *Philosophen*- or *Reiseroman*." In *Insignis sophiae arcator: Essays in Honour of Michael W. Herren on His*

65th Birthday, edited by Gernot R. Wieland, Carin Ruff, and Ross G. Arthur, 57–86. Turnhout: Brepols, 2006.

Shaw, Brent. "Bandits in the Roman Empire." *Past & Present* 105 (1984): 3–52.

———. "A Hidden History of the Equites?" *Ancient Society* 50 (forthcoming).

———. "A Peculiar Island: Maghrib and Mediterranean." *Mediterranean Historical Review* 18 (2003): 93–125.

Shinomori, Daisuke. "*Testamentum porcelli:* Ein von Sklaven errichtetes Testament?" In *Aus der Werkstatt römischer Juristen: Vorträge der Europäisch-Ostasiatischen Tagung 2013 in Fukuoka,* edited by Ulrich Manthe, Shigeo Nishimura, and Mariko Igimi, 353–73. Berlin: Duncker & Humblot, 2016.

Siems, Harald. "La vie économique des Francs d'après la *lex salica.*" In *Clovis: Histoire & mémoire,* edited by Michel Rouche, 607–30. Paris: Presses de l'Université de Paris-Sorbonne, 1997.

Siewers, Alfred K. *Strange Beauty: Ecocritical Approaches to Early Medieval Landscape.* New York: Palgrave MacMillan, 2009.

Simpson, C. J. *The Excavations at San Giovanni di Ruoti 2: The Small Finds.* Toronto: University of Toronto Press, 1997.

Siracusano, Giovanni. "The Fauna of Leptis Magna from the IVth to the Xth Century A.D." *Archaeozoologia* 6, no. 2 (1994): 111–29.

Sirks, Boudewijn. *Food for Rome: The Legal Structure of the Transportation and Processing of Supplies for the Imperial Distributions in Rome and Constantinople.* Amsterdam: J. C. Gieben, 1991.

Slavin, Philip. "Flogging a Dead Cow: Coping with Animal Panzootic on the Eve of the Black Death." In *Crises in Economic and Social History: A Comparative Perspective,* edited by A. T. Brown, Andy Burn, and Rob Doherty, 11–35. Woodbridge, UK: Boydell, 2015.

———. "The Sources for Manorial and Rural History." In *Understanding Medieval Primary Sources: Using Historical Sources to Discover Medieval Europe,* edited by Joel T. Rosenthal, 131–48. London: Routledge, 2011.

Small, Alastair M., and Robert J. Buck. *The Excavations of San Giovanni di Ruoti 1: The Villas and Their Environment.* Toronto: University of Toronto Press, 1994.

Smiarowski, Konrad, Ramona Harrison, Seth Brewington, Megan Hicks, Frank J. Feeley, Céline Dupont-Hébert, Brenda Prehal, George Hambrecht, James Woollett, and Thomas H. McGovern. "Zooarchaeology of the Scandinavian Settlements in Iceland and Greenland: Diverging Pathways." In Albarella et al., *Oxford Handbook of Zooarchaeology,* 147–63.

Smith, Julia. *Europe After Rome: A New Cultural History, 500–1000.* Oxford: Oxford University Press, 2005.

Sorabji, Richard. *Animal Minds and Human Morals: The Origins of the Western Debate.* Ithaca: Cornell University Press, 1993.

Spittler, Janet E. *Animals in the Apocryphal Acts of the Apostles: The Wild Kingdom of Early Christian Literature*. Tübingen: Mohr Siebeck, 2008.

Squatriti, Paolo. "Barbarizing the *Bel Paese:* Environmental History in Ostrogothic Italy." In *A Companion to Ostrogothic Italy*, edited by Jonathan J. Arnold, M. Shane Bjornlie, and Kristina Sessa, 390–421. Leiden: Brill, 2016.

———. *Landscape and Change in Early Medieval Italy: Chestnuts, Economy, and Culture*. Cambridge: Cambridge University Press, 2013.

Stallibrass, Sue, and Richard Thomas. "For Starters: Producing and Supplying Food to the Army in the North-West Provinces." In Stallibrass and Thomas, *Feeding the Roman Army*, 1–17.

Stallibrass, Sue, and Richard Thomas, eds. *Feeding the Roman Army: The Archaeology of Production and Supply in Northwest Europe*. Oxford: Oxbow, 2008.

Stansbury, Mark. "Early-Medieval Biblical Commentaries, Their Writers and Readers." *Frühmittelalterliche Studien* 33 (1999): 49–82.

Stern, Henri. "Les calendriers romains illustrés." In *Aufstieg und Niedergang der römischen Welt*, part 2, vol. 12.2, edited by Hildegard Temporini, pp. 431–75. Berlin: De Gruyter, 1981.

Stone, David. "Medieval Farm Management and Technological Mentalities: Hinderclay Before the Black Death." *Economic History Review* 54 (2001): 612–38.

Stuttgarter Bilderpsalter, Der: Bibl. fol. 23, Württembergische Landesbibliothek, Stuttgart. Vol. 2, *Untersuchungen*. Stuttgart: E. Schreiber, 1968.

Swartz, Michael D. *The Signifying Creator: Nontextual Sources of Meaning in Ancient Judaism*. New York: New York University Press, 2012.

Sykes, Naomi Jane. *The Norman Conquest: A Zooarchaeological Perspective*. Oxford: Archaeopress, 2007.

———. "The Rhetoric of Meat Apportionment: Evidence for Exclusion, Inclusion, and Social Position in Medieval England." In *Animals and Equality in the Ancient World*, edited by Benjamin S. Arbuckle and Sue Ann McCarty, 353–74. Boulder: University Press of Colorado, 2014.

Szirmai, J. A. *The Archaeology of Medieval Bookbinding*. Aldershot: Ashgate, 1999.

Tannous, Jack. *The Making of the Medieval Middle East: Religion, Society, and Simple Believers*. Princeton: Princeton University Press, 2018.

Thomas, Richard. *Animals, Economy and Status: Integrating Zooarchaeological and Historical Data in the Study of Dudley Castle, West Midlands (c. 1100–1750)*. Oxford: Archaeopress, 2005.

———. "Supply-Chain Networks and the Roman Invasion of Britain: A Case Study from Alchester, Oxfordshire." In Stallibrass and Thomas, *Feeding the Roman Army*, 31–51.

Toch, Michael. *"Dunkle Jahrhunderte": Gab es ein jüdisches Frühmittelalter?* Trier: Arye-Maimon-Institut für Geschichte der Juden, 2001.

———. *The Economic History of European Jews: Late Antiquity and Early Middle Ages.* Leiden: Brill, 2013.

Toplyn, Michael R. "Livestock and *Limitanei:* The Zooarchaeological Evidence." In *The Roman Frontier in Central Jordan,* edited by S. Thomas Parker, 2:463–508. Washington, D.C.: Dumbarton Oaks, 2006.

Townsend, Philippa. "The Manichaean Body and Society." In Kreiner and Reimitz, *Motions of Late Antiquity,* 63–87.

Trautmann, Thomas R., Gillian Feeley-Harnik, and John C. Mitani. "Deep Kinship." In *Deep History: The Architecture of Past and Present,* edited by Andrew Shryock and Daniel Lord Smail, 160–88. Berkeley: University of California Press, 2011.

Tsing, Anna Lowenhaupt. *The Mushroom at the End of the World: On the Possibility of Life in Capitalist Ruins.* Princeton: Princeton University Press, 2015.

Ubl, Karl. "Im Bann der Traditionen: Zur Charakteristik der *Lex Salica.*" In Meier and Patzold, *Chlodwigs Welt,* 423–45.

———. *Inzestverbot und Gesetzgebung: Die Konstrucktion eines Verbrechens (300–1100).* Berlin: De Gruyter, 2008.

———. *Sinnstiftungen eines Rechtsbuchs: Die "Lex Salica" im Frankenreich.* Ostfildern: Thorbecke, 2017.

Ulrich, Roger B. *Roman Woodworking.* New Haven: Yale University Press, 2007.

Valenti, Marco. *L'insediamento altomedievale nelle campagne Toscane: paesaggi, popolamento e villaggi tra VI e X secolo.* Siena: All'Insegna del Giglio, 2004.

———. *Miranduolo in Alta Val di Merse (Chiusdino, SI): archeologia su un sito di potere del Medioevo toscano.* Florence: All'Insegna del Giglio, 2008.

Valenzuela-Lamas, Silvia, and Umberto Albarella. "Animal Husbandry Across the Roman Empire: Changes and Continuities." In Valenzuela-Lamas and Albarella, "Animal Husbandry in the Western Roman Empire," 402–15.

Valenzuela-Lamas, Silvia, and Umberto Albarella, eds. "Animal Husbandry in the Western Roman Empire: A Zooarchaeological Perspective." Special issue, *European Journal of Archaeology* 20, no. 3 (2017).

Van Dam, Raymond. *Becoming Christian: The Conversion of Roman Cappadocia.* Philadelphia: University of Pennsylvania Press, 2003.

———. *Kingdom of Snow: Roman Rule and Greek Culture in Cappadocia.* Philadelphia: University of Pennsylvania Press, 2002.

Van Duzer, Chet. "*Hic sunt dracones:* The Geography and Cartography of Monsters." In *The Ashgate Research Companion to Monsters and the Monstrous,* edited by Asa Simon Mittman and Peter Dendle, 387–435. Farnham: Ashgate, 2012.

Vanpoucke, Sofie, Fabienne Pigière, Anne Defgnée, and Wim Van Neer. "Pig Husbandry and Environmental Conditions in Northern Gaul During Antiquity and the Early Middle Ages: The Contribution of Hypoplasia Analysis." *Archaeofauna* 16 (2007): 7–20.

Vassberg, David E. "Concerning Pigs, the Pizarros, and the Agro-Pastoral Background of the Conquerors of Peru." *Latin American Research Review* 13, no. 3 (1978): 47–61.

Veen, M. van der, A. Grant, and G. Barker. "Romano-Libyan Agriculture: Crops and Animals." In Graeme Barker, David Gilbertson, Barri Jones, and David Mattingly, eds., *Farming the Desert: The UNESCO Libyan Valleys Archaeological Survey*, 1:227–63. Tripoli: UNESCO and Department of Antiquities; London: Society for Libyan Studies, 1996.

Vera, Domenico. "Dalla liturgia al contratto: Cassiodoro, *Variae* X,28 e il tramonto della città curiale." In Díaz and Martín Viso, *Between Taxation and Rent*, 51–70.

Vico, Romana Martorelli. "Gli scritti anatomici della *Collectio Salernitana*." In *La "Collectio Salernitana" di Salvatore De Renzi*, edited by Danielle Jacquart and Agostino Paravicini Bagliani, 79–88. Florence: SISMEL-Edizioni del Galluzzo, 2008.

Vigil-Escalera Guirado, A., M. Moreno-García, L. Peña-Chocarro, A. Morales Muñiz, L. Llorente Rodríguez, D. Sabato, and M. Ucchesu. "Productive Strategies and Consumption Patterns in the Early Medieval Village of Gózquez (Madrid, Spain)." *Quaternary International* 346 (2014): 7–19.

Vigil-Escalera Guirado, Alfonso, and Juan Antonio Quirós Castillo. "Early Medieval Rural Societies in North-Western Spain: Archaeological Reflections of Fragmentation and Convergence." In Escalona and Reynolds, *Scale and Scale Change in the Early Middle Ages*, 33–60.

Vitelli, Giovanna. *Islamic Carthage: The Archaeological, Historical and Ceramic Evidence.* Carthage: Centre d'Études et Documentation Archéologique de Carthage, 1981.

Vizcaíno Sánchez, Jaime. *La presencia bizantina en Hispania (siglos VI–VII): La documentación arqueológica.* Murcia: Universidad de Murcia, 2009.

Vogüé, A. de. *Les règles monastiques anciennes (400–700).* Typologie des Sources du Moyen Âge Occidental 46. Turnhout: Brepols, 1985.

Volbach, Wolfgang Fritz. *Elfenbeinarbeiten der Spätantike und des frühen Mittelalters.* 2nd ed. Mainz: Römisch-Germanisches Zentralmuseum, 1952.

Volpe, Giuliano. "Città apule fra destrutturazione e trasformazione: i casi di *Canusium* ed *Herdonia*." In *La città italiene tra la tarda antichità e l'alto medioevo*, edited by Andrea Augenti, 559–87. Florence: All'Isenga del Giglio, 2006.

Volpe, Giuliano, and Maria Turchiano, eds. *Faragola 1: Un insediamento rurale nella Valle del Carapelle.* Bari: Edipuglia, 2009.

Vokaer, Agnès. "Pottery Production and Exchange in Late Antique Syria (Fourth–Eighth Century A.D.): A Study of Some Imported and Local Wares." *Late Antique Archaeology* 10 (2013): 567–606.

Von Staden, Heinrich. "Anatomy as Rhetoric: Galen on Dissection and Persuasion." *Journal of the History of Medicine and Allied Sciences* 50 (1995): 47–66.

Vos, Mariette de. "The Rural Landscape of Thugga: Farms, Presses, Mills, and Transport." In *The Roman Agricultural Economy: Organisation, Investment, and Production*, edited by Alan Bowman and Andrew Wilson, 143–218. Oxford: Oxford University Press, 2013.

Vroom, Joanita. "Ceramics." In *The Archaeology of Byzantine Anatolia: From the End of Late Antiquity Until the Coming of the Turks,* edited by Philipp Niewöhner, 176–93. Oxford: Oxford University Press, 2017.

Wallis, Faith. "Cædmon's Created World and the Monastic Encyclopedia." In *Cædmon's Hymn and Material Culture in the World of Bede: Six Essays,* edited by Alan J. Frantzen and John Hines, 80–110. Morgantown: West Virginia University Press, 2007.

———. "'Number Mystique' in Early Medieval Computus Texts." In *Mathematics and the Divine: A Historical Study,* edited by T. Koetsier and L. Bergmans, 179–99. Amsterdam: Elsevier, 2005.

Warde, Paul. *The Invention of Sustainability: Nature and Destiny, c. 1500–1870.* Cambridge: Cambridge University Press, 2018.

Ward-Perkins, Bryan. *The Fall of Rome and the End of Civilization.* New York: Oxford University Press, 2005.

Wiemer, Hans-Ulrich. "Odovakar und Theoderich: Herrschaftskonzepte nach dem Ende des Kaisertums im Westen." In Meier and Patzold, *Chlodwigs Welt,* 293–338.

Warner, Bernhard. "Boar Wars: How Wild Hogs Are Trashing European Cities." *Guardian,* 30 July 2019. https://www.theguardian.com/world/2019/jul/30/boar-wars-how -wild-hogs-are-trashing-european-cities. Accessed 30 July 2019.

Warren, James. *Epicurus and Democritean Ethics: An Archaeology of "Ataraxia."* Cambridge: Cambridge University Press, 2002.

Wasserman, Mira Beth. *Jews, Gentiles, and Other Animals: The Talmud After the Humanities.* Philadelphia: University of Pennsylvania Press, 2017.

White, Lynn. "The Historical Roots of Our Ecologic Crisis." *Science* 10 (1967): 1203–7.

White, Sam. "From Globalized Pig Breeds to Capitalist Pigs: A Study in Animal Cultures and Evolutionary History." *Environmental History* 16 (2011): 94–120.

Wickham, Chris. "European Forests in the Early Middle Ages: Landscape and Land Clearance." In *L'ambiente vegetale nell'alto medioevo,* 2:479–545. Settimane di studio 37. Spoleto: Centro Italiano di Studi sull'Alto Medioevo, 1990.

———. *Framing the Early Middle Ages: Europe and the Mediterranean, 400–800.* Oxford: Oxford University Press, 2005.

———. "Space and Society in Early Peasant Conflicts." In *Uomo e spazio nell'alto medioevo,* 551–85. Settimane di studio 50. Spoleto: Centro Italiano di Studi sull'Alto Medioevo, 2003.

Wigh, Bengt. *Animal Husbandry in the Viking Age Town of Birka and Its Hinterland.* Birka Studies 7. Stockholm: Birka Project for Riksantikvarieämbetet, 2001.

Witney, K. P. *The Jutish Forest: A Study of the Weald of Kent from 450 to 1380 A.D.* London: Athlone, 1976.

Wolska, Wanda. *La topographie chrétienne de Cosmas Indicopleustès: Théologie et science au VIe siècle.* Paris: Presses Universitaires de France, 1962.

Wood, Ian. "Entrusting Western Europe to the Church, 400–750." *Transactions of the Royal Historical Society* 23 (2013): 37–73.

———. *The Merovingian Kingdoms, 450–751.* London: Longman, 1994.

———. *The Modern Origins of the Early Middle Ages.* Oxford: Oxford University Press, 2013.

———. "Where the Wild Things Are." In Pohl, Gantner, and Payne, *Visions of Community in the Post-Roman World,* 531–42.

Woodbridge, Jessie, Neil Roberts, and Ralph Fyfe. "Vegetation and Land-Use Change in Northern Europe During Late Antiquity: A Regional-Scale Pollen-Based Reconstruction." *Late Antique Archaeology* 11 (2018): 105–18.

Woolgar, C. M. *The Great Household in Late Medieval England.* New Haven: Yale University Press, 1999.

Wright, Lawrence. "The Future Is Texas." *New Yorker,* 10 July 2017.

Wright, Roger. *A Sociophilological Study of Late Latin.* Turnhout: Brepols, 2003.

Yvinec, Jean-Hervé. "La part du gibier dans l'alimentation du haut Moyen Âge." In *Exploitation des animaux sauvages à travers le temps,* edited by Jean Desse and Frédérique Audoin-Rouzeau, 491–504. Juan-les-Pins: Éditions APDCA, 1993.

Zchomelidse, Nino M. *Santa Maria Immacolata in Ceri: pittura sacra al tempo della Riforma Gregoriana.* Rome: Archivio Guido Izzi, 1996.

Zerbini, Andrea. "The Late Antique Economy: Primary and Secondary Production." *Late Antique Archaeology* 10 (2013): 61–81.

Zuwiyya, Z. David, ed. *A Companion to Alexander Literature in the Middle Ages.* Leiden: Brill, 2011.

General Index

Index of Manuscripts